Arendt and Adorno

Arendt and Adorno

POLITICAL AND PHILOSOPHICAL
INVESTIGATIONS

EDITED BY
Lars Rensmann and Samir Gandesha

STANFORD UNIVERSITY PRESS
STANFORD, CALIFORNIA

Stanford University Press
Stanford, California

© 2012 by the Board of Trustees of the Leland Stanford Junior University. All rights reserved.

No part of this book may be reproduced or transmitted in any form or by any means, electronic or mechanical, including photocopying and recording, or in any information storage or retrieval system without the prior written permission of Stanford University Press.

Printed in the United States of America on acid-free, archival-quality paper

Library of Congress Cataloging-in-Publication Data

Arendt and Adorno : political and philosophical investigations / edited by Lars Rensmann and Samir Gandesha.
   pages cm
Includes bibliographical references and index.
ISBN 978-0-8047-7539-7 (cloth : alk. paper)
ISBN 978-0-8047-7540-3 (pbk : alk. paper)
   1. Arendt, Hannah, 1906–1975. 2. Adorno, Theodor W., 1903–1969. 3. Political science—Philosophy. 4. Philosophy, Modern—20th century. I. Rensmann, Lars, editor of compilation. II. Gandesha, Samir (Samir Suresh), 1965– editor of compilation.
JC251.A74A75 2012
320.5—dc23

2011037323

Contents

Preface — vii

Contributors — ix

1. Understanding Political Modernity: Rereading Arendt and Adorno in Comparative Perspective
   LARS RENSMANN AND SAMIR GANDESHA — 1

PART ONE | POLITICAL MODERNITY, THEORY, AND PHILOSOPHY

2. Arendt and Adorno: The Elusiveness of the Particular and the Benjaminian Moment
   SEYLA BENHABIB — 31

3. Political Modernism: The New, Revolution, and Civil Disobedience in Arendt and Adorno
   J. M. BERNSTEIN — 56

4. From the Critique of Identity to Plurality in Politics: Reconsidering Adorno and Arendt
   DANA VILLA — 78

5. Passion Lost, Passion Regained: How Arendt's Anthropology Intersects with Adorno's Theory of the Subject
   DIETER THOMÄ — 105

PART TWO | LEGACIES OF TOTALITARIANISM, ANTISEMITISM, AND CRIMES AGAINST HUMANITY

6. Grounding Cosmopolitics: Rethinking Crimes Against Humanity and Global Political Theory with Arendt and Adorno
   LARS RENSMANN — 129

7. Debating Human Rights, Law, and Subjectivity:
   Arendt, Adorno, and Critical Theory
   ROBERT FINE   154

8. Blindness and Insight: The Conceptual Jew in Adorno
   and Arendt's Post-Holocaust Reflections
   on the Antisemitic Question
   JONATHAN JUDAKEN   173

9. The Paralysis of Judgment: Arendt and Adorno
   on Antisemitism and the Modern Condition
   JULIA SCHULZE WESSEL AND LARS RENSMANN   197

PART THREE | POLITICAL THEORY IN EXILE,
            EXILE AS A THEORETICAL PARADIGM

10. Theorists in Exile: Adorno's and Arendt's Reflections
    on the Place of the Intellectual
    DIRK AUER   229

11. Homeless Philosophy: The Exile of Philosophy
    and the Philosophy of Exile in Arendt and Adorno
    SAMIR GANDESHA   247

Notes   281

Index   347

Preface

Hannah Arendt and Theodor Adorno were undoubtedly among the most influential political theorists and philosophers of the twentieth century. And yet despite the enormous impact the work of these two contemporaries has had on political and social theory, philosophy, and the humanities more generally, this is the first book in English that takes a comparative look at both authors. This has been a long time coming. But the book would not have seen the light of day without the cast of outstanding scholars supporting our project and contributing to this volume. We owe a special debt of gratitude to them for their willingness to present original work in this volume—work cutting incisively across the rigid theoretical boundaries that have existed for far too long. We thank them, additionally, for the enormous generosity of spirit and forbearance they have shown in the face of many, often unexpected, delays. It is our hope that this volume will open the space for many more such studies that seek to compare, explore, and critically appropriate, not only Arendt's and Adorno's work, but also the profound intellectual traditions they embody.

This book is, in more ways than one, a collaborative project. It is a product of several years of the editors' joint work on Arendt and Adorno and of many fruitful discussions between them. In no small measure, the volume has benefited hugely from the intellectual and institutional environments in which it developed, environments without which long-term commitments to projects are simply not possible. We thank Simon Fraser University's Institute for the Humanities, which is approaching its thirtieth year, and the University of Michigan, in particular its Department of Political Science, for funding and institutional support, and for providing the kind of extraordinary spaces and communities in which our work could take hold and flourish.

We are also very grateful to graduate students at both institutions for their feedback in seminars on Hannah Arendt and on the Frankfurt School. The German Academic Exchange Service (DAAD), which generously co-funds Rensmann's position at the University of Michigan, has supported the production of this book in countless ways; so has the Moses Mendelssohn Center at the University of Potsdam, where he is a Permanent Fellow. The generous support of the Alexander Humboldt Foundation, which made possible Gandesha's extended stay in Germany in 2001–2, has also played a critical role in making this project possible, as has the Social Sciences and Humanities Research Council of Canada. The authors are also grateful for support from the Simon Fraser University Publications Committee.

To a considerable extent, the book owes its existence to the support and encouragement of wonderful colleagues and friends, many of them at our respective universities, who shared their ideas, pushed us to think in new directions, read all or some of the chapters and were crucial in helping us finish the book. They can take credit for whatever merits this book may possess but not the responsibility for any of its shortcomings, which are ours alone. Special thanks are owed to Ian Angus, Seyla Benhabib, Stephen Eric Bronner, Lisa Disch, Andrew Feenberg, Malachi Haim Hacohen, Donald Herzog, Martin Jay, Jennet Kirkpatrick, Mika LaVaque-Manty, Anne Manuel, Andrei S. Markovits, Christoph Menke, Douglas Moggach, Charles Reeve, Mark Rigstad, Arlene Saxonhouse, Elizabeth Wingrove, Richard Wolin, Jerry Zaslove, and Mariah Zeisberg. We are particularly grateful to our acquisitions editor at Stanford University Press, Emily-Jane Cohen, for her unwavering and relentlessly energetic support at every step of the way and her extraordinary work with us over the years, and to assistant editor Sarah Crane Newman, whose careful and diligent work made everything easier. We owe special thanks to Peter Dreyer for meticulous copy editing, and to production editor Tim Roberts. It's really hard to overstate the role they had in making this book happen. We are sure that in this difficult climate for academic publishing, our experience is far from typical.

We would like to thank a number of graduate students who helped in countless ways on this project, among them Andrew Bingham, Adela Muchova, Dennis Nattkemper, and Natalie Wing. We also thank Thomas Murphey for his insightful comments, and we owe special thanks to Suzanne Hawkins, who was instrumental to helping us bring the manuscript together at the end, and who contributed most of the index.

Last but not least, we owe gratitude to our respective families, whose presence and support mean the world to us, Rachia van Lierop, Ruby and Milan Gandesha, and Ina and Samira Klingenberg. We could not have done it without them.

Contributors

DIRK AUER is a freelance journalist and sociologist with Balkanbiro in Sofia, Bulgaria, and a former lecturer in the Department of Sociology and Institute for Sociology and Social Research, University of Oldenburg, Germany. His publications include *Politisierte Demokratie: Richard Rortys politischer Antiessentialismus* (Wiesbaden: VS Verlag für Sozialwissenschaften, 2004), *Die Gesellschaftstheorie Adornos,* with Thorsten Bonacker and Stefan Müller Doohm (Darmstadt: Primus, 1998), and *Arendt und Adorno,* edited with Lars Rensmann and Julia Schulze Wessel (Frankfurt: Suhrkamp, 2003).

SEYLA BENHABIB is Eugene Meyer Professor of Political Science and Philosophy at Yale University and a former president of the Eastern Division of the American Philosophical Association. Her many books on political theory and philosophy include *Critique, Norm and Utopia: A Study of the Foundations of Critical Theory* (New York: Columbia University Press, 1986), *The Reluctant Modernism of Hannah Arendt* (Lanham, MD: Rowman & Littlefield, 2003), *The Rights of Others: Aliens, Citizens and Residents* (New York: Cambridge University Press, 2004), winner of the Ralph Bunche Award of the American Political Science Association, and *Another Cosmopolitanism* (New York: Oxford University Press 2006). She is also the author of dozens of scholarly articles and the editor of many books, including most recently *Migrations and Mobility: Gender, Borders and Citizenship* (New York: New York University Press, 2009) and *Politics in Dark Times: Encounters with Hannah Arendt* (New York: Cambridge University Press, 2011).

J. M. BERNSTEIN is University Distinguished Professor of Philosophy at the New School for Social Research. His books include *Against Voluptuous Bodies: Late Modernism and the Meaning of Painting* (Stanford: Stanford University Press, 2007), *Classic and Romantic German Aesthetics* (New York: Cambridge University Press, 2003), *Adorno: Disenchantment and Ethics* (New York: Cambridge University Press, 2002), and *Recovering*

Ethical Life: Jürgen Habermas and the Future of Critical Theory (London: Routledge,1995).

ROBERT FINE is professor of sociology in the Department of Sociology, University of Warwick, Coventry, England. His books include *Political Investigations: Hegel, Marx, Arendt* (New York: Routledge, 2001), *Democracy and the Rule of Law: Marx's Critique of the Legal Form* (Caldwell, NJ: Blackburn Press, 2002), and *Cosmopolitanism* (New York: Routledge, 2007). He is the author of many journal articles and has edited several collections, among them "Cosmopolitanism: Past and Future," with Vivienne Boon (special issue of the *European Journal of Social Theory*, April 2007), *Social Theory after the Holocaust*, with Charles Turner (Liverpool: Liverpool University Press 2000), and *People, Nation and State: The Meaning of Ethnicity and Nationalism*, with Edward Mortimer (London: I. B. Tauris 1999).

SAMIR GANDESHA is associate professor in the Department of Humanities at Simon Fraser University and the director of SFU's Institute for the Humanities. He specializes in modern European thought and culture, with a particular emphasis on the nineteenth and twentieth centuries. His work has appeared in *Political Theory, New German Critique, Kant Studien, Philosophy and Social Criticism, Topia, European Legacy*, the *European Journal of Social Theory*, and *Art Papers*.

JONATHAN JUDAKEN is Spence L. Wilson Chair in Humanities and professor of history at Rhodes College. He is the author of numerous scholarly articles on French intellectuals and the Jewish Question. His published books include *Jean-Paul Sartre and the Jewish Question: Anti-Antisemitism and the Politics of the French Intellectual* (Lincoln: University of Nebraska Press, 2006). He is the editor of *Race After Sartre: Antiracism, Africana Existentialism, Postcolonialism* (Albany: State University of New York Press, 2008), *Naming Race, Naming Racisms* (New York: Routledge, 2009) and *Situating Existentialism: Key Texts in Context* with Robert Bernasconi (New York: Columbia University Press, 2012).

LARS RENSMANN is DAAD assistant professor in the Department of Political Science, University of Michigan at Ann Arbor. He is the author of several books, including *Gaming the World: How Sports are Reshaping Global Politics and Culture*, co-authored with Andrei S. Markovits (Princeton, NJ: Princeton University Press, 2010) and *The Frankfurt School and*

Anti-Semitism: Politics, Theory and Philosophy (Albany: State University of New York Press, forthcoming). His work has appeared in numerous journals, including the *European Journal of Political Theory, German Politics & Society, Journal of Contemporary History, Political Studies Review, Politics, Religion & Ideology,* and *Perspectives on Politics.*

JULIA SCHULZE WESSEL is assistant professor for political theory in the Department of Political Science, Technical University of Dresden, Germany. Among her publications is the study *Ideologie der Sachlichkeit. Hannah Arendts politische Theorie des Antisemitismus* (Frankfurt: Suhrkamp, 2006). She is also the author of several scholarly articles on Arendt and antisemitism.

DIETER THOMÄ is professor of philosophy at the University of St. Gallen, Switzerland. He is the author of many books, in particular on the philosophy of modernity and the philosophy of happiness. His recent ones include *Totalität und Mitleid. Richard Wagner, Sergej Eisenstein und unsere ethisch-ästhetische Moderne* (Frankfurt: Suhrkamp, 2006); *Vom Glück in der Moderne* (Frankfurt: Suhrkamp, 2003). He is also the editor of several collected volumes, including *Heidegger-Handbuch* (Stuttgart: Metzler, 2003).

DANA R. VILLA is Packey J. Dee Professor of Political Theory at the University of Notre Dame. Among his many books are *Arendt and Heidegger: The Fate of the Political* (Princeton, NJ: Princeton University Press, 1996); *Politics, Philosophy, Terror: Essays on the Thought of Hannah Arendt* (Princeton, NJ: Princeton University Press, 1999); *Socratic Citizenship* (Princeton, NJ: Princeton University Press, 2001), and *Public Freedom* (Princeton, NJ: Princeton University Press 2008). Villa is also the author of many articles and editor of several volumes, including *The Cambridge Companion to Hannah Arendt* (New York: Cambridge University Press, 2000).

ONE

Understanding Political Modernity
*Rereading Arendt and Adorno
in Comparative Perspective*

LARS RENSMANN AND SAMIR GANDESHA

Sapere aude: *Unlikely Intellectual and Philosophical Encounters*

Having experienced the fate of exile in the twentieth century, Hannah Arendt and Theodor W. Adorno reflected directly on that century's atrocities and wars, and they continue to bear ghostly witness to the twenty-first century's ensuing dislocations. Moving beyond typical disciplinary borders, few thinkers have had a more lasting influence on critical debates on the social and political dimensions of "modernity" and its myriad crises. Although they have had a highly fraught reception, there can be little doubt that Arendt's and Adorno's overall impact on the social sciences and the humanities, political and social philosophy in particular, is profound. They shared similar life experiences, intellectual origins, and even theoretical interests in light of the catastrophes they faced. Moreover, they were perhaps the most uncompromising, nonconformist public intellectuals of their day, engendering distinct modes of public criticism.

Shaped by the intellectual milieu of the Weimar Republic and their German Jewish backgrounds, both Arendt and Adorno were forced into exile by the Nazi regime and found refuge in the United States. Along with

Hugo von Hofmannsthal and Gershom Scholem, they were among the first to recognize the brilliance of Walter Benjamin. After Benjamin's terrible death in Portbou in Catalonia, both went on to edit landmark collections of his writings: Adorno edited Benjamin's *Gesammelte Schriften* in German and Arendt the volume *Illuminations* for Schocken Books in English. They both returned to Germany a few years after the Holocaust. Arendt visited frequently thereafter, and Adorno, who first prepared his return in the immediate aftermath of the war, stayed for good as of 1949. Arendt and Adorno hence became critical observers of post-totalitarian Europe and engaged critically with its public discourse. In such public engagements, the Kantian spirit, its insistence on *sapere aude*, "daring to know" or the courage to think for oneself, is what pervades Adorno's and Arendt's activities as intellectuals. In contrast to Georg Lukács, for example, whose book on the intellectual roots of National Socialism, *The Destruction of Reason*, as Adorno remarked, confirmed little more than "the destruction of his own reason" at the behest of an ever more exacting Communist party line,[1] Adorno—like Arendt—insisted on political and intellectual independence. Indeed, at times Adorno seemed to insist upon independence from politics itself, which, understood dialectically, was not without political significance.[2] As a consequence, Adorno was attacked not just from the Right, but also from the Left—as he alludes to in the preface to his magnum opus, "The author is prepared for the attacks to which *Negative Dialectics* will expose him. He feels no rancour and does not begrudge the joy in those of either camp who will proclaim that they knew it all the time and now he was confessing."[3] Adorno was, of course, also criticized for his supposedly mandarin attitude to popular culture, jazz in particular, and his less than sanguine estimation of the prospects for working-class politics—that is, his calling into question the "official optimism" of the Left. The quintessential dismissal of Adorno was, perhaps unsurprisingly, articulated by Lukács himself. The latter stated that insofar as they had placed any possible hope for social transformation in neither party nor class, but rather in what the Hungarian philosopher regarded as a "nihilistic" modernism, Horkheimer and Adorno had fatefully taken up residence in "Grand Hotel Abyss" which Lukács originally describes in *The Destruction of Reason* as "a beautiful hotel, equipped with every comfort, on the edge of an abyss, of nothingness, of absurdity. And the daily contemplation of the abyss between excellent meals or artistic entertainments, can only heighten the enjoyment of the subtle comforts offered."[4] From the Right, Adorno had to endure a scarcely veiled antisemitism in Adenauerian Germany upon his return in 1949. And, of course, he was held directly responsible for the student uprisings of 1968, which is ironic given Adorno's undeniable ambivalence vis-à-vis the students' movement.[5]

Like Adorno, Arendt earned much scorn from Left and Right alike. The Left objected to Arendt's apparent glorification of an ancient conception of political action grounded in the fifth-century Athenian polis. More important, Arendt's distinction between "politics" and the "social"—and her undeniable preference for questions relating to the former and her devaluation of the latter[6]—did not sit comfortably with the Left. At the same time, the Right bridled at her critical diagnosis of actually existing liberal democracies as exemplifying the retreat of the political. By the same token, ironically, she was later on "appropriated" by both conservatives and the Left alike. But Arendt explicitly rejected such "friendly takeovers" by various camps.[7] In addition, her account of the Eichmann trial, first serialized in the *New Yorker* and later published in book form, caused a huge public stir.[8] As Anson Rabinbach suggested, the controversy surrounding *Eichmann in Jerusalem*, "was certainly the most bitter public dispute among intellectuals and scholars concerning the Holocaust that has ever taken place."[9] She was vilified by Gershom Scholem and many others. Yet the book continues to influence debates on international law and international criminal justice and will most likely do so for decades to come.[10]

At the intersection of their political and philosophical interventions, both Arendt and Adorno developed nuanced critiques of modernity. They sought to understand modernity's relationship to totalitarianism, and, though often with different intentions, developed their respective ideas through rigorous encounters with the German intellectual and philosophical tradition of figures such as Kant, Hegel, Marx, Weber, Heidegger, and Walter Benjamin. Arendt and Adorno were shaped by this tradition, just as much as they have drawn attention to its blind spots, exclusions, and aporiae. Indeed, as much as they sought to initiate a break with this tradition of thought, both in their own ways also absorbed and critically reflected it. In particular, the philosophical conception of historical progress, which reached something of an apogee in the great tradition of German Idealism, had become suspect. For both, such a break was first and foremost necessitated by the caesura in Western civilization represented by Auschwitz. This amounted to the recognition that, as Benjamin had suggested in his final writings on the philosophy of history, modern civilization was also inextricably tied to its opposite, barbarism.[11] For Arendt and Adorno—as for Benjamin himself—such recognition was more than an abstract idea. It was lived and experienced with painful concreteness in the form of expulsion, escape, homelessness, and exile. Such experiences shaped Adorno's and Arendt's thinking to an extraordinary degree, serving as a constant point of reference and enhancing a profound sensitivity to the fate of the individual under modern conditions. Against this background, it is especially surprising that Arendt and Adorno have not yet been placed under any substantial comparative scrutiny.

Embattled Legacies: Between Affinity and Aversion

This void may be attributed to several factors. First, on philosophical grounds, the gap may be attributed to the general conflict between critical theory and phenomenology, embodied in Adorno and Arendt respectively. In many ways, the phenomenology–critical theory divide embodied by Arendt and Adorno to some extent goes back to epistemological differences between Aristotle and Plato; the phenomenology of the former remained faithful to the world of appearances and its actualization, the latter was rather concerned with "true being" behind the appearances.[12] While Arendt and Adorno are both deeply indebted to, and work through, German philosophy and German Idealism in particular, their major theoretical anchors are obviously different—in Adorno's case, Hegel, Freud, Kant, and Marx; in Arendt's, Aristotle and the experiences of the ancient Greek polis, Kant,[13] and Heidegger.[14] Yet the conversation between critical theory and phenomenology has long begun at other places and through other venues too.[15]

The second obstacle has been the striking antipathy between these two thinkers. Strangely, despite (or perhaps because of) their apparent biographical, intellectual, theoretical, and even anti-fascist political affinities, they failed to acknowledge, let alone engage with, each other's work. Arendt was never reluctant to express her own aversion, indeed hostility, to Adorno in letters and private conversations. In what has now become a fabled episode in German intellectual history, Arendt responded to the suggestion of her then husband Günther Stern (later Anders) that Adorno—Stern's *Habilitation* (postdoctoral qualification) supervisor—be invited to dinner in no uncertain terms: "Der kommt uns nicht ins Haus!" ("That one's not coming into our house!"). Arendt came to hold Adorno directly responsible for Stern's ultimately failed attempt to receive his *Habilitation* in the philosophy of music at the University of Frankfurt in 1930, which ended Stern's academic career in Germany. Moreover, early on in her French exile, Arendt accused Adorno and his colleagues at the Institute for Social Research of betraying Benjamin—who, coincidentally, was Anders's cousin—by failing to supply him with sufficient material support at his hour of greatest need. In the end, Arendt held Adorno and his colleagues personally responsible for Benjamin's suicide, which clinched her judgment on Adorno and his work.[16] She affirmed this harsh criticism several times during the postwar years. Arendt was especially forceful in a letter to Karl Jaspers, written in response to rumors about a positive article Adorno had written on Nazi music before his emigration.[17] Here Arendt accuses him of nothing less than participating in the Nazis' attempt at total coordination and forcing into line of state and society, or *Gleichschaltung*.[18] Moreover, in a letter in which she defends her former teacher and lover Martin Heidegger against Adorno's acerbic criticisms, she goes so far as to call the latter a "half-Jew and one of the most disgusting people that I know."[19] And she accuses Adorno of being the "string-puller" behind campaigns against Heidegger, who, in one of the most infamous episodes of twentieth-century intellectual history, had declared his open support for the Nazi movement in his notorious *Rektoratsrede* (rector's address) as rector of Freiburg University from 1933 to 1934.[20] Arendt also attacked Adorno and Horkheimer by suggesting that "they accused anyone of antisemitism who opposed them in Germany, or threatened to do so."[21] In the only correspondence between Arendt and Adorno, she contacted him three times in the late 1960s in connection with editing Benjamin's work. The correspondence is respectful, though cool and somewhat passively aggressive on Arendt's side. Adorno, for his part, responded in a more friendly way, but still maintained considerable distance.[22] Hence, lack of interest and indifference on Adorno's side are matched by an abiding and cultivated animosity to Adorno on Arendt's.

The third reason for the striking absence of comparative analyses can be said to follow from the second: it is not uncommon that such deep-seated personal antipathies have a profound impact on the subsequent reception of the writers in question. Their celebrated personal animosities have been reproduced in myriad ways by their followers over the years. For instance, Dagmar Barnouw contrasted Arendt's presumed assimilation into American society to Adorno's alleged "autocratic snobbism" and "paranoid resentment."[23] In turn, critical theorists in the Frankfurt School tradition largely either ignored Arendt or rejected her "non-dialectical" theorizing and her robust opposition to Marx and Hegel. Thus far, such differences seem to have prevented theoretical dialogue between the contributions of Arendt and Adorno. An exception is, of course, Jürgen Habermas who has sought almost from the beginning of his career to instigate a shift from the relation of subject and object to intersubjectivity, from the paradigm of consciousness philosophy to that of communicative action.[24] Significantly, Habermas argues that his own Frankfurt predecessors (and Adorno in particular) represent the final aporia of the philosophy of consciousness.[25] That is, the argument of Adorno's and Horkheimer's *Dialectic of Enlightenment* gets caught within the snares of a performative contradiction insofar as it presupposes the very form of reason that it denies in its substantive claims. Crucially, this shift of paradigm—one that has been taken over and deepened by Axel Honneth's theory of recognition—is underwritten not only by the speech-act theory of Austin and Searle but also by Arendt's crucial differentiation of the *vita activa* into labor, work, and action in her book *The Human Condition* (1958). Habermas has appropriated both Adorno and Arendt in his own way. Be that as it may, this book breaks with the dominant tradition of disrespect and indifference. Initiating a theoretical conversation between these two distinctive thinkers, who shaped critical thinking about the twentieth century and the modern condition as few others have, is a worthwhile and timely endeavor, we argue.

Deconstructing Arendt and Adorno

In our view, the stand-off between Arendt and Adorno, reproduced by myriad followers, represents a false either/or. This stark opposition may have served different intellectual and political needs in the latter half of the twentieth century, but it now appears well and truly obsolete. The time has come, therefore, for a rethinking of the affinities between these two traditions and their theoretical relevance.[26] Only in North America has this dichotomy occasionally been challenged or deconstructed by some prominent theorists for some time.[27] Yet this has not led to more systematic comparative investigations that fully engage with the relationship between their theoretical concepts. As will be suggested in what follows, we think that the systematic comparison of central aspects of their work undertaken should include, though should not be limited to, a contribution to intellectual history.[28] In addition, however, Arendt's and Adorno's writings should also be taken seriously as theoretical, philosophical, and indeed political enterprises with striking contemporaneity in our own "post-metaphysical" global age.

The first reason for a new interest in both thinkers, and indeed a posthumous theoretical dialogue between them, is the recovery of the substance of their work, on which a comparative perspective may shed new light. In so doing, the implications of their work for present-day social and political philosophy should be reconsidered beyond the canonical, often superficial and at times stereotypical receptions of each thinker. Adorno, for example, has been portrayed, in reference to his collaboration on Thomas Mann's *Dr. Faustus*, as the Mephistophelean representative of Arnold Schoenberg's "emancipation of dissonance," as the figure who threatened to "take back" Beethoven's Ninth Symphony (Lyotard); or he has been characterized as a "dark," "melancholic," and, above all, "apolitical"[29] theorist of a "gloomy cultural pessimism"[30] and the inexorable implosion of Enlightenment. In contrast, Arendt has often been portrayed as the theorist of "civil society" par excellence, of the capacity of men and women to engage in genuine political action and, therefore, as the one political theorist who most inspired the revolutions of 1989. To be sure, recent scholarly work has led to first fissures in this hegemonic intellectual and public view. As Russell A. Berman and Alex Demirovic have shown, Adorno was a far cry from the image of the isolated *Flaschenpost* (message in a bottle) thinker that many followers and critics like to uphold. Upon his return from exile, for instance, Adorno was tirelessly engaged in attempts to reform the hierarchical structures of the German university from within. He participated in radio and television lectures and discussions, intervened in public debates, and dedicated much time to a series of public lectures on issues pertaining to "working through the past" and educational reform. While Adorno himself refuted the charge of cultural pessimism that has repeatedly been launched against him, Arendt, sounding a pessimistic note, was herself deeply concerned about the fate or "decline" of culture. Therefore she lamented the loss of the meaningful resources of what she called "the world"—a secure, diverse public realm in which people appear, speak, and enact their identities—in the face of the ever-more gargantuan appetites of the "entertainment industry." Furthermore, as Claude Lefort points out, Arendt has always approached modern representative democracy from a critical distance,[31] sharing Adorno's radical democratic intentions. In particular, she diagnoses the "lost treasure" of modern American democracy[32] and the decline of the modern republic, most radically so in her critical discussion of the Pentagon Papers.[33]

Arendt and Adorno's approaches are premised upon some significantly different philosophical assumptions and presuppositions, which should not be downplayed here. Their different epistemologies and interests structure the authors' critical investigations in distinctive ways. We can contrast Arendt's existentialism and political republicanism, highly critical of Hegel and Marx, with Adorno's materialism and dialectical thinking. We may emphasize their very different relationship to the *sensus communis* (in Kant's sense of an understanding shared by all) and to common sense—both of which are important reference points for Arendt and the object of scathing criticism for Adorno. Or we may point out their opposing notions of (political) power: whereas Adorno accepts Weber's modern instrumental understanding of power, Arendt distinguishes power conceptually from domination *over* someone. For her, power is shaped in the plural, based on cooperation, agreement, and mutual recognition between distinct actors who recognize their equality. Thus she separates power from authority, force, coercion, and violence. In an anti-Weberian turn and at odds, not only with Adorno, who understands power in a continuum of domination, coercion, and (structural) violence, but with much of the tradition of political thought (most strikingly with Carl Schmitt's antagonistic concept of the political),[34] for Arendt power corresponds to "the human ability not just to act but to act in concert"; in fact, it springs up "wherever people get together and act in concert."[35] Adorno, in turn, shares and expands Arendt's critique of violence. Yet he provides only a rudimentary concept of the political, and hardly any developed political theory that invests much theoretical interest in the act of political founding and the institutions that protect freedom. He does point, however, to some general parameters. These prominently include his relentless support for a free, democratic public sphere. In it, universalistic commitments are considered genuinely universal when they are critical and do not efface the nonidentical.[36]

Be that as it may, the often constructed, seemingly stark oppositions between Arendt and Adorno are, at best, only part of the story. For a start, they overlook that Arendt and Adorno are also driven by similar or overlapping critical paradigms and critiques of modern culture and the social sciences: from the critique of the "administered world" (Adorno) to the critique of government turned into "administration" (Arendt); from Adorno's diagnosis of the reification of memory and a modern "barbaric lack of relations" in modernity to Arendt's understanding of the modern "collapse of worldliness and the accompanying erosion of individual and collective memory";[37] from Adorno's critique of capitalist domination permeating all spheres of life to Arendt's critique of a laboring society that extinguishes politics, freedom, and the public sphere; and from the critique of "romanticist" identity politics and sovereign willpower to the critique of liberal notions of self-interest and what Adorno calls "blind particularism." In fact, the aforementioned antagonistic readings have—for too long, as we argue—obscured perspectives on intriguing shared motives, theoretical undercurrents, and implications of their work, which are grounded in common concerns for politically transformative human solidarity, difference, spontaneity, and plurality. Some of them this book seeks to uncover.

The Revival of Critical Political Theory

The project of exploring bridges between Arendt's and Adorno's respective bodies of work may be ripe for a second, and in our view especially compelling, reason, the social "untimeliness" of such an enterprise in critical political theory notwithstanding.[38] It is a shared yet distinct quality that both theorists critically and productively engage with political modernity's ambivalences, antinomies, and paradoxes. For a start, they echo Edmund Husserl's *The Crisis of the European Sciences,* in which he argues that under the spell of modern progress, humanity has made great leaps in knowing how things work. But we no longer know what things mean because we have lost touch with human experience. For Arendt and Adorno, then, the loss of experience and the false abstraction from particulars—and their meaning—is a constitutive motive of their critique of modernity. However, Arendt's and Adorno's reflections about the modern condition point far beyond Husserl's lament. Conceiving the modern condition in terms of historical dangers and possibilities that are difficult to disentangle, they offer philosophical and theoretical responses to modern conundrums. But they do not give in to the temptation to postulate comprehensive authoritative political or legal solutions. Furthermore, their critique is driven by claims to freedom that are seen through a self-critical and distinctly modern and egalitarian lens, and they reconstruct the philosophical tradition accordingly. But they are also thoroughly critical of modernity's false universals, and acutely aware of its contradictions, violence, and potential abyss.

After the "cultural turn" and the predominance of postmodernism, poststructuralism, and postcolonialism—with their critiques of what Jean-Francois Lyotard calls totalizing "meta-narratives" and the attack on the very idea of political subjectivity—interest in what has been defamed as "grand theory," namely, theorizing that is critically organized by a notion of totality and seeks to understand the constitutive features of society as a whole, appears to be reviving.[39] We argue that Arendt and Adorno offer some key theoretical resources for such a revival in light of contemporary conditions. Indeed, the implosion of the Soviet Bloc and the process of postindustrial globalization have prompted Perry Anderson to suggest that capitalism's "ideological triumph appeared to vindicate just the kind of legitimating narrative whose obituary Lyotard had sought to write."[40] Instead of "only" subverting objectifications expressed in narratives of fixed cultures, identity, or the nation-state (as important as this philosophical project is), Arendt's and Adorno's anti-essentialism moves beyond such endeavors and takes it in a political direction.

Both thinkers illuminate the 'dark side' of modernity in intriguing ways. Yet they also staunchly defend the possibility of human action, subjectivity, and political transformation. Arendt and Adorno aim at understanding the complexities of modern society with its ever-present potential for, on the one hand, genuine forms of democratic "non-domination"[41] and the transformative exercise of freedom that may enable human plurality and universalism;[42] and on the other hand, the drive toward forced homogeneity, objectification, exclusion, and identity politics.[43] Much of Arendt's and Adorno's work reflects these paradoxes and challenges of the modern condition, which, one may argue, dramatically resurface in new ways in the context of globalization.[44] However, they also provide significant theoretical groundwork to rehabilitate distinctively "modern" claims to universal freedom *and* diversity in politics and society. At the same time, they suggest that such claims are often entangled in modern forms of heteronomy, disempowerment, and "thoughtlessness." Taking a fresh look at their theoretical genesis and output, the focus that inspires this book is therefore as much on the differences and similarities of Arendt's and Adorno's work as it is on their relevance for reconstructing political theory and social philosophy today.

Rethinking Political Modernity with Arendt and Adorno

Against this backdrop, one of the crucial points of departure is the recognition of the Kantian elements in both thinkers, and especially of the relevance of Kant's theory of reflective judgment.[45] Rather than simply subsuming the particular autocratically under an extant or false universal, such a form of judgment begins with the particular, out of which it then generates a universal concept. Reflective judgment also attributes relevance to subjective experience. To be sure, in particular Adorno develops a thorough critique of Kant's idealistic limitations and "formalism." Yet, like Arendt, he also defends Kant's insights into the limits of reason. With Kant, both oppose in their own ways Hegel's dictum about the legitimate primacy of the general in history, the latter's logic of consequence according to which "the particular is of the most part of too trifling value as compared with the general: individuals are sacrificed and abandoned."[46]

Thus, a central and shared motive of their theorizing is the critique of unreflective abstractions that are constitutive of modern thinking. However, at the same time, they view the anti-modern negation of abstraction, the seemingly opposite direction of particularisms and blind arbitrariness, as no less problematic. Adorno refers to the standpoint of such radical particularism as the "false concreteness" of a "jargon of authenticity." Arendt scathingly refers to such a perspective as "Romanticism." Today, we may argue, these particularisms are reincarnated in authoritarian populism and religious fundamentalism, both of which can be seen as arising in response to globalization and conditions of a profound and deepening social and psychological insecurity. Abstract formalism, in turn, may itself generate anti-modern reactions that are deeply inimical to plurality and diversity. In fact, for Arendt and Adorno, modern social modes and structures help facilitate the problematic "ontological need,"[47] that is, the need for particularistic beliefs in the "authentic" and apolitical forms of the "false concrete" or the "natural life" that conceptually eclipses the very space for freedom and politics.

The impact of Arendt's and Adorno's multifaceted work may therefore well be especially significant in that it reflects the relationship between the general and the particular in the context of the "modern predicament"—what Habermas calls the "philosophical discourse of modernity."[48] From this vantage point, Arendt and Adorno sharpen our understanding of how modern societies tend toward *both* differentiation and homogenization under the spell of, in Max Weber's terms, rationalization and disenchantment.

For Arendt and Adorno, such dynamic tensions lying at the heart of modernity demand that we rethink the relation between formal universality and substantive particularity. Such a rethinking preserves a central role for political and subjective experience, critical judgment, and the aesthetic dimension in developing a transformed conception of political freedom. In light of Adorno's and Arendt's critical models, we propose a conceptualization of "political modernity" as a constellation comprised of three major elements: the dynamics of *modernization* (modern social and political transformations and formations), the *idea of modernity* (normative claims to autonomy, self-governance, and nondomination), and *modernism* (the critical, or self-reflective, and aesthetic dimensions of political modernity).

The notion of political modernity could be said to arise in the wake of the irreversible crisis of the Hegelian philosophy of history.[49] The latter sought to show the manner in which the logic of modernization or the differentiation of society since the demise of the "beautiful unity" of the Athenian polis was at the same time a logic of the progressive realization of freedom and autonomy. Within such a philosophy of history, the contradictions and revolutionary violence of modern society would inevitably lead to a form of ethical life or *Sittlichkeit* in which universality and particularity would be, once and for all, decisively reconciled at a putative "end of history." Arendt and Adorno fundamentally challenge such a conception of history. Rather, implicit in their work is a differentiation between the aforementioned three distinct aspects of political modernity: modernization, modernity, and modernism.

First, modernization is associated with ambivalent historical processes of societal "rationalization," from the economy and politics to culture, including capitalist development, urbanization, industrialization, state formation, societal differentiation, the evolution of modern "objective" science, and secularization. It implies a universalizing tendency that connects formerly disparate parts, manifesting itself all over the world and imposing its power globally.[50] The dynamic and contradictory nature of the logic of modernization is already expressed in the *Communist Manifesto,* which in many respects represents a materialist rewriting of Hegel's philosophy of history.[51] Here Marx and Engels describe the dynamic nature of exchange relations under capitalism, in terms that in the English translation resonate with Shakespeare's *The Tempest*: "All that is solid melts into air, all fixed, fast-frozen relations, with their train of ancient and venerable prejudices and opinions, are swept away, all new-formed ones become antiquated before they can ossify."[52] What is so crucial about this account of modernization—today frequently invoked to describe postindustrial or post-Fordist globalization—is that it shows how the very dynamism of modern transformation processes may lead to new forms of domination. But they also coalesce with a critical undermining of traditional worldviews that may well be the very precondition for genuinely democratic self-rule.[53] For Adorno, this modernization takes shape under the spell of a universalized instrumental rationality that subsumes and transforms particulars according to their abstract exchange value. It follows the instrumental rationality of labor, that is, a domination and mastery over objects that bleeds into all other public and indeed private spheres. For Arendt, it is the "modern glorification of labor,"[54] which has the effect of "de-worlding the world," through which human beings regress to a merely private, atomistic self.[55] In her argument, this glorification exemplifies the central danger of political modernity and mass politics, namely, that the distinctively *human* form of life, or *bios,* regresses to life as such, or *zōē.*[56]

Second, however, there is a normative moment of political modernity: the *idea of modernity,* or the normative claim to enlightenment. For Kant, this involves man's release, his exit, from "self-incurred tutelage."[57] Above all this normative aspect invokes the idea of autonomy. It holds that I am free if and only to the extent to which I can consider myself to be the author of the law under which I live. Drawing upon Kant's and Hegel's philosophies of history, Marx believed that there was a relatively straightforward relationship between modernization and autonomy; that the development of the productive forces would reach a point at which it would be brought into a contradiction with the relations of production. This would, in turn, create the conditions in which human social relations were reconciled. The subsequent atrocities of the late nineteenth and twentieth centuries belie Marx's understanding of a directionality of history (and the belief in progress he shares with Kant and Hegel). Rather, it seems to be more consistent with Weber's somewhat less sanguine prognostics that societal rationalization could seriously backfire. Even more so, the historical experience of the "rational" efficiency of the death machines of Auschwitz and Treblinka disclosed the utmost chasm between actual historical processes, on the one hand, and the actualization of the ideal of autonomy, on the other. As Adorno famously puts it at the beginning of his *Negative Dialectics*: "Philosophy, which once seemed obsolete, lives on because the moment to realize it was missed."[58] That is to say, Hegel's "cunning of reason" shows itself to be *insufficiently* cunning to push beyond the reifications of the actual modern world.

If Arendt and Adorno are among the first theorists to conceptually detect the decoupling of any straightforward relationship between modernization and the idea of autonomy in the "modern age of genocide," they also insist that normative responses to these modern perplexities and predicaments will have to be shaped by political modernity itself. This applies equally to Adorno, trenchant critic of the dialectic of enlightenment, and to Arendt, the "reluctant modernist" (Benhabib). Though not without a certain ambivalence, both Adorno and Arendt employ critical reasoning and self-reflection and engage in forms of political practice that retain a strong foothold in modern ideals of enlightenment, nondomination, and autonomy. Such normative ideals become explicitly political in their critiques of the loss of rights (Arendt) and of society's treatment of refugees (Adorno), in their critical appraisal of difference and plurality (Adorno's critique of identity philosophy in part mirrors Arendt's methodological criticism of philosophy that misconceives man in the singular and obstructs the plurality on which the human condition and all human association is based), or in their critiques of violence. In a way that distinguishes these thinkers from the facile postmodernism with which they occasionally are associated, both Arendt and Adorno insist with different inflections that the particular cannot be thought other than in a critical relation with universality. Such an insistence leads them repeatedly back to a rethinking of the legacy of German Idealism and to the problem of the aesthetic as a principal location of that rethinking. In political terms, their reflection of common (mis-)understandings and presuppositions about modernity underscores a modern normative universalism that does not fall victim to false universals. It refuses to elide or reduce difference, contingency, and individuality.[59] Instead, such *difference-sensitive universalism* is even preconditioned by plurality; in fact, both recognize freedom's dependency on difference, the particular, and diversity. Among other things, we argue that Arendt and Adorno hereby find common epistemological ground in the claim that "the very possibility of a rationality that lies latent—although not always recognized—within experience itself."[60] For Arendt, this experience, and the capacity to judge, relies especially on one's presence within the "realm of appearances," namely, the space of the political, where difference is disclosed and enacted by speaking, acting individuals. For Adorno, residues of subjective experience can be found particularly in individual encounters with the other, as well as in the subject's "sense of solidarity with what Brecht called 'tormentable bodies.'"[61] In the "face of the totalitarian unison with which the eradication of difference is proclaimed as a purpose in itself," Adorno therefore suggests in his *Minima Moralia* that part of the "social force of liberation may have temporarily withdrawn to the individual sphere."⁶²

To be sure, only Arendt developed an influential theory of politics. In fact, critical theory's "democratic deficit" is one of the areas where Arendt may complement the work of Adorno, while Adorno's understanding of social processes may complement Arendt's aim of a retrieval of the "public world." Yet both provide serious challenges to dominant views in contemporary political theory that either prioritize false universals, which ignore autonomy and plurality, or relativistic particularism, which refuses cosmopolitanism altogether. The former can be discerned in the liberal insistence on the context-transcending nature of moral norms and law. The latter is expressed in the radical contextualism and relativism of neo-Aristotelianism, communitarianism, and some postmodern political theories. As Adorno put it, "collectivism and individualism complement each other in the wrong direction."⁶³

This, indeed, leads to the third moment of political modernity: *modernism*. Modernism—what Jay Bernstein's calls the "self-consciousness of modernity" in his contribution to this volume—serves as the basis for a critical reflection of the tensions between modernization and the idea of modernity as enlightenment and nondomination. If modernization ultimately fails to make good on realizing modernity's promises, to wit: the promise of freedom, modernist "self-consciousness" makes possible "critical interruptions." In this respect, as alluded to already, Walter Benjamin deeply influenced both Arendt and Adorno. According to Benjamin, if it was possible to realize autonomy, this would not come about through a Hegelian eschatology of a completion or the achievement of the end of history. Rather, autonomy may be actualized through a break with temporal continuity or what Benjamin called a "tiger's leap into . . . the open air of history."⁶⁴ This is reflected in Adorno's idea of an almost primordial, mimetic "shudder" that reverberates in the most "advanced" works of art.⁶⁵ We also find it mirrored in Arendt's notion of new political beginnings and in her very understanding of political action as anchored in the human condition of natality. According to Arendt, constitutionalism and the rule of law provide an important context for political action—without a guaranteed public realm, freedom "lacks the worldly space to make its appearance." For her, the political faculty of promise depends on an elaborate framework of ties and bonds for the future, such as laws and constitutions—but historical processes are also constantly "interrupted by human initiative, by the *initiuum* man is insofar as he is an acting being."⁶⁶ This may entail a fundamental break with, or significant regeneration of, a politically exhausted regime or constitution. Her reconstruction of the "lost treasures" of the American democratic-republican revolution and constitution is only one of many examples.⁶⁷ As T. J. Clark has recently argued, modernism and socialism, despite all of their serious differences, were ultimately deeply allied in seeking to "imagine modernity otherwise."⁶⁸ Such a formulation nicely captures the political valence of the aesthetic dimension of the work of Arendt and Adorno.

As developed here against the backdrop of Arendt's and Adorno's work, the concept of "political modernity" is therefore charged with critical intent. Even in light of their rather pessimistic or sweeping diagnoses about modern mass society—some of these arguments may be more valid than others today—both seek to *open the political space* for new subjectivity and agency. They do not accept the closure of human possibilities and the public sphere. Their writings point in the direction of furtive possibilities for political change, aiming at nonsovereign, nonexclusive political associations and conditions of freedom.⁶⁹ Reading Adorno and Arendt together shows more clearly that their reflections escape the Scylla of common contemporary celebrations of liberal political modernity—for example, its nation-state-centric forms of political order or liberal notions of the law, self-interest, and formal entitlement—and the Charybdis of an abandonment of the Enlightenment project of reason and universalism *tout court*. Instead of throwing out the "baby with the bathwater" and identifying modern culture (and the cosmopolitan and democratic norms it facilitates) solely as a set of arbitrary claims and lies,⁷⁰ thinking with Arendt and Adorno today, we argue, means first and foremost engaging in critical analyses that remain committed to modernity's cosmopolitan claims, promises, and its agents. This implies the political commitment to a democratic, autonomous, free existence that recognizes difference and plurality.

Such thinking is concerned with the protection and institutionalization of freedom, understood as private and public autonomy, and their societal preconditions. Yet it also means consciously facing the contradictions and paradoxes in which such claims, and modernity at large, are entangled. They stretch from societal constraints, pressures, and modern forms of violence to the contradictions of inclusion and exclusion in the institution of modern citizenship.⁷¹ The awareness of these tensions enables a critical but open mode of thinking about political order, living subjectivities, and human freedom. It facilitates cosmopolitan thinking beyond the limitations of liberal universalism, on the one hand, and of identity politics, on the other. And, as a philosophical and political project, it looks for mediations—by means of thinking, language, aesthetics, and action—of problematic dichotomies between the universal and the particular that continue to haunt political and social philosophy.

Arendt and Adorno in the Twenty-First Century: Why They Still Matter

While many of their arguments are highly controversial, Arendt and Adorno challenge shortcomings of contemporary political thought and philosophy. Defending plurality and reflective judgment, which starts with the particular while remaining committed to universalism, Arendt and Adorno can be viewed as theorists who pave the way for critical theorizing of political modernity and democracy. As we have indicated, in contrast to much contemporary political theorizing, they both do not view plurality and universalism as inevitable contradictions. Their approaches help to subvert thick communitarian and essentialist claims for the prioritizing of any "given" cultural notion of the "common good" and pre-political collective identities or other boundaries of community demarcated by 'sovereign' rule.[72] Moreover, they challenge notions of an uncontested particular individual or collective self-interest and sovereign will—as Arendt argues, "if men wish to be free, it is precisely sovereignty they must renounce."[73] Yet Arendt and Adorno also provide conceptual tools to criticize thin liberal defenses of formalized rights and procedures. They suggest that these liberal defenses largely ignore the fact that social and political phenomena are historically situated and entangled in contradictions that cannot be resolved by abstract normative or legal principles. "Thin" liberalisms also neglect substantial political problems of societal atomization, exclusion, injustice, and indifference—which have arguably become even more salient under present conditions of global modernity. Both Arendt and Adorno are decidedly non-liberal, if not anti-liberal, thinkers who are critically aware of the limitations of the "rule of law," formal equality, and "justice," as well as conscious of the extralegal sources of formalized rights and legal rule—and for that matter, of the "liberal credo, 'The less politics the more freedom,'"[74] and of "my-share-of-the-pie social and political theories."[75]

Still, if we avoid any kind of "worshipful piety,"[76] questions about Arendt's and Adorno's relevance will not find easy answers. Over time, the question marks behind theories that try to come to terms with their own age tend to increase rather than disappear. In turn, though, it is far too common that boldly posited "new paradigms" simply fall back behind a certain level of reflection that preceded them. The common talk of "new paradigms" often suggests a progression of knowledge that is rather unaware of theoretical roots and oblivious to lasting conditions or continuities within change.

The authors of the essays in this volume each examine common and distinct motifs, references, and models of Arendt's and Adorno's work, establishing connections without eliding important differences. In addition, the collection charts Arendt's and Adorno's respective influences on contemporary debates within social and political thought, from Habermas's theory of communication through hermeneutics and phenomenology to poststructuralism. Employing Arendt's and Adorno's theories, the volume also presents an attempt to conceptualize conditions and dynamics that marked the twentieth century and continue to shape the twenty-first. Indeed, in light of the baleful impasse between "empty" or formalistic universal conceptions of justice, on the one hand, and a retreat into "blind" particularity by postmodernism, on the other, the time has never been more propitious for a "stereoscopic" reading of Arendt and Adorno. In this context it may be asked, for example, if the more skeptical accounts of modernity put forward by Arendt and Adorno can generate an illuminating "force field" when contrasted with more recent sophisticated theoretical understandings of what Habermas calls the "philosophical discourse of modernity." This includes Habermas's rather optimistic understanding of the way in which processes of modernization in the life-world unleash an emancipatory form of communicative reason as an "irreversible learning process." And it entails Axel Honneth's view of the evolution of modern legal, moral, and political spheres of recognition.[77] One of the goals of this volume is to evaluate the limits and possibilities of Arendt's and Adorno's contributions against the matrix of these theories of the late twentieth and early twenty-first century to enhance our understanding of the complex and contradictory nature of contemporary political modernity's "unfinished project."[78]

Some overlap of ideas between these two European-American humanists of their time has undoubtedly historical origins. It is partly indebted to a shared time horizon, similar living circumstances, and the intellectual environment of Weimar Germany from which their work originated. But, as claimed before, there is reason to argue that a critical reappropriation of their thinking also points beyond this shared intellectual history and common "songs of experience."[79] We suggest that this reappropriation sheds light on the diagnostic force and analytic power of their theories: transcending their specific historical conditions, rereading Arendt and Adorno may challenge us to rethink political modernity in the global age. It also encourages us to reconsider the foundations for critical humanistic universalisms—conceiving the better state as one in which everyone "can be different without fear."[80] In so doing, reconstructing Arendt and Adorno may become an important part for a revival of critical political theorizing in our own time.

Another Enlarged Mentality: Revisiting Concepts and Traditions

While we find stark contrasts in the way Arendt and Adorno approach, for instance, Heidegger and Marx—neither Arendt's critical reading of Marx nor Adorno's attack on Heidegger[81] is free from misunderstandings and simplifications—there is also much common ground in their own reappropriations of philosophical and theoretical traditions. Weber, for instance, provides a key reference point for the evolution of their theories of modernity. And Hegel's systematic, "positive" dialectical philosophy—not to mention his "theodicy of history"—is subject to astonishingly similar criticisms. Arendt and Adorno confront and incorporate a shared intellectual horizon that has shaped critical thinking in the Weimar republic and beyond. However, they both reiterate *and* change the questions and concepts of "the tradition" without outright violating it. For instance, the modern experience of "worldlessness," isolation, and mass atrocities leads Arendt and Adorno to abandon the pretheoretical moral intuition that Kant conceives as the "factum of reason."[82] Adorno is in tune with Arendt's call to rethink history, after the breakdown of civilization that Auschwitz signified, when he reformulates Kant's categorical imperative in the "Meditations on Metaphysics" of his *Negative Dialectics*, namely, for humankind "to arrange [its] thoughts and actions so that Auschwitz will not repeat itself, so that nothing similar will happen."[83] Arendt, it may be argued, turned this moral imperative into a political one in reflecting on crimes against humanity under the "global condition of politics" in the twentieth century. Given the history of the late twentieth century, of the "ethnic cleansing" of Srebenica, of the killing fields of Rwanda, of the nightmarish images of terror attacks, such moral and political imperatives, sadly, retain all of their force well into the twenty-first century. Adorno's and Arendt's reappropriations of the tradition, and the implications of their thought for contemporary philosophy, are the subject of the first section of this book.

Seyla Benhabib demonstrates in her contribution that there is one shared dimension of Arendt's and Adorno's critiques of classical German Idealism that stands out: the rejection by both of false universals, posited primarily by the Hegelian system. Arendt and Adorno search for illuminating configurations of the particular, without falling either into empiricism or *Existenzphilosophie* (existential philosophy). Beginning with Adorno's essay on "The Actuality of Philosophy" and Arendt's "What Is Existenz Philosophy?" Benhabib traces the search for the elusive particular in their thought. For both, this culminates with a rereading of Kant's *Critique of Judgment*. Arendt finds in Kant's doctrine of "reflective judgment" an epistemology for elucidating the particular without missing the intersubjective and shareable quality of such judgments. For Adorno, aesthetic judgment occupies that "in-between" space, framed by the *Naturschöne* (natural beauty) on the one hand and *das Erhabene* (the sublime) on the other. Benhabib analyzes differences and similarities in the political epistemology of judgment in Arendt in comparison to the epistemology of aesthetic judgment in Adorno.

The reconsideration of judgment and its epistemology and the relationship between the universal and the particular is also an important component of Dana Villa's chapter. Villa reconstructs Adorno's major philosophical contribution as a critique of "identity philosophy," that is, the insight that conceptual rationality, identity, and universalism need to be constantly reminded of their dependence on particularity, difference, and the nonconceptual or nonidentical. Yet Villa contrasts this contribution to Arendt's interpretation of difference and plurality: while Adorno's difference-affirming utopia can exist only on a plane *beyond* politics, beyond the difference-repressing sphere of the universal or public, Arendt places difference and plurality squarely in the realm of politics and public freedom. Public freedom is "nonsovereign" in nature and does not seek to overcome the frailty and unpredictability of human affairs. Arendt thereby, Villa argues, criticizes the escape from politics between citizens that is emblematic of the great tradition of philosophy—and of Adorno in particular. She simultaneously affirms the republican institutionalization and constitutionalization of public freedom, which Adorno viewed with some skepticism. Thus Villa engages in the theoretical dialogue between the two thinkers to further clarify and reemphasize theoretical distinctions, if not incommensurability, between the two.

The constellation that comprises "political modernity," namely, modernity, modernization, and modernism, forms the basis of Jay M. Bernstein's essay, which begins with the constitutive paradox inherent in Adorno's thinking: on the one hand, as the "self-consciousness of modernity," modernism represents the shock in the arrival of the new, yet, on the other, as the project of "making it new," modernism, because based on an act of will, fails to escape the logic of the always-the-same. This is indicative of the semblance character of art—that is, the idea of the new rather than its material actualization. Nonetheless, such semblance is vitally important as modernity's promise, namely, that of a wholly secular, immanent form of life. At the same time, Adorno was unable to show how this promise, as manifested within the aesthetic, could be translated as the collective praxis of which it is a cipher. In Bernstein's view, the idea of civil disobedience epitomizes precisely such a translation, which represents, so to speak, the truth of Hannah Arendt's "critical political philosophy." It is a refounding as a renewing, which is "the uprising of the new in its double conditionality; always dependent on the very past it exceeds, always failing (ready to be lost again)."

While there can be no doubt that any critical notion of "political modernity" depends on the normative idea of autonomy, such an idea, particularly in its Kantian form (which reiterates the dualism between duty and inclination, sensibility and rational will), is not without significant problems. This problem lies at the heart of Dieter Thomä's essay. Arguing that it is misleading to think that Arendt's work is guided by the idea of *amor mundi* (love of the world), he shows that, given her Kantian starting point, for Arendt love represents an illegitimate or heteronomous standpoint. It is far too passive, far too grounded in the senses, to form the basis for freedom understood as the ability to begin a new sequence in time. Yet because the Kantian will is, at the end of the day, metaphysically construed, Arendt relies crucially on the idea of "natality," which grounds the possibility of freedom in the context of human sociality. Thomä turns this conception of natality on its head and suggests that it is the form of sociality itself that confers on natality its significance. In Adorno's language, the nonidentity of the other leads to recognition of the self's own nonidentity. The idea of pure autonomy ultimately falls prey to a fatal self-contradiction.

Modernity, Totalitarianism, and Genocide: Working Through Experiences of the Twentieth Century

The second section of this book examines Adorno's and Arendt's contributions to understanding the central experiences of the twentieth century, namely: totalitarianism, the Holocaust, and crimes against humanity. These themes are central to both Arendt's and Adorno's most important writings and their conceptions of modernity, politics, and society. In spite of the differences in their responses to Hegel and their distinct relationships to political institutions, Arendt's and Adorno's understandings are motivated by the desire to comprehend the incomprehensible, and by the recognition that they are looking at novel, unprecedented historical events and forms of domination. Hence new forms of rule, the self-destruction of society, and unprecedented forms of terror have a profound impact on their subsequent writings. Arendt's and Adorno's conceptualizations of totalitarianism and its origins, the caesura of the Holocaust and their analogous attempts to come to terms theoretically with totalitarian tendencies within mass society and politics represent core elements of their respective bodies of work and contributions to modern political thought. This section also examines what both theorists considered to be the generalizable political and normative lessons to be learned from the experience of totalitarian ideology and terror for a post-totalitarian democratic society.

As noted above, Adorno and Arendt were targets of criticism from both Left and Right. In a way, their respective analyses of totalitarianism were almost calculated to antagonize those on both sides of the political spectrum. Not only did they turn their critical attention to the rise of fascism in Europe, they detected similar threats at work in the United States itself. Adorno did so in terms of a Freudian analysis of authoritarian personality structures that were the product of an inverted appropriation of psychoanalysis—what Leo Löwenthal called "psychoanalysis in reverse."[84] Arendt did so in terms of political history. Where the intentions of depth psychology were expressed by Freud in the form of the slogan "Where id is, ego shall be," fascism turned this Enlightenment imperative on its head: "Where ego is, id shall be." If Adorno addressed the missing subjective or affective elements in a materialist analysis of the rise of authoritarianism in Europe, Arendt rooted her understanding of totalitarianism in the shifting and complex relation between state and society of nineteenth-century Europe, in particular the tendency of "the social" to explode the boundaries of the nation-state, culminating in pan-nationalism and colonialism. For both, what was crucial was the philosophy of history that undergirded and legitimized totalitarianism. For Adorno (and Horkheimer), fascist totalitarianism culminates in the attempted extermination of the nonidentical. The genealogy of this phenomenon is traced to the earliest form of myth. The repetition of myth as enlightenment hinges upon transition from mythical forms of sacrifice as the external propitiation of the gods to the progressive internalization of sacrifice. The unbearable tension that accrues as a result of such an "internalization of man" (Nietzsche) eventually also facilitates anti-Enlightenment rebellions against reason; the tensions are released on an enemy. This is, so to speak, the libidinal economy of Nazi antisemitism. Arendt, in turn, argues that both forms of totalitarianism—fascism and Stalinism—are underwritten by a philosophy of history that sacrifices the individual to the iron laws of "history" (class struggle and proletarian revolution) or "nature" (the social Darwinistic struggle for the existence of discrete racial groups). Totalitarianism, in other words, displaces "men" by "Man." It destroys the space between them, melting the plurality of "the many" into "the One." In their doubled critiques of fascism and Stalinism, Adorno and Arendt can be said to have outstripped by several years the formation of the New Left, which came into existence through outspoken opposition to the "fraternal" Soviet invasion of Hungary in 1956.

In this context, Lars Rensmann shows in his chapter that Arendt and Adorno develop a distinctly cosmopolitan response to the historical caesura of the Nazi genocide, which exploded the limits of law and morality. For both theorists, this particular experience has forced upon humanity a new cosmopolitan imperative that replaces Kant's abstract formalism, and liberal trust in legalism: namely, to prevent humans from becoming "superfluous" victims of genocide, and to make sure that nothing similar happens again. However, humankind faces a human rights aporia that has become apparent with crimes against humanity and the emergence of global political modernity. Neither the "bankrupt" nation-state system nor appeals to a global legal system have been capable of preventing mass-scale human agony. Therefore, Rensmann argues, Arendt and Adorno point to a cosmopolitics "from below" grounded in a critical understanding of global conditions, as well as situated in particular contexts and acts of human solidarity within and across borders. The universal, then, depends primarily upon its appropriation in diverse human communities and decentered associational bonds. It is first and foremost through the vernacularization of cosmopolitan claims that universality survives.

Robert Fine argues in his chapter that Arendt and Adorno confront a similar problem. They both address a basic contradiction that lies at the heart of modern society: the elevation of subjective freedom, on the one hand, and the domination of subjects through the logic of commodification inherent in the capitalist economy and the instrumental rationality of the modern state, on the other. Such a contradiction is the result of a key feature of modernity: its logic separates subject and object. In and of itself, this does not necessarily result in catastrophe; yet the avoidance of the latter requires human agency. Fine argues that for both Adorno and Arendt, the ever-present possibility of a slide into barbarism is, however precariously, held off by human institutions whose legitimacy can never be taken for granted. The writings of Adorno and Arendt provide us with vivid images of what happens when these institutions are destroyed.

In his reconstruction of their post-Holocaust reflections on the "anti-Semitic question," Jonathan Judaken shows that Arendt and Adorno develop very different theoretical paradigms to understand the problem. Despite the differences between their interactionist and socio-psychoanalytic approaches, however, they share a common problem that riddled their respective understandings of antisemitism. Both depend upon elevating what Judaken calls "the conceptual Jew." The conceptual Jew in Arendt and Adorno comes to serve as a figure of difference: a cipher for the outsider, the queer, the nomad. It is also closely identified with financial capitalism and the underside of modernity. The very processes that Arendt and Adorno sought to itemize and critique are thereby personalized, leading them to reiterate certain stereotypical constructions of Jews and Judaism. Still, Arendt's interactionist understanding and Adorno's socio-psychological critical theory provide conceptual tools for thinking about antisemitism and the modern sociological and political processes that underpin it.

In their chapter, Julia Schulze Wessel and Lars Rensmann approach Arendt's and Adorno's theorizing about antisemitism, the constitutive ideology of the Nazi regime, from a different angle. Both thinkers make a seemingly paradoxical claim: they recognize that antisemitism became more and more radical and lethal over the course of history, justifying mass crimes against

Jews in the twentieth century, yet it also became less relevant, if not "disappeared" as a subjective prejudice. An explanation of this paradox can be found in Arendt's and Adorno's focus on pathologies of modern life that paralyze human capacities for judgment. Modern totalitarian antisemitism proclaims Jews to be "objective enemies," doomed to extermination independent of their individual or political behavior. Antisemitism thus standardizes the other, completely isolating itself from the perception of its particular objects. The contents of such ideology and its victims are, however, in principle exchangeable. Shifting the focus on the form of ideology, Schulze Wessel and Rensmann suggest that antisemitism in Arendt's and Adorno's theorizing reflects a loss of experience and the breakdown of thought and judgment. Though Nazi antisemitism constituted a specific phenomenon, it was also enabled by certain modern conditions and modern political imaginaries.

Theory in Exile, Exile as Theoretical Paradigm

The profound theoretical impact of the historical phenomena of Nazi totalitarianism and the Holocaust is indisputable. In Arendt's and Adorno's cases, they also had very concrete impacts on their life and their work. Without reducing Arendt's and Adorno's work to their personal experiences and their historical context, it would be difficult to overlook them. The experience of forced exile as German Jewish intellectuals in America,[85] or their views of the concentration camps, which they barely escaped, are constitutive for their thinking. In her youth, Arendt, for instance, was hardly interested in politics or history. As a Jew, however, she saw herself thrown into politics after the Nazis took power in Germany and existentially threatened the life of Jews. After her arrest by the Gestapo, she immediately escaped to France because she did not intend "to run around in Germany as a second-class citizen."[86] This desperate experience of loss of citizenship is constitutive for Arendt's brilliant analysis of the aporiae of human rights in *The Origins of Totalitarianism*. Here she interprets the fundamental loss of the "right to have rights," the right to be a member of a political community, as the precondition of extermination. According to Arendt, the loss of citizenship also means the loss of worldliness; the loss of a polity makes humans politically superfluous and can, in the modern age of organized mankind, simultaneously be understood as an expulsion from humanity[87] that leads to the nakedness of bare life (*zōē*). While different international norms and rights of refugees and stateless have emerged since then,[88] Arendt's insight into the meaning of political membership, and the implications of its loss, remains an important, still relevant contribution that helps us understand the paradoxes of political modernity.

Adorno's escape and exile were similarly decisive experiences for his thinking. Initially, Adorno clearly underestimated the impact of the Nazi rule. Although he was forced to give up his teaching position at the University of Frankfurt in 1933, he continued to hope during the first years of Nazi rule that the *Spuk* (spook, haunting) would soon be over. Such early naïve misperceptions soon gave way to drastic implications for Adorno's thinking after his escape from Nazi Germany and the Shoah. These experiences enhanced his self-understanding as a "homeless intellectual" and the radicalization of a conceptual distance from a society that could no longer be trusted. Most important, survival of the catastrophe became a precondition and key presupposition of Adorno's future thinking. Notions of marginalization, disruption, break, collapse, and discontinuity are signatures of both Arendt's and Adorno's theoretical and philosophical endeavors thereafter and lend them an uncanny contemporaneity.[89] However, the fact that both Arendt's and Adorno's theorizing by no stretch of the imagination simply continued as if nothing happened, but was deeply marked by the unprecedented atrocities in modern Germany and Europe, was for a long time either ignored in the reception of their work, or their critical reflections on this rupture were reduced to expressions of merely individual experiences.[90]

A crucial dimension of modernity's self-awareness, as already suggested, is what Kant called the public use of reason. Hence the very concept of the intellectual whose specific origins can be traced to the Dreyfus Affair—an event with a deep antisemitic undercurrent that plays a significant role in Arendt's account of the origins of totalitarianism—is inextricably bound to the fate of the public sphere. Dirk Auer poses the question concerning the changed role for the intellectual once he or she has through exile and migration experienced a break in this relationship to a given sphere of publicity marked by language and culture. He concludes that the intellectual-in-exile occupies a strange, "neither-nor" space embodied in Adorno and Arendt's positions, "neither friend nor foe, neither inside nor outside, neither distanced observer, nor full participant."

Similarly, Samir Gandesha contends that Arendt's and Adorno's contemporary importance lies in their attempts to rehabilitate experience, and that their own specific experiences of exile are central to this project. It is precisely their experience of exile that has the most to offer us today, in a period of forced migration perhaps not seen on an equivalent scale since the interwar period, and that will no doubt increase in the near future. That is, for both Arendt and Adorno, such a *conception of experience*, while perhaps present in nascent form prior to their forced exile from Germany, undergoes an intensified development as a direct effect of their own respective confrontations with the condition of a loss of *Heimat* (home). In other words, this experience was the basis for their development in rather different ways of what Gandesha calls a "homeless philosophy."

PART ONE

Political Modernity, Theory, and Philosophy

TWO

Arendt and Adorno
*The Elusiveness of the Particular
and the Benjaminian Moment*

SEYLA BENHABIB

I

Few if any images capture the poignancy of the twentieth century better than that of Hannah Arendt and Walter Benjamin playing chess during their French exile, which lasted from 1933 to 1940.[1] Benjamin and Arendt, who already knew each other from a distance in Berlin—she was married to his cousin, Gunther Anders (Stern)—grew closer during their time in Paris, and Arendt became part of a large circle of German émigrés alongside Benjamin in the cafes of the Latin Quarter. Arendt met her second husband, Heinrich Blücher, on several occasions, among them on evenings at Benjamin's apartment, and an affectionate friendship developed among the three of them.[2] Benjamin and Arendt taught Blücher to play chess. "Yesterday I played chess with Benji for the first time in a long and interesting game," Blücher wrote. Arendt responded playfully: "I am extremely proud you beat Benji. It reflects well on my teaching."[3]

Chess appears to have been not just a pastime for Benjamin but a complex metaphor for his thinking about history, progress, teleology, and the ironies of fate. The first thesis of Benjamin's "Theses on the Philosophy of

History," composed in shock at the signing of the Hitler-Stalin pact, reads as follows:

> The story is told of an automaton constructed in such a way that it could play a winning game of chess, answering each move of an opponent with a countermove. A puppet in Turkish attire and with a hookah in its mouth sat before a chessboard placed on a large table. A system of mirrors created the illusion that this table was transparent from all sides. Actually, a little hunchback who was an expert chess player sat inside and guided the puppet's hand by means of strings.[4]

The puppet, for Benjamin, was "historical materialism." Arendt was entrusted with bringing Benjamin's suitcase, which contained this manuscript, to the United States after his death. Two decades later, she lovingly edited these and other texts of Benjamin's, translated into English by Harry Zohn, into a volume titled *Illuminations: Essays and Reflections*.

The ironic contempt for the doctrine of "historical materialism" expressed by Benjamin via the metaphor of the chess-playing puppet was undoubtedly shared by Arendt and Blücher. Blücher, who had been a member of the Spartacist league in Berlin, founded by Rosa Luxemburg, broke with his faction after her death and escaped to Paris ahead of the German police. Yet neither he nor Arendt nor Benjamin gave up the hope that one would somehow beat the mysterious little hunchbacked dwarf, that is, the chess master who seemed to pull the strings of history. "To articulate the past historically," Benjamin wrote in Thesis VI, "means to seize hold of a memory as it flashes up at a moment of danger.... In every era the attempt must be made anew to wrest tradition away from a conformism that is about to overpower it."[5]

These few lines can serve as a guidepost for understanding Arendt's own practice of historical narrative, ranging from her discussions of antisemitism and imperialism in *The Origins of Totalitarianism* to her account of the French and American revolutions in *On Revolution*, and even to *Eichmann in Jerusalem*. For Arendt, as for Benjamin, there was "redemptive power" in narrative.[6] The political philosopher, as narrator, had "to seize hold of a memory as it flashes up at a moment of danger," and undo the chess master's moves, which always seemed to outwit historical actors by suffocating the "new" under the weight of historical conformism and false teleology.

But why begin an essay on Arendt and Adorno with an account of Benjamin's theses on history and their influence on Hannah Arendt? It is the

"Benjaminian moment" in their work, I argue, that best reveals the subterranean affinities between Arendt and Adorno. It is widely known that any consideration of Arendt and Adorno as thinkers who share intellectual affinities is likely to be thwarted from the start by the profound dislike that Arendt in particular, seems to have had for Adorno.[7] In 1929, Adorno was among members of the faculty of the University of Frankfurt who evaluated the *Habilitation,* essential to secure a teaching post in a German university, of Arendt's first husband, Günther Anders (Stern). He found the work unsatisfactory, thus ending Stern's hopes of a university career. It was also in this period that Arendt's notorious statement regarding Adorno, "Der kommt uns nicht ins Haus!"—meaning that Adorno was not to set foot in their apartment in Frankfurt—was uttered.[8]

This hostility on Arendt's part never diminished, while Adorno endured it with a cultivated *politesse.* Arendt's temper flared up several more times at Adorno: first, when she was convinced that he and his colleagues were preventing the publication of Benjamin's posthumous manuscripts,[9] and secondly, after the publication in 1964 of Adorno's critique of Heidegger, *Jargon der Eigentlichkeit (The Jargon of Authenticity).*[10]

Of course, such psychological attitudes and personal animosities cannot guide our evaluations of a thinker's work, texts, and legacy. And this is particularly true in the case of Arendt and Adorno, who not only reflected upon the "break in civilization" caused by the rise of fascism and Nazism, the Holocaust, and the defeat of the working classes in Europe and elsewhere, but asked, "What does it mean to go on thinking?" after all that. They shared a profound sense that one must learn to "think anew," beyond the traditional schools of philosophy and methodology. It is this attempt to "think anew" that I will refer to as their "Benjaminian moment." Put succinctly: Arendt as well as Adorno came to believe that thinking must free itself from the power of "false universals." This means not only refuting historical teleologies but, at a much deeper level, it involves a categorical critique of all philosophical attempts at totalizing and system building. For Arendt, honest thinking can only be accomplished in "fragments"; for Adorno, thinking must resist the temptation to overpower the object, letting it instead appear and assert itself over against the epistemic imperialism of subjectivity. The "primacy of the object"[11] for Adorno and the "fragmentary constellations" for Arendt illustrating the criss-crossings of tendencies and trends in culture, history, and society, all of which might have happened differently, are central themes in their work revealing the legacy and influence of Walter Benjamin. This critique of false universals, shared by both Arendt and Adorno, frees thought to face the "elusiveness of the particular" and leads to an encounter with Kant's *Critique of Judgment*.[12] Arendt finds in Kant's doctrine of "reflective judgment" an epistemology for elucidating the particular without dismissing the intersubjective quality of all judgment. For Adorno, aesthetic judgment becomes a paradigm for thinking beyond the false harmonies of the naturally beautiful (*Naturschöne*), on the one hand, and awe of the sublime (*das Erhabene*), on the other. Can reflective judgment, whether moral, political, or aesthetic, restore the power of thought, then? Adorno's 1934 essay on "The Actuality of Philosophy" and Arendt's 1946 essay on "What Is Existenz Philosophy?" will serve as my entry points to this question.

II

On May 7, 1931, upon assuming a position in the Faculty of Philosophy at the University of Frankfurt, Adorno gave a lecture titled "Zur Aktualität der Philosophie" (The Actuality of Philosophy).[13] The opening statement of this text already indicates the militant rigor with which the young professor is ready to take on the philosophical establishment: "Whoever chooses philosophy as a profession today must first reject the illusion that earlier philosophical enterprises begin with: that the power of thought is sufficient to grasp the totality of the real. No justifying reason could rediscover itself in a reality whose order and form suppress every claim to reason; only polemically does reason present itself to the knower as total reality, *while only in traces and ruins is it prepared to hope that it will ever come across correct and just reality.*"[14] Since the left Hegelian critique (Feuerbach, Marx, Engels) of Hegel's assertion "that the actual is rational; and that the rational is actual" (Was vernünftig ist, das ist wirklich; und was wirklich ist, das ist vernünftig),[15] faith in the capacity of reason to "grasp the totality of the real" had been shown to be a chimera at best and an ideology at worst. Following this tradition, Adorno is not only criticizing the hubris of philosophical thought but also indicating that "the real" itself "suppresses every claim to reason"; the failure of philosophy is not that of the thinker alone but also that of a reality that does not permit itself to be grasped as rational. "Only in traces and ruins," Adorno writes, introducing a Benjaminian phrase, wholly unknown to philosophical discourse at the time, can a "correct and just reality" be encountered.

Adorno proceeds to survey the contemporary German philosophical scene. The question of Being, called the most "radical" by Heidegger, is according to Adorno, "powerless . . . it is nothing more than an empty-form principle whose archaic dignity helps to cover any content whatsoever."[16] By contrast, the neo-Kantianism of the Marburg School has preserved its "self-contained form as a system, but has thereby renounced every right over reality."[17] Georg Simmel's *Lebensphilosophie* is an attempt to reach out beyond the categories to the real itself, but instead it "becomes resigned to the 'living' as a blind and unenlightened concept of nature." Furthermore, Heinrich Rickert's Southwest, or Baden, neo-Kantian School tries to mediate between the extremes by producing "value" categories that sets reality in relation to these values. But their locus and source remain undetermined: "they lie between logical necessity and psychological multiplicity somewhere."

Adorno's greatest esteem in this essay is reserved for Husserl and his efforts at "transcendental phenomenology," aimed to gain "a trans-subjective binding order of being." Even if he took post-Cartesian "transcendental idealism" as his starting point, it was an "authentically productive and fruitful discovery of Husserl" that he recognized the meaning of "the non-deducible given [*unableitbaren Gegebenheit*]," as "the fundamental problem of the relationship between reason and reality." But every Husserlian analysis of the given still rests on transcendental Idealism, and it is proof of Husserl's "great and clear honesty" that "the jurisdiction of reason" (*Rechtsrechnung der Vernunft*) remains "the court of final appeal."[18]

Adorno returns once more to Heidegger in this context: whereas Husserl, despite the origins of his phenomenology in transcendental Idealism, acknowledges the problem of the "given" and the irreducibility of reality to the jurisdiction of reason, Heidegger transforms the ontology of being into "the existential analytic of Dasein."[19] "It is thus no accident," observes Adorno, "that Heidegger falls back precisely on the latest plan for a subjective ontology produced by Western thinking: the existentialist philosophy of Soren Kierkegaard."[20]

As I will show in the next section, there are astonishing parallels between Adorno's account of the collapse of objective Idealism and the transition from Husserlian phenomenology to existential phenomenology and eventually to existentialism *tout court*, and Arendt's own reconstruction of these same philosophical currents in "What Is Existenz Philosophy?" Arendt proceeds, however, from the failure of philosophy to restore a "sense of being-at-home-in the world" to the political implications of the analytic of *Dasein*, whereas Adorno draws a suggestive parallel between Kierkegaard's "leap into faith" and the Heideggerian resolve unto death: "However, a leap and an undialectical negation of subjective being is also Heidegger's ultimate justification, with the sole difference that the analysis of the 'existing there' (*Vorfindlichen*—the ready-to-hand), whereby Heidegger remains bound to phenomenology and breaks in principle with Kierkegaard's idealist speculation, avoids the transcendence of belief . . . and instead recognizes solely the transcendence of a vitalist 'thus being' (*Sosein*) in death."

Writing in 1931, before Heidegger joined the NSDAP and assumed the rectorship of the University of Freiburg, forever casting a shadow on his standing as a philosopher, Adorno, unlike Arendt in 1946, does not, of course, seek to uncover the possible links between Heidegger's Nazi politics and his existential ontology of death and anxiety. Instead, Adorno still questions how "The claim to totality made by thought is thrown back upon thought itself, and it is finally shattered there too."[21] The categories of thrownness, anxiety, and death "are in fact not able to banish the fullness of what is living," but swinging between an irrational exuberance for the "pure concept of life," and feelings of dread and anxiety in view of the finitude of *Dasein*, the pendulum of phenomenology after Husserl disintegrates through these wild gyrations.

After the failure of these attempts at philosophical system building, is philosophy itself actual? Adorno considers the efforts of the Vienna School to self-liquidate philosophy into science. Not denying "the extraordinary importance of this School," he nevertheless argues that two problems cannot be mastered by the positivist turn to the sciences: first is the meaning of "the given" itself, which according to Adorno, "is not ahistorically identical and transcendental, but rather assumes changing and historically comprehensible forms"; the second is the problem of "the alien ego," accessible for empirio-criticism only "through analogy."[22] In singling out the problem of "the given" and that of "intersubjectivity" as the two problems to which empirio-criticism can provide no answers, Adorno may have been following Georg Lukács's *History and Class Consciousness*, which, in the famous essay on "Reification and the Consciousness of the Proletariat," also highlights these two issues as pitfalls of bourgeois philosophy.[23] For Lukács, both problems had their roots in the inability of bourgeois thought from

Descartes to Kant, and through Locke and Hume, to grasp the relation of the epistemic subject to the world, not in terms of mere contemplation, but as a form of active, involved, material praxis of transforming nature in the process of socially laboring in cooperation with other human beings. Adorno does not take this materialist route of dissolving the problems of modern philosophy into a teaching of historically situated social labor.[24] Instead, he asserts that although "Philosophy will not be transformed into science" under the positivist and empiricist attack, "philosophic problems will lie always, and in a certain sense irredeemably, locked within the most specific questions of the separate sciences."[25] Adorno continues: "Plainly put: the idea of science (*Wissenschaft*) is research; that of philosophy is interpretation . . . philosophy persistently, and with the claim of truth, must proceed interpretively without possessing a sure key to interpretation."[26]

Adorno's magisterial survey of the history and actuality of philosophy has resulted in a rejection of "the power of thought to grasp the totality of the real."[27] Husserlian phenomenology confronts the non-deducible given; Heideggerian ontology leads to an existentialism of dread and death; Simmel's *Lebensphilosophie* results in an irrational exuberance toward an uncritical concept of "life"; the Marburg School of neo-Kantianism remains caught in a teaching of categories without any persuasive connection to the real; the Rickert School postulates values, neither the origin nor the extent of which it can explain; the Vienna School, like Husserl, cannot resolve the problem of the given nor of the "alter ego," of the constitution of intersubjectivity. How then is the concept of "interpretation" supposed to provide an answer to this formidable array of problems? And what does "interpretation" mean?

Interpretation is not to be confused with the problem of meaning; it is not the task of philosophy to present reality as if it were meaningful; nor should interpretation suggest a "second, secret world," behind the appearances. Referring explicitly now to Benjamin's *Origin of German Tragic Drama* (*Ursprung des deutschen Trauerspiels*),[28] on which he was then teaching a seminar, Adorno writes:

> Authentic philosophic interpretation does not meet up with a fixed meaning which already lies behind the question; but lights it up suddenly and momentarily, and consumes it at the same time. Just as riddle-solving is constituted, in that the singular and dispersed elements of the question are brought into various groupings long enough for them to close together in a figure out of which the solution springs forth, while the question

disappears—so philosophy has to bring its elements, which it receives from the sciences into changing constellations, or, to say it in a less astrological and scientifically more current expression, into changing trial combinations, until they fall into a figure which can be read as an answer, while at the same time the question disappears. The task of philosophy is not to search for concealed and manifest intentions of reality, but to interpret unintentional reality, in that, by the power of constructing figures, or images (*Bilder*), out of the isolated elements of reality, it *negates (aufhebt) questions, the exact articulation of which is the task of science.*

Although Adorno concludes this passage with a gesture toward the "strange affinity between interpretive philosophy. . . . and the thinking of materialism,"[29] his Frankfurt colleagues at that time, including Max Horkheimer, could not but have been astonished at this turn in Adorno's thinking toward this elusive concept of materialist interpretation.

In his 1937 essay on "Traditional and Critical Theory," Horkheimer would reverse Adorno's contentions: first, it is the task of philosophy to pose the questions, "the exact articulation" of which remains its (philosophy's) task. The sciences enable an answer, in that one can integrate their results into some kind of analysis of an "epoch approaching its end,"[30] but they do not supply philosophy with *its* questions; second, critical theory rejects the problem of "the given," by showing that, following Marx and Lukács, the given is constituted in and through a process of social labor and that nature is formed sociohistorically. Third, critical theory is critique in that it allies itself with the oppositional forces capable of transforming the false social totality.

Even if between his own 1931 essay on "The Actuality of Philosophy" and the 1937 programmatic essay by Horkheimer on "Traditional and Critical Theory," Adorno's thinking underwent changes, he never accepted the program of social labor subscribed to by Horkheimer and Lukács, and insisted instead on the concept of *Naturgeschichte*, with all its paradoxical implications. He defended the idea of the nature of history and of the historicality of nature, neither of which could be reduced to the intentional activities of empirical or transcendental subjects. Furthermore, Adorno resisted sociologizing philosophy. As Benjamin Snow observes,

> Horkheimer believed as firmly as Adorno that bourgeois philosophy was in a state of decay, but he seems to have concluded that if metaphysics were no longer possible, then the philosopher had to look to the social sciences in order to find truth. For Horkheimer, the problem of "the object" tended to dissolve into (Marxian) sociology, the problem of "the subject" into

(Freudian) psychology, and critical theory attempted to explain their interrelations.... Adorno ... had an almost Hegelian faith in the immanent logic of philosophy.³¹

"A configuration of reality"; "changing constellations"; the "configuration of unintentional truth" through "historical images"—these are the Benjaminian phrases that tumble out of Adorno's pen in the last pages of this magisterial essay. In a grand dialectical move at the end of the essay, however, Adorno once more returns to the problem of Being and considers the following objection that could be raised against his own efforts as well. Could it not be objected, he asks, that

> out of blind anxiety before the power of history ... I bestowed upon historical facticity, or its arrangement, the power which actually belongs to the invariant, ontological first principles, practiced idolatry with historically produced being, destroyed in philosophy every permanent standard, sublimated it into an aesthetic picture game (*Bilderspiel*), and transformed the *prima philosophia* [philosophy of first principles] into essayism.³²

Adorno admits that these objections are legitimate, and he will gladly accept the reproach of essayism. For essay writing is a form of experimentation with the "power of freshly disclosed reality," and if with the disintegration of philosophical certainties and pieties, the essay makes its reentry into philosophy, then Adorno welcomes this. "For the mind (*Geist*) is indeed not capable of producing or grasping the totality of the real, but it may be possible to penetrate the detail, to explode in miniature the mass of merely existing reality."³³ As we know, Adorno did not just practice the essay form and in many of his writings, he retained the urge toward the totality (and showed repeated failures to attain it) by making the dialectic "suffer violence in its own hands," to use a phrase of Hegel's.³⁴ Yet what I am calling the "Benjaminian moment," is not confined to this early essay but is deep and lasting in Adorno's philosophy, informing his well-known mature theses such as the primacy of the object and the nonidentical concept of the concept.³⁵

The next German thinker who uses concepts such as "configurations," "changing constellations," and "crystalline structures" in such prominent fashion is none other than Hannah Arendt in her preface to *The Origins of Totalitarianism*,³⁶ whose German title, *Elemente und Ursprünge totaler Herrschaft* (Elements and Origins of Total Rule), explicitly evokes Benjamin's *Ursprung des deutschen Trauerspiels*.³⁷

In her first preface to the book in 1950, Arendt rejected the identification of "comprehension" with "deducing the unprecedented from precedents."[38] In the 1967 preface to part 1 of *The Origins of Totalitarianism*, around the time that she was editing Benjamin's writings in *Illuminations,* she wrote of totalitarianism versus "its elements and origins."[39] Arendt is not concerned to establish some inevitable continuity between the past and present that would compel us to view what happened as what *had* to happen. She objects to this trap of historicist understanding and maintains that the future is radically underdetermined. If we recall Benjamin's chess-playing puppet, Arendt is concerned to show that the mysterious hunchback behind it does not pull all the strings of history after all. Instead, she is searching for the "elements" of totalitarianism, for those currents of thought, political events, and outlook that form a particular *configuration* and *crystallization of elements*, quite differently than they did in their original context. All historical writing is implicitly a history of the present. And it is the particular constellation and crystallization of elements into a whole at the present time that should serve as methodological guides to their past meanings. Thus, none of the elements she assesses—antisemitism, the end of the rights of man, the decline of the nation-state, or the European scramble for Africa, race-thinking, and bureaucracy—are sufficient to explain how a racially based, exterminationist Nazi antisemitism totally dependent on a well-functioning bureaucracy emerged. Arendt explains

> The book, therefore does not really deal with the "origins" of totalitarianism—as its title unfortunately claims—but gives a historical account of the "elements" which "crystallized" into totalitarianism. This account is followed by an analysis of the "elementary structure" of totalitarian movement and domination itself. The elementary structure of totalitarianism is the hidden structure of the book.[40]

In view of the deep and lasting influence of Benjamin upon their thinking, the struggle that broke out between Adorno and Arendt (and also Scholem) over Benjamin's legacy may be more intelligible in retrospect. But my point here is to identify those "Benjaminian elements" in their thinking even beyond matters of intellectual influence and at a much deeper level of orientation in their thought. And for this, we need to return to Arendt's own first properly philosophical essay after World War II, namely, "What Is Existenz Philosophy?" written in 1946 for *Partisan Review.*

III

Adorno's "The Actuality of Philosophy" is a magisterial essay, astonishing in its self-confidence for one writing so early in his academic career. The same cannot be said of Arendt's "What Is Existenz Philosophy?"[41] It is written in a halting language, probably because she was not yet fully fluent in English; it is pedagogical in tone, trying to introduce an American audience, curious about trends in "recent European thought," to themes in German Idealism. There are a few too many "firsts" and assignments of periodicity: for example, she tells us that "the word 'existence' is used in the modern sense for the *first time* in Schelling's late work";[42] that "Modern existential philosophy *begins* with Kierkegaard";[43] and that "Kant... is *the real, though secret,* as it were, founder of modern philosophy."[44] One has the sense that Arendt is trying very hard to render manageable for a general, and not necessarily philosophical, audience some of the deepest currents of European philosophy since the death of Hegel.

Like Adorno, Arendt sees the collapse of the Hegelian system as the crucial point of entry into philosophical trends of the late nineteenth and twentieth centuries. She writes that "immediately after Hegel's death it became apparent that his system represented the last word of all western philosophy, at least to the extent that, since Parmenides, it had not... ever dared call into question the unity of thought and Being."[45] But this questioning had already been accomplished by Kant; in that sense, what culminated with Hegel was not an unbroken tradition but rather the illusion of "restoring" a tradition. It was Kant who distinguished the concepts of our understanding from the sensory impressions that originate with the impact of the external world upon our sense organs—our intuitions (*Anschauungen*). The "that" of our conceptual apparatus can never explain the "what" of our sense perceptions. I may know from someone else's description what a "lilac" is and looks like, but I shall never know what a lilac smells like until I have actually smelled one!

Arendt, however, draws from this two conclusions that diverge from Adorno's: first, "If Being and thinking are no longer the same, if thinking no longer enables me to penetrate the true reality of things because the nature of things has nothing to do with their reality, then science can be whatever it likes; it no longer yields up any truth to man, no truth of any interest to man."[46] Arendt, unlike Adorno, does not envisage a division of cognitive labor between the sciences and philosophy. For her, even until her last work, *The Life of the Mind*, the task of knowledge provided by the sciences is to account for factual reality and establish "truth," while the task of thinking, generally, and philosophy, more specifically, is to generate "meaning."[47] This concept of meaning in Arendt's mature work is quite close to Adorno's concept of "interpretation." It is concerned with the illumination of constellations and with attempts to think the "break" in tradition and the emergence of the "new" and the "unprecedented," in all their moral and political ambiguity. This feature of Arendt's thought is best exemplified through her interpretations of the history of political philosophy, contained in essays such as those in *Between Past and Future: Six Exercises in Political Thought*.[48]

In her early 1946 essay, however, Arendt, unlike Adorno, turns to the implications of the disunity of thought and being for the human being as a moral and political actor, as a "doer of deeds and a speaker of words." The Kantian opposition of thought and being, concept and intuition, subjugates man himself to a set of untenable dualisms and antagonisms, she observes. As bodies in space and time, human beings, like all matter, are subject to the sciences' laws of motion; they are determined, in ways that are obscure and unintelligible to them, by forces in nature, including human nature. But they are also creatures of reason, who can determine their actions on the basis of moral principles that they alone can discover. Humans are creatures of freedom insofar as they determine their actions in accordance with the moral law; however, as material bodies in space and time, they are subject to the laws of nature. "At the same time that Kant made man the master and the measure of man, he also made him the slave of Being."[49] "With this position, which followed directly from Kant," Arendt writes, "man was cut off from the absolute, rationally accessible realm of ideas and universal values and left in the midst of a world where he had nothing left to hold onto."[50] Certainly, Arendt's reading of Kant here is not compatible with Kant's own self-understanding, which saw human dignity as residing in admitting the limits of reason when confronted with its antinomies. Such despair at the human condition, despite many pessimistic passages about the "crooked timber of humanity," is not Kant's disposition.

When Adorno himself reflects on these Kantian antinomies in other parts of his work,[51] it is to free sensuous nature and "nature as such," from being the "other" of reason—but also, more radically, to rethink the relationship of concept and intuition, form and matter, reason and the impulses in such a way as to go beyond the metaphors of "self-legislation" and hierarchical "subjugation." Here Arendt and Adorno agree:

> Just as it was decisive for the historical development of the nineteenth century that nothing disappeared as quickly as did the revolutionary concept of the *citoyen*, so it was decisive for the development of post-Kantian philosophy that nothing disappeared as quickly did this new concept of man that had just barely begun to emerge.[52]

Adorno is not reluctant to bid this new concept of man a speedy farewell, whereas Arendt is more concerned with the damage done to the shared human world, when the "citoyen" disappears as quickly as the autonomous individual.

Into this rift caused by the disappearance of the rational subject and the *citoyen* (citizen), enters Kierkegaard, who is seen by both as one who has faced the abyss created by the antinomies of Kant no less than by the disappearance of Hegelian truths. "Kierkegaard set the "individual," the single human being, for whom there is neither place nor meaning in a totality controlled by the world spirit," against Hegel's system, Arendt writes.[53] It follows, therefore, that "All essential questions of philosophy—such as those concerning the immortality of the soul, the freedom of man, the unity of the world—which is to say, all the questions whose antinomical structure Kant demonstrated in the antinomies of pure reason," can be comprehended only as "subjective truths, not known as objective ones."[54] The universal is only significant in its relationship to the singular—this is Kierkegaard's deep insight. The *self* cannot be captured through abstractions such as the rational moral being; nor can "the knight of faith," in Kierkegaard's terms, be encountered via general sociological terms referring to the average bourgeois citizen. And the "self" is most singular in the limit situations (*Grenzituationen*) in which it encounters its own singularity most intensely. "Death is the event in which I am definitely alone, an individual cut off from everyday life."[55] Arendt, at this point in her reconstruction of these currents of thought, much like Adorno, moves from Kierkegaard to Heidegger's philosophy of *Dasein* and explores how existential ontology, following Kierkegaard's example, turns into a philosophy of dread, death, and anxiety.

Through their broad brush strokes that trace the dissolution of the unity of thought and being, above all in their singling out of the *emergence of the singular as opposed to the universal*, and in their acknowledgment of the absence of easy mediations and reconciliation between the universal and the singular, Arendt and Adorno come closer to each other in their diagnosis of philosophy after Hegel than either of them recognized or may have been willing to admit. In Arendt's exposé and critique of Heidegger in this essay—her first postwar comment on his thought—we see the outlines of how she intends to think her way beyond false universals to a concept, *not of the singularity of the self, but of the uniqueness of the person.* Where Adorno will resuscitate the dignity of the other of reason through his unique form of practicing dialectics without teleology, Arendt will go back to a move she first sees attempted by Husserl—namely, the recovery of the "world" as an epistemological and even ontological category. In fact, the affectionate esteem for Husserl that both Adorno and Arendt display is noteworthy.

Arendt actually begins this essay by considering phenomenology and pragmatism (she says nothing about the latter) as "the most recent and interesting epigonal philosophical schools of the last hundred years." Arendt views Husserl's attempt to "reestablish the ancient tie between Being and thought," through "the intentional structure of consciousness"[56] as a noble failure. Even if philosophical reconstruction can enable me to understand why there are chairs and tables at all, "it will never be able to make me understand why *this* table *is*. And it is the existence of *this* table, quite apart from tables in general, that evokes the philosophical shock."[57] As we saw, Adorno saw a moment of honesty in Husserl's admission that the "non-deducible given" remains a problem for phenomenology; Arendt sees revealed in it an attempt "to evoke magically a home again out of a world which has become alien."[58] "Husserl's phrase "to the things themselves" is no less a magic formula than Hofmannsthal's "little things."[59] "By transforming this alien Being into consciousness" Arendt writes of Husserl, he "tries to give the world a human face again, just as Hofmannsthal, with the magic of little things, tries of reawaken in us the old tenderness toward the world."[60] It is this "tenderness toward the world" that Arendt saw collapse around her with the events of the twentieth century, never to be quite restored. Nevertheless, as we have seen, Benjamin asserts in Thesis VI of his "Theses on the Philosophy of History" that it is the task of the thinker to "articulate the past historically . . . [which] means to seize hold of a memory as it flashes up at a moment of danger . . . In every era the attempt must be made anew to wrest tradition away from a conformism that is about to overpower it."

IV

This reconstruction of the history of philosophy after Hegel up to the point where the existential analytic of *Dasein* emerges and the "world is well-lost," to use Richard Rorty's famous phrase,[61] inadequately captures the personal and philosophical drama behind Arendt's essay.[62] This was the first time after the war that Arendt had commented on Heidegger's political behavior during his rectorship of the University of Freiburg and established a philosophical, and not merely characterological link, between his actions and his philosophy. It was also the first time that Arendt turned to elements of Jaspers's philosophy—his concept of *Grenzsituationen* and communication—to move beyond the pitfalls of Heidegger's ontology toward a concept of the "world."

The Arendt-Heidegger saga has been recounted many times, and this is not the place to revisit it.[63] Arendt is just as skeptical in her evaluation of the Heideggerian analytic of *Dasein* as Adorno was in 1931. After crediting Heidegger with "picking up the question that Kant had broached,"[64] Arendt writes that "Heidegger claims to have found a being in whom essence and existence are identical, and that being is man. His essence is his existence." Yet, far from recovering a sense of being-at-home-in-the-world, when Heidegger argues that *Dasein* has an "ontically-ontologically pre-eminent rank," he "puts man in the exact same place that God had occupied in traditional ontology."[65] We may want to contest this interpretation, which hardly does justice to the principles of "thrownness," "temporality," and "care," all of which have their sources in more traditional philosophical theology with Augustinian roots. And we also know that Heidegger, after his "turn" (*Kehre*), much like Adorno, forfeited the epistemic priority of the subject and insisted on a receptivity and openness to Being with bucolic phrases such as "Man is the shepherd of Being."[66]

Arendt is not unaware of these other dimensions in Heidegger's thought and gives very careful reconstructions of being-unto-death and resoluteness. But she insists that

> The crucial element of man's being-in-the-world, and what is at stake for his being-in-the-world is quite simply survival in the world. That is the very thing that is denied man, and consequently the basic mode of being-in-the-world is alienation, which is felt both as homelessness and anxiety. In anxiety, which is fundamental fear of death, is reflected the not-being-at-home in the world.[67]

The *who* of *Dasein* is the unique, singular self who can only face her death as hers. But a "Self, taken in isolation, is meaningless," Arendt observes.[68] The only thing that this Self can do is to "resolutely" take its singularity into account, and this "taking into account" has no determinate moral and political content. In fact, it can only be filled with political content that is either naïve in its lack of judgment concerning the political world or mendacious in its willingness to jump resolutely to history's call.[69]

Arendt and Adorno both see in Heidegger's attempt to restore the unity of thought and being via the analytic of *Dasein* a colossal philosophical failure, which cannot recapture being-in-the-world, but moves toward a vacuous subjectivism. It is at this point that Arendt locates the intrinsic, and not merely accidental, link between Heidegger's philosophy and his politics. "Later, and after the fact, as it were," she writes,

> Heidegger has drawn on many and muddled concepts like "folk" and "earth" in an effort to supply his isolated selves with a shared, common ground to stand on.... *But if it does not belong to the concept of man that he inhabits the earth together with others of his kind, then all that remains for him is a mechanical reconciliation by which the atomized selves are provided with a common ground that is essentially alien to their nature. All that can result from that is the organization of these selves intent only on themselves into an Over-self in order somehow to affect a transition from resolutely accepted guilt to action.*[70]

With this comment Arendt is not only diagnosing Heidegger's political *parti pris* for the Nazis, the full extent of which she still did not know in 1946, but she is stumbling upon one of the leading insights of her mature thought, namely, that Heidegger's "existential analytic" of *Dasein* as Self makes it impossible to think the *site of the political*, which is always that of being-in-the-world with others, "of one's kind." Arendt does not mean being-with-others of "one's kind" naturalistically. Heidegger himself had already written: "By reason of this with-like-Being-in-the-world, the world is always the one that I share with Others. The world of Dasein is a with-world. Being-in is Being-with-Others. This Being-in-themselves within-the-world is *Dasein-with*."[71] However, concepts such as *Self* and *Dasein* are singularly inappropriate to disclose the dimension of *Mitsein*. This is the case because

> Existence itself is, by its very nature, never isolated. It exists only in communication and in awareness of others' existence. Our fellowmen are not

(as in Heidegger) an element of existence that is structurally necessary but at the same time an impediment to the Being of the Self. . . . In the concept of communication lies a concept of humanity new in its approach though not yet fully developed that postulates communication as the premise for the existence of man.[72]

Arendt's programmatic path is now clearer to see: from here on, she will reinterpret Heidegger's concept of "being-in-the-world-with" through a concept of communication, the outlines of which are not given here, but wherein she sees herself indebted to Jaspers.

It is in *The Human Condition* that the new category of 'plurality,' which brings these dimensions together, is articulated.[73] Humans inhabit a space with others to whom they are both equal and distinct. Plurality is expressed through speech. "If action as beginning corresponds to the fact of birth, if it is the actualization of the human condition of natality, then speech corresponds to the fact of distinctness and is the actualization of the human condition of plurality, that is, of living as a distinct and unique human being among equals."[74] But this is precisely the step that Heidegger does not take: although the world is always a world shared with others, although *Mitsein* is a fundamental condition of *Dasein*, all forms of *Mitsein*, other than being-unto-death are dismissed as inauthentic. They represent the fallenness of *Dasein* into the chatter (*Gerede*) of the everyday and the "light of the public [that] darkens all" ("Das Licht der Öffentlichkeit verdunkelt alles"). Although I cannot develop the point here, it is noteworthy that with the category of plurality, and her insistence on the unity of speech and action, Arendt, along with Wittgenstein, becomes one of the few twentieth-century thinkers to note the significance of language as speech, as the give-and-take among human beings. Admittedly, this concept of speech is not much developed in her thought and is interpreted instead through metaphors such as "the web of human relationships."[75]

Arendt's 1946 critique formulates an insight that is crucial to her analysis of totalitarianism: namely, that societal atomization, the breakdown of civic, political, and cultural associations, and the loneliness of the atomized masses makes them susceptible to the influence of totalitarian movements. Atomized existence in a mass society creates worldlessness. The world is constituted by our common and shared experiences of it to the degree that we can trust that the orientations and significations we follow are more or less those shared by others as well. This commonness of the world is the background against which the plurality of perspectives that constitute the political can emerge. Politics requires a background commonality as well as recognition of plurality and perspectivality of judgment on the part of those who share this common space. Although Heidegger, through his analysis of *Dasein*'s worldliness as a form of *Mitsein*, made "being-with" constitutive of the human condition, his analytic of *Dasein*, rather than illuminating human plurality, testified to the progressing atomization, loneliness, and worldlessness of the individual in the concluding decade of the Weimar Republic.

In *The Human Condition*, Arendt turned to natality, plurality, speech, and human action to open up a categorical realm for thinking the political, breaking with "western philosophy's love affair with death." It is only through this form of being-with-others as talking and acting selves that the singular can be recaptured and can free itself from the dominance of the universal. Whereas Adorno's mature thinking formulates a novel concept of the concept to reclaim the singular and the particular against false universals, Arendt sees in narrative in general, and Kant's theory of judgment in particular, a move beyond the defunct ontological unity of thought and being. The Benjaminian moment returns for her. The concluding sections of this essay suggest in general terms the outlines of these later developments in their thinking.

V

With the rise of European fascism and Nazism, for Arendt as well as for Adorno, the critique of false universals and ontological certainties assumed an urgent moral and political dimension. Although little noted, the "authoritarian personality" type is one who also singularly lacks the capacity for adequate judgment. For Adorno and his co-workers, the authoritarian personality was incapable of evaluating individuals and circumstances without being imprisoned by rigid categories. Authoritarian personality types submitted their will as well as their judgment to those higher than themselves while demeaning those who stood in a position of social inferiority to them.[76] Such personalities were prone to paranoia in that they projected their own aggressive feelings toward individuals whom they then claimed to be hostile to them, who wanted their destruction and the like. Antisemitism, Adorno and Horkheimer argued, was based on complex processes of projection and paranoia. As the *Dialectic of Enlightenment* expresses it,

If mimesis makes itself like the surrounding world, so false projection makes the surrounding world life itself. If for the former the exterior is the model which the interior has to approximate, if for it the stranger becomes familiar, the latter transforms the tense inside ready to snap into exteriority and stamps even the familiar as the enemy.[77]

The result of such psychic processes is a loss of judgment, of the capacity to assess and evaluate both the circumstances around one and the consequences of one's actions.

Whereas Adorno uses the language of psychoanalysis and social psychology to characterize this general loss of capacity for judgment, Arendt persistently interrogates the relationship between thinking and moral considerations, asking: "Might the problem of good and evil, our faculty for telling right from wrong, be connected with our faculty of thought?"[78] This is why she claimed that Adolf Eichmann's most striking quality was not stupidity, wickedness, or moral depravity, but what she described as "thoughtlessness."[79] But then this led to the further puzzle that Heidegger, who thought in a fashion no other could, and Eichmann, who in her opinion could not "think" at all, were both complicit in the Nazi regime. Could the power of thought alone, then, not only prevent one from doing evil, but also enable one to judge the moral and political salience of particular circumstances? To retrieve the specificity of the particular, Arendt returns to Kant's theory of judgment and to his distinction between determinative and reflective judgment.

The Eichmann affair showed the centrality of judgment for human affairs in many and varied ways: there was the retrospective judgment that every historian and narrator of past events exercises; there was the moral judgment of the contemporaries who conducted the trial against Eichmann and judged his actions; and there was also the lack of a faculty of judgment on Eichmann's own part.[80] Prompted by the urgency of these problems, Arendt turns to Kant's *Critique of Judgment*.[81]

Arendt's unusual and somewhat idiosyncratic reading of Kant's moral philosophy in relation to the problem of judgment has been often noted. As Richard Bernstein has remarked: "Arendt well knew that, even though she invokes the name of Kant, she was radically departing from Kant. There is no question in Kant that the 'ability to tell right from wrong' is a matter of practical reason and not the faculty of reflective judgment which ascends from particulars to generals or universals."[82]

Judgment, for Kant, "as the ability to think the particular as contained under the universal," is determinative when the universal is given and the particular is merely subsumed under it. It is reflective, if only the particular is given and the appropriate universal has to be found for it.[83] Although Kant thought that the faculty of judgment was most needed with respect to teleological judgments concerning nature and to ascertain the beautiful, Arendt insisted that judgment was a faculty of "telling right from wrong,"[84] and not just the beautiful from the ugly.

In view of our analysis of Arendt's 1946 "What Is Existenz Philosophy?" essay, we can now see that for Arendt the problem of judgment, although it was of prime importance in the moral and political realm, originated early on with her critique of the search for false universals in the history of philosophy and her attempt to move beyond the crises of philosophy by discovering a way of "thinking" the new and the unprecedented in all its particularity. The evidence for this interpretation is provided through the fact that Arendt, *already* in 1961, before the Eichmann trial, in an essay on "The Crisis in Culture," explicitly discusses Kant's doctrine of "reflective judgment" and the role of *sensus communis*, as "the idea of a sense shared by all of us . . . that in reflecting takes account (a priori), in our thought, of everyone else's mode of presenting [something], in order as it were to compare our own judgment with human reason in general."[85] She writes:

> The power of judgment rests on a potential agreement with others, and the thinking process which is active in judging something is not, like the thought process of pure reasoning, a dialogue between me and myself. . . . And this enlarged way of thinking, which as judgment knows how to transcend its individual limitations, cannot function in strict isolation or solitude: it needs the presence of others "in whose place" it must think, whose perspective it must take into consideration and without whom it never has the opportunity to operate at all.[86]

Enlarged thought (*erweiterte Denkungsart*) is not empathy, for it does not mean assuming the standpoint of the other. It means making present to oneself the perspective of others involved, and it means asking whether I could "woo their consent." Enlarged thought displays the qualities of judgment necessary to retrieve and to do justice to the perspectival and plural quality of the shared world. Judgment requires the moral-cognitive capacities for worldliness, that is, an interest in the world and the human beings who form the world; it also requires a firm grasp of where one's own boundaries lie and where those of others begin. Whereas thinking requires autonomy, consistency, tenacity, independence, and steadfastness, judging requires worldliness, an interest in one's fellow human beings, and the capacity to appreciate the standpoint of others without projection, idealization, and distortion. But there are also tensions between the faculties of thinking and judging. Tenacity of thought may lead one to ignore the others' claims upon one and to deny their perspective as valid. Often, philosophical thought suffers from a certain worldlessness, precisely because it seeks consistency, not perspectivity. But it is the task of judgment to restore the commonality of the world in its full plurality. May we say then that judgment is needed to establish "configurations" and "crystallization of elements" in their singularity as well as commonality? How can we capture these configurations? May be through building metaphors? "In other words," observes Arendt,

> the chief difficulty here seems to be that for thinking itself—whose language is entirely metaphorical and whose conceptual framework depends entirely on the gift of metaphor, which bridges the gulf between the visible and the invisible, the world of appearance and the thinking ego—there exists no metaphor that could plausibly illuminate this special activity of the mind, in which something invisible within us deals with the invisibles of the world.[87]

Thinking dwells in the language of metaphors and tries to bridge the gap between the visible and invisible realms. But the political thinker, as opposed to the speculative philosopher, must have the capacity to *share* the power of metaphor with her fellow-human beings such as to nourish and sustain the fragile plurality of the shared world, which at any moment, can disintegrate and be overwhelmed by propaganda, kitsch and the loss of common sense.

What I have been calling Arendt's "Benjaminian moment" is caught in this tension between the universal and the particular, metaphor and reality, the faculties of thinking and judging. Metaphor provides abstract, imageless thought with an intuition drawn from the world of appearances, but "whose function is 'to establish the reality of our concepts'; thus undo, as it were, the withdrawal from the world of appearances that is the precondition of mental activities."[88] Arendt is referring once more to Kant's *Critique of Judgment*, paragraph 59, "On Beauty as the Symbol of Morality." "Now," writes Kant, "I maintain that the beautiful is the symbol of the morally good; and only because we refer the beautiful to the morally good (we all do so naturally and require all others to do so, as a duty) does our liking for it include a claim to everyone else's assent, while the mind is also conscious of being ennobled."[89]

Arendt herself does not explore this connection between beauty and the morally good. It is Adorno who, through his concept of the *Naturschöne*, explores this link and introduces another mode for retrieving the particular from being swallowed by false universals.

VI

Whereas Arendt sees in Kant's theory of reflective judgment and *sensus communis* a categorical strategy for retrieving the specificity of the particular, Adorno engages in a dialectical struggle with Kant's moral theory for some eighty pages in *Negative Dialectics*.[90] Freely deploying psychoanalytic categories against Kant's theory of the self and of the categorical imperative, Adorno writes:

> According to the Kantian model, the subjects are free, insofar as, conscious of themselves, they are identical with themselves; and in such identity they are once more unfree, insofar as they stand under its compulsion and perpetrate it. They are unfree as nonidentical, as diffuse nature, and as such free, because in the stimulations that overcome them—the nonidentity of the subject with itself is nothing else—they will also overcome the compulsive character of identity."[91]

Adorno repeats here a charge brought against Kantian moral philosophy since the young Hegel's critique that the Kantian moral law, formulated through the principle of the categorical imperative, amounted to a principle of tautology. "Act only in such a way that the maxim of your actions can be a universal law for all," is translated into the principle "Act in such a way that the maxim of your actions does not contradict itself."[92] This translation of the universalizability principle in ethics into tautological identity is a rhetorical tour de force. What Adorno adds to this is that the compulsion toward identity, displayed through the search for a moral principle that does not contradict itself, actually is not autonomy, but unfreedom. The epistemic and moral subject of Kantian philosophy—"the I that must accompany all my apperceptions"—reveals this rigid search for an identity that can only be achieved at the cost of denying not only otherness but the otherness within the self as well. The Kantian moral law is a perfect instance of rigid identity-formation through repression within and without.

"Utopia," writes Adorno, "would be the nonidentity of the subject that would not be sacrificed" (Utopie wäre die opferlose Nichtidentitat des Subjekts).[93] This nonsacrificial nonidentity, however, must not be understood as "reconciliation," as "being-by-oneself-in-otherness." In Hegel's understanding of freedom "as being-by-oneself-in-otherness," otherness simply becomes the narcissistic mirror in which Spirit can contemplate itself. To be by-oneself-in-otherness can only be achieved through the aesthetic experience of the *Naturschöne*—the "naturally beautiful."[94] To be sure, one cannot interpret the *Naturschöne* as if it were an eternally given and unchanging substratum of beauty. Rather, the "naturally beautiful" is antithesis, the antithesis of society[95] and as undetermined, the antithesis of determination. It is an "allegory," a "cipher," a "sign" (*Zeichen*) of reconciliation. It is a mode in which the mediation between humans and nature, between subject and object, can be thought of; it is not a state of affairs, a final condition, but an aporetic longing that can only be captured as "allegory" and as "cipher." Adorno writes, in terms that unmistakably remind us once more of Benjamin, "The naturally beautiful is the cipher [*Spur*] of the nonidentical in things set upon their course of universal identity."[96] From the standpoint of conceptual thought, the naturally beautiful, precisely because it can only be intimated but not stated, is deficient. But the utopia of a nonsacrificial nonidentity of the subject is intimated in the noncompulsory relation to otherness that forces the subject to forget himself or herself and thus to catch a glimpse of the moment of reconciliation. As Albrecht Wellmer observes,

> Adorno sees in natural beauty a cipher of nature that does not yet exist, of nature in a state of reconciliation, which has thus developed beyond the splitting of life into mind and its object. . . . The work of art, as an imitation of natural beauty, thus becomes the image of a nature which has found its speech, a nature redeemed and liberated from its muteness, just as it becomes the image of a reconciled humanity."[97]

Yet this image requires *philosophical interpretation*.[98] It is important to properly capture the interpretive complementarity, as well as dissonance between art and philosophy: To quote Wellmer again,

> philosophy, whose utopia is "to unseal the non-conceptual" by means of concepts, but without reducing it to conceptual categories . . . remains tied to conceptual language (what Adorno calls "*die meinende Sprache*") in which the immediacy of the aesthetic presentation of truth cannot be

reconstituted. Just as a moment of blindness adheres to the immediacy of aesthetic perception, so does a moment of emptiness adhere to the "mediacy" of philosophical thought. Only in combination are they capable of circumscribing a truth which neither alone is able to articulate.[99]

Undoubtedly, for Adorno the naturally beautiful was not an aesthetic paradigm alone but a moral ideal as well; the "nonsacrificial nonidentity" of the subject suggests a life-form and a form of conduct that we can only capture only in moments of intimation.

In contrast with Arendt, and above all with Kant, there is one dimension in this experience of the naturally beautiful that is missing in Adorno: the *communicability* of this experience; the necessity that our judgments of the beautiful be communicable and shareable with others. Kant's theory of aesthetic judgment for Arendt accomplishes both the revelation of particularity and a model of communication that is not based on coercion, but upon "wooing the consent of others" in whose place we must think. Following a similar line of thinking, Albrecht Wellmer has juxtaposed a Wittgensteinian theory of the concept to what he names "the rationalistic fiction" to which Adorno subscribes, and writes that "there is a mimetic force at work in the life of linguistic meaning, a force which enables what is non-identical in reality—as Adorno would say—to be reflected as something non-identical in linguistic meanings."[100] Arendt herself saw this "nonidentical in linguistic meaning," to be revealed through the "web" of relationships, embedded in narratives, and that are constitutive of the "who" of the self and the "what" of our actions.[101] It was in this constant and inevitable tension between the standpoint of the I and the other, between what my actions mean for me and how they are understood by others, that the perspectivality of the world was lodged. And because action is speech, this perspectivality does not just shatter into so many shards of a broken glass, but can be woven, undone, and rewoven just like a web. Arendt, in this sense, anticipated Habermas's critique of Adorno, which signaled the transition from the critique of instrumental reason to communicative rationality in the history of the critical theory of the Frankfurt School.

In his 1969 article "Urgeschichte der Subjektivität und verwilderte Selbstbehauptung," Habermas wrote with reference to the utopia of the nonidentical:

> Whoever meditates on this assertion will become aware that the condition described, although never real, is still most intimate and familiar to us. It

has the structure of a life together in communication that is free from coercion. We necessarily anticipate such a reality, at least formally, each time we want to speak what is true. . . . Adorno might just as well have not assented to this consequence and insisted that the metaphor of reconciliation is the only one that can be spoken. . . . The wholly other may only be indicated via determinate negation; it cannot be known."[102]

In her critique of the false universals of the history of philosophy, Arendt herself already made this communication-theoretic turn with means derived from Kant's aesthetic theory and her not fully developed concepts of speech, action, and narrativity.

Exploring the intellectual affinities and dissonances between Adorno and Arendt, as I have tried to do in this essay, not only permits us to reconstruct what still remains one of the most impressive philosophical traditions in the history of Western thought, it also permits us to see that beyond all the dogmatisms of schools, personal hostilities, and struggles to position oneself as an Arendtian or an as an Adornian, there lies a vast horizon of philosophical moves and countermoves, which are breathtaking in their configurations.

THREE

Political Modernism
The New, Revolution, and Civil Disobedience in Arendt and Adorno

J. M. BERNSTEIN

Modernism is the self-consciousness of modernity. Modernist practices elaborate an acknowledgment of their contingency, which not only signals the disenchantment of nature, secularization, the collapse of traditional authority, and release from the authority of dead gods and dead ancestors, but equally involves the uprising of the new, the *idea* of the new, the new as itself an indeterminate sign of value. The new signals what is without foundation, what is groundless, what affirms human particularity against the universal, what thus proceeds from human doing rather than unchanging reason, what belongs to history and its development, what bears within itself the emancipation of the human from myth and nature. In German, modernity is *Neuzeit*; it was as "new time" that modernity first became conscious of itself in the eighteenth century.[1]

For a significant stretch of the past one hundred and twenty-five years, the new, in the guise of artistic modernism, reigned as a pivotal cultural site for the hopes of enlightened modernity against its ongoing societal collapse into domination. Yet, as Theodor W. Adorno asserts, there is a paradox in this: "By exigency, the new must be something willed; as what is other, however, it could not be what was willed. Velleity binds the new to the ever-same, and this established the inner communication of the modern and myth. The new wants nonidentity, yet intention reduces it to identity; modern art constantly works at the Münchhausen trick of carrying out the identification of the nonidentical."[2] This paradox is overdetermined: on the one hand, it derives from the simple fact that to be intentionally willed is for an action or object to have a ruling conception as its ground, to be determined by some schema, some idea in the mind, some universal—hence not to be new; on the other hand, since at least some art objects "feel" new, appear as if in excess of any given universal or concept, then what gives what is, after all, only a "velleity," a disillusioning charge that the new in art is only art—and not world. Because modern art is semblance, then the new in art is the idea of the new rather than its actuality; the new in art is, Adorno claims, always only a longing for the new. But since it attaches to nothing less than the promise of modernity itself, that longing matters.

As a refuge for the idea of the new, the work of art is equally a refuge for the idea of collective praxis: "the process enacted internally by each and every artwork works on society as the model of a possible praxis in which something on the order of a collective subject is constituted."[3] It would be an understatement to claim that Adorno never managed to translate the promises borne by artistic practice into political praxis. Adorno's Marxism led him to construe liberal and democratic political forms as components of capital without a rationality potential beyond it. In this respect, his conceptions of critical theory as a placeholder for an absent politics and art as a placeholder for an absent collective praxis are as much suppressions of the political as they are critical resources. If one response to this suppression is to insist that philosophy and art, as placeholders, must be understood in interventionist, praxial, and hence political terms, the other is to admit the suppression and attempt to construct a social philosophy from Adornoian materials.[4] While I think there is much to be learned from both these responses, I agree with the suppressionist thesis that Adorno's reductionist reading of democratic practice should be rejected, and that democratic thought should be reconceived in ways that match the demands of critical theory. The thesis of this essay is that, after numerous detours and false leads, Hannah Arendt's political theory can be read as accomplishing the translation of artistic practice into political praxis; in her writings, modernism for the first time takes on a systematic political visage. If one supposes that Adorno's thought is a version of philosophical modernism that is the companion proper to his continual defense of artistic modernism, then one might urge that it is modernism itself that lies at the bottom of Adorno's thought; as a consequence, one would expect that the correct way to proceed, following Adorno, is to ask the question: what might political modernism be? The answer to that question would hence become the answer to the question of a political philosophy proper to critical theory. Arendt's political philosophy is the closest approximation to a critical political philosophy matching the modernist program of first generation critical theory to have appeared.

While the new is typically aligned with experimentalism in the arts (or, worse, with mere fashion), no one has asserted the thesis that the new belongs to the very meaning of human action more forcefully than Arendt. (In this understanding, action is opposed to the cyclical, reparative activities of mere laboring through which we sustain our biological being, and work, the business of fabricating "things"—from thumbtacks to bridges, from schools to works of art—in accordance with antecedent schemas or blueprints.) For Arendt, action relates to both the contingency proper to human sociality—what she calls "power"—and our capacity for new beginnings. Both these aspects of action, aspects that are in principle available in any nonroutine, public human doing, become thematic only in political action, which entails, conversely, that political action should thus be considered as *constituted* by its role of displaying and securing the ultimately contingent character of human sociality, the contingent nature of our being together as speaking and active beings, and its promotion of the new. But, arguably, to underline the contingent character of human sociality is precisely what is involved in thinking of political praxis as no longer governed by identity thinking; that is, to view democratic praxis as involving the permanent interrogation of the being of the social, that who we are is necessarily an ongoing experiment in simultaneously creating and discovering who we are, is to think the political under the auspices of the new.

Since this essay offers a dense sliver of a much longer exposition, let me begin by simply stating my conclusion. Once Arendt relocates her political theory from Greek antiquity into modernity, then the notion of actions as beginnings, as bearers of novelty, becomes exemplified in revolution, and hence in acts that found a state. But state founding is rare. And that rarity is the point. As Sheldon Wolin eloquently states the thesis:

> The loss of the political [which is the orienting experience governing Arendt's entire project] is a clue to its nature: it is a mode of experience rather

than a comprehensive institution such as the state. The thing about experience is that we can lose it, and the thing about political experience is that we are always losing it, and having to recover it. The nature of the political is that it requires renewal. It is renewed not by unique deeds whose excellence sets some beings apart from others [Arendt's baroque fantasy synthesizing Homeric heroes with Greek democracy], but by rediscovering the common being of human beings."[5]

Wolin means these words to be a criticism of Arendt, but in fact they precisely state the content of her doctrine of civil disobedience. Civil disobedience, I argue, reveals that the truth of revolutionary founding is always a refounding. If action is essentially beginning, and beginning is best exemplified by revolutionary founding, and founding is best realized in the refounding that is civil disobedience, then civil disobedience is the fulfillment of Arendt's political doctrine.[6] Civil disobedience as refounding is renewing; renewing is the uprising of the new in its double conditionality: it always dependent on the very past it exceeds, always failing (ready to be lost again).

Civil disobedience proceeds politically in a manner deeply analogous to the way in which Adornian negative dialectics proceeds theoretically: just as the claim of negative dialectics states that there is "more" to a given particular (or range of particulars) than the concept covering them permits, and hence that the concept in question does not exhaust but rather denies the reality it determines, so acts of civil disobedience contend that there is a claim by a range of particulars that existing social practices deny. Because legal norms are at stake, acts of civil disobedience can reveal the gap between particular and concept from either direction: the presumed legal norm is not truly realized in this instance, or the norm is realized and thereby suppresses the claim of these particulars. Civil disobedience is the emphatic realization of nonidentity thinking as internal to the very logic of democracy.

The idea that civil disobedience is a refounding and renewal depends upon three distinct ideas. First, the form of sociality proper to us as beings who speak and act, that is, the form of sociality that most fully acknowledges the contingent character of modern sociality, is promising. Promising, in all its Nietzschean hyperbole, forms the absolute center of Arendt's political ontology, her account of how it is and what it means for us to be bound together in the mode of speaking and acting. Second, it is the kind of bonding that occurs through mutual promising—above all in the social contract—that constitutes what Arendt means by power. Power is the proper name for the kind of social bond realized by a community of promisors. And third, the rational force of the principles under which civil disobedients act is analogous to the kind of force possessed by a modernist work of art. Kant's calls it "exemplary validity"; in it the rational force and normative authority of an idea (concept, value, universal) is *revealed* through the particular act or work. This is what revolutionary action and constitution making share with modernist artworks. On this account, the Constitution of the United States possesses exemplary validity, a validity dependent on its revolutionary emergence, which is reauthorized—refounding our political being together—in exemplary acts of civil disobedience. Since promising and exemplary validity are political morality and rationality as always conditioned, always contingent, always failing or falling or dissolving, hence always in need of renewal, Arendt's political doctrine is unequivocally modernist. As I will argue in conclusion, this doctrine converges perfectly with the role of determinate negation in Adorno's thought.

The Power of Promising

What distinguishes Arendt's version of radical democracy from other, analogous accounts is the centrality she gives to the notion of founding, and in her account of founding, the place she accords the American Constitution and constitution making. Founding is the most direct transcription of Arendt's conception of natality and beginning into a political, collective register. She conceives natality as a constitutive aspect of the human condition. For beings who have a world through conventional practices of speech and action, the arrival of each new being into the world simultaneously signals the possibility of new words and actions. This possibility is for the most part actualized behind the backs of individuals, but it can be upheld self-consciously. We embrace our humanity by embracing our capacity to begin: "With word and deed we insert ourselves into the human world, and this insertion is like a second birth, in which we confirm and take upon ourselves the naked fact of our original physical appearance. . . . To act in it most general sense, means to take an initiative, to begin. . . . It is in the nature of beginning that something new is started which cannot be expected from whatever may have happened before."[7] For Arendt, we take responsibility for our presence in the world by acting in the full sense of the word; we take responsibility for the world itself, all that is sedimented in the institutions and practices we inhabit, when we collectively found that world, that is, when we acknowledge that the terms of our mutual habitation are not given but made, and if made then capable of being remade, refashioned, done again, done in an image of the world we project. We cannot literally make the world, but we can fashion the bounds of our being together and the terms of our encounter with the world. Politics in part involves collective taking responsibility for our being together in the world; and we take responsibility for our being together in the world by fashioning the terms of mutual belonging. Political founding is, at this level of analysis, the collective corollary of the existential fact of natality and the character of action to begin something. Part of the human meaning of politics, what I term its existential excess, is provided by the constellation that connects natality with beginning and beginning with founding.

Surprisingly, perhaps, Arendt locates the revolutionary act of founding in the American Constitution, and thereby in constitution making generally. For her, a constitution is the act through which people constitute a government,[8] which is to say, it is the act through which they constitute themselves as *a* people with binding institutional rules regulating their life together. Hence the term "constitution" always possesses a double register for Arendt: it is the *act* through which a people constitutes itself as a people, and hence a performance of some kind; and it is the *object* of that act, what is constituted, hence the legal document, the laws, and institutions that are set in place in the light of that acting. It is the two-sidedness of constitution, political and legal, act and object, performative and constative, that is at the center of Arendt's version of constitutional democracy. One can hear the existential pathos she attributes to constitution in her approving quote of John Adams: "a constitution is a standard, a pillar, and a bond when it is understood, approved and beloved. But without this intelligence and attachment, it might as well be a kite or balloon, flying in the air."[9] We might say that the plausibility of Arendt's constitutional theory turns on her capacity to demonstrate exactly how we can understand, approve, and love the constitution in order that it be a standard, pillar, and bond, so that its standing is internally related to the regard it is accorded by citizens; constitutions without constitutional patriotism are empty—kites or balloons.

Arendt begins to secure her idea of constitutional founding through a unique development of social contract theory. Arendt's route into contract theory develops out of her understanding of promising, which, in the first instance, she considers from the perspective of neither politics nor morality, but rather, as a component of her phenomenology of action/praxis. In *The Human Condition*, after distinguishing action from labor and work, Arendt argues that action possesses two intrinsic predicaments: unpredictability and irreversibility. The remedies for these two features of action lie within action itself. Forgiveness is the remedy for irreversibility, while promising is the remedy for the "chaotic uncertainty of the future."[10] Forgiving and promising are the only moral precepts "not applied to action from the outside, from some supposedly higher faculty or from experiences outside action's own reach. They arise . . . directly out of the will to live together with others in the mode of acting and speaking."[11] Promising is a potentiality of action in that promising is itself nothing other than an action. Promising, as the memory of the will, is a disposing of one's future in the present in relation to one or more others; it occurs through the medium of a written or verbal act: stating the words "I promise." To promise is a performative utterance: the making of the utterance "I promise" is binding myself to others by binding the future course of my will, undertaking now to do or forgo particular future actions.[12]

Echoing the Nietzschean remarking of promising as what distinguishes humans from other animals, Arendt avers that

> without being bound to the fulfillment of promises, we would never be able to keep our identities; we would be condemned to wander helplessly and without direction in the darkness of each man's lonely heart, caught in its contradictions and equivocalities—a darkness which only the light shed over the public realm through the presence of others, who confirm the identity between the one who promises and the one who fulfils, can dispel.[13]

In saying that promising is a form of action that depends on others, that its force arises directly out of the will to live together with others in the mode of speech and action, and that it confers identity upon the speaker, Arendt is ascribing to promising the—Nietzschean—status of being the form of our normative relation with others; it is the paradigmatic form taken by a social bond that resides firmly within the domain of sociality. For Arendt, promising is sociality itself; it is the exemplary revelation of the normative authority of speaking and acting as essentially social events, as events that acknowledge plurality and natality. Promising for Arendt is not a mere intention, undertaking, commitment, or self-binding. On the contrary, and here is the crux of the matter, it is the opposite that is the case: the very ideas of intending, undertaking, committing, and binding oneself are constituted through the intrinsically linguistic institution of promising.

The force of promising does not depend on any "inner" psychological state, say, promising in my heart, but on my word being my bond irrespective of my heart. This is why excuses, which routinely apply to actions, do not apply to promises: we cannot have promised accidentally or inadvertently or unknowingly or by mistake, our words belying or falsely transcribing an opposing inner state. *Saying* the words "I promise" abruptly places me in an emphatic spiritual relation to my speaking partner: I am bound to her by my future being bound to her. Promising words, by so binding and bonding, stake the self, hence lend that self an imposing moral stature and standing. Promising lifts me out of the "equivocalities" of my heart into a space I share with others. Hence if my word is my bond, then it is that which gives promising its terrifying character, its character of locating me, presenting me in a social relation to others that I am no longer free to dispose of as I please; that is, my words place me socially with respect to others in a manner necessarily exceeding my accompanying desires or willings (since their spiritual urgency is formed by the normative import of the words). If I forfeit my bond, I thus forfeit myself, become hollow, unworthy, and lose face and standing.

Of course, not all promises are momentous ("I promise to take out the garbage"), or difficult to keep, or of a kind where failing them is failing one's place in the world. But promises can be all that, and when they are, this is because "since no word is really mine to dispose of as I wish . . . what I forfeit is language itself. . . . Forfeiting my word when my word is my bond would be like forfeiting my body."[14] This, from Stanley Cavell, sounds exorbitant, but is plainly entailed: if promising bestows upon me a public identity in relation to others, then forfeiting a promise is forfeiting that identity (myself for others). If I have that identity in the light of the words I speak, then as promisor, I am bound to the life of those words; when I forfeit my bond, I forfeit not my word here but my standing as a speaker: having failed that promise, my words no longer have the power of binding. Since my words are just my spiritual presence for others, when my words no longer bind and bond, then I no longer possess a spiritual presence for others. Hence forfeiting my word when my word is my bond is like forfeiting my body—it is forfeiting my linguistic-spiritual body, which is my public spiritual presence for others.

The spiritual content of promising depends on the kind of institution it is, its way of binding us to others and a future that thereby, if the institution is to flourish and mean in the ways its lineaments project, solicits subjects for whom saying "My word is my bond" becomes something fateful for them and all those they address. In *The Human Condition*, promising for the most part appears simply as the moral precept intrinsic to the life of action, saving us from the predicament of unpredictability. Yet the implicit subtext of her brief remarks gives Arendt's account the wider compass I am suggesting, which becomes thematic in *On Revolution*. What is at stake in promising, what makes it an exemplary institution, especially for us moderns, is its revelation of the power, authority, stakes, and potentialities embedded in the mere fact of our speaking and acting together. Promising exemplifies the spiritual density of speaking and acting together. Cavell (whose Austin-inspired account I have been drawing on) eloquently states the thesis: "the price of having spoken, or remarked, taken something as remarkable . . . is to have spoken forever, to have entered into the arena of the inexcusable, to have taken on the responsibility for speaking further, the unending responsibility of responsiveness, of answerability, to make yourself intelligible."[15] In Arendt, this thought comes with a Nietzschean pedigree, but its salience is the same: *speaking with others is to promise*.[16] The binding power of promising is hence the power invested in the space of appearances, our appearing to one another in the modes of speaking and acting.[17]

Mutual promising is the analogue in Arendt's political theory of the Aristotelian doctrine of friendship; it is her counter to the Platonic work model of politics that has some notion of social justice at its center. For Arendt, it is mutual promising, not justice, which is to be the bond of communities. Promising is "higher than justice" because it is the condition for it. The force of the claims of social justice is, at least in part, parasitic upon mutual promising because, in a secular world, no idea or norm can be politically authoritative unless it derives from our collective deliberation. But the authority of our collectively deliberating derives from how we are bound together as a deliberating body. The substance of that body is formed by our speaking and acting having a promissory status: we are bound together as a community of promisors, and hence *our* word is *our* bond. This is the fundamental source of Arendt's anti-moralism. Morality is too individualistic, too private, to bound to the whims of conscience, to be an adequate basis for collective living.

It is speaking as promising, speaking as the positioning of oneself in social space in the mode of answerability, and hence responsibility, that finally gives substance to Arendt's notion of power—power as nothing other than the social bond formed by speaking in a promissory mode.

> In distinction to strength, which is the gift and possession of every man in his isolation against all other men, power comes into being only if and when men join together for the purpose of action, and it will disappear when for whatever reason, they disperse and desert one another. Hence, binding and promising, combining and covenanting are the means by which power is kept in existence; where and when men succeed in keeping intact the power which sprang up between them during the course of any particular act or deed, they are already in the process of foundation, of constituting a stable world structure to house, as it were, their combined power of action. There is an element of the world-building capacity of man in the human faculty of making and keeping promises.[18]

Power is Arendt's word for Spirit, for the "We" that is an "I" and the "I" that is a "We." Power is the *bond* formed through speaking and acting together; it is what normativity, authority, and intersubjective relations become when they are united, legitimately bound one to another. Arendt was continually struck by instances in which the difference between power and violence become manifest, when power overpowers or at least challenges those in possession of the means of violence: the American colonists against the English, Gandhi's campaign against the British, the Hungarian revolution, the Vietnamese against the Americans, the civil rights movement, and so on. Where traditional theory is premised on the difference between might and right, between facts and values, between force and norm—all distinctions that imply a "divided line," giving the tradition an idealist or Platonic slant—Arendt focuses on the less common but phenomenologically equally evident difference between power and violence; a good deal of the import of Arendt's distinction depends on the fact that unlike the idealist pairs, power and violence have been conflated with each other, and, at least on the surface, appear to belong to the same semantic family. Power, which is the ability to act in concert, has four distinguishing aspects: (i) Power possesses normative legitimacy in opposition to the sheer capacity for destruction in the means of violence (the single area of direct overlap with the tradition); (ii) power is the possession of a collective, it is what *emerges* in acting and speaking together—which is why in cases of power, unlike the means of violence where one with sufficient means can overcome the many, no matter how powerful, numbers matter; (iii) power is the source of authority, it is what gives authority—the capacity to be obeyed unreflectively—to governments and leaders; and (iv) power is a kind of strength, the kind that emerges from the first three items, the kind that becomes manifest in the bonding of promising.

Power is an emergent property; it is the force or strength specific to the social bond formed through word and deed.[19] Again, it becomes most visible when, for example, a government suddenly loses it, when it literally appears on the streets in opposition to a government that discovers itself stripped bare of authority and possessing only the means of violence to resist—as occurred most recently in Egypt in Cairo's Tahrir Square (Spring 2011); or when, as in Vietnam, "an enormous superiority in the means of violence can become helpless if confronted with an ill-equipped but well-organized opponent who is much more powerful."[20]

I suggested above that the bond created through mutual promising is the replacement for the Aristotelian doctrine of friendship as the antecedent to and surplus beyond justice that is the source of political community. This is not exactly correct, since power is the name of that bond. Arendt says this explicitly. Power like peace is an end in itself. To say this is not to deny "that governments pursue policies and employ their power to achieve prescribed goals. But the power structure itself precedes and outlasts all aims, so that power, far from being the means to an end, is actually the very condition enabling a group of people to think and act in terms of the means-ends category. And since government is essentially organized and institutionalized power, the current question What is the end of government? does not make much sense either." Arendt's first stretch of argument against means-ends rationality and the teleological, work model of action reaches its conclusion in her conception of power as the end in itself specific to human sociality. Government is not for the sake of anything because it has power as its fundamental condition of possibility. Since power is the emergent property of speaking and acting as promissory modes, then power and the experience of power is the existential excess accompanying all merely noninstrumental collective action.

Because power is the necessary condition for the possibility of government, it most emphatically displays itself when the very possibility of government is at issue: in revolution and in founding.

> The grammar of action: that action is the only human faculty that demands a plurality of men; and the syntax of power: that power is the only human attribute which applies solely to the worldly in-between space by which men are mutually related, combine in the act of foundation by virtue of the making and keeping of promises, which, in the realm of politics, may well be the highest human faculty.[21]

While each promise presupposes the institution of promising in general, the making of a specific promise nonetheless *institutes* or *creates* a social bond. To say a promise institutes a particular social bond between us is equivalent to saying that a promise is, in miniature, a beginning and a founding: it begins a new history in our relation by creating a bond between us that stretches out into the future. If speaking and acting together implicitly contains a promissory lining, which creates a power-imbued space of appearance wherever individuals congregate for the sake of speaking and acting together, then, conversely, mutual promising itself is the making explicit of that implicit content—the institution of power. The act of foundation is the institution of power, the creation of a particular social bond that occurs through an explicit effort of mutual promising.

Civil Disobedience as Refounding

There is one further aspect to founding: the content of the mutual promise. Directly in line with the argument of "What Is Freedom?" Arendt contends that beginning is saved from arbitrariness through the principle it discloses, and hence beginning and principle are not only related but coeval:

> The absolute from which the beginning is to derive its own validity and which must save it, as it were, from its inherent arbitrariness is the principle which, together with it, makes its appearance in the world. The way the beginner starts whatever he intends to do lays down the law of action for those who have joined him in order to partake in the enterprise and bring about its accomplishment. As such, the principle inspires the deeds that are to follow and remains apparent as long as the action lasts.[22]

There is nothing new in these words except their contextualization: principle is now equivalent to the content of the mutual promise of founding, that is, principle is now not some antique idea (honor or excellence or love of equality), but the Constitution itself. Promises can have wildly diverse contents, but typically the contents are actions that themselves have external objects. The founding promise has as its content the terms that are to regulate and govern the community formed through it; hence it provides the normative terms governing the promise itself as a founding and a beginning of a life we are to live together.

The Constitution is awesome as both a promise and the premise for living a life based on nothing but mutual promising: it is the promise to live a life with others in accordance with the norms implied by the very idea that community is fundamentally the life of a being who makes promises. Hence, on Arendt's reading, if promising is making explicit the implicit promissory character of speaking and acting together, then the Constitution is itself the social mechanism through which that making explicit of promising becomes explicitly the terms of our life together. And, again, since it is through promising that we attain a normative identity in our being with others, then the Constitution, its creation of a community of promisors, is the mechanism through which we attain an ongoing normative identity with respect to one another. We call this identity being a citizen. This is the fundamental reason for Arendt's fierce opposition to liberalism, and her equally fierce fidelity to civic republicanism: constitution making as a form of promising necessarily leaves the private individual behind. To make a constitutional promise is to become a citizen for oneself and for others; one's political responsibilities and entitlements flow from one's identity as citizen—one's identity as promisor.

Arendt is quick to point out that this promising to live a life governed by the principles of mutual promising, as opposed to living a life governed by axiomatic or self-evident truths, was only dimly grasped by Jefferson in the Preamble to the Declaration of Independence (the document that most explicitly takes up the question of the authority of the founding). It emerges in his indulging in the "somewhat incongruous phrase, '*We hold* these truths to be self-evident,'" rather than the more natural "These truths are self-evident." For Arendt, the "We hold" is momentous, since it regiments the contents held, those self-evident truths, to our mutual promising. While the whole phrase combines "in a historically unique manner the basis of agreement between those who have embarked upon revolution, an agreement *necessarily relative because related to those who enter it*, with an absolute, namely with a truth that needs no agreement,"[23] the success of the American enterprise turns on the resolving of those truths into their performative statement, that is, their being held in the manner of a promise. What were self-evident truths become principles that remain "apparent as long as the action lasts."[24] But this is insufficient as it stands: while the authority of "We hold"—our right to do so—is intrinsic to promising itself, the authority of the content cannot be exhaustively accounted for in this way since principles inspire the deeds that follow from them, and in this sense inspire from *without*. While the "We hold" makes the content relative to context and community, and further binds us to that content as something promised, to say flatly that what is held has its authority solely from being promised makes the authority of the cognitive content of the principles no different in kind than any other object of promise (taking out the garbage)—which is patently absurd.

To draw on the conceptuality Arendt would later find in Kant's aesthetics, principles in *On Revolution* possess an *exemplary validity*.[25] Art, in modernity, is the domain for fashioning authoritative, novel unique particulars, items whose worth is not dependent on falling under an antecedent concept or norm. Kant develops the idea of exemplary validity in order to explain how this is possible. How is it possible for us to judge an item that is truly new as beautiful if it transforms what beauty and what art mean? How is it possible for an item that is not the product of an antecedent concept or idea to make original sense, create new meaning? How can something new possess authority? The puzzle over the authority of the Constitution is at one with Adorno's puzzle over the possibility of there being something new, the new that was to be the bearer of the hopes of modernity; they are the same puzzle. The puzzle that art cases raise is that in them the particular precedes the universal; there is a universal only by being *instituted* by the effort of some particular item. Artworks, at least in modernity, are beginnings; and it is that which in part makes their authoritative standing continually fascinating. Analogously, the Constitution is the act of founding, hence particular, while being the authoritative universal that legitimates what is revealed through it.

Artworks are items for which no rule can be given—hence they are groundless, intentionless, and unwilled—but nonetheless themselves serve "as a standard or rule for estimating."[26] Artworks are hence paradigmatically what principles are for Arendt: a rule or standard or norm or value that becomes manifest in an item, and through that manifestation legislative for both it and what might follow. The litmus test for exemplarity, what demonstrates that an item has that authority, is succession, that is, the production of further instances that do not imitate but rather "create from the same sources out of which the former himself created, and to learn from one's predecessor only the way to proceed in such creation oneself."[27]

The burden of modernity, and hence the continuing insistence of Arendt's modernism, her allegiance, via Kant, to modernism, turns on the discovery that in the realm of human affairs the only kind of authority principles (norms, standards, values) can have is exemplary validity. To say that the kind of authority the Constitution is to possess is that commensurate with the Preamble to the Declaration in which the contents are bracketed within the mutual promise that forms it—"We hold"—is to make the authority of the principles that follow exemplary. This is to say two things. First, the manner in which the Constitution itself appears, its contents, needs to be seen as analogous to the way in which a work of art appears. The Constitution is a particular; its contents need to be understood as both rules and a blueprint for government, and as the disclosure of the world in which such a notion of government can be received and have an impact. Beginnings are the beginning of a world, are world making. But the authority of that world making is the reconfiguring of the known world in the light of its projected shape. Hence, the Constitution is an item in the world that means to redescribe the world, give it a new look and appearance. Or better, the relation between the Declaration and the Constitution makes the latter a polemical universal, the universal implied by the revolutionary contestation of English authority and the rebellion against it. In this respect, every political act, in the full sense of act, is an argument and recounting of the world where that very argument is to fit and have its force.[28] (Autonomous artworks, we say, create their own audience; likewise, constitution making must here be seen as creating the community of its appropriate regard.) This is part of what it means to think of political acts as having an aesthetic moment. (The aesthetic, as Adorno and Arendt understand the concept, is nothing other than the exemplification of the transcendental logic of contingency—the exemplification of exemplarity.)

Second, what Kant calls "succession," Arendt identifies in terms of amendment and augmentation: "Thus the amendments to the Constitution augment and increase the original foundations of the American republic; needless to say, *the very authority of the American Constitution resides in its inherent capacity to be amended and augmented.*"[29] What Arendt is crediting to the American Constitution, albeit with a retrospective glance, is recognition of the only kind of authority available under conditions of modernity. Call it revolutionary authority. Revolutions typically fail, Arendt avers, because they seek to make absolute their founding moment. The genius of the American Revolution was the recognition that it formed *a* beginning, not the beginning, and that any beginning is just a beginning, hence contingent, hence in continual need of preservation, augmentation, and amendment.

Now if legitimate authority is essentially revolutionary authority, if founding is the quintessential political moment, then what happens *after*? What gives Arendt's account in *On Revolution* a utopian cast is her supposition that the current state of affairs is deficient for lack of an appropriate commitment to a pyramidal ward or council system. But what such a system amounts to in Arendt's thought is the continual dissolution of the poiesis of democratic praxis back into itself, as if every moment of democratic politics could be the realization of its three moments (founding, empirically continuing, refounding), as if the council system in Hungary would not have rigidified into a static, bureaucratic structure if it had lasted longer than twelve days, that it was only in virtue of its twelve-day life span that the revolution was made to appear complete in itself; as if, then, any council system in time would not become another bureaucracy; as if the size and complexities of modern societies permit something other than representative democracy; as if the components of any state power—scientific, technological, economic, and cultural—would not generate and perpetuate some form of elitism, and hence some formations of power that would be used both for *and* against people.[30] Perhaps the problem is methodological: Arendt's practice of historical phenomenology always tends to purify the elements she seeks to celebrate, and hence to distort their empirical reality. Whatever the reason, in *On Revolution*, Arendt still had the idea of an ideal polity—as there represented by an idealized construction of the American Revolution—against which contemporary reality might be measured. In so doing she in fact robs her theory of its modernism, and hence its own intrinsic radicality.

It is just this that she comes to recognize in her essay "Civil Disobedience" (1970). Action, in distinction from work and labor, involves a beginning. In political life, the idea of beginning becomes emphatic in revolutionary founding. In order to conceive of revolutionary founding as a beginning, two notions are necessary: first, we found through mutual promising, where promises are precisely the kind of speech acts that *institute* a new bond among agents that binds them to a future beyond themselves; second, because the act of founding involves the binding of subjects to one another in the light of a normative horizon represented by the Constitution, the validity of the founding is exemplary. Exemplary validity not only permits augmentation and amendment, but demands it. Mutual promising and exemplary validity are not by-products of founding; rather, they are essential to the authority of modern government, which can have no legitimate authority without revolutionary authority, since promising alone is the ground of legitimate power, and the exemplary validity of the constitutional settlement is the ground of the authority of statutory laws and policies.

The fact of the fabrication of government and state, which is the product of every founding, entails that the everyday life of a modern representative democracy will necessarily detach power from the people and rigidify exemplary validity into habit, command, and coercion. Call this the tendency toward totalitarian tyranny—the rule of no one—built into every modern, large-scale bureaucratic institution. Bureaucratic rationalization is the 'natural' way modern institutions fail.

In a quiet piece of self-criticism, Arendt agrees that the Lockean conception of the social contract, in which people contract with one another, is a legal and historical fiction; but it is not an existential or theoretical fiction. Further, for the first time, Arendt acknowledges that social contract theory *implies* a notion of consent. Hence, her question becomes: how can we align the role of consent with the promissory understanding of contract? She begins with the obvious assumption of social contract theory, namely, that tacit consent is given by birth, since we are dependent on society. But tacit consent is hardly voluntary since it derives from a situation of dependency. In acknowledging social dependency, Arendt is for the first time acknowledging the empirical reality internally conditioning, everywhere and always, political life itself (as opposed to being a mere external condition). Political life does not emerge after our life of mutual dependency is settled, which is the fantasy of *The Human Condition*, nor when the life of mutual dependency is not urgent or pressing, the fantasy of *On Revolution*, but rather from *within* a world always already constituted by dependencies, social *and* political. What this means is that the tacit consent we must give to the laws and norms governing our everyday lives, the consent entailed by our participation in and benefiting from life in a representative democracy, while truly a form of consent, does not on its own match the terms for legitimacy represented by the existential and theoretical truth of contract theory. In this situation, consent can become truly voluntary if and only if we have the power of dissent (the power of voice and exit). Dissent implies consent. So dissent keeps consent alive, giving it back its actuality. However, our consent is not to statutory laws but to the constitutional settlement (and only thereby to routine laws). In binding ourselves to the Constitution, we leave ourselves free to dissent from particular laws: "Consent, in the American understanding of the term, relies on the horizontal version of the social contract, and not majority decisions. . . . The moral content of this consent is like the content of all agreements and contract; it consists in the obligation to keep them. This obligation is inherent in all promises. . . . The only obligation which I *as a citizen* have a right to assume is to make and keep promises."[31]

In making dissent the cornerstone of her theory for consent, Arendt is doing nothing more than making explicit what is already implicit in her revolutionary theory. Because she was absorbed by the idea of actions as beginnings, with founding as the primary political moment, and with mutual promising as the formative act in that founding, Arendt had previously simply ignored the fact that revolutions are, in the first instance, acts of dissent and rebellion, transgression and negation, acts of saying "No!" If consent is bound to the moment of founding, then *every act of consent presupposes a dissent made good*. Actual consenting, as opposed to tacit consent, includes the potential for dissent, and actual dissent becomes the central mechanism through which tacit consent can become actualized, appear, and become manifest. Said differently, if all founding is only a beginning and not the beginning, authentic founding entails refounding. Refounding is the *truth* of founding; it is, to use Kant's language, to create anew out of the same sources from which the original emerged; in augmenting the original founding, it reveals that founding as authoritative—as if for the first time.

Because "active support" for the constitutional settlement cannot be fully or adequately provided by the ordinary mechanisms of a representative democracy, and because the everyday world of such a democracy involves the congealing of power in government in opposition to the people whose power it is, then the paradigmatic mechanism for refounding, for the dissent proper to democrat consent, becomes civil disobedience. As she describes it, civil disobedience is the central mechanism for refounding, for augmentation and amendment in the ordinary world of constitutional democracies.

> Civil disobedience arises when a significant number of citizens have become convinced either that the normal channels of change no longer function, and grievances will not be heard or acted upon, or that, on the contrary, the government is about to change and has embarked upon and persists in modes of action whose legality and constitutionality are open to grave doubt.[32]

Civil disobedience always concerns the constitutional order itself, referring to either its augmentation or its restoration. Although dissenting from the majority, the civil disobedient "defies the law and established authorities on the ground of basic dissent,"[33] that is, as a citizen; because civil disobedience is the work of citizen dissent, it is the work of a minority standing in for a presently absent constitutional majority.

If this is correct, then civil disobedience involves, precisely, the two defining features of revolutionary authority: first, civil disobedients are a community bound together by "common opinion,"[34] rather than common interest; they are an essentially political community bound together in the mode speech and action in opposition to government. This is why, when effective (as in the U.S. civil rights movement) or nearly so (as in American opposition to the war in Vietnam), such groups appear powerful. But, second, their power cannot derive solely from their form of communal binding: the opinion, that is to say, the principle under which they act is revealed, by their being bound to it in the manner of speech and action as—potentially—authoritative. It is in acts of civil disobedience that the characterization offered earlier concerning the disclosure of principles becomes most evident. Acts of civil disobedience are efforts of both political argument and world disclosure, that is, again, the revelation of the world in which the argument is to have its place. Civil disobedience is theatrical in that it always involves the revelation of a scene where the absent majority becomes visible in or through the dissenting minority voicing the polemical principle unheeded by the actual majority. Civil disobedience is the materialization of the power of the people under the sign of the principle currently flouted by government, the principle (of equality, of justice, of law) necessary for governmental legitimacy.[35] For Arendt, civil disobedience and revolution are structurally the same; civil disobedience is thus the analogue of revolutionary founding that occurs within the ordinary world of representative, constitutional democracies.

Conclusion

The standard complaint against Arendt's political theory, especially from the Left, is that in inveighing against the social question, against the French's Revolution's politics of pity and poverty, she detaches politics from its most absorbing object: social justice. The position of promising in her theory reveals that this criticism is mistaken. Arendt is not opposed to any political content; what she opposes is the systematic and principled reduction of political action to an instrument, to a mere means for achieving ends external to it. The instrumentalization of politics, like the liberal vision of seeing politics as primarily a means for securing private ends, say, as a mechanism for coordinating action, is the instrumentalization of our life together, hence a form of self-instrumentalization. In this liberal politics is a terrible shadow of capitalist economic practices. Promising as the achievement of communal power is Arendt's conception of human solidarity, but a solidarity that is now premised on action rather than passion. This being together in the manner of plural, equal individuals, each with the capacity for initiating action, and each necessarily, albeit implicitly so doing in binding herself to the social contract, is the condition for all other political action. Political actions that fail to recognize its powerful promissory ground tend toward instrumentalization. The subtext of Arendt's critique of any politics oriented by the social question is, in this respect, pure Adorno. "Freedom can only be grasped in determinate negation [*bestimmter Negation*] in accordance with the concrete form [*Gestalt*] of unfreedom," Adorno writes.[36]

Marxist and neo-Marxist utopianism routinely instrumentalized political action—justice as a remedial virtue for societies premised on scarcity, a philosophy of history with an ideally rational telos, the withering away of the state, and all that. It was this, above all, that Arendt saw as Marxism's devil's compact with liberalism. I suspect that it was this indigenous weakness in Marxist thought that Adorno simply inherited, giving the utopian elements of his thought, as it is driven forward by an unswerving negativity, a strangely idealist cast. In opposition to Adorno, the utopian elements in Arendt's thought derive not from a hyperbolic negativity ("The whole is false," etc.), but from an absence of the negative. It is this absence that her writing on civil disobedience finally corrects, installing the negative into the center of her understanding of revolutionary founding. But, then, who ever imagined that there could be revolutionary founding without an effort of negation, without being conditioned by the state of affairs being overthrown, without being intrinsically bound to the past out of which it grows and from which it departs?

Nonetheless, because Arendt's negativity is tied to the utopian promise present in actual democratic politics—or so she believes—it can converge with and empirically anchor Adorno's binding of negation and praxis. For him, but I am urging for Arendt as well, much of what we can make of human freedom emerges from the determinate negation of unfreedom;

hence, freedom is given shape and meaning through the concrete forces of domination, repression, coercion, and reification ranged against it, and the acts resisting those forces: each separate act of resistance, each source or form of unfreedom overcome stands for and promises a life premised on freedom.[37] Once this thought is given its proper place, it becomes evident that for both Arendt and Adorno, the politics of resistance is two-sided. On the one hand, the emphatic concepts of enlightened modernity—freedom, autonomy, equality, and so on—are kept alive and their authority restored through the acts of resistance to unfreedom and inequality; the patient work of the negative that Arendt analyses under the heading of civil disobedience is the local and temporary means through which what we know of political justice attains authoritative existence. For Arendt this refounding of constitutional democracy is the truth of its founding; for Adorno, this should be one of the central means through which the emphatic concepts of Enlightenment are given empirical significance. For both, this modernist politics of interruption is a refuge for freedom. On the other hand, there could not be a refuge for freedom unless freedom (equality, justice, etc.) could be more than it becomes in the acts of resistance to unfreedom. This "more" is the utopian element in the thought of each. Both Arendt and Adorno held close to this utopian element as the counter necessary against a modernity reneging on its own promise of a wholly secular, wholly immanent form of life, a modernity that is at every moment becoming more reified, more identitarian, more subject to the rule of no one. I see no gap of substance between Adorno's social world in which life does not live, the perfected rule of identity thinking, and Arendt's thought of the totalitarian rule of no one.

I do not wish to altogether impugn the utopian moment in Arendt and Adorno's thought. However, if I am right in arguing that refounding is the *truth* of revolutionary founding, then utopia must become a more complex affair. Indeed, if what is achieved in moments of rebellion is the disclosure of the validity of a value or ideal, then utopia is nothing more than the adequate recognition of that authority, of the normative reach of an idea in relation to present curtailed reality. Arendt was wont to idealize past moments of politics and revolution; Adorno, lacking an adequate conception of ethical normativity, urged an emphatic notion of truth. The panicky semantics of utopian truth makes what falls under it less rather than more plausible. If their joint commitment to modernism is the best of both Arendt and Adorno, then the orienting concepts of political modernity (freedom, equality, justice, etc.) should come to be seen as logically operating precisely as the term "art" operates in the context of modernist practices: each visible act of rebellion, whether failed or realized, both reauthorizing the claim of freedom, say, against the world of unfreedom, and in so doing refashioning what freedom means. It is because individual acts reauthorize and refashion the claim of the *orienting* concepts of political modernity, political "new time," that they reach out into an indefinite future; because they reach out into an indefinite future, their claim can seem boundless. The tradition has called that boundlessness "utopia." We modernists can see that "utopia" is just a bad name for the normative authority of what emerges as the principle (ideal, idea, value) under which a collective struggle occurs. Utopia, so-called, is just the new as it flashes up in a terrible moment of resistance, the new in its continual movement of rising up and falling. This, once more, is not to deny the promise of happiness given with our founding, orienting ideas, the promise of a different form of life; it is only to insist that these are indeed only *promises*, hence contingent, conditioned things, political things whose very nature as a mode of experience is to be something that we lose, are always losing, and thus having to be recovered, renewed, again and again and again.[38]

FOUR

From the Critique of Identity to Plurality in Politics
Reconsidering Adorno and Arendt

DANA VILLA

The years 2003 and 2006 were, respectively, the hundred-year anniversaries of Theodor Adorno and Hannah Arendt's births. It is hardly surprising that many conferences were held in their honor. However, one might be surprised by geographical preponderance of the celebrations. In Arendt's case, events were organized in America, Brazil, Sweden, France, Italy, Turkey, Japan, Finland, Norway, and, of course, Germany. Adorno's centennial was also marked in America, but the *real* celebration was in Germany. I spent a good part of 2003 in Berlin, and it seemed that hardly a day went by without some kind of Adorno event: a conference, a newspaper or magazine article, the appearance of a new biography or a new volume of correspondence.

There are a variety of reasons for this imbalance—some expected, some unexpected. The fact that Adorno's centennial generated more "column inches" than Arendt's attests to two basic facts. First, in Germany, Adorno is viewed as a *German* thinker. True, the biographies published by Lorenz Jäger, Detlev Claussen, and Stephan Mueller-Dohm during the *Adorno-Jahre* all highlight the German Jewish nature of Adorno's background. His father, Oscar Wiesengrund, inherited the family wine business in Frankfurt; his mother, the singer Maria Calvelli-Adorno, was Catholic and of Italian Corsican descent. Adorno himself was raised as a Protestant, and was confirmed at St. Catherine's Church in Frankfurt. With the rise of the Nazis, he dropped his father's surname and went solely by his mother's, retaining the "W" of Wiesengrund as a middle initial.[1]

But the biographies also tell Adorno's life story in terms of a somewhat predictable yet nevertheless revealing narrative arc. First, there is a happy and loving childhood and precocious intellectual apprenticeship in Frankfurt, an idyll interrupted by forced exile (in England and America) during the *Nazizeit*. Exile is followed by Adorno's return to Germany—episodically in the period 1949–53; for good thereafter—and, finally, by his ascent to the status of Germany's preeminent intellectual and critic in the period 1955–69. It is this narrative of exile and return that accounts, at least in part, for the disproportion in the attention lavished on Adorno compared to Arendt. For the German popular and popular intellectual press, Adorno was and is a figure of unquestionable stature in the intellectual, cultural, and philosophical worlds. The extraordinary range of his activities—from music theorist, to neo-Marxist philosopher, to literary critic, to sociologist and cultural critic—attest to the kind of "universal genius" Germans have traditionally celebrated in their most notable thinkers, from Kant and Goethe on down.

Adorno's Jewish heritage, and, more pointedly, the fact of his return after the Holocaust testified to the possibility of another Germany—a Germany vastly different from the one Adorno knew during his childhood, to be sure, but a Germany capable of understanding and transcending the pathological impulses toward romantic nationalism and racial purity that propelled it into Hitler's arms. As a postfascist political entity, the Federal Republic was hardly Adorno's cup of tea. But that, precisely, was the point. Adorno saw the preservation of the utopian urge—in the face of unprecedented catastrophe of the Nazi era *and* the "business as usual" charade of the Adenauer regime—as his primary duty.

Seen from the standpoint of the German popular and intellectual press, then, Adorno's story is yet another chapter in the ongoing saga of *Was ist deutsch*? In certain respects, his critique of identity philosophies—most compactly expressed in *Negative Dialectics* (1966)—explodes that question.[2] At the same time, however, this critique provides a therapeutic ascesis that enables the question to be asked anew, in a postnationalist, postmilitarist, and postreligious way. Adorno's philosophy can be viewed as an insistent plea to make room for "otherness" in the face of various tyrannizing collectivities (nationalism, fascism, totalitarianism, the "administered society," late capitalism). As he put it in one of the most enduring lines from *Minima Moralia* (1951), "An emancipated society . . . would not be a unitary state, but the realization of universality in the reconciliation of differences."[3] It would be a society in which "people could be different without fear." The resonance with contemporary German and non-German celebrations of multiculturalism is clear.

Arendt, on the other hand, has only become popular as a *theorist* since the 1980s. Insofar as her path-breaking critique and reformulation of the Western tradition of political thought has surfaced in Germany since then, it is especially thanks to Jürgen Habermas's theory of communicative action. That theory, like Habermas's earlier work on the public sphere, owes a tremendous intellectual debt to Arendt, one he has been quick to acknowledge.[4] Her broadly neo-Aristotelian distinctions between labor, work, and action in *The Human Condition* enabled Habermas's break with the "work model of action" that deformed the Marxist tradition and—ultimately—led to the theoretical cul-de-sac of Adorno and Horkheimer's influential *Dialectic of Enlightenment*.[5]

Habermas was Adorno's assistant following the latter's return to Germany. He later went on to become the most celebrated of the "second generation" of Frankfurt School theorists. His intellectual identity is, as a result, more bound up with Adorno and the Frankfurt School than with his borrowings from Hannah Arendt. For the longest time, Arendt the *theorist* had been more influential as an analyst of totalitarianism and as an investigator of the nature of totalitarian evil (*The Origins of Totalitarianism* and the Eichmann book). In contrast to Adorno, who taught in Frankfurt, her major works of political theory, *The Human Condition* (1958), *On Revolution* (1963), *Between Past and Future* (1968), and *Crises of the Republic* (1972) became canonic in German political theory only in the early 1990s.

The result of this constellation of circumstances is that the Adorno and Arendt centennials had the somewhat strange effect of monumentalizing Adorno (as a universal genius and preeminent political and social critic) while relegating Arendt to an interesting, yet second-tier status. This is unfortunate for a couple of reasons. First, and most obviously, because it reveals the relatively small impact Arendt's work has had on the practice and development of contemporary German political theory; second, because it attributes to Adorno a kind of expertise (in political theory) that he clearly did not have.[6]

Whether perusing Adorno's oeuvre or the *Adorno-Jahre* biographies, one is struck by how little contact he had with the main currents of Western political thought. Of course, he knew his Marx and Freud, as well as his Weber, Durkheim, and Nietzsche. His absorption of the Kant–Hegel–German idealist canon is also unquestionable. But there is little reference to either the leading lights of civic republicanism (Machiavelli, Harrington, Montesquieu, Rousseau, et al.) or liberalism, whether French or English (Locke, Constant, Tocqueville, Mill). Indeed, in *Negative Dialectics* the *political* theory of Kant and Hegel is dealt with either in passing or in semi-caricatured fashion. Thus, for example, the long section entitled "World Spirit and Natural History: An Excursion to Hegel" reiterates some obvious liberal criticisms of Hegel's historical and social ontology, albeit in language far more dense than one normally encounters in Anglo-American writers.

This lack of familiarity with, or concern for, the two main traditions informing modern Western political thought has myriad consequences. Perhaps the most baneful is that Adorno's political thought—if we can call it that—continues and deepens Marxism's traditional lack of concern with the problem of *how to institutionalize freedom*—both personal and political—in the modern world.[7] In Adorno's hands, political thought is reduced to cultural critique and reiterated complaints about the "falseness" of late capitalism and the "total society." In addition, there is certain amount of vague but elusive gesturing toward a possible but not probable future in which "reconcilement"—with nature, ourselves, and others—is achieved. The substantial political deformations wrought by Marx's conflation of praxis with labor or work are "overcome" by a retreat to the realm of aesthetics.

In what follows, I outline Adorno's critique of identity philosophies, as well as his cultural critique of "late capitalism" and the administered society. I then contrast his anti-identitarian stance with the explicitly *political* notion of plurality Arendt develops in her major theoretical works. My hope is that this contrast will reveal some of the reasons why a "differential ontology" is not adequate as a political theory and can—in certain formulations—actually inhibit political thinking. Political thinking is, of course, what Arendt devoted her life to after the debacle of 1933. In this respect, the "unreconciled" exile may have more to offer Germans (and the rest of us) seeking to understand the possibilities and problems of civil society and a democratic polity in "late modern" times.

Adorno: The "Total Society" and the Critique of Identity Philosophy

As readers of Adorno and Horkheimer's *Dialectic of Enlightenment* (1947) know, "classic" Frankfurt School theory largely derives from Max Weber's theory of modernity and his "formalization of reason" metanarrative. According to Weber, the modern age has witnessed the tremendous growth of subsystems of formal rationality in law, economics, the state, and bureaucracy generally. The "right reason" invoked by the Enlightenment and the early modern philosophical tradition—a reason that was *substantive* in nature, implying both an idea of justice and a standard of the common good—gave way to a strictly purposive or means/end rationality (*Zweckrationalität*).

Weber's analysis demonstrated how the rise of the modern state, positivistic science, and capitalist economics worked in tandem to dissolve reason's immanent connection to the Just and the True. Such a "metaphysical" conception of reason was anathematized as prescientific and dogmatic. It had to be purged of its indefensible prejudices and traditional norms. What was left were interlocking political, economic, and legal structures, rationalized and systematized so as to better generate power, efficiency, and profit (a point underlined, albeit critically, by Max Horkheimer in his *Eclipse of Reason* and Habermas in his *Reason and the Rationalization of Society*). This new constellation of formally rational subsystems set the pattern for Weber's famous "iron cage." The late modern age witnessed not merely the triumph of bureaucratic rationality, but the birth of the "administered society."[8]

Dialectic of Enlightenment appropriates Weber's metanarrative and—in the retrospective light provided by two world wars and the extermination of European Jewry—hypothesizes an internal link between *rationalization* ("enlightenment") and renewed barbarism. As Horkheimer and Adorno famously—and, it must be acknowledged, correctly—observed at the start of their "Concept of Enlightenment" essay, "the wholly enlightened earth is radiant with triumphant calamity."[9] How could a *rationalized* world— one in which superstition, tradition, and magical thinking had largely been vanquished; one in which science, technology, and formal reason loomed so large—give birth to such a new, and seemingly unlimited, form of barbarism?

The answer was not the familiar conservative one–namely, that a social form uprooted from tradition, faith, and an unquestionable set of moral presuppositions is bound to regress as it slides down the slippery slope of "relativism." Rather, *Dialectic of Enlightenment* posits a much more interesting "immanent" explanation. In Western culture, reason emerges out of myth and—in fully developed scientific, unreflective, and "total" form—reverts back to it. In Adorno's brilliant allegorical reading of Homer's *Odyssey*, the primordial roots of Western *ratio* are traced back to the unending struggle for self-identity and self-preservation in the face of hostile (and/or seductive) natural forces. These forces threaten not only to overwhelm the emerging ego but—in the form of the powerful natural drives and the lure of an instinctual ("animal") happiness—prevent it from forming itself in the first place. The gradual consolidation of the ego in the face of such forces, together with an increasingly powerful ability to use simple forms of instrumental rationality to cope with, if not yet dominate, nature itself, opened the human horizon to possibilities beyond sheer survival (on the one hand) or animalistic regression (on the other). In an almost literal sense, reason gives birth to civilization. Then, thanks to the philosophers, it gives birth to the idea of a civilization *not* predicated on domination—a "polis without slaves," to use the preferred German idealist locution.

Yet, as Nietzsche had seen in *On the Genealogy of Morals*, the forces that gave rise to Western *ratio* permanently distort its subsequent iterations, no matter how advanced. Because reason first emerged as a tool in the struggle for self-preservation, it winds up insisting—throughout its long history—on the need for ever-renewed repression of nature and instinct, which *is* man. It winds up, in other words, insisting on the need for renewed discipline and increased self-denial in the social totality.

Thus, even though we have long since learned how to dominate our external environment, we find ourselves—like Odysseus and his men—either chained to the mast or endlessly laboring to keep the social totality afloat. Our ancestors' fear of the ego-dissolving powers of instinctual "desublimation" remains, anachronistically, one of the most powerful forces in the present. The result is that our "rational" society is still predicated upon political domination and instinctual repression. The master/slave dialectic—allegorized in Homer's depiction of Odysseus and his men evading the Sirens' song—is one that knows no *Aufhebung* so long as society structures itself as a vehicle for self-preservation in the face of a hostile (external and internal) natural forces.

This is the analysis behind Adorno and Horkheimer's otherwise confusing claim that "Enlightenment . . . is mythical fear radicalized."[10] Society becomes a system not just in order to generate profit and power (the traditional Marxist analysis), but in order to repress the ever-threatening "other" of reason permanently—whether that "other" be instinctual drives, insufficiently rational ("bourgeois") behavior, or insufficiently "rational" peoples, cultures, and races. The realization of a fully rationalized, "enlightened" social form is thus the realization of a fundamentally repressive totality that enforces conformity and is savagely punitive with respect to anything—behavior, cultural norms, political movements—that questions its instrumental orientation or implies that social existence might take another form, more genuinely in tune with "the needs and powers of men."[11]

In Adorno and Horkheimer's hands, then, Weber's idea of an "administered society" becomes the contemporary reality of an integrated, systematic "total society" that incorporates technologized science, art, and a thoroughly prudentialized morality as essential components of its unreflective drive to reproduce itself and expand its power. Its advent renders moot the gradual disaggregation of various value and life spheres (e.g., art, science, morals, politics, economics, religious, and erotic life) that Weber famously posits as one of the defining characteristics of the modern age in his "Vocation" lectures. It is not that some meaningful new principle has been found to take the place of a vanished theological (unifying) hierarchy. Rather, the "system" itself is the new *ordo*. Its only principles—its only values—are efficiency, power, and operational integration.

The image of a "total society," while illuminating in many respects, is also deeply problematic. In the case of *Dialectic of Enlightenment*—and, indeed, much of Adorno's subsequent work—it led to the effacement of a variety of distinctions and innovations that Western political thought and practice had labored—often quite painfully—to articulate over the course of seventeenth, eighteenth, and nineteenth centuries.

First and foremost, the idea of a "total" society effaces the basic distinction between state and civil society (the sphere of economic and associational life). This effacement is, of course, no accident. Rather, it conveys one of Adorno and Horkheimer's primary points: in "late" capitalism, the Hegelian distinction between the two realms has become more or less illusory. To be sure, the interpenetration of state and society in advanced

Western societies has been substantial. Nevertheless, the leveling of the state/society distinction—presumed by the entire analysis of *Dialectic of Enlightenment* and by the very idea of a "total" society—also effectively levels the distinction between "managed" liberal capitalist regimes and totalitarian systems like the Soviet Union. Adorno and Horkheimer were hardly unaware of the differences between the two. Nevertheless, *Dialectic of Enlightenment* presents both systems as iterations of the Janus-faced "total society" brought about by the basic process of societal rationalization and economic-governmental integration.

Second, Adorno and Horkheimer's influential idea of the "culture industry"—of TV, radio, and popular culture as highly effective and ubiquitous agents of ideological programming and social integration—reduces the public sphere (understood here as the discursive arena "between" state and society)[12] to a stage set for media, advertising, and relentless psychological manipulation.

The "mass deception" propagated by the culture industry produces individuals who are, to use the Kantian term, almost entirely heteronomous. The only individuality that exists—or, rather, the only individuality that is produced—is "pseudo individuality," an individuality born of consumer appropriation of various style or demographic signifiers.[13] Schooled in a "positive" attitude by media and socially integrated through the consumption of mass culture, inhabitants of the "total society" find themselves bereft of the capacities for judgment, deliberation, and the filtering of information, which are vital to active or autonomous citizens.[14]

Third (and following from the first two), the category of the "total society" renders the idea of collective political action—*praxis*—either a bad joke or an unattainable ideal. One of the defining experiences of Frankfurt School neo-Marxism was the failure of the proletariat to live up to the role assigned it by classical Marxist theory. Working-class support for Hitler in Germany and the distinctly unrevolutionary character of American working-class politics both pointed to new and theory-resistant forms of "false consciousness." *Contra* Marx and Engels, the analysis of *Dialectic of Enlightenment* induces skepticism about the idea that there is any "epistemological kiss" that could awaken *this* Sleeping Beauty (the working class in the "total society") from its ideologically induced slumber. Lacking the space, motivation, and consciousness requisite for society-transforming *praxis*, the working class takes its disciplined place as a set of cogs in the well-oiled social machine—a machine whose primary products are (once again) profit, domination, and the relentless subjugation of nature (both external and internal).

It is against this theoretical backdrop that Adorno's *Minima Moralia: Reflexionen aus dem beschädigten Leben* (1951), translated by E. F. N. Jephcott as *Minima Moralia: Reflections from Damaged Life,* must be read. Composed largely in exile during the period 1944–47, it is informed throughout by the revelation of Nazi extermination camps in central and eastern Europe.[15] Like *Dialectic of Enlightenment*, it takes the "barbarism of the present" as an established and undeniable fact. It also takes the reality of the "total" or "false" society—the social form created by fully developed postliberal capitalism in both Europe and America—as a given. Social evolution has created hyperintegrated, instrumentally rational societies, societies that are conformist and collectivist down to their innermost components.

This development not only overturns Marx's Schilleresque notion of fully rounded social individuals forming a "free association of producers" but also makes the Hegelian idea of "ethical life" (*Sittlichkeit*) radically suspect (a point nicely elucidated by Jay Bernstein in his *Adorno: Disenchantment and Ethics*). Under contemporary conditions, Adorno states, social and political life *cannot* be the locus of anything approximating an ethical existence. The "false society" makes us all complicit in horror, exploitation, and domination.[16] The Hegelian vision of an institutionally situated and practically realized "ethical substance" is given the lie by the consummate bastardization of public and social existence in the mid-twentieth century. Hyperorganized warring collectivities know no such thing as either the "good life" or "ethical life."

The "fact" that the public and social spheres are clearly domains of systemic immorality and injustice means that the philosopher must practice a renewed and radical withdrawal. He has no choice but to turn to whatever fragments remain of a shattered, alienated subjectivity in *private life* if he is to recover the semblance of a life worth living—or, to put it more in line with Adorno's epigraph from Ferdinand Kürnberger, a life that can be *lived*.[17] This project is neither simple nor straightforward, particularly given the extent to which the "false society" has crept into individual experience itself. Thus, in *Minima Moralia's* "Dedication" to Max Horkheimer, Adorno writes:

> What the philosophers once knew as life has become the sphere of private existence and now of mere consumption, dragged along as an appendage of

the process of material production, without autonomy or substance of its own. He who wishes to know the truth about life in its immediacy must scrutinize its estranged form, the objective powers that determine individual existence even in its most hidden recesses. To speak immediately of the immediate is to behave much as those novelists who drape their marionettes in imitated bygone passions like cheap jewelry, and make people who are no more than component parts of machinery act as if they still had the capacity to act as subjects, and as if something depended on their actions. Our perspective of life has passed into an ideology which conceals the fact that *there is life no longer*.[18]

Yet even within a social life reduced to unending, conformist mimesis, "Reduced and degraded essence tenaciously resists the magic that transforms it into a façade." In other words, even in its distorted and caricatured form (the "sphere of consumption"), private life must be protected, contemplated, and investigated, lest what Adorno calls "the monstrosity of absolute production" prevail.

More to the point, private life—individual existence, the "particular"—must be protected from steam-rolling subsumption by the public or universal (*das Allgemeine*) if critique itself is to remain viable. "Critique" in the context of the "total" or "false" society means the articulated *recognition* that the "good life" is no longer possible under contemporary conditions: "Wrong life cannot be lived rightly."[19] Such recognition is possible only if reflection, the decomposition of bourgeois society, and the contingencies of existence conspire to promote a richness of individual experience that can—however briefly and vulnerably—serve as an alternative pole to the difference-effacing "totality." If, as Adorno remarks in one of his most famous aphorisms, "the whole is the false," then the particular offers the only path to (partial) truth.[20]

This withdrawal to the standpoint of the particular—to individual (damaged) experience—has struck many more traditional Marxists as existentialist, "liberal," or worse. It seems to privilege a reality—individual experience—that, from a Marxian perspective, is either obfuscating or reactionary. Yet Adorno was clear as to the nature and extent of his "deviation," articulating precisely the stakes involved in his inversion of the usual Hegelian-Marxist ontological hierarchy. To be sure, this does not lead him to embrace "atomism," that catch-all term denoting both social contract methodology and the bourgeois ideology of "individualism." But it does lead Adorno to a focus on the creaturely "particular" and to an (admittedly tactical) appreciation of liberal political institutions and protections:

> We owe our life to the difference between the economic framework of late capitalism and its political façade. To theoretical criticism the discrepancy is slight: everywhere the sham character of supposed public opinion, the primacy of the economy in real decisions, can be demonstrated. For countless individuals, however, the thin, ephemeral veil is the basis of their entire existence. Precisely those on whose thought and action change ... depends, are indebted for their existence to the inessential, illusion; indeed to what, measured by the great laws of historical development, amounts to mere chance. But is not the whole construction of essence and appearance thereby affected? Measured by its concept, the individual has indeed become as null and void as Hegel's philosophy anticipated: seen *sub specie individuationis,* however, absolute contingency, permitted to persist as a seemingly abnormal state, is itself the essential. The world is systematized horror, but therefore it is to do the world too much honor to think of it entirely as a system; for its unifying principle is division, and it reconciles by asserting unimpaired the irreconcilability of the general and the particular.[21]

This passage is not simply a protest against Hegel's privileging of the universal and the Marxist "base and superstructure" model. It is also an "immanent" critique of Adorno and Horkheimer's own tendency to reify contemporary (late capitalist) society as a "system." To do so risks depicting a society so infernally "total," so utterly successful in the work of integration that the very possibility of resistance or change evaporates.[22] Adorno's focus on the individual, and on the irreducible discrepancy (real or potential) between the particular and the universal, is his answer to those critics who see the analysis of *Dialectic of Enlightenment* as a paradigmatic instance of "totalizing" critique, one that leaves critical theory trapped in a cul-de-sac.

But what, exactly, is the "message in a bottle" implied by such a focus? It is the damaged individual's capacity to imagine an "emancipated society" in which the common or universal would no longer involve the effacement of particularity or difference. Such a society would protect and promote their articulation through "the reconciliation of differences." The result would be a society in which "people could be different without fear," one in which the fixation of identity (rooted in the struggle for self-preservation of both individual and society) would finally give way to a more relaxed, open, and differential form of identity.

Where, one might ask, does the image of such an "emancipated" society come from? How does the individual—how does Adorno—manage to articulate it? The charge of "totalizing critique" so often leveled at *Dialectic of Enlightenment* (and made most pungently by Habermas in his *Philosophical Discourse of Modernity*) is correct insofar as the formalization of reason metanarrative leaves few *social* grounds for immanent critique and the teasing out of utopian possibility. What is left—and what Adorno's biographers and other German commentators pointed out repeatedly during the *Adorno-Jahre*—is the memory of a loving and protective bourgeois family. Thus, throughout *Minima Moralia,* we find nostalgia not only for the more humane practices and everydayness of the bourgeois past, but—more tellingly—for a childhood that was loving, supportive, and "affirmative of difference" (as we would say today). That Adorno himself was conscious of this linkage is made clear by passages like the following:

> To a child returning from a holiday, home seems new, fresh, festive. Yet nothing has changed there since he left. Only because duty has now been forgotten, of which each piece of furniture, window, lamp, was otherwise a reminder, is the house given back this sabbath peace, and for minutes one is at home in a never-returning world of rooms, nooks, and corridors in a way that makes the rest of life there a lie. No differently will the world one day appear, almost unchanged, in its constant feast-day light, when it stands no longer under the law of labour and when the home-comers duty has the lightness of holiday play.[23]

This passage can be read as a sign of rank sentimentalism, or as an indication of Adorno's "regression" behind the critique of the bourgeois family contained in the *Communist Manifesto* and other writings by Marx and Engels. What really stands behind it is less private nostalgia than Adorno's fear is that the so-called "autonomous" individual (produced by the bourgeois family in its heyday, albeit in distorted and "atomistic" form) is giving way to a collectivist herd-man, one incapable of rising above, or indeed contemplating alternatives to, the system that creates him. Thus,

> With the family there passes away, while the system lasts, not only the most effective agency of the bourgeoisie, but also the resistance which, though repressing the individual, also strengthened, perhaps even produced him. The end of the family paralyzes the forces of opposition. The rising collectivist order is a mockery of the classless one: together with the bourgeois it liquidates the Utopia that once drew sustenance from motherly love.[24]

The explicit reference to a "Utopia that once drew sustenance from motherly love"—a comforting reality shattered by the two world wars, the extermination of European Jewry, and the rise of the "administered society"—suggests that, as critical theorist and *Adorno-Preis* winner Albrecht Wellmer has put it, "Adorno did not have a political theory—he had a dream."[25] This is the dream of a society which is relational and nonrepressive, a society no longer characterized by a political *state* and all the other modern institutions (media, monopoly capitalism, interlocking governmental, and corporate directorships) that help create the illusory reconciliation of the "universal and the particular" in the present.

For some readers, this gesture on Adorno's part will no doubt recall the young Marx's indictment of the state and representative institutions (in *On the Jewish Question*) and the "alienating" division of labor in modern capitalist society (in *The German Ideology*). Marx's critique famously left the outlines of the future socialist society as vague as possible. One thing it did make clear, however, was that an emancipated future would be irreconcilable with the continued existence of a political state and (indeed) a political domain that transcended strictly administrative functions. Such a postpolitical world may seem implausibly utopian, but in terms of Marx's theory, at least, it makes perfect sense. If the state and its associated institutions boil down to the "executive committee of the bourgeoisie"—if modern politics itself is nothing other than the clash of particular or sectional interests, which themselves emanate from class differences—*then* the abolition of those differences will create the conditions under which a truly general and *social* interest can, at last, emerge, more or less naturally and spontaneously. In a classless society, the General Will would no longer be a contractual fiction—a "political lion skin." Rather, it would be the animating spirit of a social form whose essential principle is cooperation rather than competition.

Is Adorno saying the same thing as the young Marx? Not really, despite his yearning for the day when the "law of labor" is finally suspended and the struggle for material existence is (as Marcuse would later put it) "pacified." Capitalism is not the central problem in the late modern age—the virtually unchecked reign of the "total" or "administered" society is. The inflexibility of the division of labor is less important than the tyranny of the systematic "universal" in all its varied forms (social, economic, scientific, and philosophical). Adorno's retreat from the (utterly false) public sphere in *Minima Moralia* thus makes perfect sense in terms of his and Horkheimer's overall analysis. Even more than traditional Marxism's "overcoming" of the political, it represents the abandonment of the public and an institutionalized political sphere for what is, essentially, an ethical-critical *attitude* or *Stimmung*.

This attitude—critique that purges itself of the kind of conceptual domination invariably practiced by the *maîtres penseurs* (Kant, Fichte, Schelling, Hegel, and Marx himself)—is nicely captured in a section from *Minima Moralia* entitled "On the morality of thinking":

> Even when sophistication is understood in the theoretically acceptable sense of that which widens horizons, passes beyond the isolated phenomenon, considers the whole, there is still a cloud in the sky. It is just this passing-on and being unable to linger, this tacit assent to the primacy of the general over the particular, which constitutes not only the deception of Idealism in hypostasizing concepts, but also its inhumanity, that has no sooner grasped the particular than it reduces it to a through-station, and finally comes all too quickly to terms with suffering and death for the sake of a reconciliation occurring merely in reflection—in the last analysis, the bourgeois coldness that is only too willing to underwrite the inevitable. Knowledge can only widen horizons by abiding so insistently with the particular that its isolation is dispelled. This admittedly presupposes a relation to the general, though not one of subsumption, but rather almost the reverse. Dialectical mediation is not a recourse to the more abstract, but a process of resolution of the concrete in itself.[26]

This passage not only provides a reformulation of dialectical mediation and the critical ethos for an age dominated by the "universal." It also points toward the critique of identity philosophy that Adorno carried out in *Negative Dialectics*. Before turning to Arendt, I want to conclude this section by saying a few words about that ethical-aesthetic project.

As Brian O'Connor and others have pointed out, Adorno's critique of identitarian thinking has turned out to be his most enduring legacy. Together with the Heidegger's metahistory of philosophy, as well as Emmanuel Levinas's *Totality and Infinity* (1961) and Jacques Derrida's *Writing and Difference* (1967), it provides the theoretical basis for overcoming the "identity of identity and difference"—an identity that characterized not just Hegelian Idealism, but *all* dialectical approaches to history, contingency, particularity, and difference. The difference between Adorno and these other thinkers—including his erstwhile philosophical enemy Heidegger—is that they followed Nietzsche in attempting to "overcome" metaphysics, while Adorno strove to maintain a solidarity between his thinking and "metaphysics at the time of its fall."[27] In other words, he remained a rationalist, despite his critique of both speculative and instrumental reason.

The critique of philosophical systematizing and Western *ratio* is, however, taken quite far in Adorno's work. Indeed, as demonstrated by both *Dialectic of Enlightenment* and *Negative Dialectics*, it was extended to the genealogical roots of conceptual rationality itself. The historical emergence of the concept as a tool in the struggle for self-preservation meant that conceptual rationality, and the scientific-Enlightenment spirit generally, would always proceed via the "liquidation" of differences.[28] Adorno, however, adamantly insists that the limits of conceptual rationality–its difference-leveling nature, its tendency to obliterate the nonconceptual as such—can be addressed adequately only by means of an artfully contrived "constellation" of concepts.

The *nonidentity* of identity and difference can be expressed adequately only through a play of concepts that takes as its first duty the need to preserve the thought—and the reality—of the nonconceptual. This is the imperative that drives Kant's otherwise clumsy talk about the "thing in itself" (*Ding-an-sich*). While acknowledging the correctness of Hegel's critique of this notion (in which the "naïveté" of a primordial and unbridgeable split between the cognitive subject and its object is preserved), Adorno nevertheless aligns himself with the *symbolism* of Kant's critical effort, his "system of stop signals."[29] Conceptual rationality—subsumptive and dialectical rationality, the rationality that achieves its most sophisticated and yet frightening expression in Hegel's *Science of Logic*—must be constantly reminded of its dependence on the nonconceptual.

But, we must ask, is this in any way a *political* project, and can *Negative Dialectics* and the critique of identity philosophy be viewed as a form of *political* theory? Readers approaching Adorno's notoriously difficult text for the first time may be forgiven if their first impulse is to demur. Much of *Negative Dialectics* is given over to arid and at times impenetrable polemics against Heidegger and other philosophical competitors. The long sections on Kant ("Freedom") and Hegel ("World Spirit and Natural History") seem, at first glance, merely to state the obvious. Adorno criticizes the Kantian conception of man's radical (noumenal) freedom, arguing that it is purchased at the price of eliminating *worldly* contingency and spontaneity. In the *Groundwork of the Metaphysics of Morals* and *The Critique of Practical Reason*, Adorno points out, freedom is reduced to the individual's *obedience* to ostensibly self-given laws. In a similar vein, he argues that the Hegelian ideas of Spirit and history as the progress of freedom are, after Auschwitz and other twentieth-century catastrophes, no longer plausible.

The apparent obviousness of Adorno's criticisms of Kant and Hegel is, however, misleading. While a good part of *Negative Dialectics* is devoted to questioning Kant's serial reduction of freedom to will (and will [*Wille*] to "pure practical reason"), as well as the triumphalist character of Hegel's philosophy of history, these are sideshows. The real thrust of the work—the thing that has made it enduring—is Adorno's strenuous attempt to reformulate dialectical thinking as "the consistent sense of non-identity."[30] In layman's terms, this means holding onto Hegel's insights concerning the "myth of the given" and the omnipresence of mediation (through thinking, concepts, language, and culture), while fending off all Hegelian or Hegelian-type urges to subsumption, closure, and systematicity.

In Hegel's hands, dialectics—which mimics the movement of thought itself—is a tool that repeatedly reveals the otherness of the other (whether this be the "object" of the cognitive subject, the God of Christianity, or the laws and institutions of society) to be our own construction, our own work.[31] In Adorno's hands, the dialectical approach becomes a tool that dissolves the illusion of complete integration fostered by the "total" society. It does this by consistently pointing out the *ethical* priority of the material and the "other." If, as vulnerable and creaturely particulars, we are to escape the fate of being "subsumed" by either an instrumentally rational society (Weber's "iron cage") or rationalist fantasies of total transparency (Hegel's system, Marx's classless society), *then* it is imperative that we resist the "compulsive" urge to efface the difference between every object, thing or entity and its concept. The myth of the concept's "adequacy" to the thing it names is what Adorno calls "the primal form of ideology."[32] Such is the absorptive or proto-totalitarian character of *all* philosophies of identity. As a result, Adorno urges, we must "be suspicious of all identity."[33]

As a "logic of *dis*integration," Adorno's negative dialectics formalizes this suspicion and turns it into a kind of methodology. The ethical trespass—the tendency to reduce a thing, individual, or group to some allegedly inclusive universal—begins with the logic of identity. It begins, in other words, with the movement of conceptual rationality itself.[34] But, as Adorno notes, even though "we can see through the identity principle," the fact remains that we cannot think without identifying."[35] Identity, definition, and conceptual thought can hardly be abandoned. And, in fact, the logic of identity—which otherwise seems so repressive[36]—actually contains a kernel of truth:

> To define identity as the correspondence of the thing-in-itself to its concept is hubris; but the ideal of identity must not be simply discarded. Living in the rebuke that the thing is not identical with its concept is the concept's longing to become identical with the thing. This is how the sense of nonidentity contains identity. The supposition of identity is indeed the ideological element of pure thought, all the way down to formal logic; but hidden in it is also the truth moment of ideology, the pledge that there should be no contradiction, no antagonism. . . . The untruth of any identity that has been attained is the obverse of truth. The ideas live in the cavities between what things claim to be and what they are. Utopia would be above identity and above contradiction; it would be a togetherness of diversity.[37]

This passage indicates as well as any what Adorno is up to with his reformulation of dialectical thought as "the consistent sense of nonidentity." The point is not simply to underline "the resistance otherness offers to identity" à la Derrida or Levinas.[38] Rather, it is to preserve the tension between the identical and the nonidentical, while imagining a social state—a "totality"—that is nothing more than the "togetherness of diversity." In other words, the point is to reimagine society as a collection of differences whose "reconcilement" does not in any way demand their erasure.

The image of a difference-oriented Utopia has been the official ideology of progressive (or "politically correct") academia for some time now, both in Germany and America. Viewed against the backdrop of the "tyranny of the Universal"—of the French revolutionary terror and its Soviet and Maoist offspring—its appeal is self-evident. What makes it problematic, at least in Adorno's version, is that the critical notion of the "tyranny of the Universal" is meant to apply as much to liberal democracy as it is to the republican cult of civic virtue, various inflamed nationalisms, and Stalinist communism. The "total society" knows many forms, even—some might say especially—liberal democratic ones.[39]

This brings us back to Weber's "formalization of reason" metanarrative and his "iron cage" metaphor. The obvious problem with both is that they encourage us to see the institutions of the late modern age—the market, law, government agencies, corporations, constitutional arrangements, the public sphere itself—as of a piece. Surface tensions aside, they all supposedly work together to form a more or less seamless web of domination. That this "classic" Frankfurt School take on Weberian sociology is not entirely off target is confirmed by Weber's own insistence that politics is inseparable from domination.[40] Nevertheless—and this is crucial—Weber saw the arena of political struggle as one important area in which something like freedom could continue to manifest itself.[41] "Rule by officials," while increasingly likely, is by no means a foregone conclusion.

Adorno's self-conception is that of a theorist who has stepped beyond this "liberal" illusion. The struggle of parties and politicians does not limit the reach of the "total" society; rather, it is one of its more familiar (and misleading) manifestations. Moreover, even if the struggle of parties offered more than a choice between Tweedledee and Tweedledum—even if the agonism of liberal democratic electoral politics *meant* something—it would still be far from the utopia of unconstrained difference that serves as Adorno's critical-ethical lodestar. The reason for this is simple. Liberal and republican political institutions, constitutional structures, ideological vocabularies, and party formations all work to constrain "difference," even if they do not do so in anything like the proto-totalitarian fashion of the Jacobins (let alone the concretely totalitarian fashion of the Bolsheviks or the Chinese communists). For this reason, Adorno's difference-affirming utopia, like Marx's "free association of producers," can exist only on a plane *beyond* politics, beyond the difference-repressing sphere of the public or general (*Allgemeine*).

As a member of a polity or a public, a liberal or republican *citizen* is someone who has been "educated to the universal" (to use a Hegelian turn of phrase). Of course, this hardly means that such a citizen is a member of a homogeneous mass, or that political membership turns on universal acceptance of one or even several accepted definitions of the "common good."[42] The latter, as any member of a liberal or republican democracy knows, is an "essentially contested notion," one created through an ongoing process of definition and redefinition, argument and debate. This process, this *struggle*, is part and parcel of the liberal-republican attempt to *institutionalize* freedom. As such, it can never be reduced to the expression of *pure* difference, nor can it effect a totally nonrepressive "reconcilement" of differences. Institutionally articulated differences—what Hannah Arendt indicated by the general term "plurality"—are, on the other hand, its lifeblood. To step, however episodically, into the public realm—to step outside the "home" provided by individual or group identity—is to bid farewell to Adorno's utopia of unconstrained yet reconciled difference. It is to engage others on the basis of the common or "universal"—that is, on the basis of the public realm and its institutions.

Arendt: Political Action and the Public Realm

At first glance, Arendt's insistence on the priority of the public realm and *political* membership may seem like regression to a difference-hostile form of civic republicanism. As anyone familiar with *On Revolution* or her conception of the public realm can attest, Arendt was indeed quite influenced by the republican tradition. However, she was also well aware of its deficits, particularly when it came to the question of human plurality and the expression of a range of different opinions on public matters and the common good. Arendt's theories of political action and the public sphere—theories that focus on politics understood as speech between diverse equals on matters of public (common) concern—*presume* human plurality not only as a precondition, but also as the *achievement* of political speech and action. Through acting and talking together, plural individuals articulate their perspectives on common things more precisely and more richly. It is that richness of *discursive* difference—of political speech—that constitutes Arendt's utopia.[43]

Arendt's insistence on plurality as the origin and goal of a genuinely discursive public realm is given pungent expression in a famous passage from *The Human Condition*:

> The reality of the public realm relies on the simultaneous presence of innumerable perspectives and aspects in which the common world presents itself and for which no common measurement or denominator can ever be devised. For though the common world is the common meeting ground of all, those who are present have different locations in it, and the location of one can no more coincide with the location of another than the location of two objects. Being seen and being heard by others derive their significance from the fact that everybody sees and hears from a different position. This is the meaning of public life, compared to which even the richest and most satisfying family life can offer only the prolongation or multiplication of one's own position with its attendant aspects and perspectives. The subjectivity of privacy can be prolonged and multiplied in a family, it can even become so strong that its weight is felt in the public realm; but this family "world" can never replace the reality rising out of the sum total of aspects presented by one object to a multitude of spectators. Only where things can be seen by many in a variety of aspects without changing their identity, so that those who are gathered around them know they see sameness in utter diversity, can worldly reality truly and reliably appear.[44]

This passage is remarkable for a number of reasons, not least of which is that it stands in stark contrast to Adorno's presuppositions. Plurality—"the fact that men, not Man, live on earth and inhabit the world"[45]—is not simply a precondition for action and speech, our distinctively political activities. It is the sine qua non of the public realm itself, understood as the institutionally articulated public space where diverse citizens meet and discuss their common affairs. This activity takes the form of different opinions on common "objects," opinions that themselves are a function of the diversity of perspectives enabled by a *shared* public world—what Arendt, in her Greek or quasi-Heideggerian mode, calls a "space of appearances."

A public space that enables and encourages the debate and deliberation of diverse equals is thus the place where *publicly significant differences* come into being and achieve their fullest articulation. The public realm is a sphere of opinion, not truth, and any public realm that approximated unanimity would cease, in Arendt's view, to be truly *public*. A nearly unanimous or "mass" form of public opinion—the kind of thing our pollsters currently measure and Tocqueville warned about—is not really *opinion* at all. This is because *opinions* (in contrast to *interests*) are always the property of *individuals*. They are formed through the type of discursive mediation and argument that a robust public sphere enables.[46]

Well and good, Adorno might say, but how can anyone in the late modern age assume the reality of a robust public sphere, let alone thoughtful citizen-individuals? Isn't it the case that our public sphere has been "structurally transformed" (to borrow a phrase from Habermas) to the point where governmental, corporate, and advertising interlock, creating a bogus public realm that operates strictly through plebiscitary acclaim for particular persons or interests?[47] Doesn't mass culture operate, as *Dialectic of Enlightenment* famously argues, as a form of *mass deception*? Relentlessly assaulted by the ideological content purveyed by TV, radio, and mass media generally, modern individuals are, in Adorno's phrase, "spellbound without exception." They are caught up in a false reality, which they are unable to see through.[48] The "diversity of perspectives" Arendt presumes doesn't exist, precisely because the agencies of mass integration are so infernally good at what they do.

Of course, Arendt, like Adorno, was well aware of the pathologies of mass public opinion. And, like Adorno, she was attuned to the dangers of advertising, popular culture, and "hidden persuaders" generally.[49] However, unlike him, she never viewed adult citizens as patients in need of therapy or children in need of paternalist-pedagogical guidance.[50] She acknowledged—indeed underlined—the fact that there are many forces currently undermining *our* public realm and its (potential) diversity of perspectives. Not least of these is the modern evolution of an increasingly "economic polity," one focused more on questions of material reproduction and social "housekeeping" than on creating and preserving spaces and opportunities for democratic self-governance.[51] Alive to the threats posed by economic or administrative despotism, she resisted intensely the critical strategy of radical de-differentiation practiced by Adorno and (in more recent times) Michel Foucault.[52]

From Arendt's perspective, this strategy—in which the distinctions between civil society, state, the economy, the public realm, and mass media are undone—merely reflects the "inclusive" logic of an ever-expanding social realm, one devoted to material and biological reproduction.[53] In the face of the modern "rise of the social" the important thing is not to further efface these distinctions. Rather, it is to preserve or recover crucial distinctions such as those between public and private, the social and the political, and labor, work, and action. Only by working *against* the subsuming logic of modern economic life and the "total society" can one begin to recover the idea (and practice) of an authentically public realm that provides a space for the speech and action of diverse equals.

Framing Arendt's theoretical project in this manner may make it appear that her central task was to question the tendency to reduce politics to economics—a tendency both orthodox Marxism and Frankfurt School neo-Marxism reflect. This is indeed an important dimension of her thought, as any reader of *The Human Condition* knows. However, seeing her project in these terms greatly foreshortens it, robbing us of the depth of her analysis and concealing the extent of her ambition as a political theorist. For while Arendt certainly wanted us to stop and "think what we are doing" in the midst of our relentless expansion of economic and market forces, her *primary* task was to reveal, not just one, but several deeply rooted cultural and philosophical prejudices against politics and human plurality itself. The late modern tendency toward a bureaucratically managed economic polity is but the latest manifestation of a rage against the contingency and non-sovereignty that characterize the worldly, tangible freedom born of human plurality, the public realm, and genuinely *political* relations.[54]

The roots of this tendency—of what Arendt, in a term of art from *The Human Condition*, calls "world alienation"—go back to Plato and Aristotle's philosophical impatience with a public sphere constituted by diverse equals. Where human plurality is able to find public-political expression (as it did in Athenian democracy), it gives rise to a decidedly noisy and open-ended politics, a politics of unceasing argument and decidedly rhetorical debate. This is a politics of constantly evolving opinions, shifting ideas of the common good, unpredictable consequences, and (last but not least) apparent moral irresponsibility.

The philosophers' response to the messiness of Greek democracy—to what Arendt terms its "futility, boundlessness and uncertainty of outcome"—was a systematic recoding of political action as a kind of *making*. The political actor was not to be regarded as one speaker amongst many, engaged in the never-ending process of persuading equal but diverse fellow citizens. Rather, he was to be viewed as a kind of expert craftsman or artist, one who possessed the specialized moral and political knowledge necessary to form both character and a harmonious polity. Political action, rightly understood, is a form of *rule* based on expert knowledge. As a result, it is hierarchical in its very nature. Such is the fundamental argument of Plato's *Republic* and *Statesman*. In Arendt's view, this is an argument Aristotle dilutes but does not fundamentally question (his distinction between praxis and poiesis notwithstanding).[55]

The conversion of a plurality-laden praxis into a specialized form of poiesis has numerous advantages, at least from a philosophical point of view. Indeed, as Arendt writes in *The Human Condition*,

> It has always been a great temptation, for men of action no less than men of thought, to find a substitute for action in the hope that the realm of human affairs might escape the haphazardness and moral irresponsibility inherent in a plurality of agents. The remarkable monotony of the proposed solutions throughout our recorded history testify to the elemental simplicity of the matter. Generally speaking, they always amount to seeking shelter from action's calamities in an activity where one man, isolated from all others, remains master of his doings from beginning to end. This attempt to replace action with making is manifest in the whole body of argument against "democracy," which, the more consistently and better reasoned it is, will turn into an argument against the essentials of politics.[56]

When plurality reigns in the public realm—as Arendt argues it must if relations are to be nonhierarchical, carried out through modes of speech and persuasion—the actor is also always a sufferer. "To do and to suffer are like opposite sides of the same coin."[57] When plurality is effaced—whether through a Platonic or bureaucratic claim to expert knowledge, or by more traditional forms of authority—the political actor need not worry about the unpredictability introduced by the presence of other actors in what is an essentially discursive medium. Dominating the "public" by virtue of his knowledge and authority, he can issue commands for others to execute. He, or the ruling group of which he is a part, is, as the modern political tradition puts it, "sovereign"—a patriarchal presence in the midst of a "national household." The "power" of such an actor is, seemingly, greatly enhanced. So, apparently, are the chances that his action will achieve its intended goal. It is such an essentially strategic or instrumental conception of action that Weber had in mind when he famously defined political power as "the ability to impose one's will upon others."[58]

The problem with this conception—dominant, in one form or another throughout the Western tradition of political thinking—is that it neglects the *political* dimensions of both *action* and *power*. Political action, as Arendt never tired of repeating, is a form of *acting together* through the medium of speech and persuasion.[59] *Political power* is something such acting together generates. As such, it is to be radically distinguished from the *strength* or *force* available to a single ruler or ruling elite.[60] By transforming political power into a commodity possessed by a ruler or ruling class, the tradition effaces the troublesome dimension of human plurality and turns the exercise of such power into a relation of domination. Freedom, understood as a tangible reality arising between diverse equals in a public realm, disappears from the political landscape.

The point about such *public freedom*—the freedom of *citizens*—is, to repeat, that it is nonsovereign in nature. The reality of freedom—its very possibility—hinges on our ability to see that *sovereignty* and *freedom* are not species and genus, but *antonyms*. As Arendt put it in her essay "What Is Freedom?" "if men wish to be free, it is precisely sovereignty they must renounce."[61] This, however, is easier said than done. The attraction of rulership (the ancients) or of the sovereign will (the moderns) is that they promise to overcome all of action's "calamities"—the "futility, boundlessness, and unpredictability of outcome" that attends all political action in the public-plural realm and that makes it so uncertain and (seemingly) ephemeral. Indeed, Arendt observes, the obsession with overcoming "the frailty of human affairs" is so strong that "the greater part of political philosophy since Plato could easily be interpreted as various attempts to find theoretical foundations and practical ways for an escape from politics altogether."[62]

The topos of an escape from plurality and politics is what underlies Arendt's wide-ranging critique of the Western tradition of political thought, a critique developed most fully in *The Human Condition*. This critique is aimed at both ancients and moderns, at the "great tradition" from Plato to Marx.[63] No matter where she turns—whether it's to Plato and Aristotle, Augustine and Aquinas, Hobbes and Rousseau, or Hegel and Marx—Arendt finds ample evidence of a desire to bracket human plurality and "escape from politics altogether."

Encountering this critique for the first time, the casual reader may wonder whether Arendt has exaggerated the "anti-political" tendencies of the "great tradition." To be sure, these tendencies *are* substantial. Arendt's vehement anti-Platonism (imbibed, in large part, from Heidegger and Nietzsche) effectively highlights the tradition's bias against plurality, opinion, and the decidedly messy deliberation of civic equals. But it fails to have much critical purchase on those political thinkers—one thinks of Constant, Tocqueville, and Mill—who also warred against the fiction of a univocal "sovereign" or "general" will.

Why does Arendt leave such thinkers out of her story? There are two basic reasons. The first is that Constant, Tocqueville, and Mill are self-consciously *liberal* thinkers, for whom civil rights and individual liberties ultimately trump public freedom and the claims of civic action and democratic self-government. The second and more involved reason is that Arendt, like Adorno and many other Weimar intellectuals, acquired early on a prejudice against the liberal tradition, equating it with the materialistic agenda of the European bourgeoisie. Nowhere is this (ironically Tocquevillian) prejudice more in evidence than in the treatment of the "political emancipation of the bourgeoisie" contained in *The Origins of Totalitarianism*. Truth be told, it colors Arendt's entire oeuvre, an oeuvre animated by two discrete and somewhat opposed loyalties. The first allegiance is to Heidegger and his depth critique of the Western philosophical tradition. The second is to the civic republican tradition, with its heavy emphasis on civic virtue, public freedom, and the primacy of the political.

Arendt, it should be emphasized, does not share Heidegger's German romantic nostalgia for a more genuinely reconciled or "natural" relation to Being. But she does take up his general thematic, the better to highlight what she sees as the "world and earth" alienation of the moderns.[64] We are alienated from the "world"—from the public dimensions of our culture, society, and polity—insofar as we set up the self as ultimate reality and measure. And we are alienated from the earth—the "object" that is the fundamental precondition of human existence—insofar as our science adopts a cognitive standpoint *beyond* the confines of earthly existence (the "Archimedean point"). Both tendencies—the inflation of the subject or self to ultimate reality, the reduction of the earth to the status of one more object—testify to the fundamental Baconianism of the "modern project." Our resentment of finitude—of the limiting conditions under which human life has been given to us—lead us to deploy science and technology in order to increase our power and (ultimately) to conquer the *conditions* of human existence itself.

It is at this point—namely, in the Heidegger-inspired critique of modern science and technology that she mounts in the last part of *The Human Condition*—that Arendt most closely approaches central themes from *Dialectic of Enlightenment*.[65] Yet the thematic proximity is in many respects misleading. In *Dialectic of Enlightenment*, Adorno is working out the implications of Weber's formalization of reason metanarrative, borrowing from Nietzsche and Freud in order to extend this narrative back to the primordial origins of Western *ratio*. In contrast, Arendt borrows from Heidegger in order to expand and extend an old civic republican theme regarding the *cultural* forces that have contributed to the decline of the *vita activa* and the public realm in Western civilization. Like Machiavelli, Montesquieu, Gibbon, and Hegel, Arendt underscores the enormous Christian contribution to the cultivation of "world alienation" in the West. In contrast to them—and largely because of her historical position—she stresses how modern scientific worldliness (of the sort celebrated by the philosophes) turns, in the late modern age, into something else entirely: an enormously "successful" expression of resentment against the limiting conditions of human existence.

This difference regarding the significance and cultural origins of world and earth alienation points to another, more radical divide between Arendt and Adorno. This is Arendt's central concern (again born of the civic republican tradition) with the *institutionalization* and *constitutionalization* of public freedom. This concern—which, as Jeremy Waldron has forcefully pointed out, is often overlooked by commentators focused on the dramaturgical concept of action found in *The Human Condition*—is manifest in *The Origins of Totalitarianism* (1951), where Arendt stresses again and again how totalitarian dynamism effectively destroys stable structures of law and institutions, the necessary prerequisites of a *civilized* life.[66] It comes fully into its own in *On Revolution* (1963), where Arendt theorizes the initiatory action of the *modern* revolutionary tradition in terms of its creation ("founding") of a constitution and a "new space for freedom."⁶⁷ As *On Revolution* makes clear in a hundred places, Arendt thought that public freedom in the modern world demanded the kind of institutional home that only a complex, multilayered federal constitution could give it.

For Adorno, constitutionalism, civic republicanism, and the institutionalization of freedom are all nonstarters, not only because they have been neutered by the "structural transformation" of the public sphere, but for the even more telling reason that they participate in the difference-repressing logic of the *Allgemeine*. Here we must note that, when it comes to political theory, Adorno takes his bearings almost entirely from his reading of Hegel's *Philosophy of Right*. The result—filtered through the experience of the *Nazizeit*—is that he was unable to see legal and institutional structures as anything other than the concrete instantiations of a steam-rolling and difference-effacing Universal.⁶⁸ This, more than anything else, constitutes the Achilles' heel of Adorno's "political" theory.⁶⁹

Arendt's capacity to do justice to the enormous achievement of the so-called "bourgeois revolutions" gives her political theory an undeniable advantage over Adorno's.⁷⁰ Her utopia—if we can call it that—remains a recognizably political structure, one in which legal and constitutional boundaries are taken with the utmost seriousness; one in which *individual* and *political* rights are seen as worldly creations in need of institutional articulation and vigilant citizen protection and oversight. The "utopian" element is not found in the dream of "reconcilement." Rather, it is found in Arendt's idea of an institutionally articulated public space, one that provides an arena for the articulation of politically salient differences. The ground of such differences is not competing sets of values, identities, or moods. Rather, the ground is found in the fact that we occupy different positions in a shared world. Arendt's utopia is thus one in which diverse perspectives, no matter how opposed, find their raison d'être in a shared "care for the public world."

Conclusion

In many respects, the centenary celebrations of 2003 and 2006 wound up telling us more about where we are politically than about either Adorno or Arendt. In Germany, Adorno's status as the "last" genius received universal assent, even as some voiced reservations about his political judgment.⁷¹

Grounding this evaluation was the palpable gratitude of an entire generation of German university students from the 1960s, a group whose revolutionary sentiments Adorno mistrusted but whose moral-political *Bildung* drew heavily from the most radical moments of Frankfurt School theory. Looking back from positions of social, political, and intellectual prominence, this generation expressed thanks to Adorno as a German Jewish intellectual who—unlike Heidegger and many others—remained untainted by the moral corruption of the *Nazizeit*. In light of reunification, it is also important to note that Adorno's unease with "the total society" made him skeptical of both Soviet and Chinese communism (unlike Georg Lukács and Jean-Paul Sartre). If his criticism of these societies in *Negative Dialectics* looks tame beside that of André Glucksmann or Michel Foucault, it is because he never fully came to grips with the magnitude of the crimes committed by ostensibly Marxist regimes. Nevertheless, he *did* criticize them, and this—more than anything else—makes his political thinking during the 1960s look eminently sane when compared to the Maoist enthusiasms of the time.[72]

Arendt, of course, was under no illusions as to the extent of these crimes, as *The Origins of Totalitarianism* makes plain. However, her fame as an analyst of totalitarianism made her subsequent work an object of suspicion among the *marxisant* intellectual cultures of Western Europe in the 1960s and 1970s. It is only post-1989 and the fall of communism that her work has received something like the level of attention due it in European intellectual circles. Yet that attention remains hobbled—in Germany, at least—by the absence of a genuine institutional presence. Indeed, insofar as Arendt *is* taken seriously as a political thinker, it is thanks to the appropriations performed by second- and third-generation Frankfurt School thinkers.

This fact, more than any other, reveals the difficulty confronting an oeuvre that still remains either "second best" or terra incognita for many in Germany and Europe. With due credit to the intellectual contributions of both thinkers, from the standpoint of *political* thinking, this situation is more than unfortunate. Interest in Arendt as a political thinker in her own right is growing. It will be some time, however, before she comes to occupy the same plane as Adorno.

FIVE

Passion Lost, Passion Regained
How Arendt's Anthropology Intersects with Adorno's Theory of the Subject

DIETER THOMÄ

As readers of Hannah Arendt's letters to Karl Jaspers and Heinrich Blücher will know, *The Human Condition* emerged from a project whose first provisional title was *Amor mundi*.[1] Indeed, *amor mundi* has served as a kind of motto for Arendt's work in general since Elisabeth Young-Bruehl chose *For Love of the World* as the subtitle of her 1982 biography of Arendt.[2] Even though there is evidence for the particular significance Arendt attributed to the phrase *amor mundi*, the question remains of why she did not choose it as the title of what became *The Human Condition*, one of her most important books.[3]

Whether the provisional title *Amor mundi* actually fits the book later called *The Human Condition* and serves genuinely as a motto for her philosophical journey in general obviously depends on the status of the terms "love," "world," and "love of the world" in Arendt's work as a whole. Given that "love" belongs to the realm of the "passions," it is rather startling find it considered for the title of a book dedicated to an analysis of human agency. Agency and passion are not as clearly opposed as activity and passivity, but their common ground is not necessarily self-evident either. It is also unclear how *Amor mundi* relates to *Vita activa*, the German title chosen by Arendt for *The Human Condition*.

I begin this paper with a discussion of these issues (§ 1). That there is a certain ambivalence in Arendt's account of "love of the world" is apparent from her notebooks of the 1950s, which show her engaged in a kind of theoretical experiment that she eventually was to eschew in the final version of *The Human Condition*. By tracing this detour (§ 2), we hit a blind spot in Arendt's theory of the person: her account fails to recontextualize agency or activity with reference to the "internal ocean"[4] of emotions and their social implications. Yet, as it turns out, a critical analysis of her account of agency can take its cue from certain hints given by Arendt herself (§ 3). As we are invited to think with Arendt contra Arendt, we are tempted to think with Adorno contra Arendt as well. Although it contains its own difficulties, his critical discussion of modern subjectivity and autonomy aptly complements the systematic considerations of agency and interaction that have been the fruit of our discussion of Arendt (§ 4).

"Amor mundi" and the "Human Condition"

The natural starting point for considerations of the "love of the world" in Arendt is her doctoral dissertation *Der Liebesbegriff bei Augustin (Love and Saint Augustine)*, first published in 1929, in which Arendt describes a transformation of love that passes through three stages. In the first stage, I live "by desiring and depending on things 'outside myself'";[5] this life is characterized by "dispersion," by dependency on external "goods," by "habituation" in a "world to which we would flee" if conscience had not put us off.[6] Love as *cupiditas* does not deserve to be qualified as *amor mundi*, because the loving person actually vanishes behind "desires" that "pull" her "outward."[7] Her obsessions do not do justice to the openness of the "world."

If, at this stage, I may be lost to things external, I attempt to turn to myself again in the next stage. Augustine's "I became a question to myself" (*quaestio mihi factus sum*) is the result of withdrawing into myself and "gather[ing] the self from the dispersion and distraction of the world."[8] Following Augustine, this quest is guided by God, as the return to my "createdness" is to be regarded as a "return to the creator."[9] However, this reflexive turn will not lead to isolation or "estrangement from the world." In the third stage, I gain access to a "new togetherness . . . defined by mutual love . . . , which replaces mutual dependency."[10] It should be mentioned that *amor mundi* and *dilectio mundi* appear in Arendt's dissertation,[11] yet do not clearly refer to the highest state of sublimated love. "Love of the world" is said to be "never a choice, for the world is always there and it is natural to love it," but higher "social life" is based on an act of "choos[ing]": true love is "selective" in the sense that it requires a conscious embracing of my own and my neighbor's being.[12]

It is all too evident that Arendt's approach is indebted to the three-step strategy of "falling," "individuation" or "solitariness," and authentic "Being-with" put forward in Heidegger's *Being and Time*. Yet instead of expanding upon these affinities,[13] I shall turn to one of the relatively infrequent allusions to the early dissertation in Arendt's later work. In *The Human Condition*, she writes: "It was Augustine who proposed to found not only the Christian 'brotherhood' but all human relationships on charity."[14] This kind of "community" is now regarded as a strangely restrained and distorted form of social life by Arendt. It does not allow for the creation of a public sphere, a "world" shared and shaped by current, former, and future members of a community. From her perspective, a community based on charity "corresponds to the general human experience of love" and shares with it the distinctive feature of "worldlessness" or "unworldliness."[15] That love can do *without* the "world" casts some doubt on the claim that loving is a preferable attitude *to* the world—a claim that is implied in Arendt's own estimation of *amor mundi*.

Arendt's later notion of the world as open space and public sphere relies on the distinction between the public and the private, which cannot possibly apply to a Christian conception of "social life," where everybody is regarded as a "neighbor." Arendt's late turn against "worldlessness" is inconceivable without an argument that associates love mainly with this private sphere. This argument was not articulated in *Love and Saint Augustine*, but came soon afterward. In her book *Rahel Varnhagen: Lebensgeschichte einer deutsche Jüdin aus der Romantik* (1959), Arendt analyzes the worldlessness of romantic love.[16] Here it is seen as a restriction that needs to be overcome. Unfettered sociality goes beyond the "fixation on a single thing."[17] The "world" as a public sphere is to be defended against indulgence in private matters and emotional exuberance. (In later writings, Arendt claimed that the public sphere is also threatened by consumerist self-centeredness.)

There is an uncanny coalition of threats to the "world" and to worldliness. Arendt scrutinizes the worldlessness of privatized emotions in *Rahel Varnhagen*. She takes issue with the worldlessness, that is, the antipolitical turn of consumerism, in nineteenth-century America in *On Revolution*.[18] And she blames totalitarianism for destroying plurality and generating worldlessness on a large scale in the *Origins of Totalitarianism*:[19] under totalitarianism, "self and world . . . are lost at the same time."[20] Whereas "world" is defined as a sphere shared by human beings presenting and "disclosing"[21] themselves in front of their fellow men, "love" is attributed to a dyadic structure that unifies human beings in a state of the highest emotional intensity and intimacy. In the light of Arendt's definition of worldless romantic love, the phrase "love of the world" looks rather heterogeneous, if not oxymoronic. The verdict from *The Human Condition* reads as follows: "Love, by its very nature, is unworldly."[22] Yet instead of simply dismissing *amor mundi* at the outset, we are called upon to look for a meaning of "love" that is more fitting in relation to the "world." What Arendt may have in mind is an attempt to transpose the disclosing powers of love to a broader social framework and to apply the idea of whole-hearted commitment to a sphere transcending private relations. "Love," like friendship, would then be regarded as a stance of affection, inclination, or fondness aptly described by Ralph Waldo Emerson in a passage used by Nietzsche as a motto for his *Gay Science*: "To the poet, to the philosopher, to the saint, all things are friendly and sacred, all events profitable, all days holy, all men divine."[23]

Arendt's notion of "love of the world" is not all-embracing, however. It is clearly not directed at things within the world, but at the world *as such*. This appreciation goes along with aversion: the defense of the 'world' as an open sphere constitutes the basis for an attack on totalitarian or rather privatized attempts of destroying the "common." This meaning of the "love of the world" is in line with the stance taken by Arendt in *The Human Condition*, and we find related comments in her other writings and in her correspondence. Yet it must be said that this charitable reading of worldly affirmation is not supported by detailed elaborations on the notion of love itself in *The Human Condition*. They point to love's negligence of the qualities of a person, of "*what* the loved person may be."[24] The link between love and the narrative identity of a worldly individual cannot thus be anything but weak. Given that love does not play a significant role in the final version of the book at all, it does seem plausible or even necessary that Arendt changed the title from *Amor mundi* to *The Human Condition* (or rather to *Vita activa*). But why exactly does Arendt retreat from love? And is this retraction or omission reversible? In order to settle these questions I shall now focus on the period during which Arendt conceived and wrote *The Human Condition*.

The "Internal Ocean" of Emotions

In an entry from December 1952 in her notebook, the so-called *Denktagebuch*, Arendt briefly refers to the "fundamental activities," or the "active modes" of human life. This entry seems to be one of the earliest harbingers of the book published six years later as *The Human Condition*. Four Greek terms are listed: *pathein, prattein, poiein, ergazesthai*.[25] The last three easily translate into the triad of "action," "work," and "labor" familiar to every reader of *The Human Condition*: *prattein* mainly stands for political action, *poiein* for productive or creative activities, and *ergazesthai*, like "labor" in Arendt's sense or *ponos* in Greek equals the efforts to secure self-preservation. Yet *pathein*, the first term in the list above, comes as a surprise (and it seems to have eluded those who have commented on the *Denktagebuch* so far).[26] It is not self-evident that *pathein* or suffering could be regarded as an "active mode" at all. One of the short explanations given by Arendt at the time reads as follows: "*pathein*: suffering; paramount 'relation': love."[27]

In an entry from April 1952 we encounter the same triad of "action," "work," and "labor," this time not complemented by passion, but, without further explanation, by "love" itself.[28] Arendt is critically concerned with "labor," which is seen as being confined to the necessities (*anankaia*) of life; its restriction to an "animal"-like existence is said to be "truly pernicious."[29] She draws rather sketchy distinctions here, as these are obviously her first shaky steps into uncharted territory. "Work," "love," and "action" are said to be superior to "labor" as they seek to overcome necessity in one way or the other. Their efforts are only partly successful though. "Work" culminates in creative "initiatives," yet these remain episodic and fall short of reaching the goal of truly "mastering" life.[30] "Love" is able to transcend natural instincts by turning "necessity" into erotic "needs," but it also fails to establish self-mastery. Autonomous "action" stands out as being the strongest antidote to natural "necessity."

Arendt experiments with various hierarchical orders between those four fundamental activities. In a rather enigmatic passage she states:

> As *active beings* who can act only within a jointly inhabited world and by explicitly realizing their being-together, men are truly "men" in the sense of a specific humanity. And as [a] *lover*, who, as One, need[s] the Two in order to receive, as a gift from nature, the Three etc., by immediately moving from singularity to plurality . . . , every man is—in an unfathomable ironical way—*the* man as well.[31]

I must confess that I do not really grasp the sense of irony associated with the "humanity" of the lover.

It may be that this is an allusion to the transcendence of individuality in sexual union and reproduction, or rather to the fact that every human being resembles the other in being seducible by *eros*. Suffice it to say that, next to "action," "love" is acknowledged as a particular mode of being *human*.

Arendt comes back to the systematics of "fundamental human activities" one more time in October 1953. Now the list gets even longer: "Labor," "work," "action," and "love" are complemented by "thinking."[32] This emendation is not far-fetched, as *theoria* is famously regarded by Aristotle as being the highest form of praxis. This time, the distinctions drawn by Arendt are based on slightly different criteria. The contribution of "thinking" to "humanity" is attributed to its capability of encompassing the "others" by way of generalization. "Action" is praised for creating the "common world." But "love" is now said to lead to "worldlessness,"[33] which surely affects its association with a "specific humanity."

This extension of the list is later revoked when Arendt finally turns to the triad of "labor," "work," and "action." "Love" is dropped from the list of activities for the first time in February 1954, when Arendt settles for the abovementioned triad.[34] In an entry entitled "book" from May 1954, this triad already forms a sequence in a provisional table of contents.[35] This corresponds to the detailed information provided by Arendt in a letter to Heidegger from May 8, 1954, where she talks about the planned "analysis" of the variants of *vita activa* as opposed to *vita contemplativa*.[36] It is only *after* "love" disappears from the list of fundamental activities that *amor mundi* comes up—in entries from April and July 1955.[37] It is safe to say that in the early 1950s, the systematics that would eventually serve as the organizing principle of *The Human Condition* were still in the making. The findings from the later "career" of those temporary entries in Arendt's list of activities present mixed results. "Thinking" is actually recognized as *vita contemplativa* in *The Human Condition* and, as a consequence, is left out intentionally;[38] it is later scrutinized in volume 1 of *The Life of the Mind*. Arendt's arrangements for "love" are less forthcoming than those for "thinking." Two questions remain: we still need to understand how "passion" or "love" could qualify for the realm of "activities" in the first place; and we are confronted with the fact that they eventually disappear from the screen as if they had never existed.

The answer to the *first question* is comparatively simple and rests on two hints given by Arendt in an entry in the *Denktagebuch* from March 1953.

Here, she reminds us of the notion of *thymos* encompassing action and passion.[39] However, she does not expand upon this broad conception of *thymos*, except when, without actually mentioning the Greek term, she celebrates Homer for his discovery of the "heart": "The organ of endurance (passion) is the heart."[40] In her brief remarks on "heart" or *thymos* Arendt seems to take the side of anti-dualism. This can be regarded as preparatory to admitting "passion" to the realm of activities. Another hint given by Arendt proves this point, when she draws on the distinction between *pathein* and *algein*: "Only *algein* corresponds to suffering; *pathein* is passion."[41] By keeping bodily reactions and passions apart, she paves the way for a broader notion of human agency, which includes the latter. On this occasion, she could have also turned to the Stoic discussion of *euthymia*, which includes *euprattia* as well as *eupathia*. But Arendt does not go down this path.

Instead, Arendt presents a brief to an appeal court, which then rescinds the emancipation of passion. This court is convened in the notebooks themselves. In April 1955, she declares that "passion is the exact opposite of action."[42] This does not coalesce with earlier considerations on "love" and "action" as different forms of actualizing the "human." The revocation is not complete: The allusions to passion in the early notebooks resonate in some of Arendt's later remarks on love, which I shall reconsider below. Yet, for the time being, and in *The Human Condition*, love or passion is banned from the realm of activity. In light of the earlier remarks on "love," it is striking to see how Arendt then talks about "intimacy" or "privacy" virtually without reference to passions and emotions. "Intimacy" is said to be "directed first of all against the leveling demands of the social," the discussion of "privacy" is pitched at "property," and so on,[43] some sketchy remarks on "family life" notwithstanding. The exclusion of love or passion is in accordance with two main features of the anthropology put forward in *The Human Condition*: the *connection between teleology and autonomy* and a specific approach to *human interaction*. The first point will be discussed at length, the second very briefly.

Teleology and autonomy. Strangely enough, any systematic reasoning on the essence of human agency is missing from *The Human Condition*: we learn that labor, work, and action are "three fundamental human activities,"[44] without ever obtaining any information on what exactly an "activity" is or why there could not be more than these three. It seems that the feature shared by these activities is their *teleological* structure. In the realm of "labor," the *telos* is fixed: activities serve the purpose of self-preservation or the satisfaction of needs. In "work," we aim at external products, and our freedom consists in transcending the realm of necessities. Whereas this individual goal-setting still depends on the availability of objects, the teleology in the realm of "action" is truly self-sufficient: Our actions have their purpose in themselves; they stand for the pure exertion of autonomy. The hierarchy culminating in "action" (or praxis) is known from Aristotle's ethics, but Arendt adds an additional twist to the concept of "action." Purposeful behavior is based on the ability of setting a purpose, an ability that Arendt attributes to a human being empowered to set new "beginnings." She establishes a link between Aristotelian praxis and *archē* (beginning)[45] and further elucidates *archē* by bringing together Augustine's "Initium ut esset, creatus est homo" (That a beginning be made, man was created)[46] and Kant's definition of freedom as the "faculty of absolutely beginning a state."[47] She claims that Kant's "spontaneity" is "closely related" to Augustine's "beginning,"[48] and (sloppily) quotes Kant's definition of freedom in the German version of *Origins of Totalitarianism* without mentioning his name; the quotation is missing from the English version.[49]

The initial, inceptive freedom of human action serves as a bulwark against determinism, yet it is also a source of irritation for those who are at odds with dualism—and Arendt might be expected to be one of them. Following Kant, freedom is based on a rigid distinction between reason and the senses; any intrusion from the side of the latter puts into question the moral validity of the agent's intentions. Saving the "passions" from becoming a mere subsection of our bodily nature is unthinkable in this context. This explains why Arendt, in her concern to defend true freedom against animal-like consumerism, focuses on autonomy and leaves passion aside. Later, in *The Life of the Mind*, she is adamant about that: "The opposite of deliberate choice or preference is *pathos*, passion or emotion, as we would say, in the sense that we are motivated by something we suffer."[50]

Drawing a sharp distinction between liberation by reason and enslavement by passion is as common as it is unclear. Firstly, this kind of initial freedom, which comes "out of the blue," does not really serve the purpose of explaining the genesis of "strong evaluations" and practical orientation;[51] its power to enable agency is disputable. Secondly, the seemingly unrestricted freedom creates constraints of a hitherto unknown kind, as it entails the *labor* of forcefully excluding the emotions. Arendt is no stranger to considerations of this kind; she actually blames Plato's "idealist" dualism for preparing the turn to materialism.[52] In her remarks on biography and the "process character of action" she alludes to a notion of personal identity that stresses the central role of historic embeddedness.[53] Yet this does not mean that Arendt withdraws from a strong notion of freedom. By tracing back Kant's "beginning" to Augustine's *initium*, Arendt seeks to identify the birth of a human being as a primal scene of freedom. Next to the concept of the "world," the idea of "natality" as "beginning" may actually be the single motive that is to be found in all stages of Arendt's work.[54] It is virtually the "last word" of both *Origins of Totalitarianism* and *The Life of the Mind*. Yet even though many commentators are intrigued by Arendt's concept of natality,[55] this apparent cornerstone of her theory of agency is, in actuality, a stumbling block.

Natality remains a fuzzy category in Arendt—it is a "miracle," something that is possessed of "startling unexpectedness" and, as a result, defies our comprehension.[56] When working on the German translation of *The Human Condition*, she seems to have been slightly unsatisfied with what she had written on "natality:" the relevant paragraph in the German version is much longer than the English original, and the strong expression "fact of natality" is twice added in the book.[57] Several relevant insertions are to be found in the German version: "The singularity [of the individual] is not based on certain qualities or on the unique combination of already familiar qualities within an 'individual,' yet it rests on the fact of natality that is the foundation of all human togetherness. . . . Due to this singularity implied in the fact of birth it is as if in every human being the creative act of God is reiterated and reconfirmed."[58] The English phrase "Men . . . are . . . born . . . in order to begin" is complemented in German by a clause reminding us of the fact that their ability "to begin" exists only "as long as the proper personal-human substance [*das eigentlich personal-menschliche Substrat*] that comes into being with them is not pulverized."[59] The expression "personal-human substance" is one of the rare occurrences of a rather scholastic, artificial term in Arendt's vocabulary; we may take it as an indication of some kind of quandary.

How are we to understand the fact that human beings are endowed with freedom, that is, the ability of setting purposes, of making deliberate decisions, and so forth? If we attribute this ability to every individual, to every member of the human species, their coming into being could be regarded as an instance of freedom. In this perspective the fact of birth itself does not assume any particular meaning though. Uniqueness, newness, spontaneity are regarded as qualities of the human being as such, they are linked to a person, not to a particular event or "fact." Freedom is defended based on an essentialist anthropological claim, and Arendt's "personal-menschliche Substrat" is in line with this kind of argument. Yet her emphasis on "natality" obviously points in a different direction.

What exactly does it mean then that "action as beginning corresponds to the fact of birth" or, as the German version reads, that "action as beginning corresponds to the birth of somebody", to the birth of "a Somebody" or "a person" (Geburt des Jemand)?[60] Arendt claims, "with each birth something uniquely new comes into the world." This newness serves as a kind of a role model for practical beginnings, as "action" is categorized as the "actualization of the human condition of natality."[61] "The very capacity for beginning is rooted in *natality*, and by no means in creativity, not in a gift but in the fact that human beings, new men, again and again appear in the world by virtue of birth."[62] Arendt feels the urge to authenticate the newness, uniqueness, or singularity of human life as something given. In the midst of "customs and standards of behavior solidified through tradition"[63] a person is supposed to regain agency and accountability by reminding herself of her new beginning. By linking spontaneous "freedom" to "natality," she seems to seek a backing for moral autonomy. The newborn is presented as the "founding father" of freedom.

Arendt is caught between two strategies here, which are both self-defeating. She could expect the "fact of birth" to provide some kind of biological basis for freedom. Yet this would blur the difference between the birth of a human and the birth of an animal—a difference that Arendt seeks to uphold. So she defends a strictly anti-biological reading of the "fact of birth," yet this reading is based on metaphysical qualifications of the human being that have virtually nothing to do with the "fact of birth" as such. By linking freedom to this "fact," Arendt suggests that freedom is based on some kind of evidence, on something given. But the ontological status of this "fact" is anything but clear. "Natality" remains purely metaphorical.

As birth is meant to be more than biological "delivery," it cannot be an empirical fact, but entails a social and emotional encounter that Arendt does not talk about at all. I would therefore turn the tables and state that instead of taking "birth" as the "foundation of all human togetherness," it is rather a certain understanding of "human togetherness" that prepares us for feeling overwhelmed and entranced when we see a newborn or a baby. And it is not a simulation of God-like creativity that we appreciate in this moment; rather, we respond to the baby's innocent frailty, neediness, and curiosity. There is no "fact" of natality that causes such behavior; the "discovery of childhood" is a cultural achievement.[64]

While revising the English text of *Love and Saint Augustine*, Arendt actually comes close to such a cultural reading of freedom. Here she talks about the "temporal extension" of the life process and about man's ability to unite "into a whole his own existence" by the means of "memory" and "remembrance."[65] Based on these tentative remarks that correspond to her concept of narrativity, we can start thinking with Arendt against Arendt. When remembering, we may actually go back to the "fact of birth," but it is not this fact that ensures freedom but the fact of remembering itself, because it belongs to a process of self-interpretation defying causality. Not just "expectations and desires" but any intentions "are prompted by what we remember and guided by a previous knowledge," and this being "prompted" and "guided" is not to be conceived of in a deterministic manner. When privileging remembrance over expectation, Arendt explicitly turns against "Heidegger's approach"; one might also say that she confronts Heidegger with Proust.

Theory of interaction. Remembrance is based on a shared vocabulary. Instead of singling out spontaneous agents reenacting spontaneous natality, we need to recontextualize agency and turn to the human togetherness that enables the appreciation of spontaneity and freedom. Arendt states: "The freedom of spontaneity is part and parcel of the human condition. Its mental organ is the Will."[66] It is as if she wanted to conceal the dualism implied in her concept of freedom by short-circuiting the spontaneity of the will and the "fact of birth"—a "fact" that comes close to Kant's "fact of reason." By referring to "natality," Arendt seeks to identify an autonomous core within the teleological structure of human agency. Yet instead of singling out spontaneity and autonomy, the phenomenon of "natality" leads to a theory of human interaction and a reappraisal of the constitutive role played by passions or emotions. In this perspective it is particularly unfortunate that the passions have been excluded from the discussion of agency and interaction in *The Human Condition* from the outset. Interaction, in Arendt's perspective, is almost exclusively confined to the exchange in the public sphere.[67] In *The Human Condition*, within the triad of labor, work, and action, the link between "action" and interaction actually makes sense, because, due to their dependency on goods and things, labor and work do not qualify for true interaction between human beings. Nonetheless, Arendt's discussion of interaction appears to be rather narrow. The discussion of economic exchange, for example, is displaced to the chapter on "work,"[68] even though this "exchange" is by no means confined to the sphere of production. Arendt's elucidating remarks on the "frailty" of human affairs and the indissoluble intertwinement of "doing" and "suffering"[69] notwithstanding, interaction is associated first and foremost with the public deliberation on the common wealth.[70]

Even if I readily take her side in defending the public sphere, I feel that her account of interaction remains inconclusive. Arendt *instrumentalizes* "natality" for *backing* autonomous action, which, in turn, is *prioritized* in the sphere of interaction. The notion of "natality" gets distorted when forced to play this role. Moreover, there are forms of human interaction that *neither* comply with the requirements of autonomy put forward by Kant and Arendt *nor* belong to subsections of the spheres of "labor" or "work" only. Among those forms of interaction, affectionate, passionate relationships (among parents and children, lovers, etc.) stand out. The exclusion of passion and love from *The Human Condition* affects the accuracy of Arendt's account of natality *and* of human interaction. This is the price paid for a single-minded defense of autonomy: dimensions of human life not complying with its premises are subdued. Arendt's attempt to provide a firm anthropological foundation for normativity suffers from descriptive shortcomings. Morality is brought into play in a strangely blunt, precipitous manner. However, this criticism is not the "last word" on Arendt.

Passion Regained

The title of this chapter "Passion Lost, Passion Regained," which, of course, references John Milton's *Paradise Lost* and *Paradise Regained,* seeks to suggest that the defeat of passion is not final. In scattered remarks, Arendt gives precious hints as to how the argument on the status of love or passion could proceed. With regard to the teleological structure of action, I shall briefly hint at a passage from *The Life of the Mind*; with regard to the theory of interaction, I turn to an early entry from the *Denktagebuch.* In the following, I focus exclusively on love, which seems to be the mode of passion most fiercely defying reduction to passivity.

Teleology reconsidered. Even though Arendt insists on the distinction between passivity (including passion) and intentional activity, "love" comes into play in her reasoning on the "will" one more time. A critical point is reached when she draws upon the characteristics of *vita activa* as "'unquiet,' *nec-otium, a-skholia*."[71] Does that mean that men are condemned to unrest or even disconcertment? This may be true for those activities oriented toward goals in the future, but not for those having their purpose in themselves. This self-sufficiency is not a state of immobility, but a state of tranquility *in the course* of performing an action. Examples of situations granting a fulfillment of this kind come readily to hand, although these experiences are usually temporary and volatile. They find their limits when confronted with the temporal dynamics of the external world interfering with self-stabilizing agency. A natural reaction to such external intrusion consists in turning away from the world and maintaining a state of fulfillment or ease in the independent sphere of pure thinking or contemplation. Be that as it may, those who are not willing to shut down the exchange with the world will continue their search for situations in which they can relate to something without falling prey to the volatilities of external affairs. They will quickly turn their attention to *love*.

The object of "succeeding" love does not alter, nor does the lover who is moved and carried on by his or her affection. Of course, this claim requires further argument, inasmuch as it inevitably brings to mind Shakespeare's famous line "Love is not love that alters when it alteration finds" and Amélie Rorty's rebuttal "Love is not love that alters not when it alteration finds."[72] If I talk about love's constancy, I do not mean to say that it is entrenched against qualitative changes. The winds of change may alter the persons concerned and their feelings, yet love is not just an object to historic change, but prescribes a certain mode of living through changes in relations. I return to this in the next subsection, on "interaction reconsidered."

The account of love given here cannot claim to be a faithful reconstruction of Hannah Arendt's argument. However, it is supported by one passing remark in *The Life of the Mind*, which proceeds in three steps. First, Arendt states that happiness cannot consist in sheer "passivity," because human life entails agency. She goes on to say that the endlessly pressing "will" asks for "redemption." (This is what I would call the need for overcoming unrest.) She eventually identifies love as the source granting such redemption; it does not demolish will or agency, because it "is still active, though without restlessness, neither pursuing an end nor afraid of losing it."[73] Arendt prefers transforming the will into love more than overcoming the will altogether (or, to put it differently, she prefers Augustine to Thomas Aquinas). Interestingly enough, and in spite of her equaling passions and passivity, she describes a "transformation of willing into *loving*" that is made possible by the fact that love is an "activity," as well, "that has its end in itself." Love stands for constancy, for a "self-fulfilling, everlasting movement."[74] In *The Human Condition*, Arendt's teleological account of agency eventually culminates in spontaneous freedom, which makes it impossible to admit love. In her latest work, she seems to be willing to expand the realm of activities by attributing self-fulfillment to love, that is, she comes back to the position tentatively taken in the early entries from the *Denktagebuch*. So far, I have mainly discussed the internal perspective and the attitude of lovers themselves. Human agency and love do not only raise issues of teleology, they bear on interaction as well.

Interaction reconsidered. In May 1953, when Arendt was still toying with the idea of putting love or passion on her list of fundamental human activities, she notes:

> The eternity of love exists in world*lessness* only. . . . Love becomes the "most human" of mankind, namely a humanity that exists without a world, an object (the beloved is never an object), and a space. Love *absorbs*, namely the world, and gives an inkling of what a world-less man would be like. . . . Love *is* life without world. As such it turns out to be world-creating; it creates or produces a new world. Every love is the inception of a new world; this is its greatness and its tragedy, as in this new world . . . it will perish. . . . Only because love itself creates a new world, it stays in the world (or the lovers return to it). Love without children or without a new world is always destructive (anti-political!); but it produces a pure form of authentic humanity.[75]

In some respects these remarks connect to what has been said earlier about the self-fulfilling "activity" of loving. But the firm, immediate connection between the lover's emotional stance, on the one hand, and the reliable relation to and response of the beloved, on the other, is now read as a vanishing of the world. This worldlessness is introduced by Arendt as a unique premise of world making, in the course of which we encounter the self-destruction of love. Arendt's comments are hard to grasp, but she seems to allude to the idea that stepping out of the world (by experiencing worldless love) enables us to reshape it from outside or reenter it in a new way. But why is love said to be "worldless" in the first place? From Arendt's perspective, the vanishing of the world results from the collapse of distinctions between the agent and his or her reference point and, therewith, the reduction of plurality to singularity.

Along the lines of my brief references above to Shakespeare and Amélie Rorty, I would describe these phenomena slightly differently. The lovers' claim that their love be everlasting does not mean that alterity, alteration, or plurality elude them. Following Aristotle's definition, true friendship or love does not refer to specific qualities (like those other forms of friendship based on utilities), but to the "person as a person." The difference drawn between a person and her qualities makes sense only if we grant a person the right and the ability to generate new qualities. This means nothing else than the ascription of a kind of internal plurality or otherness. Loving means to be committed to someone and to affectionately welcome the next steps taken or experienced by the beloved. This is how the endurance of love corresponds to the continuing existence of the beloved. The lover encourages the beloved to appear as he or she is *and becomes*.[76] By thinking with Arendt contra Arendt, I can rely on her interpretation of "Amo—volo ut sis" (I love—I want you to be)—a phrase that she borrowed from one of Heidegger's early love letters.[77]

The variety of individual characteristics does not disappear from the screen if we recognize a "person as a person." Maintaining the attention to individual characteristics goes against Arendt's contention that love is directed at the "*who*" of the beloved, remaining "unconcerned . . . with *what* the loved person may be."[78] This being "unconcerned" strikes me as odd, as does the opposition between the worldlessness of "love" and the worldliness of "action." The fact that, in the *Denktagebuch*, Arendt regards "love" as a passionate *and* active phenomenon leads us to the conclusion that it does belong to the realm of interaction; this runs against the distinction between agency and love holding sway in *The Human Condition* and also against her claim that love itself is "worldless."[79] Arendt's account of love further informs us about the difficulties of combining descriptive ambitions and normative claims or, in her case, of crafting an anthropology pitched at the defense of the "political." The presupposition of spontaneous freedom ("natality") remains an empty claim if not complemented by an analysis of social contexts in which individual freedom is granted and recognized. Love plays an important role in these contexts as it is not just a counterpart to free agency, but an attitude enabling and encouraging human functioning.

"Rien faire comme une bête"

How does all of this relate to Adorno? I have described Arendt's detour through the domains of love and passion undertaken in the *Denktagebuch* and, on rare occasions, in other writings. As I see it, this theoretical experiment *intersects* with Adorno's considerations of subjectivity. As if Adorno were talking about *amor mundi* as well, he muses about "abandonment," about surrendering oneself to the world when discussing Wilhelm von Humboldt's theory of the person.[80] After defending him against the "cult of the individual" established by his conventional epigones, Adorno quotes the following passage from Humboldt: "Merely because . . . thought and . . . action are possible . . . only by virtue of the representation and elaboration of something, of which the authentic and distinguishing trait is that it is not-man, i.e., is world, man tries to grasp as much world as possible and to join it with himself as closely as he can."[81] Following Adorno, this kind of worldliness is an antidote to a "congealed and rigidified" concept of selfhood.[82] Again the concept of individual agency is linked to a theory of interaction or the person's relation to the world. In this section of my paper, I seek to explore the correspondences between Adorno and Arendt's discussions of these matters. If the analysis of Arendt's anthropology was conducted along the lines of the notions of interaction, on the one hand, and individual agency, on the other, Adorno's main thrust is to revise the concept of the individual. He stresses the violence involved in the making of the modern individual: a violence directed against external and internal nature. His critique of the forcible character of the subject culminates in the following statement: "What is merely identical with itself is without happiness."[83] The identity of the autonomous person has its downside. In *Dialectic of Enlightenment,* Horkheimer and Adorno write:

> Men had to do fearful things to themselves before the self, the identical purposive, and virile nature of man, was formed, and something of that recurs every childhood. The strain of holding the I together adheres to the I in all stages; and the temptation to lose it has always been there with the blind determination to maintain it. The narcotic intoxication . . . is . . . an attempt of the self to survive itself. The fear of losing the self and consequently the border between the self and other life . . . is intimately associated with a promise of happiness which threatens civilization at every moment.[84]

This leads to something like a tragic reversal: "Man's domination over himself, which grounds his selfhood, is almost always the destruction of the subject in whose service it is undertaken; for the substance which is dominated, suppressed and dissolved by virtue of self-preservation is none other than that very life as functions of which the achievements of self-preservation find their sole definition and determination: it is, in fact, what is to be preserved."[85]

Adorno's rebuttal of dualism leads him to a critique of the "repressive" side of Kantian moral philosophy[86]—a critique that he would have turned against Arendt if mutual hostility had not prevented any substantial exchange between them. While Arendt, to a certain extent, defends the Kantian concept of freedom by inserting the would-be spontaneity of "natality" into the world of social customs and constraints, Adorno suspects that "freedom" turns against the very person who is supposed to enjoy it. Following Adorno, this freedom creates an internal rift within the person and an oscillation between autonomy and heteronomy.[87] It is safe to say that Arendt herself does not leave Kantian spontaneity unaltered: she temporarily acknowledges the reach of passions, elucidates the transition from "will" to "love," and seeks to reconcile freedom with a "web of relationships."[88] Adorno could have acknowledged these advances, but he would argue that, by and large, this reconciliation is confined to a language-based contextualization and continues to be based on dualistic premises.

But what is the alternative that Adorno has to offer? With his analysis of the intrinsic violence of self-determination the contention that morality implies agency does not go away. If Arendt defends the primacy of agency, one is inclined to ask: How could one do otherwise, given the urgency of moral judgment and commitment? Adorno's critical discussion of the repressive subject gives rise to the suspicion that he undermines the protagonist of practical judgment and destroys the foundations of morality. Yet he still upholds the "strength of the individual" and of "critical consciousness."[89] We should not rush to conclusions here, but should further scrutinize his appeal to the "living"—a gesture that is still very much in need of further explanation.

The "living" seems to be a label for those aspects of human life that evade practical determination; sometimes Adorno chooses the phrase "not expressible in terms of exchange value" for these matters.[90] Whereas Arendt strictly distinguishes between "action" and the "living process,"[91] Adorno moves into a broader realm of human functioning. He does not settle for a defense of heteronomy or a critique of self-constraint, but strives for a moral reorientation circling around the notion of the "living." It takes refuge in the terms impulse, suffering, compassion, and reconciliation.

Impulse. Adorno's take on the biological side of human nature differs from that of Arendt. She discusses bodily needs under the heading of "labor" and establishes a connection between self-preservation and modern consumerism, which "threaten[s]" to blemish the political purity of the American Revolution.[92] Adorno's critique of consumerism is as fierce as Arendt's,[93] but given that he finds the split between freedom and nature suspicious, he is not willing to confine the discussion of the "body" to a sphere of animal-like existence. Instead, he goes back to the notion of "impulse" or, with Schelling, "urge" (*Drang*) and describes "mental" processes as "modified physical impulses."[94] The "impulse" is said to be "the rudiment of a phase in which the dualism of extramental and intramental was not thoroughly consolidated yet."[95] Agency emerges from a process steered by an "impulse" that is "intramental and somatic in one," Adorno says.[96] By means of the peculiar concept of "impulse," he adds an ethical twist to his critique of the "subject." Whereas Arendt eventually brushes the "passions" aside in order to establish a clear hierarchy of activities culminating in moral autonomy, Adorno doubts that this autonomy could serve as a consistent guideline for living a life. He could have quoted Spinoza at this point: "[T]hose who know how to carp at men, and to reprove vices rather than to teach virtues, and not to strengthen the minds of men but to crush them—these people are irksome to themselves and to all others. The result of this is that many people, on account of excessive impatience of mind and a false zeal for religion, have preferred to live among the beasts rather than among men."[97]

Adorno takes a step back from the agency of the "living" and grants passion a constitutive role in moral reasoning itself. This reasoning is linked to situations and experiences where knowledge is inseparable from taking a stance. Christoph Menke rightly draws a line from Adorno's concept of moral "impulses" to John McDowell's definition of "virtue" as an "ability to recognize requirements that situations impose on one's behavior."[98] Adorno's foundation of agency on "impulse" may remain as tentative as Arendt's reference to the passions remains temporary. Yet Adorno helps us to regain ground from which Arendt and others have departed for no good reason. The area of passions also encompasses moral sentiments, which directly bear on human action.

Suffering and compassion. Adorno's acknowledgment of "nature" in a broad sense entails the appreciation of self-preservation and survival. They do not count as biological phenomena only (as in Arendt), but belong to the project of achieving humanity; this makes him say that one should try "to live so that one may believe himself to have been a good animal."[99] The line from *Minima Moralia*—"There is tenderness only in the coarsest demand: that no-one shall go hungry any more"[100]—is complemented by a reorientation of materialism that aims at "abolish[ing] suffering."[101] In line with the attention to suffering is Adorno's adherence to compassion, and if the former is directed against Kant's moral "duty of apathy,"[102] the latter is at odds with Kant's "contempt for pity."[103] Compassion clearly belongs to the realm of moral motives, which is why it deserves Adorno's attention. I cannot contextualize Adorno's scattered remarks on compassion in the light of Adam Smith, Arthur Schopenhauer et al. here. (This would also require a critical discussion of Horkheimer's late writings.) Anyhow, it would be wrong to imply that Adorno's reorientation of agency knows of passions only in the sense of suffering; my comments on the notion of "impulse" should have made that clear.

Reconciliation. In the moral realm to which a person is committed, she is held responsible by others, and seeks to live up to her and others' normative expectations. But this is not the only sense in which persons matter for morals. It is a moral aim in its own right to recognize and to defend personal integrity, both with regard to moral motivations (i.e., an inclusive understanding of the moral agent) and with regard to human functioning and flourishing (i.e., an inclusive notion of the passionate, suffering human being). Adorno is committed to this aim: the theory of impulses focuses on the overlap of intra- and extramental phenomena, and the concept of suffering and compassion transcends agency.

Adorno is confronted with a situation similar to that of Hannah Arendt. They have to redefine the connection between the individual and the social sphere. After returning from the detour to the passions and to love, Arendt argues for a "love of the world" that strangely outbids the love of individuals. The defense of the "world" as public sphere marginalizes human relations that do not serve this purpose. At least temporarily, she considers theoretical amendments, both on the individual and on the social level, mainly under the headings of passion and love. Adorno maintains a broader perspective on agency and the "living" and argues for a reappraisal of nonrational impulses. I have already mentioned his defense of pity, which connects to the theory of sympathy. This could transform the world of interaction into a world of "inter-passion" (if I may put it that way). Adorno would certainly not go down this path, but if Arendt's comments on agency and interaction are compelling, Adorno's contributions to these matters are sketchy. Anyhow, when discussing issues of education and individualization, Adorno states: "It is with the experience of the non-self of the other that individuality . . . grows."[104]

Jürgen Habermas claims that Adorno's idea of reconciliation with its particular focus on nature tends to marginalize intersubjectivity and communication, whose modes of reconciliation lie in the social sphere.[105] However, it seems to me that, instead of neglecting sociality and focusing on the domination of (and the reconciliation with) nature, Adorno is eager to build bridges between different modes of reconciliation. This becomes evident in a famous aphorism from *Minima Moralia* that alludes to Rousseau's *Rêveries du promeneur solitaire*, to Maupassant's story *Sur l'eau*, and to Hegel's *Logic*. In this aphorism, which actually bears the title "Sur l'eau," Adorno writes:

> *Rien faire comme une bête*, lying on water and looking peacefully at the sky, "being, nothing else, without any further definition and fulfillment," might take the place of process, act, satisfaction, and so truly keep the promise of dialectical logic that it would culminate in its origin. None of the abstract concepts come closer to the fulfilled utopia than that of eternal peace.[106]

Adorno's argument seems to be in line with Arendt's description of the transition from restless action or "will" to serene "love." It should not go unnoticed that Adorno's considerations culminate in a reference to "eternal peace." The meaning of this term is certainly not confined to the peace that we find in nature. In this respect Adorno is a true follower of Rousseau, whose appraisal of nature cannot be separated from social and political theory. I would read Adorno's allusion to "peace" as an attempt to *reconcile*, as it were, different modes of reconciliation. The experience of "lying on the water" may be a world apart from the sphere of interaction, but it is not meant to *dilute* the political agenda and turn "peace" into a somewhat lofty, otherworldly ideal. Adorno takes it to be a reminder of an experience of balance and harmony that helps *broaden* our understanding of the social sphere. This is in line with his remarks on the "living," the "impulses," suffering, and compassion.

Based on the preceding analyses, we can identify patterns of subjectivity and sociality in Adorno that complement and compete with the patterns of passion/action and interaction that we have discovered in Arendt's theory, both in its center and at its margins. I do not want to present a conclusive list of these patterns here, but solely refer to a distinction between two extremely different modes of sociality as it is drawn by Adorno and Horkheimer in the *Dialectic of Enlightenment*.

They criticize a mode of social exchange that takes a person into account only insofar as she acts accordingly and meets external expectations. Under these circumstances a person is identified with "what she now is" or "for what she could possibly be used."[107] As Horkheimer and Adorno say (anticipating Charles Taylor's critique of the "punctual self"),[108] "individuals are reduced to a mere sequence of punctual presences." This punctual self abolishes "the concept of human life" and the "unity of a human being's history": "Any [internal] unanimity and continuity of conscious memory or spontaneous remembrance" is gone.[109]

This critique is complemented by an alternative account of individual life and sociality. Horkheimer and Adorno turn against the preponderance of agency and remind us of a broader notion of the "living" of the individual. A stumbling block for such agency is the past, which evades or forestalls active determination: the historicity of the individual. Although neglected by Horkheimer and Adorno, there is a literary scene that, I believe, effectively unites the transcendence of agency and the turn to historicity. What I have in mind here is the scene depicting Odysseus's return to his home and to his wife Penelope. Horkheimer and Adorno briefly refer to this scene, but do not exploit the potential that it contains.[110] Central to this scene of recognition is the bed that Odysseus had built, using the stump of an old olive tree, before he left. When Penelope asks him to move the bed a little, Odysseus does not get caught in this trap and proves his identity. Historicity does not only help Penelope to overcome her distrust, but is reassuring for Odysseus himself who, during his adventures, was on the brink of becoming a "nobody: Moreover, the bed as a symbol for their marriage also stands for togetherness and intimacy. Our account of Odysseus's identity should not be confined to strategic rationality and the sacrifice of sensuality, but should include the ending of this story, which also stands for an appreciation of mutual recognition and emotional commitment.

The systematic premises of Adorno and Arendt's theories are worlds apart, but the phenomena that they discuss are closely related, as is their inconclusive coverage of these phenomena. Arendt seems to be struggling with the tensions between the potential of a broader anthropological approach and her focus on agency; Adorno's dialectic of subjectivity brings to the fore the "living," which not only evades rational determination but also eludes his aporetic setting of autonomy and heteronomy. In their respective accounts of interaction, Arendt and Adorno seek to spell out the implications of their different concepts of the person and the subject without ever doing justice to the juxtaposition of the urge for action and the perseverance of passion. The convergence between Arendt and Adorno lies in areas where their attempts remain tentative and fragmentary; this may prove the point that the seismic center of theoretical dynamics does not lie in the center of philosophical systems, but at their margins.

PART TWO

Legacies of Totalitarianism, Antisemitism, and Crimes against Humanity

SIX

Grounding Cosmopolitics
Rethinking Crimes against Humanity and Global Political Theory with Arendt and Adorno

LARS RENSMANN

Take a moment and think back to 1967. In that turbulent year, Hannah Arendt corresponded with a German student, Hans Jürgen Benedict. It was a frank exchange about revolutionary movements and republican loyalty, imperialism and transnational solidarity, and multiple issues of world politics—from the war in Vietnam to political violence in Iran. In her response to Benedict's urgent call to action on pressing international political problems of their time, Arendt writes a striking passage in which she seems to challenge the very possibility of global responsibility: "No doubt that it's our business that the situation in Persia, Vietnam and Brazil is horrible, but it's really not our fault. This, it seems to me, is some sort of reversed megalomania . . . You can't change *the* world because you can't be a world citizen; and most people who lean toward world responsibility do so because they fear, for understandable reasons, taking responsibility of what happens in their own world."[1] Normative concerns complement her realistic reservations about "megalomaniac" cosmopolitics. Even in her appraisal of Karl Jaspers's philosophical and legal cosmopolitanism, she asserts that it is important to think and act within *limits*. While she is rather equivocal about the principle of "territoriality," as her appropriation of Pericles' funeral oration shows,[2] Arendt conceives of bounded political communities and circumscribed citizenship as elementary preconditions of meaningful public life.[3] She also rejects the establishment of a world republic, which "far from being the prerequisite for world citizenship, would be the end of all citizenship. It would not be the climax of world politics but literally its end."[4]

Arendt's skeptical view about globalized authority and all too idealistic or lofty cosmopolitan concepts finds company, from a different angle, in Theodor W. Adorno's work. He criticizes the homogenizing ideal of a cosmopolitan "melting pot,"[5] which reflects problematic tendencies inscribed into the "global societal constitution" of modernity.[6] In Adorno's work there is also no shortage of comments criticizing the global power system and its protection by the legal mechanisms in which contemporary liberal cosmopolitans invest so much hope.[7] Thus, Arendt and Adorno aren't cosmopolitan political theorists in any conventional sense. Nor did they understand themselves as such. Prima facie, it may therefore seem hardly surprising that in current discussions about "cosmopolitics," both thinkers have received little attention. Theorizing that seriously engages with Arendt in the context of global political theory is, if at all, in its nascent stage.[8] Likewise, Adorno's status in cosmopolitan theory is one of pariah, although his work has gained some traction in critical globalization studies.[9]

By contrast, I argue that it is a mistake to neglect Arendt's and Adorno's contributions to the subject. Both theorists have much to offer to the contemporary debate about cosmopolitics. In fact, their peculiar marginalization is unjustified for at least two reasons: First, both intend to draw conceptual and moral-political consequences from the Holocaust, which they understand as a civilizational breakdown with global meaning. Much of Arendt's and Adorno's work is an attempt to come to terms with the worldwide crisis of humankind embodied in the extermination of the European Jews. In the very moment of this crisis, both theorists suggest that "humanity" has become a pressing concern and emerged as a political reference point. Understanding the universal implications of the particular experience of genocide that has affected all of humankind is a central undercurrent—indeed a normative driving force—of Arendt's and Adorno's theoretical endeavors. In their view, the Nazi genocide has forced upon humankind the political responsibility—a reconstructed categorical imperative after Kant—to prevent future crimes against humanity, and similar atrocities. Yet according to Arendt and Adorno, modern genocide has also dramatically exposed constitutive antinomies of global modernity and international law, and especially what can be seen as the modern aporia of universal human rights: namely, that such rights often do not matter when it matters, and that they depend on the very institutions of the "sovereign" modern nation-state that has continuously deprived humans of their rights and proved unable to guard them.

Second, Arendt and Adorno develop profound arguments that speak to substantive problems of contemporary cosmopolitan thought. Their admittedly fragmented contributions to global political theory help generate critical perspectives that work as correctives to hegemonic variations of cosmopolitics, if not providing robust alternative models. My main proposition is that Arendt and Adorno are cosmopolitan in the particular mode with which they address novel crimes against humanity—crimes that have exploded the limits of (international) law—and how they reflect on the "new global political situation."[10] Their critical interrogations start with the particular: by reflecting sociohistorical conditions, political contexts, and particular human experiences. Rather than delegating global challenges primarily to formal legal principles or appealing to abstract morality and principles of justice, Arendt and Adorno first and foremost turn to situated political responsibility and particular politics of human dignity in order to realize, and rectify, the universal: the unconditional prevention of genocide and, ultimately, the possibility of human freedom. In this lens, critical cosmopolitics are acutely aware of the perplexing situation of human rights while looking for—and locating—cosmopolitan agency that *vernacularizes* human dignity and political inclusion from below, making them relevant within and through the particular.[11] Call this Arendt's and Adorno's *grounded cosmopolitanism*. The articulation of "authentic" claims to human dignity, however, may challenge allegedly preordained, reified cultural self-understandings and the boundaries of existing law; and such vernacularizations are not limited to prepolitical territorial confines either.[12]

What I offer in the remainder of this chapter is not a comprehensive reconstruction of Arendt's and Adorno's writings in relation to the cosmopolitan question.[13] Rather, I provide a sketch of theoretical motives and moves. I thereby try to sort out different layers of Arendt's and Adorno's—never entirely straightforward—cosmopolitan responses to the global human predicament, which is distinctly marked by the experience of genocide and crimes against humanity.

Between International Law and Politics: Arendt's Cosmopolitan Response to Crimes Against Humanity

According to Arendt, the historical experience of the Nazi genocide exploded all existing politics and law. The extermination of the European Jews fully exposed the antinomies and limits of international law and national sovereignty.[14] This human atrocity signified a historical caesura of global proportions. But it also marked, in Arendt's terms, the "end of the rights of man," or what can be called the modern *aporia of human rights*: that human rights, and the right to have *any* rights, ultimately depend on the very institution (the sovereign nation-state, embedded in the Westphalian international system and law) that has itself undermined such rights either by expelling its own citizens or by denying rights to a new multitude of stateless people. Preceded by other crimes against minorities and "others," the emergence of statelessness as a mass phenomenon and the reality of genocide negatively constituted humankind because humanity in its entirety—different levels of guilt and responsibility notwithstanding—failed to guard the victims of terror. The former became complicit in the latter's expulsion from organized humanity. But this also produced a new, common human predicament that requires new forms of political responsibility in the face of the nation-state system's failure. Thus the *particular* event necessitates thinking about "humanity as a whole."[15] Let us have a closer look at Arendt's response to the Nazi genocide and the way she understands the historical perplexities it discloses.

Even though Arendt was, as previously indicated, an outspoken skeptic of a world state, she simultaneously diagnoses the "bankruptcy of the nation state" and objects to its restoration.[16] Arendt is acutely aware that the Westphalian nation-state system, "always carried within itself the seeds of exclusionary injustice at home and aggression abroad."[17] For Arendt, in fact, the atrocities of the twentieth century can be traced back to national sovereignty's inherent contradictions, as well as to the antinomies of international law. In the Westphalian system, virtually only the nation-state survived as an organized political community in which citizens were granted rights and a meaningful space among equals. Yet it was the exclusive principle of nationality—a key founding element of the nation-state from the onset—that ultimately dissolved the European nation-state as a legal institution capable of safeguarding its members' civil and political rights. The supremacy of "nationality" sanctioned the nation-state's expulsion of some of its citizens and minorities, rendering them superfluous and transforming them into stateless *outlaws*.[18] They could neither cling to their national rights, of which they were deprived, nor have recourse to any international authority. The nation-state system as a whole turned out to be incapable of "providing a law for those who had lost the protection of national government."[19] Even where the "sovereign right to expulsion" was not exercised,[20] nationally circumscribed and international law failed to prevent the worst, because both the expulsion of and genocidal violence against nonmembers was no one's business. According to international law, it was the *legal* privilege of the sovereign German nation to declare the racial Nuremberg Laws of 1935 against its Jewish minority, and international law offered no tool to deal with statelessness or enforce human rights.[21] Expulsion from one's nation-state also implied expulsion from humanity at large.

In Arendt's view, then, the widespread decline of the nation-state and its inner legal integrity—rendering millions of denaturalized people superfluous, stateless, and without the fundamental "right to have rights"—has not only shown that the nation-state system is bankrupt and has failed humans. It has also proven that human rights are anything but "inalienable."[22] The loss of the right to have rights in a political community—primarily the Janus-faced modern nation-state—also means the automatic loss of all (enforceable) rights. But Arendt doesn't stop there: deprivation of political membership does not "just" entail loss of a legal status and thus of specific human individual rights. The loss of your polity includes the more fundamental loss of *human dignity,* the "essential quality as man," which is dependent on a place in the world "which makes opinions significant and actions effective"[23]—a worldly context in which human life can have meaning and in which humans recognize one another as free and equals. For Arendt, therefore, appeals to allegedly "universal" human rights remain a moral and legal abstraction; inadequate, empty, and with little meaning beyond the "shadowy existence as an appeal in individual exceptional cases."[24] The stateless and the victims of genocidal persecution have nowhere to turn in the system of international law; and the only remaining place for meaningful membership, the sovereign nation-state, is at the very root of the human rights aporia—and thus the condition of statelessness—itself. The nation-state and international law's sovereignty principle should therefore not be absolutized. In fact, behind all past and present "nationalistic phraseology," "national sovereignty is no longer a working concept of politics, for there is no longer a political organization which can represent or defend a sovereign people, within national boundaries. Thus the 'national state,' having lost its very foundations, leads the life of a walking corpse, whose spurious existence is artificially prolonged by repeated injections of imperialistic expansion."[25]

Conventional international law protects the "walking corpse" of particularistic national sovereignty, which is mostly indifferent to *human* rights. Yet materializing "abstract" human rights by creating a new universal law—a world state, global public law, or other forms of unbound, superior universal jurisdiction—is not a realistic response to statelessness and genocide. Nor is it desirable to transfer power to some global authority that is so vast in its reach that it can't be checked by republican means and thus makes a meaningful (political) existence impossible, while it conceals its own political bias. The human predicament that surfaced with modern genocide, Arendt argues, is by no means solved if the political unit that identifies law with what is good for the whole is as large as mankind itself; for it is "conceivable" that a politically organized humanity might persecute minorities and conclude "by majority decision . . . that for humanity as a whole it would be better to liquidate parts thereof."[26] While the hitherto existing right to have rights ends at exclusive national boundaries—which is why, in the face of genocide, we ultimately need organized humanity to guarantee it—new forms of abstract universal law and morality alone would be unable to protect this fundamental human right. Instead, such global law in itself even threatens to replace the very freedom, dignity, and diversity it is supposed to guard, namely, by an uncontrollable global tyranny of the majority. Arendt seeks to make us aware of this aporia, or seemingly insoluble contradiction, of human rights in the modern, postgenocide world. It seems impossible to square this circle—at least "in theory" and by means of abstract legal or political principles.

Still, Arendt seeks "worldly" spaces in the *hic et nunc* for a more effective prevention of the unprecedented historical challenge of modern genocide. Though she clearly recognizes the shortcomings of "legalism," she is far from being generally anti-state and opposed to "the rule of law," or *Rechtsstaatlichkeit*. Sustainable freedom as a political reality ultimately depends on a constitutional framework, "for the space between men as it is hedged in by laws, is the living space of freedom."[27] Arendt hereby invokes older conceptions of constitutional law that house public freedom, in opposition to laws according to which "crimes against human rights . . . can always be justified by the pretext that right is equivalent to being good or useful for the whole in distinction to its parts."[28] Furthermore, as Seyla Benhabib points out, over time Arendt did display a growing faith in international law and institutions.[29] Her continuing ambivalence about universal human rights declarations notwithstanding, she began in 1963 to employ the categories of the international Genocide Convention of 1948. She conceived the crime of genocide as *the* "crime against humanity" or "with greater accuracy, a 'crime against the human status'": an attack upon human diversity, aimed at eradicating the very concept of the human being.[30] Consequently, she supported, albeit reluctantly, international tribunals and an international criminal court to prosecute such distinctly new crimes against humanity.[31] In light of the failure of hitherto existing (criminal) laws to deal with them,[32] she calls for nothing less than the cosmopolitan "emergence of an international penal code."[33] Against the background of the novel historical experience of genocide, some legal institutionalization is required that reflects a new categorical imperative—namely, for humanity to address such crimes and to find tools against their recurrence. Yet human rights and international law remain caught in contradictions. And law cannot inspire action, or itself replace human action, freedom, and dignity.[34]

Skeptical of overambitious, paternalistic, and democratically "unattached" global constitutionalism, Arendt leads us to contemplate new ways to address the fragility—indeed the aporia—of human dignity in the context of modern global conditions. It has become imperative to prevent genocidal persecution and the expulsion of humans from a polity—and thus, in a completely organized world, from humanity. For Arendt, this is *the* genuine cosmopolitan legacy of the twentieth century. It is not the product of an abstract moral reflection but a particular response to "unprecedented"[35] human atrocities. Like Adorno, she refers to specific "inhuman acts"[36] rather than to the violation of a legal or moral principle.

Dealing with the legacy of these unimaginable crimes against humans, then, requires some new forms of cosmopolitan responsibility that legitimately cut across sovereign borders. Humankind is hereby no longer an ideal state in a "far-distant future" where human dignity coincides with the human condition—as it was for Kant.[37] Like it or not, Arendt says, these experiences show, alongside other aspects of an emerging new global political situation, that "humanity, which for the eighteenth century, in Kantian terminology, was no more than a regulative idea, has today become an inescapable fact."[38] Consequently, Arendt argues, in order to reconstitute human dignity, which depends on the fundamental "right to have rights"—the right to meaningful political inclusion and voice—it is not possible to simply restore the principle of nationality that allowed the deprivation of human dignity and the persecution of stateless masses in the first place. Rather, "the right of every individual to belong to humanity, should be guaranteed by humanity itself," while Arendt concedes "whether this is possible" is by no means certain.[39]

In retrospect, it is rather questionable to claim that the "phraseology of the rights of man" has been completely "compromised."[40] In spite of their abuse, human rights claims have in fact become an increasingly powerful political tool of the excluded and persecuted. Arendt's response to crimes against humanity, however, contributes to our understanding of the problem by exposing some constitutive contradictions that human rights continue to face in international law and in the global order. Arendt thereby points beyond an exclusive focus on legal abstractions (and Karl Jaspers's unequivocal idealization of cosmopolitan law), and forces us to think about crimes against humanity, human rights and dignity in political terms.[41] She also reminds us that international power politics—and their extralegal ends—often hide behind seemingly neutral legalisms and the rhetoric of human rights.

As indicated, Arendt is also critical of any "pacification from above," which she finds neither feasible nor desirable.[42] A superior global institution possibly bolsters global despotism; it may provide a justification for the elimination of "enemies of humankind" in the name of humanity.[43] Consequently, the institutionalization of an uncontrollable, centralized global authority might not be helpful in preventing humanitarian crises but play a part in creating them. Conversely, Arendt turns to the intersection of law and politics. She emphasizes how crucial extrajudicial, *political* actions are in ensuring solidarity with those who are victims of crimes against humanity. In this view, human dignity is not primarily protected by legal reforms or institutions from above, let alone through extreme legalism.[44] Even though she does endorse international legal reforms addressing crimes against humanity, in an Arendtian lens, the preservation of human dignity first and foremost relies on living subjects who act in diverse public spaces, through whom the idea of cosmopolitan responsibility and the practical solidarity of world citizens can emerge.[45] As Robert Fine aptly puts it, worldly cosmopolitan solidarity is not "forged simply through the progression of legal and institutional reforms but through our capacity as actors in the public sphere to come to terms with our cosmopolitan existence."[46]

For Arendt, then, we cannot fully resolve the antinomies of the bankrupt nation-state system and globalized responsibility *in abstracto* or by appealing to moral and legal principles. An abstract conceptual solution would be incompatible with her "aporetic way of thinking."[47] Only political action can resolve the seemingly mutually exclusive dichotomies of globality and political community, or cosmopolitan norms and meaningful citizenship. First and foremost, Arendt's worldly perspective redirects the focus to the specific responses of particular communities in action, and to political subjects—independent of their political and legal status—who take responsibility in situations where life and freedom are at stake. She reminds us that we cannot primarily rely on global institutions, abstract legal formulas, or allegedly neutral judges and enforcement mechanisms.[48] Rather, genocide prevention and the realization of human dignity especially depend on political struggles and voices of contestation, and may at times even hinge upon extraordinary politics of transgression that break with existing—illegitimate or insufficient—legal principles on the national and international level.

Beyond National Sovereignty and Legal Formalism: Adorno's Cosmopolitan Categorical Imperative and the Legacy of Genocide

Cosmopolitan requirements do not emerge from abstract moral philosophy and abstract principles of justice for Adorno either. The new cosmopolitan demands on politics and morality are superimposed to mankind by the force of contingent events and, in particular, by the Holocaust. At the critical juncture of this global crisis, "humanity's prospect opens up in the face of its extinction," Adorno asserts.[49] "Humanity," then, is no longer just a regulative ideal (Kant). Rather, pace Kant, it also indicates both the need, and the material political possibility, to *reorganize* human relations in a changing world, and thus to fulfill humanity's and enlightenment's hitherto unfulfilled promise.

Adorno formulates the modern aporia of human rights diagnosed by Arendt—that the persecuted who need human rights to be enforced have nowhere to turn to and depend on the same sovereign nation-state that undermines their rights—in a different and arguably even more radical fashion. The particular historical experience of the Nazi genocide evokes renewed critical self-reflections that expose the limits of (inter)national law.

Furthermore, he displays even less trust than Arendt in the capacity of legal systems to rectify the new global situation in which "superfluous masses" are subject to genocidal persecution.

First of all, in the face of the Nazi genocide, Adorno develops an even more radical critique of the principle of national sovereignty upon which conventional international law still rests. He fundamentally calls into question any absolutization of national sovereignty claims, since they have efficiently served to enable human atrocities. Hitler demanded "the right to practice mass murder in the name of the principle of sovereignty under international law, which tolerates any act of violence in another country," Adorno argues.[50] Taking issue with Hegel's glorification of the nation-state—seemingly equipped with a natural quality, an ethnic substrate embodied in the "national spirit"—Adorno pushes further Arendt's critique of the political organization of the nation state and its underlying prepolitical, mythical idea of common origin. Against the background of the crimes committed in the name of collective superiority, he calls nationalism and the concept of national sovereignty a politically regressive, irrational yet persistent "anachronism." Particularly fierce in places "where 'cosmopolitanism' is a term of abuse,"[51] this anachronism, to be sure, has so far survived its own death.

Adorno also radicalizes Arendt's critique of Kantian moral and legal abstractions. Political theory that relies too much or exclusively on abstract general maxims and "legal formalism" fails to fully recognize the scope and character of the cosmopolitan challenge created by modern genocide.[52] Without rejecting the legal form altogether, Adorno is skeptical of any naïve trust in (the reform of) international law and top-down global institutions that are entrenched in the global power system. Adorno shares key presuppositions of Marx's critique of the legal form, most explicitly articulated in his *Contribution to a Critique of Hegel's Philosophy of Right*, and the contradictory foundation of law.[53] Like Arendt, to be sure, Adorno does not ignore the significance of a constitutional framework and universally formalized civil rights, which have largely been the product of political and social struggles. Nor does he dismiss the formal principle of *Rechtsstaatlichkeit* that is encapsulated in constitutional democracies. For Adorno, such rejection of juridical protection would be an indeterminate, abstract negation that fosters direct heteronomy. Instead, he supports a constitutional legal framework that safeguards individual freedom from arbitrary rule (habeas corpus), civil liberties, and rights to due process in a "universal legal system" that has been one of the progressive functions of the democratic nation-state.[54] Moreover, in a way reminiscent of Arendt's republican criticism of unfettered majority rule,[55] Adorno defends the concept of separation of powers "upon which every democracy is based, from Locke to Montesquieu and the American constitution up to today," as an institutionalized context for critique and political responsibility: "The system of checks and balances, the reciprocal overview of the executive, the legislative, and the judiciary, means as much as that each of these powers subjects the others to critique and thereby reduces the despotism that each power, without this critical element, gravitates to."[56]

Yet as long as constitutional and international law are entangled in a system of domination, Adorno argues, formal legal principles and claims also have the function to conceal injustice—among other things, the material exclusion of "superfluous" masses and vast global inequalities of power and wealth—in the language of equality and universality. And when push came to shove, both nationally circumscribed law and instruments of international law have seriously failed to assist those who are excluded and persecuted. Without throwing the baby out with the bathwater,[57] Adorno claims that we need to be aware of the limits of (inter)national law and legal abstractions—at least as long as they that do not originate in freedom and do not reflect on, but are deeply entrenched in, forms of domination that the alleged neutrality of legalism conceals: "Justice gives way to law. . . . The blindfold over the eyes of Justitia means not only that justice brooks no interference but that it does not originate in freedom."[58] True as an idea, liberalism and liberal cosmopolitanism are constitutively oblivious to the limits of positive law and the ways it curtails freedom—and in how far it perpetuates social domination, exclusion, and violence. In a global system shaped by universal domination, Adorno argues, the failure of universal human rights to really matter also affects and undermines the very meaning of its promise: "The purpose of human rights was to promise happiness even where power was lacking. Because the cheated masses are dimly aware that this promise, being universal, remains a lie as long as classes exist, it arouse[s] their anger; they feel themselves scorned."[59]

In Adorno's view, the idealization of institutions and legal procedures allegedly designed to protect human rights may also serve as an apology for the existing order by "assuming the unity of humanity to have been already realized in principle."[60] Thus neither legal forms and legal institutions nor "formalized" universal human rights claims should be renounced.[61] But rather than actually defending human lives and humanity, legal mechanisms and formal entitlements are often at risk of cloaking powerful interests and injustices at play in global politics and society. In "large measure" the legal sphere is a "medium in which evil wins out on account of its objectivity and acquires the appearance of good."[62] From Adorno's perspective, then, legal formalism denies its political character; its claim to impartiality is deeply problematic, especially as long as it is oblivious to substantive injustices it takes part in and leaves unaltered. Even though "[p]ositively [law] does protect the reproduction of life," a legalistic and neutralistic understanding of positive law fails to address the reality of genocide and the conditions complicit in it, which would require taking sides and being partial. While a lawless society needs to be prevented because it will "succumb to pure license, as it did in the Third Reich, the law in society is . . . always ready to resort to terror with the aid of quotable statutes."[63]

Hence, the interlocking of freedom and (cosmopolitan) law is to be taken seriously. Yet the idea of a legal system that consistently reigns supreme also entails a potential threat to freedom—and while it consistently protects the existing system of power and domination, when it matters, laws often let down those excluded and persecuted human beings who count and depend on it the most. Although Adorno attributes critical functions to a universal legal system and its formal abstractions, the sphere of law, "even when it formally subserves the idea of protecting freedom and guaranteeing it, contains the tendency to abolish freedom. The relationship between freedom and the law is not a well-balanced, rational compromise, but possesses dynamic elements on both sides."[64] The protection of constitutionalized formal political equality therefore need not be narrowly construed but paired with an awareness of the shortcomings and limits of the "rule of law's" legal abstractions, which are in many cases deceptive. Consciousness of the extralegal sources and dynamics of formalized rights, as well as of the fundamental antinomies and injustices liberal cosmopolitan thought avoids addressing, also makes clear that the human rights aporia itself cannot find a remedy by purely legalistic means. In Adorno's view, appeals to universal jurisdiction fare no better in overcoming the human rights aporia. Those "superfluous" individuals who are expelled from a polity or subject to persecution have, when push comes to shove, neither national nor international law to turn to. According to Adorno, both are often applied unjustly under the pretense of being neutral. And in existing society and the global system, laws ultimately tend to guard powerful interests and the prevailing social order. The delegation of pressing concerns like genocidal threats to legal principles, even if the latter claim to guard liberty and civil rights, can ratify indifference to the victims of persecution rather than foster awareness of their suffering.

In all forms of existing law the formal principle of equivalence becomes the norm. Yet formal equality, in failing to address structural and substantive injustices, can also serve to promote and reify inequality and exclusion, and undermine diversity—specific experiences and needs not shaped in advance.[65] Its abstract universal morality, as a principle, does injustice to the particular case—a deficiency that requires political rectification.[66] Adorno even doubts if new forms of international criminal law against genocidal perpetrators can achieve *any* justice. This is a thought-provoking but in my view exaggerated and problematic claim when we look at the history of international tribunals and prosecutions of crimes against humanity.[67] Adorno does, however, articulate an important theoretical intuition here: genocide cannot be exclusively delegated to abstract legal principles, an exclusively judicial approach, or to professional judges, as recently suggested by Jürgen Habermas.[68] These matters of life and death are also political and point beyond the sphere of law.

The material, bodily impulse of concrete solidarity with particular victims of torture and genocide escapes, and ultimately challenges, any allegedly superior solidarity with state institutions and political order (which for the Hegel of the *Philosophy of Right* is a good a priori; it does not have to answer to the living subjects exposed to it).[69] For Adorno, this critical impulse cannot be fully absorbed into a new rational synthesis, such as a reformed international legal system. Rather, the "sense of solidarity" that is immanent to any genuinely moral conduct is actualized in irreconcilable extremes: the spontaneous, nonrationalized political "unwillingness to let the horror go on"—one's readiness to act—which is juxtaposed to the theoretical discernment that "shows us why the horror goes on anyway, ad infinitum."[70] This insight, and the antinomy it reflects, grounds a cosmopolitan revision of Kant's categorical imperative in response to the Nazi genocide. According to Adorno, such revision is not an expression of abstract reason. It is grounded in the experience of, and solidarity with, living subjects. Implicitly distinguishing between specific legitimacy and abstract legality, it is concerned with neither the violation of moral laws and rights nor the transgression of legal boundaries. Cosmopolitan morality survives, Adorno says, not in abstract principles applied to the conduct of men, but in the specific reflection and rejection of inhuman conditions. Such a revision of Kant cares first and foremost about human beings, not about the violation of laws—which are always, at best, a means. In particular, morality is resuscitated in the unmediated impulse to stop violence from happening *anywhere in this world*.

Reflecting on the aporia of human rights that is deeply ingrained in the social system and international law, it is now, against all odds, the unconditional imperative for humans "to arrange their thoughts and actions so that Auschwitz will not repeat itself, so that nothing similar will happen."[71] The terror that materialized in genocidal crimes against humans has, in Adorno's view, forced this revised categorical imperative upon humankind. Though universal in its requirements for human conduct, this cosmopolitan imperative is distinct from the mere rehabilitation of abstract moral and legal principles. It turns to those who are excluded, marginalized, terrorized around the globe—while being aware that "sovereign" nation-states and the global powers of civilization that claim to represent "humanity" tend to turn a blind eye to the continuous domination and persecution of those branded as inhuman or culturally different.[72] The new categorical imperative reflects concrete human pain and agony that cannot be tolerated—anything similar to the extermination of the European Jews must not happen again. Contrary to Kant's moral cognitivism, Adorno says that this is not anything that can be discursively argued for or about. Indeed, articulating uncompromising solidarity with tortured subjects, this historically situated imperative absorbs the insight that abstract universality—the universality of coherent legal and moral principles that misrecognize particular suffering and have been incapable to stop it—has *also* failed us.[73] Adorno's revised imperative, driven by a materialistic motive, "gives us a bodily sensation of the moral addendum—bodily, because it is now the practical abhorrence of the unbearable physical agony to which individuals are exposed."[74]

Adorno, thus, reconstructs a defensive but categorical—that is, universal and unconditional—imperative that "nothing similar" should happen[75] as a primary cosmopolitan response to the particular experience of the Nazi atrocities. In this understanding, cosmopolitan solidarity is driven by the unmediated, urgent impulse to stop terror against humans. Making sure that genocide is prevented, and that no similar crimes against humanity are committed, may be all that we can politically achieve for the time being. But it is also the least we can do. However, Adorno also suggests that global societal organization and its laws will ultimately have to be transformed as well, but critical reflection makes us aware of the conditions that prevent this from happening.

Global Political Theory from Below: On Cosmopolitan Agency in a Decentered World Society

Arguing from different angles, Arendt and Adorno both see existing international law as tarnished, and too limited, in the face of crimes that affect humanity in its entirety. The principle of national sovereignty has too long legalized the toleration of "any act of violence in another country" (Adorno). Consequently, any wholesale rejection of cosmopolitan norms as moralistic, apolitical and metaphysical universalism, or tools of Western hegemony, expressing nothing but moral imperialism or a "dogmatic postulate of Western ethical rationalism,"[76] is irreconcilable with Arendt's and Adorno's ideas. In their lens, such fundamentally anti-universalistic suspicions are themselves metaphysical in presupposing a cultural closure—and ultimately a closure of politics—by prioritizing dominant collective norms and existing forms of "collective existence" in an aprioristic fashion. They also ignore that universalistic claims to human rights, freedom, and justice have often been appropriated and mobilized by the victims of exclusion and persecution themselves.[77] Cultures and customs are in flux; instead of being reified, they need to be exposed to critique and contestation from both within and "outside."[78]

Yet both Arendt and Adorno are rather equivocal about the prospects of abstract moral universalisms, epitomized in calls for international legal and institutional reform from above. Their theorizing questions the focus on formal legal principles and human rights appeals as a remedy to the aporia, as valid as such claims may be. From this perspective, then, a cosmopolitics that responds to the legacy of genocide can find refuge neither in legal formalism or abstract universal morality alone nor in existing—and repressive—customary norms based in heteronomous exclusionary practices. Moreover, Arendt and Adorno suggest that the human rights aporia they diagnose in the face of a "superfluous humanity" is embedded in other fundamental antinomies of the "global societal constitution."[79] Despite the emergence of universal human rights norms, the phenomena of human superfluousness, statelessness, and genocidal politics indicate that the precarious status of human beings—and the aporetic situation of their claims to dignity—seems to have worsened overall rather than improved under conditions of global political modernity.[80] While the "bankrupt" concept of national sovereignty continues to be the major foundation of international law, power has increasingly shifted to global economic imperatives and new historic blocs, in which human rights and dignity hardly fare better.[81] In Adorno's view, global class society helps produce massive social injustices and new forms of subjugation even where citizens are formally free. And it creates masses of superfluous human beings who can no longer be utilized and are excluded from global integration.[82] Under disparate circumstances, Arendt points out, we watch the development of "homelessness on an unprecedented scale, rootlessness to an unprecedented depth," while powerlessness has become a "major experience" of humanity.[83] In Arendt's and Adorno's view, the antinomies of global modernity thus provide fertile soil for crimes against humanity to happen again; in a world in which multitudes are nowhere "at home," they can become subject to persecution.[84]

However, even in light of these contradictions—and contrary to some superficial readings—neither Arendt and Adorno advocate any unrelenting pessimism or political retreat.[85] Rather, they engage with a bottom-up view of cosmopolitan agency in a decentered world society as the main vehicle for a new guarantee of universalized conditions of human dignity and freedom, or "the right to have rights." Their critical interrogations first and foremost point to cosmopolitan perspectives from the margins. Subverting the dichotomy of globality and national sovereignty *from below*, cosmopolitan norms gain relevance if they are appropriated in specific, situated struggles by citizens, denizens, and noncitizens—within and across existing constitutional and territorial boundaries—who reinterpret these claims and make them their own. Seen through this lens, cosmopolitan claims to human dignity need to become political and *vernacularized,* that is created, translated, adopted, or "authenticated" by multiple agents in diverse languages and communities in order to be significant and legitimate. Arendt and Adorno's global political theorizing is grounded in a distinct understanding of such cosmopolitan plurality and authenticity.

This theoretical and political move can be unpacked with the help of Walter Benjamin's essay on "The Task of the Translator."[86] "Authenticity" cannot be articulated through any self-assured, steadfast cultural "jargon" (Adorno), or it becomes shallow. Claims to authenticity—especially to "ethnic," "cultural," and "religious" authenticity—are often essentializing discourses to legitimize domination and political exclusion. Foundational discourses of moral universalism, to be sure, can also have problematic, essentializing aspects. Yet we can think about "authenticity" in a different way with Benjamin, who inspired both Arendt and Adorno, and who is mirrored in their work. In this reading, you get closer to the "authentic," that is, to genuinely human purposes and experiences, if you add more layers—more voices, more languages, and more translations—to the original text or claim; not by eliminating new interpretations, reducing them to an abstract commonality, or seeking to "recover" the presumed "original" meaning or justification. In this sense, the pluralistic *vernacularization* of cosmopolitan norms points to the politico-cultural contextualization and emergence of "authentic" claims to human dignity from both within and without existing boundaries of politics, meanings, and constitutions.[87] These new and "authentic" appropriations make such claims significant by actually articulating them in the process of reclaiming public spaces.[88] In this understanding, however, there is also no inevitable trade-off between local collective "autonomy" and cultural specificity, on the one hand, and transnational agents and deterritorialized publics, on the other. The latter may also add "authenticated" arenas—in Benjamin's sense—that may help give voice to the excluded and persecuted whose claims and rights are denied; to advocacy by the victims themselves.[89] Transnational public spaces do not necessarily undermine political autonomy from outside but, instead, can also empower local actors.

Claiming cosmopolitan plurality and "authenticity," then, means neither glorifying repressive cultural customs nor superimposing a full-fledged universal legal system (though some forms of universal jurisdiction may be legitimate). One cannot invent a code that goes against the ethos of one's own age and against a specific societal and political context; to simply dismiss existing norms without taking into account the reality that underlies them, Adorno suggests, leads often "to a regression."[90] Nor can we merely conform to existing prevailing norms and customs within a confined political community: according to Adorno, a responsible human being, "cannot simply declare himself satisfied with the norms that prevail in a particular society."[91] Our political task, then, is to confront prevailing norms with our own situated consciousness and to measure each against the other.[92] This task also points back to the faculty of judgment—in Arendt's words: "the manifestation of thinking in the world"[93]—and its inherently cosmopolitan character. For Arendt and Adorno, reflective or independent judgment presupposes an enlarged mentality that transcends particular interests and perceptions; it seeks to *represent all others* and to reflect everyone else's perspective—including that of noncitizens—in a world that is now, in light of the experiences of the twentieth century, to a considerable extent shared by humanity. Even though judgment is local, it reflects a multiplicity of perspectives. It also strives for universality and entails the idea of being world citizens, and thus of human solidarity.[94]

While Benjamin and Adorno help articulate these theoretical intuitions, it is Arendt who explores this further politically. Paraphrasing and affirming Rosa Luxemburg, Arendt claims that "'pressure for action' always comes 'from below.'"[95] Instead of turning to abstract principles and global institutions, Arendt looks at living struggles epitomizing a "completely different principle of organization, which begins from below."[96] It needs locally grounded agents and empowerment for human dignity if it is to be robust and meaningful, and if global responsibility is not to become an "unbearable burden" for humanity.[97] While human rights have become "formally" universally accepted concepts, they still remain equipped with different meanings and are contested in practice.[98] Most people exposed to violations of even their basic rights, to extreme poverty, or statelessness, cannot rely on international law or human rights regimes.[99] Actualizing human dignity therefore requires vernacularized politics of human dignity, that is, political struggles for equal treatment before the law or for inclusion in a political community. Yet Arendt's bottom-up understanding of associational politics is not limited to territorial borders. True political spaces are established between people organizing themselves for a purpose, "no matter where they happen to be."[100] And human action always establishes new relationships and has an inherent tendency "to force open all limitations and cut across all boundaries."[101] If grounded in bottom-up associations and struggles, transnational communities in action may help engender cosmopolitan advocacy for human dignity and freedom "at home." This entails, in the words of Jeffrey Isaac, an "associational politics that exists beneath and across frontiers, shaking up the boundaries of the political and articulating alternative forms of allegiance, accountability, and citizenship."[102] Seen through this lens, "authentic" and pluralistic cosmopolitics from below relies on new politics of human dignity facing the new human predicament. They may find their space within contingent communal bonds as well as transnational associations acting in solidarity with embattled groups and individuals; they cannot be exclusively delegated to the realm of laws but possibly even have to transcend existing legal frameworks. Human rights claims, to be sure, can be tools in this struggle for human dignity and equality.

Both Adorno and Arendt shift the focus from global institutions and laws to cosmopolitan agency on the margins and to situated struggles to empower human dignity. Yet they recognize that global challenges—and first and foremost crimes against humanity—require forms of globalized solidarity and responsibility, whatever specific political shape they may take: "The forms of humanity's own global societal constitution threaten its life, if a self-conscious global subject does not develop and intervene. The possibility of progress, of averting the most extreme, total disaster, has migrated to this global subject alone."[103] We need, in Adorno's words, "to transcend the idea of a political subject defined by the nation-state."[104] While Adorno and Arendt refuse an abstract ontology that is often underlying moral universalisms and universal rights discourses, they both argue that the global condition necessitates new forms of cosmopolitan political subjectivity. For Adorno individual freedom necessarily presupposes the freedom of all. It presumably cannot be conceived "in the absence of social freedom,"[105] but will ultimately—his critique of Kant's formalism notwithstanding—have to be linked to the "Kantian universal or cosmopolitan concept, not one of any particular sphere of life."[106] Critical cosmopolitanism, then, now entails the ideal that "there is no longer any homeland other than a world in which no one would be cast out any more, the world of a genuinely emancipated humanity."[107] Along with that, Adorno makes related substantive claims beyond (formal) political equality. For instance, he raises the "the coarsest demand: that no-one shall go hungry anymore."[108]

In Arendt's view, too, in order to guarantee human dignity, the atrocities of the twentieth century and human rights challenges may ultimately have to translate into new political formations, a *new nomos of the earth*, that transcend the nation-state:[109]

> Antisemitism (not merely the hatred of Jews), imperialism (not merely conquest), totalitarianism (not merely dictatorship)—one after the other, one more brutally than the other, have demonstrated that human dignity needs a new guarantee which can be found only in a new political principle, a new law on earth, whose validity this time must comprehend the whole of humanity while its power must remain strictly limited, rooted in and controlled by newly defined territorial entities.[110]

Though "strictly limited" in its scope of power and evolving from below, such a new nomos of the earth, however, would require some kind of universally binding political agreement: "Politically, the new fragile unity brought about by technical mastery over the earth can be guaranteed only within the framework of universal mutual agreements, which would eventually lead into a world-wide federated structure."[111]

To be sure, Arendt and Adorno are aware that any such solution remains, in Kantian terms, only a hypothetical, that is, conditional possibility. Creating a "global situation in which . . . reason and freedom have been realized" cannot be taken "directly as a norm by which to govern" human behavior, that is, we cannot directly take a just idea or norm and apply it to the creation of a just society as a whole.[112] Moreover, the relationship between the advocated universal and the particular—particular social contexts and actual human beings, including the victims of what is being done in the name of universal justice—needs to be transparent and give voice to those affected; and "the particular interests of individual human beings must be made to prevail here and now, just as much as that global interest."[113]

Hence, for Arendt and Adorno cosmopolitanism has ultimately become a *political* question, and human dignity will have to be addressed primarily politically. In this perspective, morality and ethics have traveled beyond the false alternative between the seemingly humane moral relativism of prevailing customary norms (Hegel), on the one hand, and abstract, ahistorical laws and duties that tend to be isolated from the empirical world and human experience (Kant), on the other. For Adorno, anything that we can "call morality today merges into the question of the organization of the world. We might even say that the quest for the good life is the quest for the right form of politics, if indeed such a right form of politics lay within the realm of what can be achieved today."[114]

Arendt and Adorno, however, insist on the significance of decentered politics.[115] The threat of a "forced unity" from above—embodied, for instance, in centralized, imperial powers in the shape of an unchecked global authority—is to be taken seriously as a threat to democratic diversity and ultimately humankind. Adorno is especially critical of the ideal of the melting pot, which in fact tends to establish a repressive universal standard that swallows up the nonidentical. Human freedom cannot be conceived of as "a unitary state," but only as "the realization of universality in the reconciliation of differences."[116] Arendt shares this fear of forced unification and assimilation, which could extend the problems of national sovereignty to a global level. Consequently, she argues, the unity of mankind and its solidarity "cannot consist in a universal agreement upon one religion, or one philosophy, or one form of government, but in the faith that the manifold points to a Oneness which diversity conceals and reveals at the same time."[117]

The new global constellation that has constituted "humanity as a fact" hereby also provides new (cosmo)political opportunities to build new associations, while exercising "decentered" human responsibility that may universalize the "right to have rights." In contrast to mainstream political theory, Arendt and Adorno are far from brushing over the existential threats and exclusions that shape our modern condition. However, the two theorists point to communication technology and other organizational advances that may open new spaces to ground such cosmopolitan solidarity and global political responsibility.

In *History and Freedom,* Adorno argues that "the task is not simply to conserve the concrete essence of human relations in the transitory form of the different nations . . . but to bring about [a] concrete state of human community on a higher plane." By that he does not mean a "mechanical union of superpowers joined together in even more gigantic blocs. This would, if anything, just worsen the disaster."[118] Adorno rejects any universal, "abstract organization" that threatens to reinforce global heteronomy. Like Arendt, he fears a "tyranny of a world empire."[119] Instead, he spells out the contours of different forms of decentered cosmopolitan responsibility and organization, which is by no means "as utopian as it sounds on first hearing, if only because modern technology already opens up the possibility of decentralization that actually makes it unnecessary to bring societies together in gigantic hierarchical entities."[120] Devoid of any teleological confidence, Adorno suggests a change in the form of society itself that enables cosmopolitan subjectivities grounded in dispersed, decentered "homelands without frontiers."[121] In the meantime, it would already be "possible to organize societies . . . in much smaller units that could collaborate peaceably with one another. . . . But, oddly enough, it is precisely the technical advances towards decentralization that have been neglected."[122]

Arendt, too, discovers cosmopolitical opportunities generated by Janus-faced modern technology. Her focus is on altered communicative conditions that have changed the shape of political communities and helped humanity to recognize its common fate. Largely due to technology, we have arrived at a point in history at which "all peoples on earth have a common present [and] no event of any importance in the history of one country can remain a marginal accident in the history of any other."[123] Because they provide means of global communication, the same technologies that have taken part in the depoliticization and privatization of public spaces also allow for new forms of a "solidarity of mankind."[124] They can help facilitate new transnational, shared public spaces and diverse venues of political responsibility on which such solidarity depends.[125]

Thinking from the Margins: Grounding Cosmopolitics After Arendt and Adorno

Neither Arendt nor Adorno offers an entirely straightforward cosmopolitan model. Their critical interrogations remain a far cry from solving the conundrums of human dignity and democracy in world politics. Conversely, their focus is on raising critical awareness of precarious conditions in the world of human affairs, rather than designing a canonical cosmopolitan "plan for the good life,"[126] or setting up an abstract "ought" that has "no proper topos or place in the world."[127] Their cosmopolitan thinking reflects on particular experiences of human agony—the Holocaust as an unimaginable crime against human beings that has exploded the limits of hitherto existing law and morality—and the critique of false universals. They do so without either making strong foundationalist claims about universal rights entitlements or dismissing universality altogether and falling prey to moral relativism.[128] The particular historical caesura of the genocide against the European Jews has hereby forced upon humanity a cosmopolitan imperative that replaces Kant's abstract morality: namely, to prevent humans from becoming "superfluous" victims of genocide, and to make sure nothing similar will happen again.

Arendt's and Adorno's cosmopolitan reflections are grounded in two different ways: First, they object to highly stylized and abstract cosmopolitan normative theory. From their perspective, meaningful theorizing needs to be situated in the historical circumstances of politics, law, and society in which it is entangled. Consequently, we are forced to conceptualize the conditions thereof.[129] Although both theorists are critical of the dominant behavioral approaches to empirical sociology, they engage with sociological understandings of the global condition—the distinct configurations and constitutive antinomies of global political modernity in an age of genocide.[130] In a negative way, the experience of genocide has inevitably constituted humanity as a reference point, fostering cosmopolitan responses and rendering any absolutized principle of national sovereignty and existing international law bankrupt.[131] But Arendt and Adorno also diagnose a continuous aporia that a critical cosmopolitics faces: neither the system of sovereign nations that has expelled millions of humans nor any world authority or paternalistic legal reform from above is able—or could be trusted—to guarantee human rights and dignity, let alone fulfill the promise of meaningful citizenship among free equals.

Second, against this backdrop both theorists point to a decentered cosmopolitics that shifts the perspective to those political agents of world society who are marginalized and subject to domination, exclusion and persecution. Reflecting on tensions between the universal and the particular, I have argued that Arendt and Adorno thereby primarily turn to pluralistic, vernacularized forms of cosmopolitan solidarity; and to some tantalizing organizational, technological, and communicative possibilities that are emerging in a decentered world society. Both theorists ultimately gesture toward some new nomos of the earth and cosmopolitan subjectivity. Yet, recognizing that universality cannot first and foremost be realized through abstract formal principles, they are skeptical of grand schemes of global constitutionalism and global authority, which are also in danger of strengthening heteronomy in the name of standardized rule and morality. In turn, Arendt and Adorno's theorizing points to the enabling conditions of decentralized, diverse associations and actions that can effectively challenge the antinomies of international law—and that subvert the hegemonic dichotomy of globality and national sovereignty *from below.* Cosmopolitan norms can matter if they are contextualized; if they can be articulated, and appropriated by citizens and noncitizens who reinterpret and translate these claims, adding new "authentic" layers rather than recapturing or agreeing to any "original" justification. In this reading, "universal" values become especially meaningful in situated, local struggles for freedom, justice, and inclusion. To improve the conditions for such political inclusion has become a globalized concern, however, and "universal" values also find a voice in emerging, inclusive transnational associations, organizations, and publics that cut across conventional forms of political membership. How far a universal "right to have rights" and the "coarsest of demands," that is, a life of human dignity and without hunger, can ultimately be universally actualized very much hinges upon such forms of cosmopolitan human agency and their conditions. In the pressing case of genocide prevention, local struggles to reclaim rights, grassroots initiatives and NGOs fostering a political consensus on the "responsibility to protect"—to halt crimes against humanity—in specific contexts, are more promising than any global legal framework or enforcement mechanism. This, to be sure, does not exclude active support from "outside" or "above," or appeals to formal rights and principles. But it is first and foremost through particular acts of solidarity and associational bonds that universality survives. The universal, then, depends primarily upon its bottom-up appropriation by a multiplicity of diverse human communities and agents—on its vernacularization from below, within and through the particular, within and across existing political borders.

While Arendt and Adorno make us aware that cosmopolitics cannot exclusively rely on delegation to seemingly neutral legal mechanisms alone, Adorno in particular tends to go too far in his criticism of "legal formalism." Forms of universal jurisdiction may actually serve as an important element of genocide prevention and critical cosmopolitics. To be sure, Adorno himself warns against throwing the baby out with the bathwater. He credits both Kant's formal universalism and the universalization of legal norms with emancipatory qualities that are to be preferred to blind affirmation of particular cultural customs and uncontested conformity to national(istic) social norms. Still, he seems to underestimate how much claims to "formal" universal rights claims can matter in the protection of individual lives. His repeated denigration of "formalism" and the false universals of legal "abstractions," to a considerable extent shared by Arendt, raises some questions. Are the "formalism" of law and universalized legal principles the problem—or isn't it rather a matter of specific substantive norms, injustices, and exclusions that *existing* forms of (inter)national law defend? Isn't the primary issue the shortcomings of *institutional realities* of international bodies—such as the United Nations—that are "unchecked," often protecting partial, powerful interests instead of humans in need? Arendt's and Adorno's emphasis on (cosmo)*politics* and grounded political responsibility over legal formalism offers an important corrective to the delegation of global challenges to only seemingly impartial international legal mechanisms and institutions. Arendt and Adorno have, rightly, little trust in existing and hitherto emerging global institutions. But, partly dissolving the dialectical tension that they themselves expose and illuminate, the theorists tend to be too skeptical of the potential of cosmopolitan jurisdiction and international human rights regimes as vehicles that can engender both transnational and local struggles for human dignity. Contradictions notwithstanding, such legal tools—if emboldened by public pressure and agency from below—can play a significant role in the fight for individual freedoms and minority rights, and against crimes against humanity.

However, both theorists open spaces and critical new directions for cosmopolitan thought pointing to a cosmopolitics that is both humble and radical. Humble, in that such cosmopolitics is acutely conscious of the precarious status of human life in international law and the global power system and the often aporetic situation of human rights therein, making us aware of the limits human agency faces in global political modernity. Humble also, as such a cosmopolitics shifts the perspective to the margins of world society, toward the outlawed, excluded, and persecuted who need to become the focus of humanity. Mobilizing situated responsibility and self-reflection, this means abstaining from authoritarian "self-assertiveness" (Adorno) or "pacification from above" (Arendt).[132] While Arendt and Adorno anticipate the potential of new communicative and organizational spaces that challenge territorial confines and language barriers, their difference-sensitive cosmopolitanism also points to the need of cultural appropriation—not forced assimilation—and the vernacularization of human dignity from below. Their thought is modest in recognizing the defiant contingencies of human beings and associations that are vehicles for cosmopolitan "spaces of hope"[133] in a fragmented world society, and reluctant to offer grandiose institutional designs and prescriptions. Political thought, indeed, "can nowhere provide the guidance to the possibilities of the century, or an adequate response to its horrors."[134]

Cosmopolitics after Arendt and Adorno is radical, however, in challenging conventional political theory and its confines. Legitimate responses to genocide and the human rights aporia, for instance, may also include actions that transcend existing legal-political boundaries—the politics of human dignity as politics of transgression. They thereby question narrowly construed positive (inter)national law. Furthermore, Arendt and Adorno are radical in their decentered mode of thinking about freedom, solidarity, and civic responsibility. Yet they also recognize that ultimately new forms of human association are possible—and necessary—to actualize these goods for good. They remind us that, after all, global political modernity also presents us with unprecedented possibilities for alternative political organizations in which individuals and groups can be "different without fear."[135] Without precluding the possibility of radical transformations of global/local relations, such a cosmopolitics may seek, for the time being, to empower particular collective and individual struggles for human dignity—while understanding the limits they face, and will continue to face, on this war-torn planet.[136]

SEVEN

Debating Human Rights, Law, and Subjectivity
Arendt, Adorno, and Critical Theory

ROBERT FINE

Read together, Adorno and Arendt confront the vast contradictions of the modern age that at once elevate the freedom of the individual as its supreme value and subordinate individuality to forces of instrumental rationality and economic determination. On the one hand, the modern age reaches toward maximizing the scope of subjective freedom and giving shape to this principle in the form of rights of personality and property, romantic love and individual responsibility, the voice of conscience and pursuit of self-interest, portraiture in art and character in literature. On the other hand, it elevates both the state and capital into something akin to "earthly gods," which set in motion forces capable of destroying all that has previously given shape to our subjectivity. If the promise of the modern age is that these opposites can be reconciled, the wonder of it is that we can live with this contradiction at all. At every critical moment, we are confronted with the question of how to handle the hypertrophy of freedom the modern age bestows and the atrophy of freedom it constantly threatens.

In their own distinctive ways, Arendt and Adorno both sought to understood the barbarism of their times in terms of the disintegration of mediations between freedom and domination—mediations such as rights, law, civil society, public life, political argument, the state, and, not least, the activities of thinking, understanding, and criticizing. The logic of this disintegration leads both Arendt and Adorno to equally terrifying scenarios. One is the triumph of the will over external limitations, that is, the logic of the camps abstracted from any rational purpose. The other is the triumph of technology and administration over all subjective experience, that is, the logic of the machine abstracted from any human values. The logic of the camps was to apply the principle that everything is possible by demonstrating that everyone can be murdered. The logic of the machine was to apply the principle that freedom, if it exists at all, is just one more cog in a self-perpetuating and self-valorizing system.

Of course, neither Adorno nor Arendt had to invent these scenarios. They were confronted by them. They did not have to leap over "what is" to imagine a dystopia of human beings gone mad with their own power and technology, primed for nothing other than annihilation, for this is precisely what much of the world had become. The task undertaken by Arendt in the name of political theory and Adorno in the name of philosophy was to comprehend this actuality. It was as if the worst nightmares nineteenth-century social critics had foretold of the future had come true: the fetishism of the commodity turned the human being into no more than a thing and the fetishism of the subject destroyed humanity by virtue of its own excess.[1] Nietzsche's premonition of a world in which "the highest values devaluate themselves" proved to be an understatement. The camps above all became the site where "the aim is lacking" and "'why?' finds no answer."[2] One really did experience "a total extermination and uprooting of culture" in which "everything, contemporary art and science included, serves the coming barbarism."[3]

Arendt and Adorno understood that the barbarity of civilization was neither a temporary blip on the long road to modernity nor modernity's hidden truth, the inevitable result of some preceding process of "rationalization," for there is always a gap between the process and its outcome that depends on human agency. However, they both knew that totalitarianism did not come from Mars, but was rooted in the core relations and institutions of modern society, including the forms of revolt that these relations and institutions provoked. For these writers, I would suggest, the hallmark of the modern age out of which Auschwitz and the Gulag were born lay in its capacity for division: between subject and object, person and thing, politics and economics, life-world and system, free will and determination. If in the modern age the possibility of barbarism is all too precariously held off by human institutions whose legitimacy and stability are far from certain, Arendt and Adorno provide us with enduring images of what can happen, and what did happen, when these human institutions are declared invalid, overridden from above, or undermined from below.

The human institutions I shall examine in this paper are those that circulate around juridical ideas of right, law, and legality. Arendt and Adorno addressed the breakdown of these institutions to help us understand why horror persists in the modern world: the genocide of Jews in Europe, the European colonization of non-European societies, and racial segregation within the United States itself. My topic here is the role the idea of "right" played for Arendt and Adorno in their understanding of barbarism and their response to it. My intuition is that by reading Arendt and Adorno together, the aim of this collection, we may uncover a breadth and depth that is not present when we look at each in isolation from or opposition to the other. My emphasis is on their common ground, not their distinction.

In their compelling determination to make sense of the seemingly senseless, Arendt and Adorno wrestled with their own nightmares. For Arendt, the experience of the camps had to do with the divorce of cruelty and murder from any criteria of instrumental rationality: "It was as though the Nazis were convinced that it was of greater importance to run extermination factories than to win the war."[4] For Adorno, the nightmare is of the administrative murder of millions, that is, of human beings murdered, like Jews under Nazism, as if they were "merely the object of technical and administrative measures" and of perpetrators combining "utmost technical perfection with total blindness."[5] It is the nightmare of eternal recurrence in which "each shock not inwardly absorbed, is a ferment of future destruction."[6] In Adorno's words, both writers "balk at squeezing any kind of sense, however bleached, out of the victims' fate" and shudder at the "indifference of each individual life" bespoken by the camps.[7] And yet they assume the task of understanding what happened, however difficult this might be, and find some kind of human link between the subject and the world in the very activity of understanding itself.

Critical Theory and the Idea of Right

Let me try out the following proposition: that the critique of rights is not the same as the trashing of rights, and that they should rather be seen as opposites. Trashing has as its end the devaluation of the value of rights, by demonstrating the chasm between the concept and its actual existence: between the concept of representing universal human freedom and the actuality of concealed material interests, political domination, and cultural prejudices. By contrast, the *critique* of rights has as its end the *revaluation* of the idea of right, exploring the conditions not only of its downfall but also of its reconstruction. My second proposition is that Adorno and Arendt were on the side of critique, not trashing, and that an important element of their critique was targeted at a "spiritless radicalism" that substitutes trashing for critique.

One vital aspect of the Arendt-Adorno project was to understand the sense of revulsion thinking people felt at the gulf between the rights bourgeois society espoused and the mechanized murder, violence, misery, and indifference it proved capable of practicing. It was to acknowledge how justified disgust can be in a society permeated with the double standards of the bourgeoisie and how readily these feelings can be transmuted into the hope that the whole culture might go down in storms of steel. It was to understand how anti-humanist and anti-liberal instincts are fostered, not only in the mob or the crowd, but within the intellectual elite itself. There was nothing new in the hostility to the idea of right that appeared in radical circles in the interwar years. The founders of critical theory, Kant and Hegel, had confronted precisely this phenomenon in their own times. What was perhaps more specific to the twentieth century was how welcome hostility to rights could be to ordinary people infuriated by the award of equal rights to people viewed as undeserving of them, and to a bourgeoisie tired of managing the tension between their words and their deeds and prepared to reveal a more naked brutality. Arendt and Adorno explored how the condition of this hostility to rights was prepared by changing forms of capitalism and political community in the modern age.

Arendt's Narrative of the Decline of Human Rights

In the era of imperialism, Arendt suggested, the principle of unlimited accumulation of capital was from the first accompanied by that of unlimited accumulation of power and by the substitution of violence for law in the running of the body politic. In this context the devaluation of rights and law was, to be sure, contested, but it became the practical spirit of the age.

Attacks on Jews, at last granted equal rights in European nations, were symptomatic of a larger endeavor to destroy the duplicity on which existing society seemed to rest and to explode the false equality that infected the legality of republican institutions.

Arendt's most widely cited discussion of hostility to rights is to be found in a chapter in *Origins of Totalitarianism* entitled "The Decline of the Nation State and the End of the Rights of Man." The narrative on which this discussion is based addresses the disintegration of the old multinational empires that once dominated central and eastern Europe (the Austro-Hungarian, Ottoman, Czarist, and Prussian empires) at the close of World War I and the emergence in their place of nationalist movements and new nation-states commonly opposed to the old empires but otherwise lacking any solidarity among themselves. Arendt's use of the phrase "decline of the nation state" may sound surprising in a context of transition from empires to a raft of new nation-states, but it makes sense as a reference to the normative decline of the nation-state from an instrument of law in its republican conception into an instrument of nation marked by the growing supremacy of the will of the nation over all legal institutions.[8] It also makes sense as a reference to the instability of nation-states in the face of movements that had no respect for the sanctity of national boundaries, the legitimacy of national institutions, or the integrity of national culture. The old empires were dead but the postimperial nation-states fell short of the republican model the eighteenth-century revolutions had fought to inaugurate. The idea of "the rights of man and citizen," once the epicenter of the republican state, was subordinated to the rights of nations to self-determination claimed by nationalist movements and validated by Woodrow Wilson in the West and Lenin in the East. Everyone became convinced that the rights of man could only be attained through the prior winning the right of national emancipation, however much one tried to prove that this could be a fool's paradise.

Once the balance of nation and state shifted from state to nation, once it was the nation that determined the state, rather than the state that determined the nation, the egalitarianism of law ceded place to new forms of civic stratification. Within populations, internal divisions replaced any idea of universal citizenship. There were "state-peoples" who won the right to self-determination; "equal partners" who were formally equal but not in fact not; official "minorities" whose recognition signified that only nationals could be full citizens and the rest needed a law of exception; and those who had no place in the new political order—"displaced persons" deprived of state, country, home, and work. The pariah status of displaced persons was reinforced when the countries of western Europe responded to the influx of large numbers of refugees from the East by abandoning the right of asylum, the sole means by which rights of individuals were recognized at the international level, and by adopting police measures in their place. It was but a short step to ascribing the rightlessness of scruffy refugees arriving on the doorsteps of the West to their own natural deficiencies, not least their endemic "homelessness." They were seen as nonpersons, that is, they were shorn of the right to have rights that had once been put forward as a universal attribute of all human beings as such. The final step in this process of was to deprive all citizens of legal status and rule them through administrative, military, police, and party instruments.

Arendt argued that it was by no means assured that restoration of human rights would follow from national self-determination. Even those who still had their own work, home, and country found their belief in universal human rights sorely tested when they were confronted with people who had lost everything: "who had indeed lost all other qualities and specific relationships—except that they were still human . . . the world found nothing sacred in the abstract nakedness of being human."[9] Arendt acknowledged that the idea of "the rights of man and citizen" was contradictory from the start: it referred to the inalienable dignity of man no power on earth could deny but declared that it is the nation that grants rights and there are no rights apart from those granted by the nation. Kant revisited the exclusions embodied in the rights of man and citizen and sought the means to redress them from a cosmopolitan point of view. In the history of the modern age, however, the contradiction inherent in the rights of man and citizen was played out in a far less enlightened mode.

This was not the only narrative Arendt offered in her effort to understand the "end of the rights of man" in modern Europe, though it is the most read and cited. The broader question she asked is why "the very phrase 'human rights' became for all concerned—victims, persecutors, and onlookers alike—evidence of hopeless idealism or fumbling feeble-minded hypocrisy."[10] To answer this question, she looked in part to subjective factors: human rights were sponsored by marginal figures; the victims of human rights abuses shared the disdain for human rights shown by the powers that abused them; Left and Right brimmed with hostility to all values, including human rights. Arendt's main line of argument, however, was less subjective. It was that the new political order in Europe *seemed* to support

Edmund Burke's characterization of the rights of man and citizen as a mere abstraction compared with the "entailed inheritance" of rights that sprang from within the nation and which one could pass down to one's children, in his case, "as an Englishman." This is how the world appeared. However, Arendt found no "unsuspected profundity" in Burke's preference for the "Rights of an Englishman" over the inalienable rights of man.[11] On the contrary, she repudiated the inclination she found in Burke, on the one hand, to treat law as "an outgrowth of a unique national substance which was not valid beyond its own people and the boundaries of its own territory" and, on the other, to leave "conquered peoples to their own devices as far as culture, religion and law were concerned." According to Arendt, this Burkeian inclination among the British served only to strengthen "the new imperialist consciousness of a fundamental, and not just a temporary, superiority . . . of the 'higher' over the 'lower' breeds."[12] It goes some way toward explaining why the British proved incapable of governing their colonies "in accordance with the general standards of justice and liberty at home" and why they were not interested in shifting from the application of decrees to the making of laws in the colonies.[13] She discerned a "curious touch of race feeling" in Burke's conception of the superiority of the "rights of Englishmen" over the "rights of men" and contrasted this touch of race feeling to the "practical attempts" of the European Enlightenment to "include all the peoples of the earth in their conception of humanity."[14]

When Arendt turned her attention to totalitarianism itself, the image she painted was not drawn from Weber's "iron cage" of legal and bureaucratic rationality, and the alternative she put forward did not prefigure a postmodern ethics committed to breaking out of the iron cage and reconfiguring the moral point of view in opposition to legal and bureaucratic rationality.[15] Arendt's account of totalitarianism emphasizes by contrast its "defiance of positive laws," even those it has itself established, in the name of a "higher form of legitimacy which . . . can do away with petty legality."[16] She argues that totalitarian claims to legitimacy hang on essentially nonlegal grounds, "the rule of justice on earth—something which the legality of positive law admittedly could never attain," and attack the very "sources of authority from which positive laws received their ultimate legitimation."[17] In place of establishing a legal framework within which human actions can take place, the only "law" totalitarianism recognizes is a permanent law of killing. Ideology and terror take the place of positive laws.[18] In its attempt to establish a direct reign of justice on earth, totalitarianism claims obedience to "supra-human ... laws of History or Nature" to which everybody's self-interest must be sacrificed. This notion of justice is effected through a conscious break with "that *consensus iuris* which ... constitutes a people and ... the civilised world."[19]

Arendt's Response to the Decline of Human Rights

My contention is that Arendt's point of view had nothing in common with the disdain for rights expressed in the use of dismissive phrases such as "the so-called sacred and inalienable rights of man" and that Arendt's writings afford us no warrant for "abandoning the fundamental concepts through which we have so far represented the subjects of the political (Man, Citizen and his rights)."[20] This puts Arendt herself at odds with many of her current commentators, critics, and admirers. The fact that Arendt explored the role played by contempt for rights in her study of the origins of totalitarianism does not mean that today one can invoke the authority of Arendt to endorse a new form antinomian radicalism. Such a conclusion would invert the understanding of rights Arendt sought to develop. Indeed, it was the blurring of boundaries in Arendt's own time between Marxist notions of "critique" and what I have called the "trashing" of rights that made her wary of the term "critique" itself.

One of Arendt's responses to totalitarianism was to look for ways in which the "juridical person in man" could be reconstructed. This was a multifaceted and lifelong enterprise, of which I can only outline some basic principles here. My contention is that we can hear echoes of Kant's cosmopolitanism in Arendt's writings: his support for republican forms of state based on the separation of powers, the rule of law and constitutional government; his defense of the right of all peoples to republican government and not just advanced western European nations; his attack on the abuses intrinsically associated with European colonialism in the non-European world; his insight into the limitations of existing international law and his call for its radical reformation; his conception of an all-inclusive Federation of Nations and of a framework of "cosmopolitan rights," including the right of asylum for refugees; and his understanding of the modern world as one in which "the peoples of the earth have entered in varying degrees into a universal community" so that "a violation of rights in one part of the world is felt everywhere." All these thematics reappear in Arendt's work.

True, Arendt was skeptical of the unworldliness of "Kantian" idealists who spoke of global government and universal human rights without confronting the barbarism around them, but she was a better reader of Kant than the "Kantian" idealists she criticized. She looked to Kant precisely because he was not a heady idealist for whom talk of "human rights" and "world government" served only as means of "evading reality."

In the Preface to her *Origins of Totalitarianism* Arendt demonstrates her indebtedness to Kant in articulating the requirements of a new legal and political order:

> Anti-Semitism . . . imperialism . . . totalitarianism . . . one after the other, one more brutally than the other, have demonstrated that human dignity needs a *new guarantee* which can be found only in a new political principle, a new law on earth, whose validity this time must comprehend the whole of humanity while its power must remain strictly limited, rooted in and controlled by newly defined territorial entities."[21]

The problem Arendt saw with the norms of international law existing at the time of her writing was that while new declarations of human rights expressed the "conscience of mankind" in the wake of the totalitarian catastrophe, international law continued to operate largely through treaties and agreements between sovereign states. She commented on the "conspicuous lack of reality" these new declarations conveyed.[22] "Contrary to the best intentioned humanitarian attempts to obtain new declarations of human rights from international organisations . . . this idea transcends the present sphere of international law . . . *for the time being* a sphere that is above the nation does not exist" (my emphasis).[23] The principle to which Arendt looked for a resolution of these issues also involved a restatement of Kant's philosophy of right: it was that "the right to have rights, or the rights of every individual to belong to humanity, should be guaranteed by humanity itself."[24]

Kant had a sharp eye for the *abuse* of the language of rights, that is, for confusing the simulacrum of rights with the genuine article. He criticized the so-called "right of sovereignty" in *ius gentium* as in effect a license for rulers to go to war as they please, use any means of warfare they deem necessary and exploit colonies as if they were lands without people. Equally, he criticized the abuses unleashed on non-European peoples in the name of the "right of hospitality," on the pretext that they mistreated European "travellers" who were actually armed invaders.[25] Arendt had the same sharp eye for the abuse of the language of rights. She described the notion that "what is right is what is good or useful for the whole" as essentially barbaric—whether the whole is the German people, the world proletariat, the workers' state, or even humanity as such. Arendt put the matter thus: "It is quite conceivable, and even within the realm of practical political possibilities, that one fine day a highly organized and mechanized humanity will conclude quite democratically—namely by a majority decision—that for humanity as a whole it would be better to liquidate certain parts thereof."[26] Arendt had a strong sense of the dangers of living in "one world" where there was no longer an "uncivilized" spot on earth and "loss of home and political status become identical with expulsion from humanity altogether."[27] And she drew from Kant his conclusion that in this globalizing context, freedom requires a complex architecture of rights—private, public, international, and cosmopolitan—including the right of "citizens of the world" to visit other countries, initiate communication with other peoples, try to engage with them in commerce with them, and appeal to them for help when fleeing from misery or oppression.[28]

Arendt appears to break from Kant's immersion in the natural law tradition according to which "rights spring immediately from the 'nature' of man" and are independent of history. She argues for the obsolescence of this way of thinking. With the experience of the so-called "laws of nature and history" behind us, she maintains we have good reason to doubt the existence of natural laws as well as to see their sinister aspect. The new situation Arendt sees is one in which "humanity has in effect assumed the role formerly ascribed to nature" and the philosophical anthropology of the human condition, with its repudiation any notion of human nature or human essence, takes the place of natural law. The question this leaves us with, however, is whether Arendt actually breaks from the natural law tradition or rather takes Kant's formalization of natural law one step further in its anti-essentialist conception of the human condition. Kant writes that "the student of natural right . . . has to supply the immutable principles on which all positive legislation must rest."[29] These immutable principles cannot be based on what the law happens to say in any particular place or time; they can only be drawn from the realm of natural laws defined as laws to which "an obligation can be recognized *a priori* by reason without external legislation."[30] This was crucial to the *critical* content of Kant's philosophy of right, since if universal principles were based simply on what the law is empirically, in the manner of positivist jurisprudence, they would offer no more than an endorsement of the status quo. It is difficult simply to isolate the principle Arendt puts forward of "the right of all human beings to have rights" from this conception of natural law. I wonder whether her relation to this tradition was less one of radical rupture than of engagement and dialogue. Kant's acknowledgment that the education nature actually offers us is "harsh and stern," to the point of nearly destroying the whole human race, is surely one Arendt would have endorsed.[31]

Adorno's Narrative of the Decline of Human Rights

Adorno was, like Arendt, a critic of natural law. What appears to distinguish him from Arendt has to do with the explicit link he makes between history and freedom. He writes: "freedom . . . is a historical category par excellence . . . The concept of freedom is itself the product of history and has altered with history."[32] However, Adorno equally explicitly contrasts his own approach to the "entire dialectical tradition of Hegel and Marx," when he maintains that the challenge facing the philosophy of history is to "preserve the permanent component" of such concepts as freedom throughout all the changes they undergo.[33] That permanent component consists of the ties that bind freedom to the individual, however much the concept of the individuality is turned into a symbol of conformity in commercial society. Adorno by no means ignores the history of the idea of freedom, say, the limited scope of the Spartacus uprising or of Babeuf's conspiracy, or the expanded scope of freedom in a future society without want, but his core suggestion is that the concrete possibilities of freedom can be found at every moment of history, that is, whenever individuality genuinely asserts itself. He grants that individuality is itself a historical category in the sense that it refers to different forms of individuality over time, but the possibility of exercising one's freedom is not itself historically conditioned. Adorno and Arendt may be closer to each other than they appear at first sight.

Adorno draws his notion of the dialectic from Hegel's *Philosophy of Right* but gives it a famously "negative" twist. Adorno sees before his eyes the vastly increased subjection of the particular freedom of individuals in modern bourgeois society, whether to objective norms of behavior or to the overweening power of the state or the totalitarian movement. Adorno was transfixed by the "consummate negativity" of the existing system of right. It produced a world of chained and defeated figures, walking through social life as in a prison yard, and then, adding insult to injury, representing this state of subjection in the guise of human freedom. Even National Socialism, he wrote, sometimes paraded itself as the supreme bearer of freedom. Adorno's image of the totally administered society drew from Hegel's *Philosophy of Right*, which he read through a lens partially crafted by the young Marx as a mirror of a social reality in which the bourgeois principle of autonomy, which meant something in the high period of bourgeois ascendancy, had declined into one of mass conformity, terror, and the mere illusion of autonomy.

Adorno recognized that Hegel's aim in the *Philosophy of Right* was to reconcile the particular with the universal, the subjective rights of the individual with the power of the collective, but he insists in passage after passage of *Negative Dialectics* and *History and Freedom* that Hegel invariably reconciled this opposition in favor of the "universal" against the "particular." Whilst Hegel's *Philosophy of Right* may have started off as a momentous effort to conceive a form of state which would preserve the rights of property-owners, resolve the conflicts of civil society, and embody the universal will, he ended up according to Adorno with an "inexcusable paean" to a state that cared nothing for free institutions.[34] Adorno was by no means the first to read Hegel's *Philosophy of Right* in this fashion, but where Adorno differed from Hegel's liberal critics (Karl Popper et al.) was in attributing this outcome to the dynamics of modern capitalist society. As class conflicts grew more intense, it seemed that the only solution within existing conditions was indeed to turn the state into an increasingly independent power.

What Adorno admired in Hegel was above all his realism. It was as if the hard-headed Hegel knew what had to be done if the capitalist state was to achieve the necessary integration. Hegel's "betrayal" of his philosophy of freedom appears as a mirror of the reality of bourgeois society. It was bourgeois society, rather than Hegel, that turned the state into an object of worship and degraded individuals into its executors. Hegel is said to have dissolved this experience of degradation from a higher philosophical vantage point: identifying rationality with obedience to the state, disguising decisions of state as democratic procedures emanating from the people, holding that the individual is always in the wrong whenever he or she fails to "recognise his own interest in the objective legal norm," labeling all criticism as mere "fault-finding" and associating it with an inferior type of consciousness.[35] Adorno thought that Hegel's own apparent degradation of the individual corresponded to the actual indifference of modern states to the lives of individuals. He described the world the *Philosophy of Right* attempted to sanctify as "an endless procession of bent figures chained to each other, no longer able to raise their heads under the burden of what is"; a world that compresses the particular "like a torture instrument."[36]

According to Adorno, then, Hegel put philosophy at the service of the state. His "transposition of the particular into particularity follows the practice of a society that tolerates the particular only as a category, a form of the supremacy of the universal."[37] Hegel is said to have mystified the political primacy of the state over the individual by translating it into the logical primacy of the universal over the particular in speculative thought. Passages in Hegel that seem to respect the freedom of the individual are said to be a mere "slip of the pen," things Hegel "blurted out," since he was always basically on the side of the objective legal norm against individual conscience. The secondary benefit of this mystification, according to Adorno, was to reveal the individualistic illusions of liberal thought in contemporary capitalist society. The "Hegel" Adorno constructs for this narrative of decline is a philosopher who prefigures the shape of modern society when he "blackens" the rights of individuals "as a form of narcissism—like a father chiding his son, 'Maybe you think you're something special.'"[38]

In the language I used earlier, the problem with Hegel's *Philosophy of Right* for Adorno is that it allowed for a slippage from the critique of rights to the trashing of rights. I would place "Hegel" in quotation marks, since it seems to me that Hegel does not fit the role Adorno allocates to him.[39] On the one hand, Adorno writes that Hegel's sympathies always lean to the universal, and that the individual is always "fobbed off with the assurance that the universal sustains itself by destroying him"; on the other hand, he continues to praise Hegel as a great philosopher to whom he is hugely indebted. The difficulty is to see what there is to praise in a philosophy that automatically dismisses an individual's criticism of historical events, say the development of fascism in Adorno's time, "as the grumblings of the disaffected or the irrational protest of someone who feels pangs of emotion," and puts the sense of "awareness" always on the side of the collective and not on that of the individual.[40] Adorno wants to praise Hegel but finds little to praise in such a "Hegel" except the mirror of society he offers.

The difficulty Adorno creates for himself is to think that the institutional nexus of rights, morality, family, law, civil society, state, and so on, are all too compromised by their own false promises and dialectical inversions to provide a way forward for critical theory or emancipatory politics.

This leads Adorno on a journey of relentless integrity from one difficult path, or aporia, to another. Sometimes Adorno looks to the overcoming of the modern bourgeois system of right as a whole only to acknowledge that the overcoming would be marked by the same distortions as that which is overcome. Sometimes Adorno claims that the attachment of freedom to the legal notion of "right" no longer has substance only to acknowledge that the divorce of freedom from the idea of right makes matters worse. Sometimes Adorno presents the idea of the formally free individual subject as an anachronism going back to the "high period" of bourgeois society, only to acknowledge the impossibility of abandoning the idea of the formally free individual. Even in contexts in which the entire sphere of morality has been abolished, Adorno comments, "We necessarily apply yardsticks of good and evil to behaviour."[41] At times, Adorno faces up to the negativity of the existing system of right from what he calls the "standpoint of redemption," in the hope that this will delineate the "mirror-image of its opposite," but he immediately goes on to reject this approach because

> it presupposes a standpoint removed . . . from the scope of existence, whereas we well know that any possible knowledge must not only be first wrested from what is, if it shall hold good, but is also marked for this very reason by the same distortion and indigence which it seeks to escape. The more passionately thought denies its conditionality for the sake of the unconditional, the more unconsciously, and so calamitously, it is delivered up to the world.[42]

One further strategy is to separate out the positive moments in bourgeois society (and in Hegel's thought) from its negative forms by searching for new forms of individualism beyond abstract right, new forms of association beyond civil society, and new forms of self-determination beyond the state.[43] One can try to overcome the existing system of right for the sake of the rational concepts generated by it. However, Adorno understands very well that this utopian vista fails because all such attempts at radical separation leave us with an irrational "is" and a purely abstract "ought." In the words of Simon Jarvis, it leaves the "ought" without substance and the "is" without intelligibility.[44]

There appears to be no way through these difficulties. Adorno always returns to the immediate idea of individual freedom he cannot find in Hegel. He declares in many different ways that "social analysis can learn incomparably more from individual experience than Hegel conceded," as if Hegel conceded nothing. He appears reluctantly to admit that "[i]n the face of the totalitarian unison with which the eradication of difference is proclaimed as a purpose in itself . . . part of the social force of liberation may have temporarily withdrawn to the individual sphere," as if Hegel would not even concede a temporary withdrawal.[45] He too defends Kantian formalism, as if Hegel would have no truck with it, on the grounds that it incorporates "recognition of the bourgeois equality of all subjects" and contrasts it with "the allegedly a priori differences that are supposed to exist between people according to fascist principles."[46] He then points out the contradictory character of rights, that equal rights in law means social inequality in practice, as if Hegel had no notion of any of this. From the beginning to the end of this immense intellectual journey, Hegel serves Adorno as his Doppelgänger. Adorno can appeal to the immediacy of individual freedom to counter the fetishized forms of social life Hegel seemingly validates. While the social forces conceptualized by "Hegel" reduce human action to the "twitching of fleas," Adorno finds a touch of humanity in an inhuman world in the shapes and forms of the individual's "damaged life."

In all of Adorno's troubled dialogues with Hegel's *Philosophy of Right*, the *substance* of right, the social forms of its existence in the modern world, are largely downplayed in favor of an omnipresent dialectic of the particular and the universal. Hegel turned philosophy toward social science. He explored the idea of "right" as the determinate social form of freedom in the modern age, arguing that in the course of its development, the idea of right assumes various new shapes, and that the task of philosophy is to observe and analyze "the proper *immanent* development" of these shapes of right.[47] For Hegel, the idea of right was not only the beginning of this journey but also, as he put it, "the soul which holds everything together and which arrives at its own differentiation only through an immanent process."[48] The dialectic, as Hegel defined it, is the movement of the idea of right through its various concepts and shapes: personality, property, contract, morality, love, family, law, association, civil society, state, interstate relations, global institutions, and so forth. It is not an "external activity of subjective thought," not a method that gives its user privileged access to the truth, but a process of development we can observe and do our best to understand.[49] In relation to the "subjective" forms of modern society, the task of philosophy, as Hegel saw it, is to detect the "inner pulse" that beats within the wealth of forms that constitute the field of right as a whole.[50] It is not to side with the "universal" against the "particular," but to trace the tensions and conflicts human beings confront as the system of right becomes ever more differentiated and complex. In political terms, the major challenge Hegel points to concerns, on the one hand, the fetishized power of the state, its proclivity to imagine itself as some kind of divinity, and, on the other, political hostility to the very idea of rights, law, and the state. The concreteness of Hegel's exploration of the legal and political forms of modernity is not what seems to interest Adorno, not because such matters appear outside the realm of philosophy, but because social forms appear as such as the imposition of the universal on the particular.

This is not to say that Adorno dismisses the importance of an institutional framework of legal rights for freedom. In his lectures on *History and Freedom*, he makes passing reference to the right of habeas corpus—or rather the effects of its absence under totalitarian domination:

> when someone asks what freedom is . . . tell him that he needs only to think of any flagrant attack on freedom. . . . I am content to be able to say of freedom . . . that being free means that if someone rings the bell at 6.30 a.m., I have no reason to think that the Gestapo or the GPU or the agents of comparable institutions are at the door and can take me off with them without my being able to invoke the right of habeas corpus.[51]

Adorno seems to look two ways. On the one hand, he highlights the irrational side of Kant's *Metaphysics of Justice,* which lies in halting the advance of reflection, establishing fixed standards of legality and imposing them on subjects irrespective of their will or welfare. As Adorno put it, "freedom calls for reflection, which rises above the particular categories of law and chance."[52] On the other hand, he demonstrates that Kant's formalism is not merely false, as it was presented by those who "have shown their bloody colors in the fascist practice of making blind phenomena, men's membership or non-membership in a designated race, the criteria of who was to be killed."[53] Adorno comments that in "the universal legal norm . . . despite and because of its abstractness, there survives . . . something of substance: the egalitarian idea."[54] Drawing on such experiences of terror, Adorno makes reference to the difference between a lawful state based on the separation of powers and a regime based on terror and ideology. He recognizes that even the total "Hegelian" state, where legal structures are little more than "concrete instantiations of a compressive and liquidating Universal," is not the same as National Socialism or totalitarianism.

Arendt and Adorno: Judgment and the Generative Effects of Law

In reading Arendt and Adorno today, my contention is that we may have to test the limits of their own theoretical predilections to understand precisely how the idea of right functions as the social form of freedom in the modern age. We have in a sense to rediscover Kant and Hegel. Neither Arendt nor Adorno abandoned their belief in the value of rights and critique. Neither in my language was or became a "trasher" of rights. In his discussion of "critique" in *Critical Models,* Adorno acknowledges the importance of a constitutional order of checks and balances for the practice of critique:

> The conception of the separation of powers upon which every democracy is based, from Locke and Montesquieu and the American constitution up to today, has its lifeblood in critique. The system of checks and balances, the reciprocal overview of the executive, the legislative and the judiciary, means as much as that each of these powers subjects the others to critique and thereby reduces the despotism that each power, without this critical element, gravitates to.[55]

In her discussion of student protest movements and New Left intellectuals in the 1960s, Arendt writes in similar vein of the vital role played by the constitutional framework of rights in protecting freedom and resisting exploitation:

> What protects freedom is the division between governmental and economic power, or to put it into Marxian language, the fact that the state and its constitution are not superstructures. What protects us in the so-called "capitalist" countries of the West is not capitalism, but a legal system that prevents the day-dreams of big-business management of trespassing into the private sphere of its employee from coming true. . . . Our problem today is not how to expropriate the expropriators but rather how to arrange matters so that the masses dispossessed . . . in capitalist and socialist systems can regain property. . . . It has to do with what kind of state one wants to have, what kind of constitution, what kind of legislation, what sort of safeguards for the freedom of the spoken and printed word. . . . Freedom is freedom whether guaranteed by the laws of a "bourgeois" government or a "communist" state. From the fact that communist governments today do not respect civil rights and do not guarantee freedom of speech and association, it does not follow that such rights and freedom are "bourgeois."[56]

Arendt and Adorno both reaffirm juridical values, emphasizing the stabilizing effects of law in "the public affairs of men." As Arendt puts it, lawfulness sets limits to human action but does not inspire them. It tells us what we should not do but not what we should do. It does not provide a "principle of action" beyond its own negative yardsticks or address the problem of the "movement of the body politic and the actions of its citizens." This seems to me a restrictive view of rights and lawfulness, for the generative capacities of law—its ability to inspire action even in the absence of any positive legal framework—may also be at work even in situations in which positive laws are notable only for their absence.

Arendt and Adorno had the same anxiety, namely, that the "Kantian" individual capable of thinking for him or herself was giving way to the mass man who hides behind conformity to the collective. Both in their own ways, however, try to resist any mechanistic notion of descent into subjugation. Arendt poses her opposition to totalizing forms of critique by positing a moment of freedom that intervenes between the elements of political life and their "crystallisation."[57] For her the "mysterious" faculty of judgment always remains a possibility, so that even under conditions of terror "most people will comply but *some people will not*."[58] For Arendt, reflective judgment is the ability to tell right from wrong "even when all people have to guide them is their own judgment," and even when their own judgment "happens to be completely at odds with what they must regard as the unanimous opinion of all those around them."[59] She writes of those few individuals who in the face of terror were still able to tell right from wrong: "They went really on their own judgments, and they did so freely."[60] Her case study was a certain Sergeant Anton Schmidt who helped Jewish partisans by supplying them with forged papers and military trucks, without asking for money.[61]

Adorno's equivalent to Arendt's Sergeant Schmidt was Fabian von Schlabrendorff, a member of the German resistance involved in the attempt to assassinate Hitler on July 20, 1944, who "just couldn't put up with things the way they were any longer" and "followed the idea that anything would be better than for things to go on as they were."[62] In *History and Freedom*, Adorno calls such acts of resistance "the true primal phenomenon of moral behaviour" and argues (contra Kant) that they occur when the element of impulse joins forces with the element of consciousness to bring about a spontaneous act."[63] In *Problems of Moral Philosophy*, he writes that this reveals the ever-present possibility that "things may be so intolerable that you feel compelled to make the attempt to change them."[64] Both Arendt and Adorno are confronted with what they see as an irreducible human faculty, as impulsive as it is intellectual, capable of finding the resources to tell right from wrong.

To my mind, the force of these compelling examples is stronger than the analysis offered by Arendt and Adorno. These instances of resistance may be understood as revealing not just the exercise of reflexive judgment but also the exercise of the imagination—a faculty capable of representing to these individuals an idea of right that was established in the modern world but had no visible presence in the immediate society around them. In focusing on the stabilizing functions of law, we should not ignore the generative capacities of the idea of right to inspire action. This is perhaps one way in which we can read what Arendt refers to in her lectures on Kant's *Philosophy of Judgment* as our "cosmopolitan existence." She defines it as the ability to "take one's bearings from the idea, not the actuality, of being a world citizen."[65] The idea of a world citizen, drawn from Kant, presupposes multilevel rights: civic, political, social, national, international, and human. It may take imagination to reproduce the idea of these rights in their absence and suppression, and it certainly takes courage to act on this judgment and translate one's sense of moral indignation, which may remain private, into an act of resistance, which is necessarily public. It seems to me that pure reflective judgment may be as mythic as pure determinate judgment: in one case, we have the myth of irreducible individuality in the face of a murderous society; in the other, the myth of being a mere cog in a killing machine. Considering the generative capacities of law to inspire action can help us understand these actions without resort to "mysterious" faculties or natural "impulses." In their vast efforts to confront a historical experience that was as personal as it was political, Arendt and Adorno strengthen our conviction that the idea of right continues to offer, not only a vital standard of judgment with which to assess the modern age, but also a category of understanding with which to come to terms with its extremes of freedom and terror.[66]

EIGHT

Blindness and Insight
The Conceptual Jew in Adorno and Arendt's Post-Holocaust Reflections on the Antisemitic Question

JONATHAN JUDAKEN

This chapter reconstructs the very different, interactionist and socio-psychoanalytic theoretical paradigms that Arendt and Adorno developed to understand antisemitism. Despite their differences, they shared a common problem that riddled their respective understandings. Both depended upon elevating what I shall call "the conceptual Jew" to the centerpiece of their paradigms. The conceptual Jew provided the critical energy for Arendt and Adorno's theoretical reflections on antisemitism, but also resulted in each of them reiterating stereotypical constructions of Jews and Judaism. These typologies of Jews prove quite similar. The hypostatized and essentialized conception of Jews that wends its way into their theorizing resulted in both cases in their insights as well as their blindnesses when it came to their respective analyses of what Adorno preferred to call "the anti-Semitic question."[1]

Hannah Arendt's Interactionism

Hannah Arendt's most significant contribution to the theorization of antisemitism is her insistence on its historicization. She was a trenchant critic not only of existential approaches like Jean-Paul Sartre's,[2] but of accounts like those advanced by the Frankfurt School that emphasize socio-psychoanalytic concepts like projection,[3] and she was utterly hostile to scapegoat theories, or worst of all, the notion of an "eternal anti-Semitism." Each of these theoretical approaches misconstrues antisemitism because each fails to examine the intertwined history of Jews, antisemitism, and the "Jewish Question" within a more general history of modern Europe. What makes Arendt's approach to antisemitism distinctive among its theorists is consequently what I call her *interactionist* understanding of it as the story of the role of Jews in relation to dominant society over the course of modernity.

In reading Arendt, I shall examine the disconnect between her theory of history as "storytelling" and the story that she tells about the history of modern antisemitism. For while her intention is clearly to write a history that brushes against the grain of conventional historiography because it seeks to destroy its object (i.e., antisemitism) rather than preserve it, Arendt nevertheless reiterates certain antisemitic motifs in her account. It is precisely in doing so that she reinscribes some of the problems that are the targets of her critical historiography.

Ultimately, Arendt's understanding of Jewish history is what forges the causal links between the elements that crystallize in totalitarianism. In her narrative, Jews are depicted as both at the origins of and the victims of modernity. Her analysis also depends upon the analogic use to which Jews are put in her account of social antisemitism, as well as her categorical insistence on the supernational character of the Jewish people. Most problematic, however, is her account of the role of Jews in the development of financial capitalism, where she recycles an image of the "Rothschild Jew" that was so widespread in the middle of the nineteenth century.[4] The stereotypes that emerge in Arendt's thought, I want to show, are themselves closely bound to the conceptual Jew that Arendt produces: a figure that permits her double strategy of condemning antisemitism but also taking on the role of the "conscious pariah" committed to an internal critique of the Jewish elite for their responsibility in bringing about the destruction of European Jewry.

Hannah Arendt's Methodology: History as Storytelling

For Arendt, writing the history of antisemitism posed unique methodological problems, for historians "had to write the history of a subject which they did not want to conserve; they had to write in a destructive way and to write history for purposes of destruction," which is "somehow a contradiction in terms."[5] The way out of this dilemma for most that had undertaken the effort before her, she maintained, was to examine the events from the viewpoint of the victims. This has resulted in a history of apologetics, a victimology, which she derisively stated, "is no history at all."[6]

Arendt thus spurned conventional approaches to history in favor of what she termed "storytelling." She was critical of any form of historical determinism that claimed to know the laws of development in history, especially those predicated upon class or race as the keys to history, which she saw as part of the latent logic that had resulted in the disasters of the twentieth century. She condemned causality as the deduction of the unprecedented from precedents. She also rejected analogic thinking as the reduction of difference to sameness, and she derided universalization as ideology built on the denial of particularity.[7] Rather, inspired by both the fragmentary historiography urged by Walter Benjamin and the *Ursprungsphilosophie* of Martin Heidegger, Arendt conceived of history as the weaving of discrete narratives framed to comprehend the events and processes under consideration. In short, the historian is a storyteller who rescues the past from oblivion, illuminating the dark times of human existence with her meaning-making narratives.

Arendt's approach was thus neither an objectivism nor a relativism, neither a historicism nor a presentism. Rather, Arendt advocated what Lisa Disch calls a "situated impartiality." Arendt sought a plural and perspectival approach to her narratology. Doing so recreated the past as a shared world where the historian never re-presented only one view on that past. Historical events are made by a plurality of individual stories that form a complex matrix of meaning. Since Arendt insisted on multiple perspectives (both within events and in reflecting on events), there are also many versions of historical truth. Situated impartiality is thus neither objective nor relative, precisely because it depends upon "perspectival differences [being] raised, contested, and situated in reference to each other."[8]

Arendt's approach to history is also critical of the "politicization of memory" that Jean-François Lyotard has called the "memorialization of the past."[9] As Seyla Benhabib has argued, what is foregrounded in her analysis is "the *politics of memory* and the *morality of historiography*."[10] Arendt not only presciently theorized a perspectival approach to history as "storytelling" but also offered multiple exemplary exercises in this approach to the past. She analyzed individuals, memorials, anecdotes, concepts, incidents, and institutions. For example, she used the stories of Rahel Varnhagen, Adolf Eichmann, Rosa Luxembourg, and Benjamin Disraeli, or events like the Dreyfus Affair, to illuminate various aspects of the antisemitic past. She practiced a *Begriffsgeschichte* (history of concepts),[11] which located instances of rupture in the past in order to rethink through remembering, using the ruins of the past as the shards of history that enable us to comprehend the present. Arendtian storytelling thus makes history a praxis, as Disch puts it, "whose purpose is not to defend abstract principles or objective facts but to tell provocative stories that invite contestation from rival perspectives." The ambiguous space of historical writing thus serves to encourage debate and reinterpretation that make situated impartiality and plurality possible to begin with.[12]

Antisemitism: The Origins of Arendt's The Origins of Totalitarianism

But when we turn to the actual history of antisemitism with which Arendt opens her triptych in *The Origins of Totalitarianism*, we find she comes to violate her own historiological principles. To get at this, I want to return to Eric Voegelin's famous review of *The Origins of Totalitarianism*. While Voegelin certainly understood origins, causes, and the relation of parts of the book to the whole differently than Arendt,[13] his account of her multifaceted text is quite acute, even though as a review it only emphasizes the central strand in her pastiche of stories.

Voegelin opened his review by stating that the *Origins* "is an attempt to make contemporary phenomena intelligible by tracing their origin back to the eighteenth century." Doing so, Voegelin suggested *avant le mot* that Arendt's work is a *genealogy* of totalitarianism in the Foucaultian sense, with its point of departure as a history of the present. He correctly indicated that while the three parts of the text are roughly chronological, the overlaps in time in her story are important:

> Anti-Semitism begins to rear its head in the Age of Enlightenment; the imperialist expansion and the pan-movements reach from the middle of the

nineteenth century to the present; and the totalitarian movements belong to the twentieth century. The sequence is, furthermore, an order of increasing intensity and ferocity in the growth of totalitarian features toward the climax in the atrocities of the concentration camps.[14]

He indicated quite rightly that the center that animates Arendt's discussion is the destruction of European Jewry. He proceeded to elucidate the governing theme as the rise and fall of the nation-state until its virtual dissolution, creating the mass society of the twentieth century. With every transformation new sections of society become superfluous and their legal, social, and economic status is therefore threatened: centralization of the nation-state and the rise of bureaucracy made the aristocracy superfluous; growth of industrialization and new sources of revenue made Jews as state bankers superfluous; and every industrial crisis created superfluous human beings through unemployment. In the twentieth century and still today, wars and totalitarian regimes create millions of refugees, which Arendt called the "stateless": those who are unmoored from their communities by the processes of modernity, becoming what Giorgio Agamben has called "bare life," the rightless "scum" whose only logical place ultimately became the internment and slave labor of the concentration camps, the laboratories of a totalitarian society. As Voegelin described it, each section of Arendt's his-story is the necessary, although not sufficient condition for the future synchronic structure of totalitarianism as it crystallized in the twentieth century.

In her opening chapter, "Anti-Semitism as an Outrage to Common Sense" Arendt criticizes both eternal antisemitism and the scapegoat theory as hopelessly unable to account for the problem of Jew hatred. She then lays out her own thesis that it is the role of Jews in relation to dominant society and reciprocally the history of the Jews' relation to the nation-state that is the basis of antisemitism in the modern period. It is as such that her model can be characterized as interactionist.

Arendt suggests that the so-called Jewish problem constitutes a reversal of cause and effect and is thus an outrage to common sense. She insists that two approaches to dealing with antisemitism in particular have masked this outrageous history: the scapegoat theory and eternal antisemitism. Arendt refutes the scapegoat theory because it implies that there could have been another scapegoat and thereby denies the particular history that resulted in the persecution and extermination of Jews.[15] She derides the scapegoat theory with a joke that functions as a reductio ad absurdum: "An antisemite claimed that the Jews had caused the war; the reply was: Yes, the Jews and the bicyclists. Why the bicyclists? asks the one. Why the Jews? asks the other."[16] She argues that whenever you try to explain something by the scapegoat theory, you have to begin to reconstruct the historical events. As soon as you do so, the scapegoat in its abstraction is left behind and you become "involved in the usual historical research—where nothing is ever discovered except that history is made by many groups and that for certain reasons one group was singled out." In addition to its inherent ahistoricism, Arendt also repudiates the scapegoat theory because "it upholds the perfect innocence of the victim," in this case, making the Jewish scapegoat blameless, which thereby "discharges the victim of responsibility."[17] While this is certainly the case, interactionist approaches risk the reverse, which is to blame the victim, as we shall consider in more detail below.

If the scapegoat explanation is one means to escape the interactionist history of antisemitism, then "eternal anti-Semitism" is another. This is the claim that hatred of Jews and Judaism is transhistorical, operating according to the same modes and methods over time. This makes antisemitism a natural reaction, to which history gives only more or less opportunity. Eternal antisemitism answers the question "Why the Jews?" with the question-begging reply, "eternal hostility."[18] For Arendt, the fact that "eternal anti-Semitism" is the doctrine adopted by professional antisemites to legitimate their position serves as a significant warning against it use. After all, if everywhere Jews have lived at all times, they have been hated, despised, or criticized, the reasoning of the antisemite claims that there must be a natural, transhistorical ground to these attitudes to Jews and Judaism that legitimates them.

In a mirror image of the antisemitic position, Arendt maintains that Jews use the notion of eternal antisemitism as a means of cohering Jewish identity. She argues that since at the same moment that antisemitism arose in the nineteenth century, Jews were threatened from without and from within, the claim of eternal antisemitism emerged as a way to keep them together.[19] Hence, eternal antisemitism enabled both antisemites and Jews to remain blameless for antisemitism. Arendt calls instead for an approach to antisemitism that examines the interactions of Jews with the dominant society, which she proceeded to write in the following three chapters.

In Arendt's chapter 2, "The Jews, the Nation-State, and the Birth of Anti-Semitism," she points to the source of modern antisemitism in the underlying double binds at the origin of Jewish emancipation. There are two aspects to Arendt's argument. First, she insightfully maintains that there are latent contradictions between nation and state as they developed in modernity. These contradictions became manifest in the equivocalities of Jewish emancipation. Zygmunt Bauman has elegantly rearticulated this Arendtian argument, contending that

> the order modern Europe built was to be the nation-state order, and that involved political powers waging cultural crusades against ethnic minorities, regional customs and local dialects, so that the myth of national self-sameness could be made into the legitimizing formula of political powers. Into this Europe of ... nation-states ... Jews did not fit ... [since they were] a non-national nation, and so cast a shadow on the fundamental principle of modern European order.[20]

While Arendt's first point provides an astute critique of the tensions immanent in the Enlightenment and human rights tradition that were a key basis of Jewish emancipation, it is the second aspect of her narrative that contains her blind spot. For Arendt also contends that it was Jewish finance from the seventeenth century onward, in the pivotal role played by the court Jews and later by Jewish bankers and financiers, that was central to the development of the nation-state. This point is adumbrated by her claim about the internal contradictions of the nation-state. Consequently, her central claim is that "emancipation of the Jews, therefore, as granted by the national state system in Europe during the nineteenth century, had a double origin and an ever-present equivocal meaning."[21]

This "double origin" and "equivocal meaning" structure what she describes as the simultaneous rise and decline of the nation-state and places European Jewry at the heart of her story of modern antisemitism. In this story, there is a consistent interplay in the relationship of the Jewish community to the state. It is determined by privileges bought for financial favors granted the state, which in turn aid its development. The result was the simultaneous decline of the Jewish community and the rise of wealthy Jewish individuals as the weakening of the nation-state unfolded and the rise of the imperialist order unfurled.

Arendt outlines four phases in her story. First, in the seventeenth and eighteenth centuries, the nation-state developed under absolute monarchs with the financial aid of court Jews. After the French Revolution, the nation-state required far more capital than individuals could provide. This phase necessitated the combined wealth of western and central European Jewry in the form of Jewish bankers. This assistance of the Jewish community was then rewarded with the privileges of emancipation being extended from a few advantaged individuals to the community as a whole. The third phase was characterized by the decline of the nation-state and the rise of imperial capitalist development. Imperialism marked the transition from the nation-state's domination of power to its domination by capital interests. As Jewish wealth became superfluous, political antisemitism increased. The Jews served as a target of hatred because of their identity with the state and financial capitalism. All social classes that conflicted with the state or were distressed by capitalist transformation turned their wrath on the Jews: "Jews became the symbols of Society as such and the objects of hatred for all those whom society did not accept."[22] The third phase overlaps with the final stage that Arendt describes, when the Jews themselves declined as a group in the period before World War I. This decline was characterized by Jewish atomization "into a herd of wealthy individuals." As a result, "the non-national, inter-European Jewish element became an object of universal hatred because of its useless wealth, and of contempt because of its lack of [real] power."[23]

In this socioeconomic and political story concerning the origins of antisemitism via the interrelations between the Jewish community and the nation-state, Jews are consequently positioned as "double origin" and "equivocal meaning": both cause and effect, benefactors of the drive toward equality and assimilation and victims of their own separation and exclusion, caught between the underprivileged and overprivileged, positioned between what Arendt terms, after Max Weber and Bernard Lazare, the "pariah" and the "parvenu." This ambivalent position of Jews also corresponds to the two forms of antisemitism that Arendt distinguishes—social and political antisemitism: the first caused by the growing political equality of Jews with all other groups, and the second by the ongoing legacy of Jewish separatism and difference.

Arendt develops this analysis in Chapter 3, "The Jews and Society," a cultural history of Jewish social exclusion and the simultaneous efforts at acculturation that structured the Jewish condition in the modern period. She uncovers and assesses the *mentalités* that corresponded to Jewish assimilation and that haunted this process throughout modern European history. This is encapsulated in the strictures between pariah and parvenu. The modern Jewish situation produced a complex psychology: "Jews felt simultaneously the pariah's regret at not having become a parvenu and the parvenu's bad conscience at having betrayed his people and exchanged equal rights for personal privileges."[24] Based on these antinomies, antisemites would simultaneously construct the "'Jew in general,' 'the Jew everywhere and nowhere' with those qualities which the parvenu must acquire if he wants to arrive—inhumanity, greed, insolence, cringing servility, and determination to push ahead."[25]

As in Arendt's story of Rahel Varnhagen[26] and her subsequent article on "The Jew as Pariah,"[27] in the *Origins,* she continues with an emphatic emphasis on the double binds of the project of emancipation, where even culturally integrated Jews were unconsciously forced to maintain the appeal of the pariah's oriental strangeness and marginality: "Jews were exhorted to be educated enough not to behave like ordinary Jews, but they were, on the other hand, accepted only because they were Jews, because of their foreign, exotic appeal."[28] Thus Arendt brilliantly conjoins her analysis of the precarious balance between society and state upon which the nation-state rested to the individual situation of Jews who were integrating. For them it meant "they always had to pay with political misery for social glory and with social insult for political success."[29] On an individual level, this meant mastering the paradoxical process of knowing "how to play the role of what one actually was."[30]

According to Arendt, the result of the paradoxes of assimilation was a Jewish type, defined psychologically, rather than nationally or religiously, "the sum total of which was supposed to constitute 'Jewishness.' In other words, Judaism became a psychological quality and the Jewish question became an involved personal problem for every individual Jew."[31] It was this step from Judaism to Jewishness that made possible the next step to seeing Jewishness as a vice. "The Enlightenment's genuine tolerance and curiosity for everything human," Arendt maintains, "was being replaced by a morbid lust for the exotic, abnormal, and different as such."[32] She offers two examples: her section on Disraeli entitled "The Potent Wizard," which explores how race became the basis of Jewish identity in the context of Jewish secularization, and her section "Between Vice and Crime," which focuses on Proust.

Marcel Proust and his account of Swann, Charlus, and the Guermantes in *Remembrance of Things Past* best illuminated for Arendt the mechanism of social antisemitism and condensed her discussion of the disintegration of modernity, where the public realm is obscured by the shadows of the social, engendering dark times. Born to a Jewish mother and a Catholic father, and thus, as Julia Kristeva puts it, "Both Jewish and Catholic, neither one nor the other or perhaps both simultaneously . . . [Proust was] destined to live through the historical events that overwhelmed the turn of the century—the Dreyfus Affair and the First World War."[33] He was "ambivalence incarnate,"[34] which made him emblematic of the epoch. Through her reading of Proust, Arendt argues that the fin-de-siècle marked a period of transition from the crime of Judaism signified in Christian thought by the deicide charge into the vice of Jewishness. This was dangerous in the extreme, for "Jews had been able to escape from Judaism into conversion; from Jewishness there was no escape. A crime, moreover, is met with punishment; a vice can only be exterminated."[35]

Proust epitomized the socially articulated vices of the period: "'the greatest witness of dejudaized Judaism,'" she notes, he represented not only the racial vice of Jewishness, but also the sexual vice of homosexuality.[36] Insightfully, Arendt makes much of the overlaps between the sexual and the racial other. The vice of Jewishness and the vice of homosexuality are compared to each other, where "their reflection and individual reconsideration became very much alike indeed."[37] What Eve Kosovsky Sedgwick has called "the epistemology of the closet"[38] applies for Arendt equally to the racialized category of Jewishness and the sexualized category of "inverts":

> The complicated game of exposure and concealment, of half-confessions and lying distortions, of exaggerated humility and exaggerated arrogance, all of which were consequences of the fact that only one's Jewishness (or homosexuality) had opened the doors of the exclusive salons, which at the same time had made one's position extremely insecure. In this equivocal situation, Jewishness was for the individual Jew at once a physical stain and a mysterious personal privilege, both inherent in a "racial predestination."[39]

Arendt consequently suggests that Jews and inverts, in their equivocal situations, have the same behavioral patterns: both feel different from the norm (in a superior or inferior way), both believe this difference to be the result of birth, both justify not what they have done but what they are, both waver between an apologetic attitude and the claim that they are an elite, and both Jews and inverts embody clannishness.

So by the time Arendt came to consider the Dreyfus Affair as the dress rehearsal of the twentieth century in the last chapter of her story of antisemitism, she had shown how antisemitism was the result of an interaction of Jews with the forces shaping the larger world of which they were a part: the economic transformations of capitalism, the rise of the nation-state as the central political structure of modernity, and the social and cultural attitudes that found Jews dangling on the horns of the dilemmas involved in Jewish emancipation.

Arendt's Conceptual Jew

This brief sketch I have given of *The Origins of Totalitarianism* helps us to appreciate Arendt's general narrative in the section on "Anti-Semitism." Let us now pause to consider how Arendt's story, which ascribes to Jews an equivocal causal function, rather than systematically destroying the antisemitic system of thought that she assesses, actually reinscribes Jews within prevalent Judeophobic typologies. I shall offer three brief examples. In the section "Between Vice and Crime" just considered, Arendt posits what seems an uncritically digested parallelism between homosexuality and Judaism that verges on reiterating nineteenth-century images of "the Jew" as perverted, promiscuous, debauched, lecherous, and feminized: in short, as the inversion of the norm. Arendt's point is surely to emphasize how the fin-de-siècle constituted mass identities and that queers, whether Jews or inverts, were accepted only because they were fascinating, exotic types. But the conflation of the stereotypes of these two queers is reiterated by Arendt rather than problematized: "it is true that to the recording onlooker the behavior of the Jewish clique showed the same obsession as the behavior patterns followed by inverts," she notes, as if this were a natural fact.[40]

In addition to reiterating rather than evaluating the discursive construction of the queerness of Jewishness, she does not adequately undermine the notion that Jews were inherently a queer nation—the alien-nation, outsiders, foreigners, the nation within the nation—since she constantly identifies Jews as the paradigm of the supernational group. For her, Jews, "remained an international element whose importance and usefulness lay precisely in their not being bound to any national cause."[41] Arendt's position stems in part from her insistence that political antisemitism was not essentially a nationalist but rather an imperialist, supranational "pan- movement."[42] Not only does Arendt underemphasize the importance of nationalist antisemitism, but Jewish assimilation appears as always already foreclosed, not only as a result of the historical processes of nation-state formation, but because of Arendt's positing of the inherent character of Jewish internationalism and cosmopolitanism. She also significantly underplays the importance of Zionism in all its permutations, a topic that was a significant preoccupation of her thought in the period preceding the *Origins*.[43]

Finally and most problematically, in her account of the Jewish role in fostering the economic activity of the state, Arendt suggests that financial alliances are the only bond that "ever tied a Jewish group to another stratum in society."[44] Pierre Birnbaum contends that "by adopting—strangely—the analyses of the French antisemitic writer Édouard Drumont which, as far as the role of the Jews is concerned, are akin in some respects to those of a Marx, Arendt postulates a purely economic interpretation of the Jews' place in the state," which he rightly calls a "flawed hunch," only partly valid with respect to Germany and questionable as a description of French history.[45] Like Marx's *Sur Judenfrage*, Arendt places the Jewish Question at the center of her early critique of modernity, too closely identifying Jews with financial capitalism and financial capitalism with the dissolution of politics, the nation-state, and individuality. This breakdown threatened to degenerate into the atomistic, antagonistic egoism that destroys species-being in Marx and produces the loss of what Arendt terms world-being.[46]

To sum up my reading of Arendt, I have tried to show how in her description and analysis of antisemitism, Jews are identified as not only symbols of what society does not accept, but at the origins of the degenerating influences of modernity—financial capitalism, the nation-state, and the bourgeoisie. Jews are situated in the interstices of the fundamental bifurcations that constitute the central categories that structure Arendt's thinking: between past and future, tradition and innovation, anti-modernity and modernity, state and nation, and society and politics. In short, Jews are caught in the double binds between the pariah and the parvenu, between being Jewish and assimilating into European society and culture.

There is an ambivalence in the story that Arendt tells that makes it difficult to determine whether her account is caught within contradictions produced by her own distinctions or those of the Western tradition that she seeks to analyze. It is sometimes difficult to demarcate in Arendt's story when she echoes the antisemitic tradition she is dissecting and when her analysis of it offers a nuanced description of the paradoxes of the Jewish condition in modernity. This is because Arendt's insights traverse the dichotomies that structure her understanding of antisemitism, politics, and modernity, even as "the Jew" that underpins her interpretation ambivalently transgresses these distinctions, occupying an ambiguous, often contradictory situation. Arendt notes of other thinkers that "fundamental and flagrant contradictions rarely occur in second-rate writers, in whom they can be discounted. In the work of great authors they lead into the very center of their work and are the most important clue to a true understandings of their problems and new insights."[47] Like Arendt's own story, which is itself fraught with the tensions and ambiguity of her own universality and particularity, Germanness and Jewishness, her political theory and her histories that focus on sociocultural singularities, the relation between her theory of history as "storytelling" and the story of her history of antisemitism demands to be reevaluated and rethought. In the chiasmus that I have traced between Arendt's perspectival approach to history and the perspectives she unfolds in her history of antisemitism, her account of the "double origins" and" equivocal meaning" of modern Jewish history opens her-story to internal contestation and reinterpretation, at the same time as revealing the importance of the interactionist approach to antisemitism that Arendt pioneered.

Theodor Adorno's Socio-Psychoanalytic Critical Theory

It was the deployment of psychoanalytic categories and the psychologization of antisemitism by Adorno and the Frankfurt School that Arendt rebuffed, although she never dealt with it systematically. Adorno and his colleagues at the Institute for Social Research would come to their socio-psychoanalytic approach to antisemitism only haltingly, however. Despite their founding promise to study the problem, the members of the Institute did not directly analyze antisemitism in the 1930s, notwithstanding the anti-Jewish policies and terror enacted in Nazi Germany, including the boycott of Jewish businesses and legislation against Jewish professionals in 1933, the Nuremberg laws of 1935, and the Kristallnacht pogrom of 1938. According to Friederich Pollock, institute members did not want to "advertise" the Jewish Question; nor were they willing "to draw unnecessary attention to the overwhelming Jewish origins" of the Institute's members.[48]

While the Frankfurt School largely neglected the problem of antisemitism in the 1930s—Max Horkheimer undertaking the first significant analysis by an Institute member only in 1939—by the early 1940s, antisemitism had developed into a major concern. As early as August 1940, for example, Adorno wrote to Horkheimer that he could not "stop thinking about the fate of the Jews any more. It often seems that everything that we used to see from the point of view of the proletariat has been concentrated today with frightful force upon the Jews."[49]

In 1939, the year his essay "The Jews and Europe" appeared,[50] Horkheimer began to discuss the possibility of a large collective research project on antisemitism, to be directed by himself and Adorno. An early version of this plan was drafted by Adorno as the "Research Project on Anti-Semitism" and published in the spring of 1941 in *Studies in Philosophy and Social Science*, the English-language continuation of the *Zeitschrift für Sozialforschung*, now published in New York. The project was to show the saturation of antisemitism within Western culture historically and to develop research methodologies for measuring its contemporary forms.[51]

As early as September 1940, Adorno began to send Horkheimer samples of his early theoretical ruminations on antisemitism as they were developing. These unpublished reflections indicate how he assigned Jews to conceptual categories that recycle well-worn typologies, even as this enabled him to unpack the socio-psychic structures of antisemitism. He opened by picking up on the old trope of the wandering Jew, the perpetual peripatetic, as both at the origin of antisemitism but also its ultimate victim. "The survival of nomadism among the Jews might provide not only an explanation for the nature of the Jew himself, but even more an explanation for anti-Semitism,"[52] he wrote to Horkheimer. Jewish nomadism, Adorno claimed, constituted Jewish nature, or at least so Jews have been constructed in the antisemitic imagination.

He put this association to work by offering it as a twist on Freud's claim in *Moses and Monotheism*. Freud had argued that anti-Jewish hatred was a function of the identity of Jews with the difficult ethical imperatives of monotheism, which elicited wrathful loathing by those who agreed with these ideals, but could not fulfill them personally. Providing a Marxian turn, Adorno shifts the terms from ethics to labor, but the Freudian insight remains: the Jewish identification with the quality of nomadism elicits contempt from those condemned by monopoly capitalism to the daily grind and misery of work, which is a by-product of settlement. "The Jews are the ones who have not allowed themselves to be 'civilized' and subjected to the priority of work," he claimed. "This ban is the origin of anti-Semitism, the expulsions of the Jews, and the attempt to complete or imitate the expulsion from Paradise." Jewish exclusion and the image of the Jewish parasite and the Jewish miser are invoked and explained at a stroke.

The insight is powerful. For on the basis of this simple set of assumptions, Adorno can provide an account as well of why Jews were a key antitype for nationalists and empire builders in the nineteenth century. He can also account for why Jews are the targets of those whose lives are strained by the conditions of the modes of production in late modernity. The cultural and the economic imperatives at work behind this image of the Jew are thus illuminated. But to offer the interpretation, Adorno echoes the claim that Jews are condemned to exile and wandering, even if this is only in the cultural unconscious of the West. Adorno's conceptual Jew as nomad is naturalized by his gloss on why this captures fascists' imaginations and what it explains in their lives. This way of conceptualizing antisemitism by reiterating the stereotype of the conceptual Jew would repeat itself in the more developed works by Adorno as well.

Antisemitism: A Social Disease

These works of Adorno's would only reach full fruition after the war. Writing in the Preface to *The Authoritarian Personality*, Horkheimer noted that the research project on antisemitism initiated in 1939, combined with "a series of discussions with the late Dr. Ernst Simmel and Professor R. Nevitt Sanford of the University of California [five years later that] laid the basis for the present project."[53] The conference that Horkheimer alludes to took place in San Francisco in June 1944. Convened under the auspices of the San Francisco Psychoanalytic Society—the California Constituent Society of the American Psychoanalytic Association, it was arranged by Ernst Simmel, a psychoanalyst who had emigrated from Germany and had been practicing in Los Angeles since 1934. He sought to "invite a group of scientists to participate in a symposium on antisemitism."[54] The results were published in 1946 in a work Simmel edited and introduced: *Anti-Semitism: A Social Disease*. In the acknowledgments, he expressed his "special thanks" to "Dr. T. W. Adorno, who gave me the benefit of his experience in arranging the material of this volume."[55]

Adorno's contribution, "Anti-Semitism and Fascist Propaganda" was the bookend to Horkheimer's opening chapter, "Sociological Background of the Psychoanalytic Approach." Horkheimer and Adorno had been invited as sociologists, since the symposium sought "the collaboration of sociologists and research psychologists who accepted the basic psychoanalytic concepts." It also included Otto Fenichel, another psychoanalyst who had fled Germany in 1933, whose paper on the "Elements of a Psychoanalytic Theory of Anti-Semitism" would influence Horkheimer and Adorno's own analysis of "The Elements of Anti-Semitism" in the *Dialectic of Enlightenment*. Also represented at the symposium were Else Frenkel-Brunswik and R. Nevitt Sanford, the core of the Berkeley experimental psychologists, who were the key partners in developing *The Authoritarian Personality*. Their joint paper was a research report tellingly titled "The Anti-Semitic Personality."

Horkheimer's chapter served as an introduction to the guiding principle of the symposium, which argued that psychoanalysis was a necessary element in any approach to antisemitism. "A mere appeal to the conscious mind does not suffice," Horkheimer insisted, "because antisemitism and the susceptibility to antisemitic propaganda spring from the unconscious." What experimental psychology could contribute, therefore, was "the character structures of anti-Semites" and a set of antisemitic types, including "religious and philosophical antisemitism," "the paranoid," "the vanquished competitor," "the Jew baiter," and the streamlined, up-to-date "fascist anti-Semite."[56]

It was the fascist antisemite who was the focus of Adorno's chapter. His observations were based upon studies by Institute affiliates Leo Lowenthal and Paul Massing working alongside him on West Coast antisemitic agitators, examining their rhetoric in their pamphlets and weekly publications and radio addresses. In this analysis of fascist discourse, Adorno makes the remarkable claim that it is the fascist mode of propaganda that makes them fascist rather than an economic plan or mode of politics. And he itemizes three key mechanisms that are at the heart of fascist antisemitic propaganda: (1) "It is *personalized* propaganda"; (2) "All these demagogues substitute means for ends"; and (3) "propaganda functions as a kind of *wish-fulfillment*."[57]

Personalized propaganda operated in a number of ways. "Fascist propaganda attacks bogies rather than real opponents," Adorno avowed. "That is to say, it builds up an *imagery* of the Jew, or of the Communist, and tears it to pieces, without caring much how this imagery is related to reality."[58] In accord with the volumes title, Adorno concurs that antisemitism is a social disease. But its origins are psychic. It is a form of neurosis that has been transformed into a commodity and marketed with propaganda. As such, Adorno terms it "a kind of psychotechnics" that is reminiscent of how other mass commodities are packaged in movies, sporting events, and other forms of mass entertainment.

Adorno also put great emphasis upon the ritualistic aspects of fascist propaganda (which, again, is only a version of the administered production of all products created by the culture industry). The ceremony of the ritual operates through the crowd "having their own minds expressed to them." It depends upon a politics of identity: the follower identifies with the leader, who embodies "a kind of institutionalized redemption of their own inarticulateness through the speaker's verbosity." Fascist discourse is also bifurcated, based upon the Schmittian "dichotomy of black and white, foe and friend."[59] These binaries are trotted out as formulas that are laced together to shape the ideology.

This ideology is built upon wish fulfillment, the concept Freud developed to explain dreams. It is the form of fascist propaganda that is ultimately so gratifying, Adorno continued, for it provides the enchanted dream that is the basis of the fascist worldview. Moreover, Adorno maintained that "at the hub of the fascist, anti-Semitic ritual is the desire for ritual murder," sacrifice that is made sacrosanct. And it is made sacred through the sacraments of fascist propaganda. Adorno consequently concluded, that "Psychologically, all fascist propaganda is simply a system of such symbols. . . . The unconscious psychological desire for self-annihilation faithfully reproduces the structure of a political movement which ultimately transforms its followers into victims."[60]

Studies in Antisemitism

The full development of this line of analysis would eventually culminate in *The Authoritarian Personality*, alongside the other volumes of the five-volume *Studies in Prejudice* series. This whole endeavor was made possible because in March 1943 the Institute was funded by the American Jewish Committee to support its multifaceted research project on antisemitism on the basis of a proposal rewritten by Franz Neumann and Herbert Marcuse. After it was accepted, several key members of the Institute began to conduct the research.

Published in 1950, the *Studies in Prejudice* series, based on multi-institutional, interdisciplinary efforts, but intended to "constitute one unit,"[61] made an important contribution to the study of racism and discrimination. It included *Rehearsal for Destruction,* Paul Massing's description of the genesis and development of antisemitism in Germany before World War I, and Leo Lowenthal and Norman Guterman's *Prophets of Deceit,* the full-length analysis of the techniques of mass persuasion and manipulation by the West Coast agitators that Adorno had discussed in 1946. The other three volumes extended the experiments with psychoanalysis, considering the psychological elements that predispose individuals to prejudice and racial hatred. In total, this enormous endeavor sought to broaden the categories for conceptualizing prejudice, racism, and antisemitism by incorporating psychoanalytic elements into Marxist social theory.

Certainly the most ambitious undertaking of the series was *The Authoritarian Personality.* The title linked it terminologically to the work of Erich Fromm in the Institute's first collective publication, *Studies on Authority and the Family* where "the concept of the 'authoritarian personality' was put forward as a link between psychological dispositions and political leanings."[62] Institutionally *The Authoritarian Personality* was a joint undertaking of the Berkeley Public Opinion Study and the Institute of Social Research, combining Berkeley's experimental and empirical academic social psychology with the Institute's sociological and philosophical bent. Adorno was specifically responsible for formulating the "sociological dimensions related to personality factors and characterological concepts concomitant with authoritarianism," as well as qualitatively analyzing the ideological dimensions of the interview material in the study.[63]

In doing so, Adorno also addressed the danger of the work head-on in his methodological chapter on "Types and Syndromes." For he was keenly aware that to suggest that there was an "authoritarian personality" risked collapsing the problem into an essentialism that located the origins of antisemitism in a characterological type encapsulated in the title of the volume. Any doctrine of types, wrote Adorno, could "tend towards pigeonholing and transform highly flexible traits into static, quasi-biological characteristics" just as fascist typologies tended to do.[64] And it is certainly the case that at times Adorno and the other contributors did box their interpretations into the categories of their analysis.

But the drive to locate the etiology of the authoritarian personality— and its correlate types—the antisemite, the fascist, the xenophobe—was justified according to Adorno, since the social conditions of modernity were themselves typed. All social processes of modernity tended toward standardization and mass production, including the personality types of individuals. "Only by identifying stereotypical traits in modern humans, and not by denying their existence," Adorno therefore averred, "can the pernicious tendency towards all-pervasive classification and subsumption be challenged."[65] Social types were the products of social rubber stamps.

How these rubber stamps were constituted as socially produced phenomena was the basis of Adorno's specific anthropology of antisemitism in the three substantive chapters he authored in *The Authoritarian Personality*. In these chapters, Adorno's first principle for understanding antisemitism as a social disease was to appreciate that the object of prejudice—that is, "the Jews"—is *not* what provokes the syndrome. This is precisely why Adorno insisted upon "the 'functional' character of anti-Semitism." The social functionality of the stereotype depends upon what Adorno termed "stereotypy" and "ticket thinking": the social production of the stereotype, which is itself linked to psychological needs created by the "cold, alienated, and largely ununderstandable world" of modernity.[66]

The psychological motor of stereotypy is projection. The key mechanism that prompts stereotypy is the defamation of other groups as a way to code one's own status. When it comes to the paranoid delusions that shape antisemitism, Adorno suggests that "the whole complex of the Jew is a kind of recognized red-light district of legitimatized psychotic distortions."[67] The social functionality of antisemitism is that it serves as compensation for social alienation. Also key is that antisemitism is a means to personalize an explanation of the complicated contradictions that engender the social and psychological discomfort and unrest that are the outcome of alienation. The ineloquence or confusion of social life can be unraveled in an instant through a set of stock images. "The stereotypes just discussed," Adorno says, "have been interpreted as means for pseudo-orientation in an estranged world, and at the same time as devices for 'mastering' this world by being able completely to pigeonhole its negative aspects."[68]

Adorno also suggested that antisemitism functions partly as a site for the internal contradictions of individuals—their inner conflicts between id and superego. Stereotypes are the externalization of these inner conflicts, which are themselves the internalization of the contradictions of global capitalism. This is why many positive stereotypes are closely linked to their negative shadow side. For example, the contention that Jews are solidly entrenched in family values has its double in the assertion of Jewish clannishness. This double set of values ascribed to the stereotyping of Jews fits Adorno's "basic hypothesis": "the largely projective character of anti-Semitism," whereby "the Jews are blamed, in social terms, for those properties which by their existence, sociologically ambiguous though it may be, impinge on sensitive spots in . . . class identification."[69] In contrast, those subjects who were low scorers on the various scales of prejudice measured by the Berkeley group intuitively understood that prejudice was a mechanism of social organization and thus focused their critique not on the object of hatred—the Jews, the blacks, the Japanese, the communists, and so on—but on the social conditions that produced the stereotype itself.

The Dialectic of Enlightenment

The *Studies in Prejudice* series consequently showed clear evidence that Adorno and the Frankfurt School were expanding the understanding of antisemitism to include a critique, not only of monopoly capitalism and fascism, but of modernity more generally. The fullest fruit of these efforts was Horkheimer's and Adorno's *Dialectic of Enlightenment*, published in 1947 with the concluding segment on the "The Elements of Anti-Semitism" added in 1949. Here, they considered antisemitism squarely within the development of Western civilization, rationality, and the administered society of modernity. They argued that Western rationality is dialectically entwined with ideological obfuscation (i.e., myth), in particular in the domination of nature. They trace this imbrication from ancient Greece through the Enlightenment and into the mass culture of modernity. Against this long-term theoretical and historical backdrop, they conclude with a discussion of eight intertwined "elements of anti-Semitism." As in *The Authoritarian Personality*, their foundational thesis is that antisemitism is a paranoid projection of fascism's own worldview.

Adorno and Horkheimer argue that for National Socialism's fascist creed, Jews are "the embodiment of the negative principle," and that "the portrait of the Jews that the nationalists offer to the world is in fact their own self-portrait."[70] The National Socialists crave total domination and unlimited power, and they project this desire of total domination onto the Jewish Other.

In establishing this as their basic premise, however, Horkheimer and Adorno nonetheless blame the Jewish victim for having become the target of fascist domination, claiming that their "inflexible adherence to their own order of life has brought the Jews into an uncertain relationship with the dominant order."[71] In fact, a guiding thread of this entire piece is that the persecution of the Jews is linked to a system of domination that undergirds that persecution, a system for which "the Jews" have some specific culpability. They present a dialectical unfolding of how Jewish history placed the Jews in the unique historical position of simultaneously playing a key role in the dialectic of civilization and ending up as its victims. As in Arendt's more truncated history of modernity, representing the Jews as both the origin and end of the dialectic of enlightenment provides a certain narrative arc through all eight theses.

Horkheimer and Adorno explain this in a dense historical overview of the dialectic of religion within civilization that is significantly indebted to Max Weber's *Ancient Judaism*.[72] Within this dialectic, God simultaneously represents liberation from nature and what explains the mythical forces of nature. In the unfolding of the dialectical relationship with God, pagan ritual sacrifice is altered in Judaism. Christianity represents the spiritualization and universalization of this process, which is in turn transformed to determine the division of labor under capitalism: "its new form went on to determine the labor process. Sacrifice is rationalized on this basis. The taboo becomes the rational organization of the labor process."[73]

Adorno and Horkheimer thus argue that the capitalist mode of production is the sublimation of ritual sacrifice. What is sacrificed in this modern "ritual of civilization" is the surplus labor of the industrial proletariat. In this sweeping dialectical movement, therefore, Jews and Judaism constitute the source of the domination of the capitalist mode of production and its concomitant exploitation—their transmutation of ritual sacrifice is the root of the ritual sacrifice that constitutes modern industrial capitalism.

Adorno and Horkheimer's argument that antisemitism is the culmination of Western civilization's instrumental rationality reaches its apotheosis in § five, where they argue that civilization has progressed by organizing and controlling through mimesis, especially in work. Mimesis is the imitation of nature in order to control nature, and the principle of the mimetic impulse is "the absorption of the different by the same."[74] The scientific gaze that orders the world according to a process of observed regularity exemplifies the mimetic impulse in the modern period. Scientific reification inherently functions to stereotype—to order through classification, compartmentalization, reducing humanity to one-dimensionality. The Nazi racial state with its emphasis on mental and physical hygiene and purity is the zenith of society ordered by the technological logic of this scientific gaze.

Adorno and Horkheimer contend that antisemitism is "the mimesis of mimesis": "There is no antisemite who does not basically want to imitate his mental image of the Jew, which is composed of mimetic ciphers."[75] The antisemite is accordingly the mimetic double of his image of "the Jew." Every aspect of this mental image corresponds with the conscious or unconscious desires of the fascist: "The fantasies of Jewish crimes, infanticide and sadistic excess, poisoning of the nation, and international conspiracy, accurately define the anti-Semitic dream."[76] Every aspect of the image of the body of the Jew is the antisemite's own desires embodied by the Jew: the nose "the physiognomic *principium individuationis*," the smell, a "longing for the lower forms of existence, for direct unification with circumambient nature, with the earth and mud."[77] The same is the case with the voice of the Jew, the hand gestures, all of which are mimetically reproduced by the fascist. In fact, the whole apparatus of the fascist order—the fascist formulas, the ritual discipline, and the uniforms—are the quintessence of mimetic behavior, the construction of community around "monotonous repetition." And "this machinery needs the Jews," who stand as the opposite of the values of equality, humanity, non-alien nation, and sameness.[78]

The question remains, why are the Jews the victims of this drive for order and rational classification? Here the blindness of Horkheimer's and Adorno's dialectic of enlightenment that I have traced again becomes apparent. It is precisely because "the Jews themselves have taken part in this process for thousands of years." They are "the oldest surviving patriarchate ... who transformed taboos into civilizing maxims when others still clung to magic.... they defused magic by its own power—turned against itself as ritual service of God." Jews are therefore accused of something they "were the first to overcome: the lure of base instincts, reversion to animality and to the ground, the service of images."[79] Once again, the Jewish civilizing impulse, which is the negativity that is itself the ur-moment in the dialectic of enlightenment, is responsible for the victimization of the Jews. In short, antisemitism as the ultimate result of the logic of the dialectic of enlightenment, and reflective of the limits of enlightenment, simultaneously has its origins and its end in a Jewish impulse.

Horkheimer and Adorno's complicated argument can thus be reduced to its basic dialectical principles: (1) mimesis (i.e., imitation of nature for control over nature) is the central impulse of civilization; (2) Jewish civilization is at the origins of mimesis; (3), antisemitism is the mimesis of mimesis, and the antisemite equals the mimetic double of his image of "the Jew." According to this dialectical logic, Jews and Judaism are fatefully linked as the starting point and the deadly outcome of mimesis. At crucial moments in the text, then, rather than critically undermining Western civilization's image of "the Jew" and Judaism, Adorno and Horkheimer reinforce it by repeating the negative construction of Jews that facilitated their destruction. In fact, the destruction of European Jewry remains an overdetermined silence within the *Dialectic of Enlightenment*.

Adorno's and the Frankfurt School's anti-antisemitism itself emerged out of their silence in the 1930s. When they did speak, "the Jews" in their analysis were caught not only between the Scylla and Charybdis of Western history and antisemitism, but within the double binds of Adorno and Horkheimer's own dialectical unfolding of that history. In the process of this dialectic, Jews are defined, not only with a nature that is dominated, but also with dominating civilization: as the dominant civilization's "colonizers for progress."[80] In the end, the aspects of Jewish tradition and Jewish history that are outside or an alternative to Western civilization are erased as the specificity of "the Jew" becomes the very negativity that animates the dialectic: the principle of nonidentity itself.

"The Jew" functioning as the placeholder of nonidentity is a quintessential case of the conceptual Jew, and it places Jews and Judaism at the origin and at the end of the dialectic of enlightenment, in a parallel fashion to the story that Arendt tells about the role of Jews in modernity. While certainly not antisemitic—indeed the point is that the conceptual move is made to think antisemitism—it does assign Jews to a rather damning position. For Jews come to function typologically and this can have the unhappy consequence of leading to the reiteration of antisemitic motifs, reproducing a paranoid image of Jews and Judaism who are culpable for the pathologies that ultimately result in their victimization.

As in my discussion of Arendt's story of antisemitism, then, Adorno and Horkheimer's effort to theorize about the underlying causes of antisemitism in order to explode it at a foundational level serves as a useful case study of what I am calling the conceptual Jew. It shows that Jews as well as non-Jews, even its most sophisticated and insightful critics, can become entangled within the nefarious logic of antisemitism in their efforts to oppose it. The ways in which Adorno and Arendt homogenize and universalize a notion of "*the* Jews" results, in part, in their reiteration of anti-Jewish stereotypes in their critical post-Holocaust reflections on the "anti-Semitic question." In the process, antisemitism as a unique phenomenon is superseded by their efforts to understand modernity more generally, so that antisemitism becomes merely a symptom of larger sociopolitical and cultural processes.

The problem of the conceptual Jew, I want to suggest, is built into the structure of thinking about antisemitism. Like all thinking, there is necessarily a hypostatization and abstraction that is entailed for the generalization that philosophical thought demands. Adorno and Arendt both insightfully warned us in different ways that this was the case and cautioned us to be sensitive to its machinations. However, how one fills the content of the conceptual Jew determines whether or not this figure of thought will overlap with antisemitic typologies. In the cases of both Arendt and Adorno, a certain Christological supersessionism shadows their thought, as the conceptual Jew is reworked as both at the origins and ends of their speculative reflections on modernity.[81] The conceptual Jew in Arendt and Adorno comes to serve as a figure of difference: a cipher for the outsider, the queer, the nomad. As in Marx's secularization of earlier Christian thinkers identification of Jews with Mammon and materialism, in Arendt and Adorno, the conceptual Jew is also too closely identified with financial capitalism, and financial capitalism with the underside of modernity. The very processes that Arendt and Adorno sought to itemize and criticize are thereby personalized. Nonetheless, as we have seen, Arendt's interactionist understanding of antisemitism and Adorno's socio-psychological critical theory provided foundational conceptual tools for thinking about antisemitism and the modern sociological and political processes that underpin it.

NINE

The Paralysis of Judgment
Arendt and Adorno on Antisemitism
and the Modern Condition

JULIA SCHULZE WESSEL
AND LARS RENSMANN

For Hannah Arendt and Theodor W. Adorno, the emergence of "total war," the brutal exercise of modern totalitarian terror, violence on a global scale and, perhaps most important, the Holocaust epitomized a profound crisis of modern politics and society. In particular, it was the Nazi genocide that required a critical reexamination of modernity. The historical rupture signified by the extermination of the European Jews, taking place in the midst of modern civilization, shattered all the optimism and trust in the idea of progress, conventionally associated with the modern enlightenment project. In Arendt's and Adorno's view, this unimaginable atrocity necessitates new and more chastened ways of thinking about politics and society, and ultimately a critical rethinking of the modern condition.[1] The breakdown of modern civilization was so deep and fundamental that it demands new categories of analysis and understanding, even experimentation with new epistemology. This is reflected in both Arendt's and Adorno's work.[2] Indeed, according to these theorists, we can "no longer afford to take that which was good in the past and simply call it our heritage" or just "discard the bad and simply think of it as a bad load which by itself time will bury in oblivion. The subterranean stream of Western history has finally come to the surface and usurped the dignity of our tradition."[3] In contrast to many of their contemporaries in the field of political and social theory, both thinkers were unwilling to perceive the Holocaust as a merely accidental event, or *Betriebsunfall*, of Western history and political modernity;[4] rather, the unlimited genocidal terror against the Jews of Europe was a historical caesura to which thinking had to adjust.

The annihilation of the European Jews especially induced Arendt's and Adorno's critical reflection on the destructive tendencies of modern society; while Arendt developed such a critique mostly in political and historical terms, Adorno framed it primarily in sociological and philosophical categories. Their analyses of modern antisemitism[5] and the mass atrocities of the Holocaust point to particular circumstances and events, including specifically German and European constellations and contradictions. Yet the development of antisemitism and its totalitarian formation also needs to be understood in the context of modern history's entanglement in practices of domination and, against enlightened modernity's own promises, the eradication of public freedom among political equals. Arendt and Adorno also offer specific critiques of modernity and modern enabling conditions of the totalitarian and antisemitic abyss. Those conditions point to problems of "normal politics" in modern times[6] and some of the very principles of modern societal integration.[7]

Auschwitz can be seen as the final act in a long-drawn-out European, and especially German, hostility to Jews. Discrimination against Jews, pogroms, attacks, exclusion, and violence against Jewish minorities have certainly been a staple of European history, and a specifically German context and legacy contributed to the rise of totalitarian Nazi antisemitism.[8] Yet both Adorno and Arendt reject the assumption that Auschwitz was simply the culmination of a continuously developing history of antisemitism in Europe, with the Holocaust as its final expression. To the contrary, both assert paradoxically that antisemitism narrowly conceived, that is, hatred of Jews as individuals, was beginning to fade away just at the time when the policy of annihilation was set in motion.[9] Thus, just when antisemitism seemed to be manifesting itself in the most radical, destructive, and devastating ways imaginable (or, rather, beyond the "faculty of imagination"), both Adorno and Arendt suggest its virtual "disappearance" as a subjective emotional attitude. In this respect they stand well apart from historical approaches that attempt to derive modern antisemitism and the Holocaust simply from a tradition—however radicalized—of subjective prejudices. Moreover, Arendt and Adorno do not interpret the atrocities exclusively as acts of antisemitism (though that too). Their argument about the interplay of modern conditions with totalitarian antisemitism implies that enthusiastic cooperation in, and support of, the mass atrocities committed against the European Jews did not even require all perpetrators to be antisemites.

Both Arendt and Adorno clearly agree with the argument that antisemitism as individual resentments directed against Jews is less significant than antisemitism as an ideological system. In their various works, both authors portray peculiarly *modern* kinds of perpetrators who were delighted to help advance the policy of annihilation without necessarily being anti-Jewish in the conventional sense. Arendt's version of this character is exemplified in Adolf Eichmann, the "deportation specialist," whom she deemed quite "unideological."[10] In *The Authoritarian Personality,* Adorno depicts the "manipulative type," which signifies the potential modern, bureaucratic mass murderer, in strikingly similar ways. In his study of this type, Adorno goes so far as to see this variation of an authoritarian character as the—in Max Weber's sense—ideal-type of late modern subjectivity.[11] One can also discern profound parallels in Adorno's and Arendt's respective conceptions of antisemitism, despite the almost diametrically opposed intellectual traditions and approaches to which they are committed. To be sure, Arendt vehemently rejects all psychological explanations for specific forms of human behavior,[12] whereas Adorno emphasizes that, for a start, the section on "Elements of Antisemitism" in the *Dialectic of Enlightenment* (written by him, Max Horkheimer, and partly by Leo Löwenthal)[13] is strongly indebted to Freudian theory and thus puts "the psychological aspects in the proper light."[14] But both Arendt's and Adorno's notions of antisemitism seem to involve the following paradox: both thinkers recognize that antisemitism became more and more radical over the course of history—ultimately turning into policies of expulsion and extermination—yet they also note its peculiar "disappearance" in the age of mass crimes against Jews. Such a paradox needs to be explored. Reconstructing central arguments and exploring the lens of Arendt's and Adorno's theorizing of modern antisemitism, this essay will investigate and illuminate several aspects of this perplexity: the complex ties between the critique of modernity and the historical origins of antisemitism; the analysis of a modern type of perpetrator who is allegedly not necessarily driven by a subjective "ideology" and resentment in the conventional sense; and the specific meaning of the claim about the "disappearance" of antisemitism as a set of prejudices as presented in Adorno's and Arendt's writings.

Points of Departure: Approaching Elements of Antisemitism

In tracing out the historical origins and elements of a hitherto unknown form of human domination, which was responsible for radical evil, Hannah Arendt is looking at history from a definite, unmistakable historical location: the aftermath of Auschwitz and the death camps. But rather than seeking those origins in factors that would explain why National Socialism almost necessarily had to emerge, she seeks to explore seemingly secondary routes running alongside the main tracks of history. She hopes to bring to light subterranean and presumably long buried histories that might illuminate those dreadful events and developments. Auschwitz, Arendt insists, irrevocably destroyed all contexts of meaning, including those that had given history its sense and continuity. In other words, Arendt intentionally avoids characterizing any inevitable continuity between the past and the present, but rather emphasizes the novelty of historical events.[15] What happened did not have to happen. To think otherwise, and construe an unavoidable historical logicality, obscures our understanding of historical realities. The decline of the public sphere and the road to totalitarianism cannot be understood as a "history of decline" (*Verfallsgeschichte*). She therefore conceptually and methodologically distinguishes between "comprehension," which characterizes her approach, on the one hand, and, on the other, "deducing the unprecedented from precedents, or explaining phenomena by such analogies and generalities that the impact of reality and the shock of experience are no longer felt."[16] Seyla Benhabib has coined the expression "fragmentary historiography" to characterize Arendt's methodological procedure in the *Origins of Totalitarianism*.[17] The main task of the historian as storyteller in Arendt's eyes is to descend into the rubble of history, much like Walter Benjamin's pearl diver,[18] and discover "pearls" of past experiences with their sedimented and hidden layers of meaning, "so as to cull from them a story that can orient the mind in the future."[19]

In her specific historical account of antisemitism, Arendt recounts episodes from a variety of different European historical arenas, scenes, conflicts, and distinct social and political strata that at first glance seem of rather secondary relevance. She does so precisely in order to understand the disparate origins of the rise of antisemitic ideology and Nazi terror; thus to comprehend the threads, historical events, and discontinuities in this historical genealogy—in which "origins" and "elements" never direct a predetermined outcome.[20] In all of those often seemingly marginal stories, she recognizes fragmentary elements that would later, and in the quite different context of totalitarian rule, disclose their destructive, inhuman potential when unleashed by totalitarian agents.

Arendt thus reconstructs the history of antisemitism in a genealogical fashion that subverts any strict historical continuity; she retells history as though its connecting threads were all severed and lacking any inherent logic. Similarly, in the *Dialectic of Enlightenment,* Adorno illuminates various elements of antisemitism that do not fit into any logic of history, but point rather to its dissolution. Adorno's historical and theoretical scope is much broader; he traces the dialectics of continuity and discontinuity that helped enable the emergence of "totalitarian antisemitism"[21] back to the origins of the civilizational process and the inhibited rationality of bourgeois subjectivity. However, he too denies that one event can initiate a logical sequence, or that one event follows logically from another. The very title of the section, "Elements of Antisemitism," shows that no general theory of antisemitism was intended.[22]

We might therefore ascribe Arendt's categorical claim that there is no connection between religious anti-Judaism, which she largely situates in the realm of personal prejudice and religious intergroup conflict, and modern antisemitism, which she views as a problem of an entirely different nature, to her political and philosophical way of looking at these phenomena, rather than regarding it as a historically tenable assertion.[23] Focusing on the novel elements that history generates, she locates the beginnings of *modern* antisemitism in the early years of the nineteenth century, when debates raged in political and social circles about whether Jews should be given legal and political rights equal to those held by Gentile members of society. For Arendt, this is the point at which an entirely new development commences, one that breaks decisively with the past. She argues that modern antisemitism did not draw its sustenance from the religiously based anti-Jewish tradition of subjective prejudice; in fact, she claims that the latter proved to be quite insignificant in molding the ideology of modern antisemitism.

In this respect she is at odds with Adorno, who glimpses the old religious anti-Judaism beneath the veneer of modern antisemitism. Even though religious antisemitism plays only a marginal role in modern anti-Jewish propaganda, Adorno thinks it still contains elements of the old religious forms of *ressentiment* (understood as a sense of inferiority and hostility vis-à-vis a source of grievances, constructed as an enemy to whom one feels morally superior)[24] directed against Jews:

> To accuse the Jews of being obdurate nonbelievers is no longer enough to incite the masses. But the religious hostility which motivated the persecution of the Jews for two millennia is far from completely extinguished. Rather, anti-Semitism's eagerness to deny its religious tradition indicates that tradition is secretly no less deeply embedded in it than secular idiosyncrasy once was in religious zealotry. Religion has been incorporated in cultural heritage, not abandoned.[25]

In fact, Adorno insists that modern antisemitism, which is expressed in the extermination of the European Jews, *also* reiterates a traditional matrix, "a well-rehearsed pattern, indeed, a ritual of civilization, and the pogroms are the true ritual murders."[26]

Of course, it was knowledge of the unprecedented crimes against humanity that radically altered Arendt's view of history and antisemitism, and that fixed her gaze so unwaveringly on the break with tradition—more radically, if you will, than Adorno's, who emphasized dialectics of continuity and discontinuity (forms of a negative *Aufhebung*) as the enablers of the unimaginable. Going against the grain of earlier accounts of antisemitism, she was determined to show that Auschwitz represented something entirely new: that the atrocities committed against the European Jews implied a radical break with all previous history. Her resolve to "think about the break" in history evolved into a method that she also used to come to grips with the elements and origins of total domination.[27] Because Auschwitz has called all truisms into question, Arendt argued, even matters that once appeared clear and obvious now need to be challenged and rethought. In spite of differences in understanding the nature and evolution of antisemitism, Adorno likewise was convinced that Auschwitz—the systematic, organized extermination of six millions Jews in the midst of modern civilization—affected all culture and thought, forcing us to revise all traditions and arrange the world in such a way that it does not happen again.[28] This entails the search for a new understanding of the nature of antisemitism. Adorno, to be sure, interpreted the impact of the Holocaust on such reflection in a dialectical fashion, emphasizing the entwinement of tradition, modernity, and the breakdown of civilization in general; and the entanglement of traditional prejudice, modern antisemitism, and the systematic extermination of the European Jews in particular.

Standardizing the Other: Antisemitism as Leveling

Although Arendt stresses the discontinuity between anti-Judaism and modern antisemitism, she acknowledges that the latter grew more and more radical and ideologically charged over the course of its history. She locates its origins in the first half of the nineteenth century, when the Jews' legal and political emancipation was just getting under way. Arendt suggests that there was a connection in premodern history between the subjective behavior of Jews and the situation in which the Jewish population found itself, including hostile attitudes toward them. Framing the problem in the context of intergroup relations and assimilation, Arendt believes in some historical complicity of Jews in shaping those attitudes during the early phase of modern antisemitism. In her book *Rahel Varnhagen,* she addresses the ambivalence of assimilation and especially criticizes those Jews who try to put aside their past and their historical identity in order to fit into societies dominated by a Christian majority.[29] For Arendt, Jewish assimilation poses the danger of sacrificing one's identity and of assimilating into an antisemitic society. Adorno subjects the idea and practice of Jewish assimilation to a similar criticism. In fact, he goes so far to label Jewish assimilation a "second circumcision," although he also recognizes some ambivalences, in that assimilation is marked both by the cruelty and the freedom inscribed in modern societal "progress": "The dialectical intertwinement of enlightenment and power, the dual relationship of progress to both cruelty and liberation, which has been brought home to the Jews no less by the great exponents of enlightenment than by democratic popular movements, manifests itself in the makeup of the assimilated Jews themselves."[30] In contrast to Arendt, however, Adorno hardly ever links antisemitism to the actual behavior of Jews, though he discusses their different reactions to and relationship with dominant society; Jewish responses include "fear." Rather, Adorno grounds antisemitism in society's objectified *perceptions* of Jews throughout history, which are preconditioned by forms of necessarily false consciousness; and he links hostility against Jews to their objective situation as a marginalized group that has been caged up in certain circumscribed spheres of society.

Consistent with these arguments, however, Arendt and Adorno further develop their notions of *modern* antisemitism in the framework of a critique of modern "leveling."[31] Such wholesale societal leveling is seen by both as a distinctly modern phenomenon. Arendt lays bare the increasing tendency of the nineteenth century to organize, assimilate, and standardize everything. As she interprets it, the refusal to tolerate whatever is different in one's milieu, the impulse to assimilate things that by their very nature are heterogeneous, perverts the majestic ideal of political and legal equality, transforming it into an institution of forced and legally enforced social normalization.[32] In this process of modernization, the "other" is defined, pinned down and homogenized through the construction and ascription of a uniform, unmistakable identity; the "other," which fails the test of standardization, stands out. This sort of forced normalization and "naturalization" has posed a special danger to Jews as it generates dichotomies of natural/unnatural or friend/foe, which are ultimately transferred to the modern political realm, rendering Jews "unnatural" and "hostile" to the social order. In an analogous way, Adorno notes that idiosyncrasy attaches itself to the peculiar, with whatever captures our attention and appears to be different, whereas "the universal, that which fits into the context of social utility" and normalcy, passes for nature, or for what just seems right.[33] Indeed, whatever is not quite assimilated, Adorno suggests, "is felt as intrusive and arouses a compulsive aversion."[34] Consequently, Adorno proposes that antisemitism is intimately linked to societal leveling and a repressive, collectivist egalitarianism, or repressive *égalité*, that is directed against "others";[35] as a popular political movement, then, antisemitism is driven by the urge to make everyone the same.[36]

Both thinkers would deny that it is just sheer coincidence that Jews were chosen as the victims of persecution and annihilation: genuinely modern assimilation pressures, forces of standardization, and leveling particularly affect them because they are seen as historical others among peers. As Arendt points out, an ideology that has to persuade and mobilize people "cannot choose its victims arbitrarily."[37] And, according to Adorno, Jews were historically locked up in a position of "otherness" and marked by this exclusion in multiple ways. Moreover, both theorists regard the precarious status and special position as minorities, intermediaries, and intellectuals that have been forced upon Jews as one factor in the precarious relationship between the majority and Jewish minority groups in modern society. Adorno also suggests that the—real or imagined—nonconformist and cosmopolitan aspects of the Jewish existence, or indeed the way of life of the Jews, throw into question the universal societal principles with which they do not conform. Simultaneously, Jews do not only epitomize a professional existence as "intermediaries" but also personify all presumably negative aspects of modernity. Jews had become largely associated with the rise of modern political formations such as constitutional democracy, which granted Jews equal rights. They had also become wrongly identified with the rise of modern capitalism, through their forced existence in the circulation sphere. Modern antisemitism thus developed in a fundamentally different way from other resentments, because it based itself upon the Jews' association with modernity and the idea that they were the secret force pulling the strings of modern society.[38] Unlike any other resentment, antisemitism functions as a conspiracy theory that offers an "explanation" of the modern world in its entirety. Furthermore, the modern anti-Jewish image stands for largely unfulfilled promises of emancipation that are associated with modernity: in another objectification of reality, Adorno claims, Jews have come to represent individuality and hopes of a different, free life, that is "happiness without power, reward without work, a homeland without frontiers."[39] The banker and the intellectual, money and mind, in fact, are *also* the "disowned wishful image of those mutilated by power."[40] In all of these dimensions, Jews appear to escape the "natural" order and normalization pressures, while they are simultaneously objectified, standardized and naturalized as the quintessential "others."

Much more strongly than Arendt, Adorno emphasizes the hopelessness and powerlessness of the Jewish population; the latter "attracts the enemy of powerlessness."[41] As Adorno puts it, all the great achievements of their prominent members notwithstanding, Jews were not admitted to the peoples of Europe or granted fully equal citizenship, and having "been prevented from putting down roots they were then criticized as rootless." At best they were "protected Jews, dependent on emperors, princes, or the absolutist state,"[42] while they primarily remained objects at the mercy of others.

By contrast, as noted above, Arendt emphasizes the ways in which Jews had a hand in shaping their own history, at least until modern times. She disputes the representation of Jewish history merely as a tale of suffering and exclusion in which—allegedly—Jews passively endured whatever the world around them meted out. Instead, she portrays them as active agents or subjects of history, thereby establishing a link between the origins of antisemitism and actual Jews.[43] For Arendt, Jews are neither arbitrary scapegoats, nor is antisemitism "eternal." The growth of modern antisemitism in particular, she argues, was accompanied by and interconnected with processes of Jewish assimilation and secularization as well as anti-Jewish violence, through which Jews as a group were "threatened by physical extinction from without and dissolution from within."[44] She points out that many Jews did not wish to let go either of their religion or of the privileges attached to their special political and social situation. In that sense, she discovers a moment of truth in "original" antisemitic opinions about Jewish particularity. For Arendt, the first stirrings of modern antisemitism reveal the tensions latent in the goals of the emancipation movement itself: the granting of political equality to socially unequal groups.[45] However, both theorists concede that antisemitism is not *only* a matter of Jews being defined and constructed by gentiles; rather, it also reflects, though in a twisted and distorted fashion, the way Jews defined themselves, and their cultural and religious differences, all of which the societal majority defames. To a lesser extent, Adorno also recognizes that the (legitimate) insistence on difference attracts the discrimination by dominant society and helps instigate its hostility in light of conformist hegemonic norms and standardizations: "The inflexible adherence to their own order of life has brought the Jews into an insecure relationship to the prevailing one."[46] Nevertheless, he parts company with Arendt on this point by asserting the hopelessness of the situation that society had imposed on Jews, independent of their actions; Jewish agency ultimately did not matter. Arendt herself of course has no intention of imputing any guilt to the Jews. She simply refuses a narrative that construes Jewish history as a pure history of victimization.[47]

Influenced by the arguments in existential philosophy that she had absorbed in her student days, Arendt is convinced that life—and history—always offers new beginnings, takes unpredictable courses, and holds open more than one possibility. She insists on the contingency of history, which for her entails more than just the rejection of historical determinism.[48] Even under unlikely and difficult circumstances, humans can potentially intervene in events at any given point in history. Arendt stresses this point so forcefully because she seeks to emphasize discontinuity; she wants to distinguish the first phases of antisemitism quite rigorously from the totalitarian antisemitism and domination of later years that, ultimately, *would* destroy all space for agency and, indeed, make it impossible for Jews to act at all. Totalitarian rule destroys everything that makes human beings human (and in that it is modern, specific, and unprecedented). And for Arendt this also means that it negates the possibility of acting so as to alter the destiny of one's own life or the course of history. This verdict applies in its most extreme form to the Jews as the primary victims of Nazi terror, who were stripped of all possibility of action in the extermination camps.

Antisemitism as Delusion and a Modern Means of Rule

There is no question, however, that Arendt and Adorno believe antisemitism can also be employed deliberately and strategically as a means of domination. Adorno, for example, underscores its usefulness to the ruling strata as a tactic of distraction.[49] For Arendt, in the modern era, antisemitism becomes a weapon in sociopolitical conflicts. In spite of Arendt's skepticism of traditional scapegoat theories, she recognizes that antisemitism is an effective tool for bringing the masses into the streets and inciting pogroms, in which the Jews are made to appear guilty of all the crises of the day. Adorno also challenges scapegoat theories while recognizing antisemitism's potential functionality in modern forms of rule. Antisemitism can be particularly effective because of a widespread social willingness to personify the rise of modernity and capitalism with Jews. Against this backdrop, the attribution of modern social malaises and abstract social domination to Jews by emphasizing the identification of Jews with modern capitalism and its crises corresponds to a specific form of reified social consciousness.[50] According to Arendt, an entire system may indirectly come under attack, because antisemitism's emotionally charged rhetoric is capable of enflaming mass hatred, with strategic antisemitism and traditional hatred of Jews mutually complementing each other.[51]

Yet, Arendt and Adorno insist on the distinction between "emotional" and "rational" antisemitism. They distinguish between these two "forms" of antisemitism to gain a better analytical grasp of the phenomenon, although the distinction also has real-world implications and political ramifications.[52] As Adorno puts it, those who have understood the power latent in antisemitism and use it as a political instrument to bring the masses into the street "neither hate the Jews nor love their own followers."[53] In Arendt's case, too, one notices that she rarely attributes anti-Jewish emotions to the leaders and inciters of pogroms. They are simply interested in combating a given political order and in pursuing their interest; they have recognized the political dynamite latent in antisemitism—its peculiar power to attract and mobilize masses around the world and "explain" social malaises of modernity—and employ it quite consciously for their own ends. As Adorno and Arendt see it, the instigators themselves appear largely immune to the emotional frenzy and irrationality that characterizes modern antisemitism and its exterminationist genocidal impulse.[54] We shall not consider whether such a sharp distinction can be maintained in reality. But as an analytic category, it is certainly useful, since it allows us to give an account of the various permutations and developments of modern antisemitism on its way from a societal undercurrent to a powerful ideology and genocide. In the last analysis, to be sure, "subjective" and "objective," idiosyncratic and presumably "rational," coldly calculating antisemitism are mutually reinforcing. In the Nazi genocide, they merged into one. And so-called objective antisemitism, as embodied in National Socialism by the SS, was actually rooted in the emotional, rabble-rousing antisemitism typified by the SA.[55] For Arendt, the Dreyfus Affair in France at the turn of the twentieth century had already signified one such modern turning point of anti-Jewish hostility: here, she suggests, the objective and emotional forms of antisemitism have indeed merged. And Adorno argues that the difference between "rationalized" and "blind" antisemitism disappears in the act of genocidal persecution, and as "completely insane or absolutely rational, [the paranoiac] annihilates those marked down as victims either by the individual act of terror or by the well-considered strategy of extermination."[56]

However, in Arendt's work on modern antisemitism, one finds the emotionalized version of antisemitism primarily associated with the modern "mob." She subsumes under this notion all the *déclassé* groups and individuals that have lost their moorings in traditional social and political structures due to various crises, scandals, and processes of inner disintegration, and ultimately the modern European "dissolution of the state into factions."[57] Now they encounter one another outside of established society.[58] It was no coincidence that the mob is so easily spurred on to acts of violence against the Jewish population. Recruiting old tropes and new resentments, the mob made the Jews its favorite target, because everything it loathed was personified in the Jews: society, because Jews were "rooted in a society which was attempting to eliminate them,"[59] while they were barely tolerated by society and in a precarious position, making them an easy target of resentment; and the (democratic) state, because the state appeared to protect Jews against society, and Jews could therefore readily be identified with the state's power:

> There can be no doubt that *in the eyes of the mob* [emphasis added] the Jews came to serve as an object lesson for all things they detested. If they hated society they could point to the way in which the Jews were tolerated within it; and if they hated the government they could point to the way in which the Jews had been protected by or were identifiable with the state.[60]

The modern mob felt that it was excluded from society and from popular representation, both of which were—seen through the lens of antisemitic resentment, this was illegitimate—allegedly open to the marginalized group of the Jews. Yet, as Arendt explains, the mob hated the Jews also because it recognized its own situation in theirs. Thus, it is not so much the other that is hated; instead, it is one's own reality and misery, things familiar or feared within it, that are directed against the Jews. Although Arendt does not like the term because of its psychological character and connotations, one may say that according to Arendt, the mob *projected* its own condition on the Jews, who were seen as both all too familiar and all too different.

Even though Arendt unequivocally dismisses all psychological explanations, there are actually striking parallels between her argument and Adorno's account of the projection mechanism that underlies antisemitism. The sixth thesis on antisemitism in Adorno's and Horkheimer's "Elements of Antisemitism" deals with the intrapsychic conflicts that beset subjects. Antisemitism is morbid projection, that is, a pathological transference phenomenon that yields no meaningful statements about the objects of hatred, but only about the projecting subject and unresolved conflicts within the self. According to Adorno, all perception and all thought is projection; the problem, however, is false projection that loses all contact with the object of perception—and that is simultaneously unable to reflect the actual distance between the subject and object of perception, merging all into one. If morbid projection is characterized by the utter absence of reflection, the morbidly projecting individual reflects neither on himself nor on the object of perception. Such projection thus loses reflection in all directions: it neither reflects the self nor the object and thus loses the ability to differentiate. The abyss that opens up between the perceiving subject and the object must somehow be bridged. For this to happen, concepts and judgments need to be interposed between the perceiver and the object. This activity of mediation between perception and object is paralyzed when the perceiving subject neither reflects on itself nor on its object: "The pathic element in [antisemitism] is not projective behavior as such but the exclusion of reflection from that behavior."[61]

To someone prone to pathological projections, his or her own traits appear alien. They are not integrated into the self and one does not become aware of them; rather, they are transferred to the "other" as something alien and offensive, and then taken as reasons to despise the other: "Impulses which are not acknowledged by the subject and yet are his, are attributed to the object—the prospective victim."[62] Here, the subject's repressed impulses, not recognized as being his or her own, are projected onto an object. In this framework of interpretation, the hostile images of Jews, as well as the wishes and fantasies associated with them, reveal stories about oneself. Their detachment from reality reinforces this objectification. In such cases, "the idea, having no firm hold on reality, insists all the more and becomes the fixation."[63] What seems repellently alien is in fact all too familiar. These impulses, in conflict with the self-ideal, have to be discredited. But the apparent "solution," the antisemitic depreciation of those features of the other that remind a person of his or her own traits, actually solves nothing; it merely intensifies paranoid anxieties.[64] Antisemitism is thus essentially socialized and politicized paranoia

> based on false projection. It is the reverse of genuine mimesis and has deep affinities to the repressed; in fact, it may itself be the pathic character trait in which the latter is precipitated. If mimesis makes itself resemble its surroundings, false projection makes its surroundings resemble itself. If, for the former, the outward becomes the model to which the inward clings, so that the alien becomes the intimately known, the latter displaces the volatile inward into the outer world, branding the intimate friend as foe.[65]

In an objectified form, these unreflected projections express the dreams and potentially violent practices of hate-mongers: The "nationalist fantasies of Jewish crimes, of infanticide and sadistic excesses, of racial poisoning and international conspiracy, precisely define the antisemitic dream, and fall short of its realization."[66]

The same train of thought may be found in Arendt's analysis. While it is questionable in how far she succeeds in offering a persuasive critique of psychology (which is the subject of repeated critical remarks by Arendt and which is especially criticized for its failure to understand antisemitism), for her, as for Adorno, the *origins* of what is experienced and condemned in the other must be sought primarily in extrapsychic phenomena and conditions. Arendt regards the situation of the mob in society as in many ways as equivalent to that of Jews. The members of the mob—grounded in disenfranchised and often unemployed social strata—recognize that Jews share the mob's own status as involuntary social outsiders. But since they detest that status in themselves, they likewise belittle, scorn, and despise it in the Jews.

It is important to bear in mind, however, that both Arendt and Adorno interpret modern antisemitism also as a problem that lies within the antisemites themselves. For Arendt, the early phase of modern antisemitism was rooted in real conflicts, so antisemitic statements still bore some resemblance to the actual situation of Jews; but history soon severed that tenuous link to reality. Modernity, and the transition from anti-Jewish prejudice to the ideology of modern antisemitism, really marks the qualitative difference. A remnant of reality still remains epitomized in the behavior of the mob, since the Jews reminded the mob's members of their real status as outsiders. But gradually even that thin thread of a connection to reality grew weaker in the process of modernization, and the modernization of antisemitism into an ideological, hermetically circumscribed, self-referential system. Especially in the later phase of modern antisemitism that is associated with race hatred and turned totalitarian, the antisemites ultimately only expressed what they themselves were, and objective conditions of Jews became irrelevant—along with intergroup conflicts and, according to Arendt, traditional stereotypes. And in a more consistent and insisting fashion, Adorno points out within his theory of false projection that in the context of modern antisemitism, the actual behavior of Jews became irrelevant to modern antisemites. Neither experience nor reality itself can make a dent in the armor of the antisemite. In its complete lack of responsiveness to reality, all forms of modern antisemitism are ultimately, in the words of Christopher Hitchens, "totalitarian by definition," because the indictment of the victim is an absolute one; it is unappeasable and total because the Jewish victim is unable to alter his fate.[67] And it is precisely this feature of antisemitism, the fact that it is somehow impervious to experience, that has posed the greatest peril for the Jews in Europe and the world over, since that sort of antisemitism, immunized from reality, can in principle never be stopped by reality.

Adorno's understanding of the diagnosed loss of the capacity for reflection and critical thinking as a crucial feature of antisemitism and the shift of mental reflection into morbid projection, also fits into Arendt's conceptualization of modern, ideological antisemitism. For her, antisemitic "opinion," even in its inception, indicates the failure to draw careful distinctions, because it equates things that simply cannot be the same. Yet within the modern context, antisemitism hardens into an ever more rigid thought pattern, the extreme expression of which—for Arendt at least—is reached in the "banal" perpetrator, Adolf Eichmann, who does not even have to "hate" the Jews to be antisemitic (and in fact lacks genuine prejudice),[68] render them worthy of extinction, and exterminate them according to hermetic ideological imperatives. Judging by her journalistic reports, his mind was little more than a lifeless, sclerotic shell following slogans, which guided his thoughtless actions.[69] In fact, Arendt emphasizes that there is a dangerous connection between his almost complete inability to engage in the critical activity of thinking, "our faculty for thought," and his inability to morally judge right from wrong.[70]

No matter how the historical origins of antisemitism are evaluated, Arendt thus concurs with Adorno that in the modern world, antisemitism is structured independently of experiences between groups and relations between majorities and minorities. Only in the sense that modern antisemitic paranoia also originates in actual political and societal processes, such as the dissolution of organized interests, does it indeed draw on experience. As a contradictory, largely contourless ideological fixation that—unlike any other (racialist) resentment—serves as an "empty vessel" into which humans pour their problems and hidden desires, modern antisemitism responds to the needs of modern human beings and fulfills a specific function in their psychological makeup. Both Arendt and Adorno, then, find ample grounds for the "success" of antisemitic thought patterns in the modern experiences of isolation, atomization, and anomie. After all, antisemitism works well in the presence of Jews; it works even better in their absence. But Arendt and Adorno's diagnosis raises a crucial question: what is the relationship between this modern, ideologically totalizing antisemitism—which according to Arendt by the twentieth century had quite emancipated and immunized itself from the real target of its persecution—and the hypothesis that antisemitism began to "disappear" about the same time, as suggested by Arendt and Adorno?[71] To answer this, we must shed more light on their respective critiques of modern society, however differently motivated these are. Both of them focus on modernity's tendency to undermine subjectivity and vitiate the subject's faculty of judgment.

The Paralysis of the Faculty of Judgment: Theorizing Antisemitism in the Context of the Critique of Modernity

On a theoretical level Arendt and Adorno consistently oppose monocausal, holistic theories and claims that there is any predetermined logic implicit in historical development; as explained previously, they recognize historical ruptures and think about history in terms of fragments, not just continuities. This insight is reinforced by the unthinkable rupture of the Holocaust, and it subsequently engenders critical forms of theorizing about antisemitism, which has to remain fragmentary. However, their critiques of modern socialization processes form a crucial connecting link in the explanations they provide for the success of totalized, modern antisemitism, as well as its alleged "disappearance" as a merely subjective prejudice and impulse.

Arendt and Adorno share an interpretation or diagnosis of the modern age that was widely held by many intellectuals of their generation. However, their critique may be distinct in its self-reflective character, as it opposes any abstract negation of modern reason, or wholesale tirades against (Western) modernity.[72] They argue that modern society has been transformed into a "mass" society in which every human being is pushed to the brink of utter isolation. Critical theory considers such anomie a constitutive element in the capitalist mode of socialization. The formation of an "antisemitic collectivity," granting some narcissistic collective gratification to weakened subjects, may serve as a desperate pseudo-antidote for rampant anomie. This pseudo-antidote simultaneously reiterates and reinforces modern subjugation and the "barbaric disconnectedness" that is induced, Adorno suggests, by an instrumental rationality and its "real abstractions."[73] Similarly, Arendt traces the isolation of modern individuals back to certain economic and political transformations in nineteenth and twentieth century societies that shattered traditional structures and overwhelmed established social and cultural arrangements. Modern mass society is a product of this structural transformation, which neither makes sense to the individuals caught up in it nor offers them opportunities to forge new social bonds and emancipate themselves from modern societal pressures, constraints, and the all-encompassing mode of labor. Loneliness allows human beings to merge seamlessly with the masses and seek refuge in forms of repressive collectivity, making them easy prey for political homogenization and manipulation, since they lack any constitutive ties with one another.[74]

In Arendt's view, the function of the masses is to provide atomized human beings an empty substitute for the communal structures and public spaces that are dying out under the onslaught of competitive capitalism, modernization, and bureaucratization.[75] The atomized individuals, believing that membership in a mass movement offers refuge from their loneliness, find in the mass little more than an impotent compensation for the self that has been undermined. The feeling of joining and being swept up in a mass movement acts as the substitute gratification for unfulfilled social needs. In that respect, such movements fulfill a purpose in the individual's psychic economy that cannot easily be replaced, as the old spaces and structures have irrevocably vanished.[76] This is the point at which, seen through Arendt's lens, antisemitism loses its specific content. The function that anti-Jewish resentment has assumed in the late modern world—leading people to believe that they can have a feeling of integration and belonging in an atomized society which has lost meaningful public spaces—has evidently become more important than that specific content itself. The masses do indeed need a concrete image of their putative enemy from which they can distance themselves, but it is at the end of the day largely irrelevant *who* plays the enemy role—as long as the negative image of the other fulfills certain political and societal functions.

First and foremost, rigid constructions of an enemy's image offer security in an increasingly insecure age that is shaped by permanent transitions, social upheavals, socioeconomic disintegration, new warfare, ideational transformations, and new political regimes. In the image of "the Jew," then, according to Arendt, stable thought patterns and personalizations—however contradictory, disparate, and obviously fabricated—of the crises and transformations one has gone through serve as a means of coming to terms with conditions of individual and societal insecurity.[77] All-encompassing antisemitism, the antisemitic world view,[78] as Arendt calls it, can supply explanations for every question of the day. It is no longer just one more opinion among many others; it tolerates no rival viewpoints and, pinning down one's identity, abolishes the distinction between public and private,[79] in that, as mentioned before, all modern antisemitism is ultimately total and "totalitarian." Since it can offer only pseudo-alternatives, while subsuming the entire world under its thought constructs, it has all the more need to present itself as the one final, exclusive answer to every question, even if this answer appears unbelievable to even the most ardent believer. To make just one admission of doubt would mark the beginning of the end. At the very center of antisemitic paranoia one finds the subject. In the words of Horkheimer and Adorno, he creates the world in his own image;

as his will permeates the entire universe, the world is simply an opportunity for his madness.[80]

Whereas Adorno notes that antisemitism and totality have been profoundly connected from the very onset,[81] the same cannot be said of Arendt's notion of antisemitism, which emphasizes discontinuity. As she portrays them, the early stages in the evolution of modern antisemitic stereotypes did not so unambiguously exhibit the tendency toward totality. That does not happen until antisemitism mutates into a holistic worldview. The tendency toward totality, however, becomes quite obvious when one examines Arendt's notion of ideology more carefully.[82] She speaks of an antisemitic *ideology* only in the context of the age of total domination. Antisemitism takes on a radically new character at this point, because it now becomes an ideology of the deed. In its early stages antisemitism may have been nourished by real events and experiences; now the exact opposite happens. Reality is remade to fit the predictions of antisemitic ideology. The lie that there are distinct human races is carried over into real-world behavior.

As Adorno remarks in the same vein, the fascists tried to make antisemitism *come true*.[83] Arendt considers it characteristic of totalitarian ideologies to predict what is going to happen. Their spokesmen pretend to be able to anticipate actual events and to set forth definitive prognoses. The terror wielded under totalitarian rule puts this idea into practice; its purpose is to prove that ideological predictions about the inevitable course of history turn out to be right. The totalitarian phenomenon, with its striking anti-utilitarian traits and its disregard for factuality, is based on the "conviction that everything is possible—and not just permitted, morally or otherwise."[84] Arendt identifies a second signifier of ideological thinking (which of course would not genuinely count as "thinking" in Arendt's normative sense) as the process of argument that is utterly "logical" in being internally consistent. Ideology, literally, the "logic of an idea,"[85] designates a kind of rigid deductive procedure that cannot be influenced by any external considerations. Everything is deduced with perfect consistency from one irrefutable postulate. The assumption that underlies this logical and consistently guided action "can be as mad as it pleases; it will always end in producing facts which are then 'objectively' true."[86] Adorno converges with Arendt's critique of forms of logicality and consistency, which are articulated in respective modern ideologies. Both authors argue that according to this modern logic, whatever contradicts the logic of consistency—every specific experience that has not been shaped in advance and whatever deviates from the abstract norm[87]—is excluded from perception and subject to oblivion or persecution. To be sure, ideological deduction is contrary to reality, since human affairs are always contingent, and there are certain limits to ideology's power to mold the world according to its system. Just as antisemitism denies human diversity, so ideology ignores the manifold complexity of the world itself. Antisemitic ideology shields its adherents from reality, forming its own separate system of concepts and thoughts, quite divorced from the rest of the world. It provides a pattern to be imposed upon every kind of knowledge and experience. Arendt regards this latter aspect, its "emancipation" from reality, as the third defining element of ideology. Since this sort of pigeonhole thinking insulates itself so completely from reality, its followers cannot possibly learn anything from the external world, especially that which might alter their preestablished convictions. Adorno also considers the loss of the capacity for experience as one of the distinctive features of modern antisemitism.[88] For both thinkers, the atrophy of the capacity to experience the world seals the fate of the subject's autonomy. The capacity to have experiences is, in Arendt's view, equivalent to the possibility of revising one's thinking and reacting to "disturbances" from without. As long as a person can still experience things, and knows that he or she is doing so, then that person retains the ability to alter or remove long-cherished convictions. Thought thrives on its own collisions with reality, as well as the constant stream of new stimulation that the latter furnishes.

From this point of view, antisemitism has gradually hardened into a totalized ideological form, which marches in step with the very loss of thought. Arendt's definition of totalitarian ideology shows that the specific content of antisemitism was fading away just at the moment when it attained its seemingly most radical expression: at the time when the Jews of Europe were exterminated. In the final analysis, it is suggested that with its most radical immunization from reality, the victims of antisemitic ideology start to become interchangeable, too. Even though the European Jews were exterminated for the sole reason of being identified as Jews, Adorno argues that these atrocities were unrelated to any actual behavior of Jews—and in that sense Jews functioned as modern place-holders of an interchangeable "ticket." For him, to be sure, the interchangeability of Jews and other victims had always been a general feature of antisemitic ideology, at least in its modern manifestation. Adorno remarks characteristically: "Rage is vented on those who are both conspicuous and unprotected [and] depending on the constellation, the victims are interchangeable: vagrants, Jews,

Protestants, Catholics."[89] For Arendt, on the other hand, this new, unprecedented form of antisemitism, originating in the modern condition, was truly actualized only in the system of total domination, and only in its most unrestrained phase.

Arendt had a chance to study in greater depth the destruction of all independent judgment and thought—which underlies her definition of ideology, and which she associates with totalitarian antisemitism—in the person of Adolf Eichmann. His trial put her in a position to encounter a person who embodied the spirit of totalitarianism par excellence as she understood the phenomenon. For his part, Adorno had no specific information of Eichmann while he was writing his study on the "authoritarian personality." Yet he describes one type of authoritarian character as a "manipulative type" almost as though he had Eichmann right before his eyes, and finds validation in the case of Eichmann; the manipulative character is distinguished by a "rage for organization, by the inability to have any immediate human experience at all, by a certain lack of emotion. . . . He makes a cult of action and [is] indifferent to the content of action."[90] According to Adorno, the "manipulative character" is fully integrated into dominant society and fulfills its demands—whatever they may be—without superego troubles; he is basically free of inner conflicts and neuroses. Adorno's manipulative type, like Arendt's "Eichmann," is also indifferent to the content of his activities.[91] Moreover, Adorno and Arendt converge remarkably in their descriptions of this kind of modern executioner, which both identify as "potentially (the) most dangerous one."[92] For both, this totalitarian executioner signifies the most radical loss, not only of experience but, along with the externalization or loss of conscience and consciousness, of the capacity for reflective judgment.[93]

Let us take one step back here before we explore the implications of this analysis of the paralysis of the faculty of judgment in one of the killers of the European Jews. One may notice from Arendt's phenomenological study, the history of antisemitism's radicalization takes clearly defined steps and is shaped by events; by contrast, Adorno's theorizing illuminates specific aspects and social implications of antisemitism without necessarily arranging them into a clear chronology, although he does make significant distinctions between old resentment, their absorption in the modern world, and new and specific features of modern antisemitism. The latter works as an explanation for the obscure, complex, and impenetrable modern world (and modern capitalism in particular). From Arendt's account, we can reconstruct the following line of development: at first, antisemitism was still just one opinion among many. It was also directed against concrete Jews, since it had emerged from actual idiosyncrasies and conflicts between the minority and the majority. Then political parties and demagogues discovered its usefulness as a weapon in their political battles. They found that it would serve them well in other conflicts besides the ones that had arisen from Jewish emancipation. As it assumed more overtly racist overtones, "antisemitism" was less and less constituted by individual prejudices. It treated Jews less and less as real human beings who could—even if denigrated as "others" and as "inferior"—still be seen as individuals capable of choice and action. "The Jew" became exclusively an expression of the modern antisemite's fantasy world and the antisemite's problems with the modern world. In other words, the antisemites attacked the Jews over conflicts or issues that no longer *had anything to do* with the actual situation or with the statements, behavior, conflicts, and social position of Jews in society. Antisemitism had lost its last residue or anchor in the specific conflicts that had traditionally divided Jews and gentiles. Having by now evolved into a full-fledged world view, antisemitism began to focus more and more evidently on the psychological, social, and political conflicts besetting its adherents independently of any living Jews, while also internalizing more and more of the social tensions of the age. In its mature ideological guise, along with the annihilation of the Jews, antisemitism finally intended nothing less than the destruction of thought and judgment. It ceased being just a personal opinion or prejudice; instead, it took complete possession of its adherents and became "objective." In Arendt's description of Eichmann, we can observe more precisely the decay or sclerosis of thinking into an "ideology of objectivity."[94]

Now, to what degree is this ideology of objectivity and its infamous representative ultimately also the product—and representative—of the modern condition at large? Adolf Eichmann is the prototypical modern mass man in that, by submerging his identity in a collectivity, he felt as though he belonged to the avant-garde of a dawning new age and a strong movement-ideology that conquered history and expressed the universal triumph of ideological laws larger than humanity. As Arendt remarks, "the wind had blown him into . . . a Movement that always kept moving and in which somebody like him—already a failure in the eyes of his social class, of his family, and hence in his own eyes as well—could start from scratch and still make a career."[95]

For both Arendt and Adorno, however, the dissolution of the subject is epitomized by the experience of integration into such a "dissociated" collectivity. The relinquishment of the self—weakened by modern atomization and anonymous, abstract powers—precedes its submergence into the mass existence of the collectivity. Adorno observes that willingness to reduce oneself to a part of an authoritarian collectivity predestines a person to think of himself or herself as passive, inert material that needs to accept its fate. Not surprisingly then, its agents treat others in just the same way: as an "amorphous mass,"[96] which incidentally also characterizes the modern manipulative types' relation to the object world.

Eichmann too made human beings into material for planning. What Arendt stresses above all in her trial report is the way Eichmann's "thinking" had ossified into a matter of administrative technique. Planning, administration, and organization simply *were* his world. Against the backdrop of the antisemitic "assumptions" of the Nazi worldview, he transformed the politics of the annihilation of European Jewry into a series of anonymous administrative actions typical of modern existence. All he could see in the murder of several million human beings was, as Arendt put it, a "staggering job of organization and administration."[97] His utterly objectified approach to the world made it possible for him to confront the work of annihilation exclusively as a problem of administration, while entirely avoiding its moral dimension; for Eichmann, this moral dimension was not even a question, because his morality was externalized and thus depended on the demands of the political system. This also created a distance between him and his victims, interposing a barrier that kept reality—that is, mass murder—at arm's length. In Adorno's theoretical treatment of modern antisemitism, he suggests that "all living things become material."[98] The self adapts to a lifeless, inert world of things. For totalitarian antisemites, the Jews represented nothing more than a fungible mass, to which anything could be done. They were accordingly put in order, deported, and exterminated.

Ultimately, Arendt and Adorno both see a direct correlation between a world dominated by modern technology and modern modes of rationalization that lack self-reflection, in which everything is converted into blind sequences of events, and the automation of mental processes.[99] As we have already seen in the case of ideologically charged antisemitism, the modern rigidity of thought is in the foreground of Arendt's critique of ideology. In her report on Eichmann, she pushes that insight in an even more radical direction: Eichmann, she notes, no longer knows anything except the world of administration. He translates reality into administrative procedures; for him there is nothing left "out there." There is a great void behind the division of the world into "schematic, administrative fields," in Adorno's words.[100]

Arendt describes the modern "desk perpetrator" par excellence as someone who no longer even takes an interest in *what* exactly is happening, but only in *how* it happens.[101] Eichmann contributed the technocratic viewpoint to the politics of annihilation, and that was all that mattered. This viewpoint did not contradict antisemitism as an ideological system and driving force of terror, but complemented it—neither had any relationship to reality or the object of persecution. In Eichmann himself, one no longer even finds the conviction that there is a "law of nature" that has to be implemented. Instead, all that remains is the "mere administration" of a predetermined process complete in itself.[102] "Action becomes a purpose in itself, cloaking its own purposelessness," Adorno writes,[103] and he discerned this in modern antisemitism as well. Adorno's observation that every living thing is degraded into material may be applied readily to Eichmann's own mental activity, because—in Arendt's view—his pseudo-thinking permits nothing living to enter into it. He deduces everything, just as Arendt says of the spokesmen for ideologies. All that remains is a single thought, a logic that is consistently followed to its final conclusion; nothing is allowed to disturb its internal consistency.

Eichmann even came out explicitly against some Nazi "true believers" who publicly engaged in open, emotion-laden persecutions of Jews. For example, he characterized the fanatical antisemite Julius Streicher, editor of the Nazi newspaper *Der Stürmer*, as an "unrealistic fool" and others of his ilk as "emotional" types,[104] in contrast to his own "objectivity" (*Sachlichkeit*).[105] "Objectivity" is distinguished by its reductive stance toward the world, rooted in administrative procedures. It is unimportant who one must deal with, since he or she will be degraded into material for planning in any case. This indifference to everything and everyone is precisely the danger that this—also specifically modern—character type poses. Hatred for a specific group is finite; in principle it would end once that group had been eradicated. In contrast, the attitude of indifference is marked by its insatiability; its boundlessness and aimlessness. It no longer acknowledges any ties between the self and the other; in a sense, it really does not matter whether the other is to be hunted down or protected, even though this can be, of course, a matter of life and death for the prospective victims. The manipulative type has no more sympathy for anyone else than Eichmann; indeed, every emotional stirring is alien to it. Instead, what distinguishes this type is precisely, "the almost complete absence of any affections," which makes him "perhaps the most merciless of all."[106]

As argued at the beginning of this essay, modern antisemitism always carried with it an urge toward leveling, standardization, and stereotyping. And in fact, it culminated in the most extreme act of stereotyping that the world has yet witnessed. In the seventh thesis on antisemitism of the *Dialectic of Enlightenment*, which he and Horkheimer added in 1947, Adorno goes so far as to suggest that little remained of the stereotyping and hatred that had always been inherent to antisemitism except the very process of stereotyping itself. For Adorno as for Arendt, antisemitism merges ultimately into a kind of rigid pigeonhole thinking. In place of an animated consciousness that could potentially change its mind and be affected by experience, the bigger threat may become the "ticket mentality" itself. From the perspective of the antisemitic subject—though not, of course, from the perspective of the victims—it is a matter of secondary importance just what the content of that ticket is. As Adorno understands it, antisemitic ideology, after having been transmitted in various forms through several centuries, ossifies in the end into the "plank in a platform" that has "ceased to be an independent impulse" any longer; there are "no longer any antisemites."[107] In Arendt's trial reports too, modern antisemitism appears to have ultimately been reduced to a mere reflex, in which the subject simply accepts an ideology without having the capacity to judge and question it, to inwardly try to substantiate its claims. For both theoreticians, subjective hatred of Jews, which still presupposes a tie between the hater and his potential victim, ultimately passes over into an ossified form of thought, imprisoned in its own rigid conceptual schemes. Hatred can discharge its venom in concrete situations such as pogroms and violence, but indifference cannot. In keeping with that observation, Adorno notes of the manipulative types: "Their goal is the construction of gas chambers rather than the pogrom. They do not even have to hate the Jews; they 'cope' with them by administrative measures without any personal contacts with the victims."[108]

The consciousness that has regressed to a "ticket mentality" resists any sort of difference; the other cannot and must not be tolerated.[109] Particularly in Eichmann's case, the capacity to make reflective judgments was completely lost. According to Arendt, "he was genuinely incapable of uttering a single sentence that was not a cliché," unless of course his comment was of a technical or administrative nature.[110] Nothing could get to him from the outside, and nothing could disrupt his objectified approach to the world or create a space to imagine the actual object, the other. What sort of counterimage or contrasting concept could be marshaled in opposition to this mélange of modern antisemitism, totalitarian ideology, and totalitarian mentality that marked both Eichmann's thinking and that of the genuinely modern "manipulative type"? In modern totalitarian antisemitism, anti-Jewish ideology and the cold-blooded business of genocidal persecution indifferent to the objects of persecution coalesce.

Rather than just referring to objective reality, Arendt and Adorno invoke heterogeneity, the plurality and difference of the world as antidotes to ossified forms of thought. All of these qualities are directly implicated in the capacity for experience. From the very outset, antisemitism tended to narrow down and vitiate experience. As an ideal type of modern individuals and perpetrators and their weakened ego capacities, Eichmann represents the final loss of all capacity for experience and thought. Someone who cannot question his assumptions because he lacks the ability to expose himself to living experience that might challenge his preconceptions loses the faculty of judgment as well; it is paralyzed.

In Arendt's and Adorno's theorizing, late modern, genocidal antisemitism therefore means, not only that the object is trimmed to fit a preexisting scheme, but that it also entails the destruction of one's very self, of one's own subjectivity. Among the adherents of antisemitic ideology, sophisticated thought capable of perceiving the full multiplicity of the world begins to atrophy. This tendency of the totalitarian mind to slip its moorings to experience is the most dangerous form of any modern ideology, because reality can no longer make any headway against it.

This immunization from reality establishes the crucial link between antisemitism and a modern condition at large that is incapable of reflecting on its rationality, and the means and ends of societal life. The nexus to the specific totalitarian domination and the specificity of the Nazi genocide, to be sure, should not be overstretched. The link between the potential modern loss of experience and totalitarian persecution or the extermination of the European Jews is tenuous. Just as nothing similar preceded the Nazi extermination of the Jews, nothing quite like totalitarian fascism has emerged since then (even though the Stalinist persecutions, the Khmer Rouge's annihilation policies and other modern genocidal politics, for instance in Rwanda, in many ways come close). Arendt and Adorno stress that the

Nazi concentration camps did not serve any "utilitarian purpose" and therefore cannot be explained in functional terms.[111] Their purposelessness point to their irrational essence; they do not serve any rational purpose, not even the thin rational purpose of domination. Adorno argues that the demonstration of its economic futility heightened rather than moderated "the attraction of the racialist panacea": it does "not help human beings but assuages their urge to destroy. The actual advantage enjoyed by the racialist comrade is that his rage will be sanctioned by the collective. The less he gains in any other way, the more obstinately, against better knowledge, he clings to the movement." Indeed, modern totalitarian antisemitism "has proved immune to the charge of inadequate profitability. For the common people it is a luxury."[112]

The Specificity of Antisemitism and the Unresolved Perplexities of Modernity

Despite the different theoretical traditions of thought that divide Adorno and Arendt, one can discern remarkable parallels in their reflections on antisemitism and the genocide of the European Jews. Aware of the rupture that this atrocity signified, their theorizing addresses the crisis-ridden, contradictory conditions of an entire age that has been construed paradigmatically as "modernity." Both situate modern antisemitism and genocide in peculiar dialectics of continuity and discontinuity. The modern condition and the emergence of modern antisemitism are linked, and the former ultimately also enables the latter. Yet there is no causality between modern origins of antisemitism and its totalitarian triumph, between favorable conditions and the act of mass murder; antisemitism, and the Holocaust, cannot be explained in any positivist fashion.

In their attempt to understand its "mysterious" character, Arendt and Adorno recognize both the specificity of modern antisemitism and its interplay with a generalized 'ticket mentality' that is reinforced by modern societal principles. Equipping Jews with presumed secret global power and personifying the "modern malaise," antisemitism is distinct from racial prejudices; it is ultimately a world explanation. Immune to reality, it thereby combines the most contradictory strains and tropes; to a large extent, it is amorphous. It also comes in more than one guise; as a societal undercurrent, antisemitism can undergo mutations and recur in very different forms, vernaculars, and at unexpected places over time.[113] Long after the Holocaust, Arendt, like Adorno, saw new, all too present emanations of antisemitism as "ugly reminders" of "something one had hoped had passed into history."[114]

While attempting to recover a critical modernist rationality, Adorno's analyses intend to lay bare the mendacity of the condition of modern society itself, including its economic organization, which presumably weakens the individual's intellectual and moral capacities and paralyzes human judgment. In the final analysis, society generates the lie of antisemitism with its own intrinsic failures and failed promises. In Adorno's view, it is not only that antisemitism distorts the modern socioeconomic order; but this order distorts human beings and undermines the always precarious capacities of modern subjects. Totalitarian antisemitism, then, is not just modernity's other: culminating in the persecution and murder of the Jews in the context of Nazism, it can be viewed as a reaction against modernity, yet it also cannot be disentangled from modern society and the "socially necessary illusions" and "ticket mentality" it generates. In Arendt's conceptualization of antisemitism one likewise encounters multiple pathologies of the modern condition that help facilitate antisemitic ideology and the rise of totalitarianism as a completely new regime form. In her report on the "banality of evil," Arendt settles accounts with the main developments of the nineteenth and twentieth centuries. The progressive decay of the capacity of judgment, originally depicted in her analysis of antisemitism, appears again, albeit in a more extreme version, in her portrait of the "deportation specialist." Eichmann represents the "totality of the human debacle in the heart of Europe in all its dreadful matter-of-factness."[115]

Ultimately, in the work of Arendt and Adorno, modern antisemitism encompasses the loss of experience and the breakdown of thought, both of which are intimately tied to the modern condition: its destructive features and specific heteronomy. While both theorists are critical modernists who do not want to give up on modern enlightenment and its claims to political equality (and thus do not throw the baby out with the bathwater by abstractly negating modernity),[116] they recognize it as part and parcel of the modern illusion that a new social order can be created by treating human beings as mere material. This mode, last but not least, also finds expression in the universalized mode of labor and exchange value.

Modern antisemitism implies a bankruptcy of the ability to judge, as well as the intellectual and psychological deterioration of its adherents, which can be traced back to modern forms of dependency and subjugation. Antisemitism denies human variety, standardizes the other, and forces individuality to fall in line, then drives the other out of society and annihilates him in death factories. It excludes difference and opposes even the very idea of contingency. Antisemitism robs its targets of their subjectivity and individuality, transforming them into abstract representatives of their "race" and imposing on them characteristics chosen by the antisemite. It distorts and denies their real identities and ultimately uses terror to liquidate them. In that, antisemitism and the Holocaust cannot simply be understood as the culmination of discrimination against and persecution of the Jews motivated by prejudice; they are also "an attack upon human diversity as such, that is, upon a characteristic of the 'human status' without which the very words 'mankind' or 'humanity' would be devoid of meaning."[117]

For both Arendt and Adorno, antisemitism is not just one more current of thought within modern society. It also expresses some of the very problems of modern society—its crises and developmental failures. And ultimately, some universalized modern objectifications overlap with antisemitic paranoia. Despite political modernity's irrevocable and significant claims to individual autonomy and public freedom that are the foundation of reflective judgment, its potential paralysis—if not total collapse, as witnessed in Nazi Germany—is also inscribed into the existing modern condition itself. In short, the theories about antisemitism proposed by Arendt and Adorno do not only point out the dangers of resentments, old and new; they implicitly put forward a radical critique of modern society as well.

THREE
Political Theory in Exile, Exile as a Theoretical Paradigm

TEN

Theorists in Exile
Adorno's and Arendt's Reflections on the Place of the Intellectual

DIRK AUER

Auschwitz, escape, exile—a thinking destined to sublimate experience into theory, as Adorno once put it, cannot remain untouched by these phenomena.[1] In fact, they mark the social negation of the intellectual in the modern world. Viewed historically, intellectuals acquire their specific role along with the development of a public domain *within* which they actively participate *on behalf of* the public. Having recourse to universal values, their interventions contribute to the formation of opinions and intentions shared in common by political communities. The loss of these conditions and contexts for public interventions, of a space in which their speeches and actions have meaning, through the breakdown of social structures and human catastrophes such as Auschwitz, is bound to affect the intellectual directly. In this essay I shall discuss the impact forced exile had on Adorno's and Arendt's respective self-descriptions as intellectuals. How did each theorize the simultaneity of intellectual activity, on the one hand, and social negation and displacement, on the other?[2]

It is often emphasized that emigration and the concomitant experience of being uprooted and isolated came to be key experiences for Arendt and Adorno.[3] A feeling of alienation and melancholy seems to be a constant element in the self-perception of intellectuals in general,[4] but for Adorno and Arendt, it became a political reality through the isolation and uprootedness forced upon them by the material experience of exclusion, expulsion, and the basic struggle for survival. Their reflections on the experience of emigration and exile add weight to Karl Mannheim's notion of the "freefloating intellectual" who transcends political and communal ties.

Nevertheless, it would be misleading to link these experiences and their theorizing too hastily and too directly. In fact, it can be shown that crucial, formative motifs in their thinking were present in both of them before 1933, and hence cannot be viewed as having been causally connected to the experience of emigration. In their work, moreover, exile is increasingly separated from its relationship to a concrete biographical experience and is ascribed an increasingly metaphorical significance. It comes to be used (1) to describe a place differentiated from the familiar practices of the social order. In order to counter the danger of hypostatizing difference, Adorno and Arendt (2) reflect on the means of preserving such a place *within* the political order. Two negative foils form the background to this: on the one hand, the situation of stateless refugees, who are forcibly isolated from political communities, and the ideology of individualism, characteristic of modern society; and on the other hand, the simultaneous tendency toward a collectivization of the world, as epitomized in modern conformism and homogenization, at the expense of plurality and difference.[5] Finally (3), both Adorno and Arendt ultimately consider the traditional role of the intellectual as spokesperson of the universal to be historically outdated. Yet as long as universal freedom is not realized, intellectuals will have to point out the limitations of the discourses of a given political community, and gesture toward alternatives. Whereas contemporary thinkers like Michael Walzer and Richard Rorty locate the intellectual fully in the immanence of the deliberative discourse of a given political community, Arendt and Adorno retain an epistemological and political position that engages with but also transcends the given context. And the tension between interior and exterior characteristic of any critical stance can best be described from the standpoint of exile.

Forced Exile and the Location of the Intellectual

Both Adorno and Arendt gained reputations as intellectuals noted beyond the context of academia. They did so especially in debates concerning the coming to terms with the Nazi atrocities and genocide that marked the twentieth century—Arendt with her reportage on the Eichmann trial and Adorno with his published interventions occasioned by the public appearance of swastika graffiti in Germany in 1959. Their previous routes of politicization, however, could hardly have been more different. Viewed from today's perspective, Adorno's long-lasting naïveté about National Socialism, documented in his correspondence with Siegfried Kracauer and Max Horkheimer, preserved in the German Literary Archive (Deutsches Literaturarchiv) in Marbach am Neckar, is almost incomprehensible. In 1932, he described the political situation as "encouraging." On May 15, 1933, just after Hitler's rise to power—hence after the Enabling Act passed on March 23, the anti-Jewish boycotts, the anti-Jewish Law for the Restoration of Civil Service of April 7, and the prohibition of all independent labor unions on May 1—he wrote Kracauer in Paris that he should return to Germany: "There is total peace and order. I believe that conditions will consolidate." One week later, he expressed doubts that National Socialism would last long, and as late as May 1935, he did not view the political situation in Germany as unequivocally disastrous, because the Nazis' *"Gleichschaltung* [forcing into line] of the workers had not succeeded." His assessment finally changed in October of the same year, *after* his emigration to England in 1934. By then he recognized that Germany had become "more dreadful than ever," the "country had become a hell, down to the smallest aspect of the everyday." Adorno followed Max Horkheimer to the United States four years later, where the latter had already reopened the Institute for Social Research.

Arendt describes herself as naïve and unworldly in her youth, but this began to change before the transfer of power to Hitler. Like the more far-sighted members of the Institute for Social Research in Frankfurt, she began to think about emigrating as early as 1932, and a lack of interest in political events had become virtually impossible for her after the burning of the Reichstag, at the latest: "Indifference was no longer possible in 1933. It was no longer possible even before that."[6] These events were "an immediate shock" for Arendt, from which point on she understood herself as "responsible": "That is, I was no longer of the opinion that one can simply be a bystander."⁷ Yet the real, fundamental shock for her was not so much Hitler's rise to power. She had known for years that the Nazis were the enemies of the Jews and that "a large number of the German people were behind them." The genuine shock was the more or less voluntary *Gleichschaltung,* or getting into line, of her non-Jewish friends, and especially intellectuals, which deeply surprised and affected her. The problem, she says, was "not what our enemies did but what our friends did. . . . it was as if an empty space formed around you." She worked briefly for the German Zionist organization, was arrested by the Gestapo but released after about a week, and left Germany thinking: "I shall never again get involved in any kind of intellectual business."⁸ Arendt fled via Prague and Geneva to Paris. On the run from the Nazis, and classified as an "enemy alien" in France, she finally escaped to the United States in May 1941—just in time.

In an essay entitled "We Refugees," Arendt describes the experience of forced emigration:

> We lost our home, which means the familiarity of daily life. We lost our occupation, which means the confidence that we are of some use in this world. We lost our language, which means the naturalness of reactions, the simplicity of gestures, the unaffected expression of feelings. We left our relatives in the Polish ghettos and our best friends have been killed in concentration camps, and that means the rupture of our private lives.⁹

From this period on, the experience of emigration becomes a shared topic for Arendt and Adorno. At first, both sought to maintain their identities against the background of the shattered continuity of their lives. Their points of departure, however, once more differed: Whereas for Adorno displacement jeopardized his identity as an intellectual, which is how he already described his place in the world at that time, exile became a topic for Arendt in view of her identity as a Jew and against the backdrop of a history of Jewish attempts at assimilation.¹⁰

Forced exile denies individuals the ability to ascertain an identity, a place in the world, and throws them back to the state of naked humanity. Besides the experience of being socially uprooted and politically disenfranchised, it was the loss of language that became an especially traumatic experience for many intellectuals. Arendt and Adorno were no exception to this. In the case of Adorno, it constituted one of the decisive reasons motivating his return to Germany after the war. Not only did he feel that his native language, in contrast to a recently learned one, permitted greater precision in expressing what he intended, but he also attributed a "special elective affinity" between the German language and the speculative element in philosophy that is essential for his thought.[11] It caused him to insist throughout his life that "the crucial things that the likes of us have to say we can say only in German."[12] Arendt, too, observed that in the speech of those emigrants who wanted to forget their native language, while they were able to speak correctly, they did so in a language "in which one cliché chases another because the productivity that one has in one's own language is cut off when one forgets that language."[13] Language is what assures continuity. It is the medium of articulation; accumulated experience and tradition that serve as the source of knowledge and self-positioning are stored up in it. Yet—as Adorno describes his situation during his American exile—the "past life of émigrés is annulled." Intellectual experience is "declared non-transferable and unnaturalizable. Anything that is not reified, cannot be counted and measured, ceases to exist."[14]

Forced emigration means the loss of familiar patterns of meaning in the living world. Yet those familiar patterns are prerequisites for the subject to orientate his or her thoughts and actions. Forced exile, as Arendt puts it, entails for subjects "the loss of the entire social texture into which they were born and in which they established for themselves a distinct place in the world."[15] The subject is forced into a state of dislocation or displacement.[16] Because of communicative ties that are severed both on the side of the agent and on the side of the agent's audience, cultural uprootedness directly challenges the inherently public position of the intellectual—of those intellectuals, at any rate, who intend to have any practical impact. Displacement means that the intellectual is transported into an environment, "that must remain incomprehensible to him . . . he is always astray . . . . All emphases are wrong, perspectives disrupted."[17] This unbearable situation necessitates a new politics of "situatedness."[18] Owing to the exile's forcible dislocation and peculiar placement between cultures, his or her situatedness is no longer self-evident, and strategies must be fashioned to create a new location from which to speak and act. Displacement and exile do not necessarily imply a permanent loss of a public space and a community of listeners, but the language and connections prerequisite to such a space have to be reclaimed and acquired. Three possibilities of such politics of situatedness present themselves: the exile can attempt to overcome his uprootedness by adapting to the majority culture of the host country; he can withdraw into the traditions of his country of origin; or he can try to create "a third place."[19] This means breaking free from the dualistic logic between assimilation to the new and attachment to the old, thus making his homelessness the basis of a new situatedness.

Both Adorno and Arendt reject assimilation, which they see as denying one's own identity in favor of adopting the culture of the country of refuge. Arendt criticizes the pressure to assimilate: "We were told to forget; and we forgot quicker than anybody ever could imagine," Arendt writes. "In a friendly way we were reminded that the new country would become a new home; and after four weeks in France or six weeks in America, we pretended to be Frenchmen or Americans."[20]

Like Arendt, Adorno observes of "the threateningly well-meaning advice" to leave behind the past, and hence one's traditions and previous experiences, that since this "cannot be transplanted, that they should write off their prehistory and start and entirely new life, merely inflicts verbally on the spectral intruders the violence they have long learned to do to themselves."[21] A fresh start of this kind, accompanied by a forgetting, meant nothing less, however, than unreflective adaptation to the cultural and economic imperatives of the host country. And this in turn means negating oneself *as an intellectual*.[22] Adorno's "reflections from damaged life," as he calls his exile work *Minima Moralia*, relate directly to his experience of being an emigrant. Damage, according to an aphorism entitled "Protection, help and counsel," is done to every emigrating intellectual—"without exception."[23] This is among the reasons why total assimilation cannot succeed, despite the most desperate efforts, since "integration is ideology, and remains fragile even as ideology."[24] The exile, according to Adorno, can never arrive, "however flawless his knowledge of trade-union organizations or the automobile industry may be; he is always astray."[25] *Forced* or compulsory assimilation can even—as Arendt demonstrates in her studies of the history of Jewish assimilation—lead to the exact opposite of what is intended: permanent insistence on the absence of a stigmatizing quality only serves to make it more apparent. In fact, the desire to extinguish one's differences, and one's Jewishness in particular, may indirectly confirm the worldview of those who think "Jewishness is a bad, ill-omened quality that must be eradicated."[26]

For Adorno and Arendt, their situation as exiles is particularly precarious because, aside from the impossibility of assimilation, direct recourse to the traditions and culture of their country of origin is no longer available. Arendt speaks of the fact that "the tradition is broken and the Ariadne thread is lost" and therefore one must engage in a "thinking without a banister."[27] This excludes the attempt to construct a Jewish identity solely by referencing a cultural tradition and making it the point of departure for political action, since that would mean the direct transfer of categories from a prepolitical domain into the sphere of politics. The political, however, according to Arendt is precisely *not* concerned with antecedent, quasi-essential identities, but instead, is the space where identities constitute themselves in and through agonal confrontations.[28] Adorno, too, views the search for "refuge on a conventional and preestablished" horizon, which he portrays as typical of the postwar period, as carrying with it the "danger of creating a new kind of blood and soil [*Blut und Boden*],"[29] that is, the rehabilitation of the ethnic-nationalist ideas and redemptive collective fantasies of a racialized homeland characteristic of the totalitarian Nazi past.

In addition, even formerly "non-conforming thoughts," including critical ideas from the Marxian tradition, may have become "conventional."[30] For Adorno, direct, immediate, or naïve recourse to the standards and emancipatory, enlightened claims enshrined in old bourgeois cultural traditions is closed off, as these claims have also been affected by the breakdown of modern civilization and the genocidal politics in twentieth-century Europe. The method of ideology critique, which draws its strength from the contradiction between bourgeois norms and factual reality, is thereby historically superseded, because those emancipatory, universalistic claims of political enlightenment and modern civil society themselves failed to prevent the rise of barbarism and are not untouched by it, if not discredited in their original form. According to the authors of *Dialectic of Enlightenment*, universalism's critical qualities can no longer be taken for granted, and critical thinking after the barbaric triumph of universal unreason has to reflect on the particular, the excluded, the exiled. It can no longer rely on old concepts that once had critical functions.

Thus the exile can neither truly arrive nor find his way back. He lives in a transitory state. Uprooted from all traditions, he finds himself in a place in-between—between two or more cultures, and between past and future. Adorno and Arendt respond to these poor alternatives by breaking free from the logic of the "either–or." They look for and create a "third space" by turning the *forced displacement into the foundation of a new placement*.[31] In Arendt's case, this move is anticipated in *Rahel Varnhagen*; the third space is that of the "self-conscious pariah," situated at the margins of society, who alone represents a responsible life. He is aware that as a Jew, he has never had a home and will never truly have one. Instead of hiding this weakness, however, he transforms his position of forced marginality into a source of strength. Only the pariah, according to Arendt, can embrace his Jewish identity and at the same time fight politically for a place where Jews can live without betraying their Jewish identity. The counterimage is that of the parvenu, who never dreams of the "transformation of poor conditions, but of a change of personnel in [his] favor, which would then, as if by magic, improve everything."[32] Uninterested in political action, he seeks to assimilate to the ruling majority culture in order finally to become indistinguishable from its mainstream members.

Adorno, who describes himself as a "professionally displaced person,"[33] also experiences exile very much as an ambivalent state and establishes a third space in response to this experience. Due to forced isolation, exile is, to be sure, on the one hand, the cause of immeasurable suffering. On the other hand, however, a certain distance from society, which is especially constitutive of the exile situation, but not dependent on it, is a necessary condition for responsible intellectual activity, since "only at a remove from life can the mental life exist, and truly engage the empirical."[34] The intellectual who resists the compulsion to assimilate and takes on exile as his destiny can thus no longer be tempted to relinquish part of his subject matter, but can give expression to his insights "without keeping an eye on success"[35] or selling off "the intellect to forms of business."[36] Under no circumstances, in contrast, must the intellectual "shape his morality from the notions of the mercantile world—that it is necessary, after all, to have some coin to offer people."[37] Only speech that does not in advance reflect on its acceptance by a potential addressee, creates the necessary distance from a praxis subjugated to the primacy of exchange value, and hence is able to shatter it in the act of reflection. "He who offers for sale something unique that no-one wants to buy, represents, even against his will, freedom from exchange."[38] That is also the reason why, for the intellectual, "inviolable isolation is now the only way of showing some measure of solidarity."[39]

Although her reflections aim in their core at the possibility of acting *within* a political community, Arendt also maintains that for the intellectual "only the onlooker occupies a position which allows him to see the whole; the agent, as a participant in the game, is compelled to play his role. . . . Therefore, retreat from direct participation to a standpoint outside of the game is a *conditio sine qua non* for any judgment."[40] Thinking, as the medium of the intellectual, permits itself distance from events; it interrupts habitual praxis and questions its unreflected preconditions. It aims firstly at an understanding of the event, and it is this will-to-understand, in contrast to action without reflection, that for Arendt defines intellectual activity.[41] For her, such reflective intellectual distance can be the precondition for gaining better insight into the unfolding of political affairs, just as "it is not uncommon for outsiders and spectators to gain a sharper and deeper insight into the actual meaning of what happens to go on before or around them than would be possible for the actual actors or participants, entirely absorbed as they must be in the events."[42]

It is this distance that is required for knowledge and judgment (*Erkenntnis und Urteilen*) which causes a certain homelessness to become a moral imperative of intellectual and political responsibility for Arendt and Adorno. If exile is usually preceded by a place of home that has been lost, and to which the exile longs to return or to arrive at an undetermined point in the future, Adorno and Arendt know that the latter sense of home can only be a deception. "Dwelling, in the proper sense, is now impossible," Adorno writes. "The traditional residences we grew up in have grown intolerable: each trait of comfort in them is paid for with a betrayal of knowledge, each vestige of shelter with the musty pact of family interests."[43]

Consequently, exile is no longer just the place of a traumatic emptiness, no longer just a stopover on the road to overcoming the loss of one's identity, but is aimed precisely at overcoming the compulsion to maintain identity.[44] Thus exile can *also* be seen as already a form of utopia that points to independence and freedom from the confines of identity. In a letter to Thomas Mann, Adorno writes that the "Californian base," to which he had returned for a time following his reemigration, in order not to lose his American citizenship, had the advantage of being all the more real: "In other words, one no longer feels at home anywhere; but then, of course, someone whose business is ultimately demythologization should hardly complain too much about this."[45]

Between Individualism and Communitarianism

To transform exile into a rhetorical device means almost inevitably facing the charge that this ignores the concrete experiences of displacement and its concomitant suffering. Thus there indeed exists, as Edward Said stresses, a great difference between the "optimistic mobility" of certain variants of a postmodern nomadicism[46] and the "massive dislocations, waste, misery, and horrors endured in our century's migrations and mutilated lives."[47] The twentieth century has produced more refugees, "displaced persons," and places of exile than any other before it in history. New articulations of globalization with their attendant waves of migration drive more and more people into a state of displacement. Homelessness, therefore, has ceased to be the fate of a minority. Against this background, it may sound cynical to valorize exile as a place of privileged knowledge (*Erkenntnis*). Instead of hypostasizing the state of exile unilaterally, Adorno and Arendt therefore insist that humans require connection to a common sphere, if they are not to lose the very medium in which they can constitute and express their individuality. This demonstrates once again the peculiar intermediate position that Adorno and Arendt hold in the discussion about modernity and postmodernism. Against an exaggerated postmodernism which, by rendering absolute the concept of difference, relinquishes the claim for reconciliation of the different, that is, the notion of social solidarity, Adorno and Arendt reflect on the *conditions* under which one can "be different without fear."[48] The classic question which is thus raised, of the relationship between the universal and the particular, between political equality and difference, can no longer be answered by the (re-)construction of universal conditions of communal life, but only in the negative via the critique of rendering absolute one side of the pair of opposites: on the one hand, hypostatizing difference at the expense of the common, as it expresses itself in the state of homelessness and the individualism that is characteristic of modern society, and, on the other, the abstract notion of equality, which negates the "human condition of plurality."[49]

For Arendt, the situation of stateless refugees, as the "newest mass phenomenon in contemporary history,"[50] becomes the point of departure from which to explore the position of the pariah. While the choice to become a pariah or a parvenu was a more or less individual decision in the past, the parvenu has since been unmasked as fictitious. Therefore, according to Arendt, all former parvenus have become pariahs and there exists "no individual way out" any more—either for the parvenu, who in the past had made his peace with a world in which, as a Jew, one was not allowed to be human, or for the pariah, who had believed herself to have been able to renounce such a world by an act of will. The realism of the one "was no less utopian than the idealism of the other."[51] The contemporary pariah is the refugee who is deprived of all elementary human rights: culturally and politically isolated, he stands outside of any law and is subject to completely arbitrary treatment, that is, de facto fair game (*vogelfrei*) until "finally the internment camp—prior to the second World War the exception rather than the rule for the stateless—has become the routine solution for the problem of domicile for the 'displaced persons.'"[52]

This state of complete abandonment, subject to being deported at any time, characterized the life of the Jewish refugee for Arendt and led her to posit "the existence of a right to have rights (and that means to live in a framework where one is judged by one's actions and opinions)."[53] Even for those who consciously live at the fringes of society, she contended, there has to exist a universal right to membership in a political community in which a person has meaning, and from which all other specific rights derive, such as the political rights that guarantee a space in which people may move freely and speak their minds. It is only within a political community that "a human may live as a human among humans—if he does not want to die of 'exhaustion.'"[54]

For Adorno, "the setting-free of the individual by the undermining of the *polis* did not strengthen his resistance, but eliminated him and individuality itself, in the consummation of dictatorial states."[55] Accordingly, he views the simultaneous liberation of individuals and installation of an ever more tightly woven system of domination as the "model of one of the central contradictions which drove society from the nineteenth century toward fascism."[56] A prerequisite for combining subjects into an amorphous, docile mass is for them to be isolated and thrown back on themselves. In this context the *principium individuationis* merely serves the purpose of depriving them of their potential for resistance and "break[s] them completely in their isolation."[57] In modern mass society, social tendencies toward individualization, according to Adorno and to Arendt, relate directly to conformist societal demands, that is, how they fit in with the means of rulers to isolate their subjects completely from one another, so that none may be able to agree and communicate with any other.[58] Individuals are thrown back on their private existence, deprived of their ability to form political judgments, which is necessarily linked to the existence of a common world, and hence are susceptible to manipulation and to conforming, so that finally they appear as "members of one enormous family which has only one opinion."[59] Adorno and Arendt recognized this phenomenon, diagnosing modern society's tendency to become what they respectively termed an "administered world" and "mass society." In its environment, all human differences are leveled in the face of an almost complete conformism as enhanced by bureaucracies. For subjects, "withdrawing behaviors" take the place of contingent, nonpreformed experiences. This causes the individual to "abandon his individuality" and become submerged in the overall life process of the species, Arendt writes.[60] She takes the diminishing of experience and the elimination of human spontaneity that she sees as characteristic of mass societies to be so radical "that man may be willing and, indeed, is on the point of developing into that animal species from which, since Darwin, he imagines he has come."[61] Action has been replaced by blind behavior according to expectations of social requirements, all of which aim to turn the individual into a predictable creature.

Against the background of this perversion, as they diagnose it, of the ideal of equality into a "classless society of automobilists, cinema-goers and fellow countrymen [*Volksgenossen*],"[62] Adorno and Arendt adopt the perspective of the excluded, the marginalized, the different. It becomes the point of departure for their furnishing of a communal space that, rather than resulting in the destruction of plurality,[63] creates loci in which "the differentiated participate in each other."[64] It is not, therefore, a normative image from which they proceed and that they contrast with a poor reality—universality cannot be gained by determining an abstract generalized stance, that is, by establishing some formal universal principle or maxim that Kant had in mind. Merely elevating equality as an abstract principle would be only "too compatible with the most insidious tendencies of society," Adorno writes. "That all men are alike is exactly what society would like to hear."[65] Arendt also criticizes the habit, characteristic of modern mass society, of regarding equality as an "innate quality of every individual," "which is called 'normal' when it is like everybody else, and 'abnormal' when it is different."[66] Equality in that sense is, for Adorno and Arendt, the prerequisite for the total domination over the particular by the communal, which views differences "as stigmas indicating that not enough has yet been done; that something has still been left outside its machinery, not quite determined by its totality."[67] Equality, according to Arendt, must instead be recognized for what it meaningfully is, a basis "for a form of organization within which distinct people have equal rights."[68] For if humans were equal from the start, equality would not be a subject of permanent political concern. In other words, because humans are unequal, their equality must be politically insisted upon and institutional measures adopted to realize it. Equality before the law can therefore exist only when it proceeds from the "fact of plurality." According to Arendt, worldliness—the state of being embedded in a human community in which one can speak and act—and the institutional guarantee of an equal right to membership open up a political space in which no one need any longer be afraid of being "either stoned or sentenced to death by starvation" by society.[69] This, Adorno says, is a prerequisite for true "communication of what is differentiated."[70]

Neither Empty Universalism nor Blind Particularism

Inasmuch as Adorno's and Arendt's thinking thus focuses on the search for the preconditions for difference and fear of losing it, the position of the intellectual has to be reassessed. Since the Dreyfus Affair, the intellectual had been regarded as one who, prompted by conscience alone, and without a political mandate, advocated for universal values in the public, political domain and drew attention to social inequality in the name of such values. However, intellectuals could no longer speak for such a common domain. Adorno and Arendt would concur that the "universal intellectual" identified by Foucault, typified since the nineteenth century by thinkers from Zola to Sartre, had been historically superseded.

With regard to the *factual dimension*, the intellectual, in setting criteria for his normative judgments, can no longer have recourse to a point of view external to society—God, nature, or the philosopher king. Arendt and Adorno place themselves explicitly in the tradition of postmetaphysical thought, in which arguments based on a critique of reason are mediated by political considerations. Arendt views recourse to universalizing generalities such as "nature" or "history" as the basis of a totalitarian (actually, totalizing) praxis, while Adorno regards attempts to "deduce the world in words from a principle" as "the behaviour of someone who would like to usurp power instead of resisting it."[71]

The intellectual must now recognize that his statements are condemned to particularity, that any universal idea he proposes invites fresh conflict, rather than leading to unity. In the *temporal dimension,* therefore, the intellectual's classic claim to represent a concrete or "realistic utopia" (John Rawls) during socially challenging times is problematized. Arendt recognized in it the ideological principle of total domination, and Adorno, too—in contrast to an oft-repeated claim—rejected any form of philosophy of history, both in its Hegelian provenance, and its opposite, embodied in the reactionary thesis of historical decline. For this point of view leaves little else than resigned agreement with the seemingly historically inevitable. According to Adorno and Arendt, it is precisely this postulated link between historical necessity and its philosophical justification that must be broken. Historical movement proceeds as contingent, without an inscribed telos that will eventually bring it to an end. Because of this, the possibility of the other, of alternatives, is always present. "Contingency," as Adorno puts it, "remains the 'Menetekel' [portent] of lordship."[72] It thus opens up, it could be said with Arendt, the actual domain of the political. Finally, in the social dimension, this argues against the intellectual's claim to a "free-floating" professional independence that, according to Karl Mannheim, makes it possible to escape the perspectivity and normativity of knowledge. Arendt and Adorno assume that knowledge is in principle bound to a particular stance and thus fallible.[73]

Adorno and Arendt would thus initially agree with social philosophers like Michael Walzer who seek to shift the self-consciousness of the social critic "from legislator to interpreter."[74] Walzer contends that the intellectual should not speak from a standpoint outside the factual, given world of morality. A context-transcending critique that distances itself too far from its recipients runs the danger of having authoritarian effects, because it tends to establish a dogma that is immunized from publicity and from democratic participation, which always serves as a corrective. Intellectuals should therefore see themselves not as explorers or inventors but as "local judges," according to Walzer, who finds the "warrant for critical engagement in the idealism, even if it is a hypocritical idealism, of the actually existing moral world."[75] The function of critique is to confront the factual state of a political order with its self-imposed claims as they are manifested, for example, in their constitution.[76] To this extent, the intellectual not only interprets the fundamental social values, but acts to remind society of its normative precepts and where it falls short of its own ideals.

Such a concept of critique is, however, not unproblematic. If critique is to be critical, it has to distance itself from criticism, and hence situate itself outside of its subject. In other words, it has to mark a difference between itself and whatever it is judging.[77] For if the criteria of critique were already immanent in the social domain, critique would be determined by the latter and hence tend to become uncritical—a problem that becomes particularly virulent politically when the established traditions have fallen under suspicion of being in themselves the germ of a new barbarism. Against the background of such a historical situation, in which thought has lost its last point of reference,[78] rather than adopting a purely contextualist view that situates critique within the deliberative conflict of a political community, Adorno and Arendt maintain that critical judgment is predicated on a certain retreat from active involvement and the partisanship of direct interest, which is "given in the world, or arise[s] out of my life in this world."[79]

Exile can thus serve as a metaphorical description of an epistemological-political position from which alone, according to Adorno and Arendt, responsible thinking and judgment continue to be possible. *Epistemologically*, to choose exile is an attempt at decontextualizing knowledge (*Erkenntnis*). The exile moves at the margins and from this vantage point is able to see things that others cannot perceive. The factually established, which appears necessary to "local inhabitants," is viewed by the exile as contingent, that is, as the result of a series of historical decisions. Dislocation counts, when viewed this way, as a condition of undistorted communication, in which social validity claims are no longer bound by a particular context, and hence gain an element of unconditionality. *Politically*, such a concept references the search for a space in which the subject can no longer be fixed by its identity and no longer needs to accommodate false loyalties. Arendt considered uncritical loyalty to a factually given collective identity "pre-political," although she contended that "in exceptional circumstances—such as the circumstances of Jewish politics—[it] is bound to also have political consequences, though, as it were, in a negative way. This attitude makes certain types of behavior impossible."[80] For Adorno, "In an intellectual hierarchy which constantly makes everyone responsible, irresponsibility alone can call the hierarchy directly by its name."[81]

The place of exile, which creates a spatial distance from the events under scrutiny, must not be thought of as an Archimedean point, from which the world becomes visible in objective form. Adorno and Arendt insist that the self-imposed solitude must not in turn hypostatize itself, that is, cut itself off from the social domain. The "humanity" of pariahs is often "dearly bought," Arendt observes,[82] the price being radical withdrawal from the world, causing them to lose contact with "the solid ground of reality."[83] Withdrawal from the world can be justified only "as long as reality is not ignored, but is constantly acknowledged as the thing that must be escaped. . . . [pariahs] must remember that they are constantly on the run, and that the world's reality is actually expressed in their escape."[84] Adorno similarly considers that one who distances himself remains "as much entangled as the active participant. . . . His own distance from business at large is a luxury which only that business alone confers."[85] If, on the other hand, the intellectual denies his dependence on the social praxis, "he hypostasizes as an absolute his intellect, which was only formed through contact with economic reality and abstract exchange relations, and which can become intellect solely by reflecting on its own conditions."[86]

The place of exile, one might then say, opens up a tension that is constitutive for any critical judgment, between social significance and becoming, between unconditionality and conditionality, that is, between unchallengeable immanence and the necessity to transcend actualities. On the one hand, Thorsten Bonacker asserts, "criticism must distance itself from the criticized, dis-place itself from it, on the other hand, it depends on contact with the criticized, on belonging to it."[87] The critic must, by his intervention, represent the shortcomings of society, and he can do this only by placing himself outside of the represented, since he can recognize shortcomings as such only when he has created some distance from them. As an intellectual, therefore, he must simultaneously be *in* society and place himself *outside* of it.

From a political point of view, this indeterminacy is precisely where his power lies, because the critic who cannot be localized undermines the clarity of dichotomous distinctions. He is neither friend nor foe, neither inside nor outside, neither all distanced observer nor all participant. He is physically close, while remaining mentally at a distance, which leads to the constant reproach for his lack of patriotic spirit and destructive influence on tradition.[88] The critic can neither be completely involved nor completely distanced, he can no longer speak on behalf of the communal, nor can he be content with being merely a particular "voice in the conversation of humanity" (in the words of Rorty, following Oakeshott).[89] It is these neither-nor's and simultaneities from which the social ambivalence of the intellectual results, and for which exile is the ultimate model.

Translated by Andreas Kahre and Lars Rensmann

We lost our home, which means the familiarity of daily life. We lost our occupation, which means the confidence that we are of some use in this world. We lost our language, which means the naturalness of reactions, the simplicity of gestures, the unaffected expression of feelings. We left our relatives in the Polish ghettos and our best friends have been killed in concentration camps, and that means the rupture of our personal lives.

—Hannah Arendt, "We Refugees,"

Every intellectual in emigration is, without exception, mutilated, and does well to acknowledge it to himself, if he wishes to avoid being cruelly apprised of it behind the tightly closed doors of his self-esteem. . . . Between the reproduction of his own existence under the monopoly of mass culture, and impartial, responsible work, yawns an irreconcilable breach. His language has been expropriated, and the historical dimension that nourished his knowledge, sapped.

—Theodor Adorno, *Minima Moralia*

ELEVEN

Homeless Philosophy
The Exile of Philosophy and the Philosophy of Exile in Arendt and Adorno

SAMIR GANDESHA

Any twenty-first-century reading of Hannah Arendt and Theodor Adorno, figures so closely tied to the questions and problems of what Eric Hobsbawm has called the "short twentieth century," immediately provokes the question of their contemporary relevance. What could we possibly hope to learn from either about the daunting problems that we face in a world that appears to bear little more than a "family resemblance" to the one that came to an end close to a decade ago? We apparently no longer live in an age in which secular ideologies confront one another on the historical stage, a time in which the threat of totalitarianism has long passed and, indeed, when the nation-state, particularly in the context of the European Union, has been superseded by a "post-national constellation." Moreover, the tradition of European modernist culture seems to have lost its confidence in the wake of the global pervasiveness of kitsch, which entered the scene through the space opened by the dismantling of the opposition between "high" and "low" culture. This has itself generated a new kind of relativism, in which the very procedure of "critique," which for Immanuel Kant formed the basis of the Enlightenment, understood as *Mundigkeit,* or the ability to speak or speak up for oneself, has become muted.

Nonetheless, before the question concerning relevance can be, if not answered, at least properly posed, it is necessary to take note of how the reception of Arendt and Adorno has changed in certain key ways in recent years. Arendt has typically been read as offering a concrete, promising engagement with the questions of real politics both in terms of her conceptual contributions, her critical journalism, and, indeed, the posthumous influence that she was seen to have in the "revolutions" that swept through the Eastern Bloc some two decades ago. Yet recently published work shows her to be deeply engaged with questions pertaining to the nature of art, literature, and culture more generally as key to understanding the conditions for the possibility of successful political action, which, after all, is situated within the context of meaning—meaningful words and deeds that persist over time and that are constitutive of what she calls the "world."[1]

Adorno, on the other hand, presents us with a dialectically inverse image. He has typically been read, first and foremost, as a co-author of *Dialectic of Enlightenment*, hence of a bleak, pessimistic, and indeed one-sided account of modernity—one that culminates in the progressive narrowing, if not outright closure, of political space, the mass deception of the culture industry, with its short-circuiting of reason in a now autonomatized schematism of the understanding and in pathological forms of projection comprising authoritarian personality structures. If hope exists at all, so the interpretation goes, it lies in the reappropriation of a mimetic relation to nature, as modeled by the most "advanced" works of modern art—so many letters in bottles, *Flaschenposten,* sent out to sea. Yet challenging this accepted view of Adorno, recent work has shown that far from a retreat from the public sphere signaled by the image of the "message in the bottle," which for Jürgen Habermas, Axel Honneth, Rolf Wiggershaus, and others, is the *pars pro toto* for the enterprise of first-generation critical theory as a whole, through his indefatigable work as an academic, administrator, and public intellectual, Adorno never actually gave up on politics. If the possibility of politics had all but withered, Max Pensky asks, why engage with the public sphere at all?[2]

Indeed, taken together, the reception of these two key figures of the twentieth century already provides the basis for an answer to the question of their contemporary relevance. And this has to do with a parallel evident in them between the requirements of understanding art, on the one hand, and the requirements of democratic politics—a parallel that, for the spirit of our times, is decidedly counterintuitive and, perhaps for this very reason, as important to emphasize as ever. The parallel is roughly as follows: art and politics both presuppose, as Aristotle already knew, the capacity for experience and, indeed, are themselves the source of new experiences. The capacity for experience is, for both Arendt and Adorno, a steadfast openness or receptivity to what is genuinely new, unfamiliar, or other. Such receptivity cannot be expected to materialize spontaneously, but is rather, paradoxically, the result of often strenuous effort. Contrary to the "common sense" of our age, the undeniable ubiquity of hollowed-out, reified cultural forms makes genuine democratic participation, central to which is, of course, meaningful communication, *less* rather than *more* likely. Indeed, the proliferation of the products of the entertainment (Arendt) or culture (Adorno) industry has contributed substantively to the actual subversion of democracy, not from the outside but from *within*.

This chapter argues that the importance of Arendt and Adorno lies in their attempts to rehabilitate experience, and that their own experiences of exile were central to such rehabilitation. It is precisely their exile experience that has the most to offer us today, in a period of forced migration perhaps unseen on such a scale since the interwar period, which will no doubt increase in the near future as a result of global climate change and its myriad effects.

For both Arendt and Adorno, the *conception of experience* undergoes an intensified development as a direct effect of their own *experience of exile*. In other words, this experience becomes the basis for their development in rather different ways of what I shall call a "homeless philosophy." The subtle differences in their respective conceptualizations notwithstanding, the basic explanation for the undermining of the Weimar Republic in the 1930s and indeed the threat to democracy in the post–World War II period for both thinkers lay in the reduction of difference to sameness that lay at the heart of the logic of the social (Arendt) or identity thinking (Adorno). For both thinkers, the roots of totalitarianism are to be located in a philosophy of history that presents the history of the human species as endowed with the structure of natural law. For Arendt, this takes the form of a social Darwinist struggle between discrete races for domination (Nazism) or class struggle (Marxist scientism). For Adorno, it takes the form of an intertwining of myth and enlightenment whereby what is common to both is the rigid, law-like regularity of "second nature," which is, in actuality, a blind repetition of first nature. Such an intersection of myth and enlightenment is allegorized, not only in the cunning guilefully deployed by Odysseus on his return home to Ithaca, but also in the clever answer Oedipus gives to the riddle of nature itself (as embodied in the feminine, monstrous figure of the Sphinx): "It is man." Similarly, for Arendt, totalitarianism manifests a similar response: the omnipotence of "Man" at the expense of difference, which is to say, the *plurality of men*.

The experience and attempt to understand the roots of the intertwinement of barbarism and civilization as it, in the words of Walter Benjamin, "flashed up in a moment of danger" was key for both. Indeed, this very experience of exile from Nazi Germany led Arendt and Adorno to rethink the concept of experience that lay at the very center of the German philosophical tradition through which each thinker had been profoundly formed. It is well known, for example, that for Arendt, the Nazi seizure of power (*Machtergreifung*) came as a terrible shock, yet more shocking for her was the utter obsequiousness of the other intellectuals around her. Prior to that moment, Arendt had been interested not in politics but rather in classical German philosophy, culminating in her apprenticeship with Martin Heidegger. As she writes in an open letter to Gershom Scholem that appeared in the aftermath of the controversial publication of *Eichmann in Jerusalem* contesting Scholem's suggestion that she "came from the German Left": "I came late to an understanding of Marx's importance because I was interested neither in history nor in politics when I was young. If I can be said to 'have come from anywhere,' it is from the tradition of German philosophy."[3] Similarly, in a lecture entitled "The Negation of the Negation," presented at the University of Frankfurt, which formed the basis for what was to be *Negative Dialectics*, Adorno provides particularly revealing insight into the relationship between exile experience and his critique of Hegel's conception of positivity. Adorno's argument is that Hegel's thesis of the negation of the negation culminating in something "positive" actually violates his own youthful critique of the "positivity"—the "self-incurred tutelage"—of the Christian religion." One cannot, of course, overemphasize the importance of the critique of the negation of the negation for Adorno's thinking. Adorno states,

> I cannot resist telling you that my eyes were opened to the dubious nature of this concept of positivity only in emigration, where people found themselves under pressure from the society around them and had to adapt to very extreme circumstances. In order to succeed in this process of adaptation, in order to do justice to what they were forced to do, you would hear them say, by way of encouragement—and you could see the effort it cost

them to identify with the aggressor—"Yes, so-and-so really is very positive . . . " And what this means is that an intelligent and sensitive person is rolling up his sleeves and washing dishes, or whatever allegedly useful social work is required of him.[4]

This passage bears an uncanny similarity to Arendt's 1943 essay "We Refugees" in which she follows Bernard Lazare and distinguishes the "conscious pariah" from the parvenu, he who is willing to tell the truth about the nature of social domination from the "upstart" who seeks to fit in to society at all costs. "Refugees driven from country to country represent the vanguard of their peoples—if they keep their identity," Arendt argues.[5] As we shall see, such a historical consciousness is consciousness of the far edges, and therefore limits, of any given configuration of culture (*Geist*) and the necessity of proceeding from the particular in such a way that its newness or nonidentity is not permitted to be subsumed or, rather, swallowed up by a purportedly universal logic of historical development.

I want to suggest in what follows that we see this new historical consciousness at work in Arendt and Adorno's *Auseinandersetzung* with the German philosophical tradition as a whole. Hegel's concept of experience is exemplary in this respect. While it has roots in Kant's "Idea for a Universal History from a Cosmopolitan Point of View," insofar as conflict between states is seen as pointing ultimately to the realization of peace, Hegel's conception goes far beyond Kant, purporting to unify the diremption, or separation, that Kantian philosophy is uniquely expressive of, and that Kant himself had acknowledged and unsuccessfully sought to transcend in the Third Critique.

In this, Hegel's arguments concerning the nature of experience in *The Phenomenology of Spirit*, particularly the preface and introduction, are of inestimable importance. Hegel explicates his concept of experience in the Preface to the *Phenomenology*. He explains the task of philosophic cognition as the systematic exposition of "grasping and expressing the True, not only as *Substance*, but equally as *Subject*," warning that such a form of cognition ought to be wary of mere edification if it lacks "the seriousness, the suffering, the patience and labour of the negative." Rather than being a superficial "imparting of moral and spiritual stability" (*OED*), corresponding to what Hegel called "positivity" in his so-called early theological writings, this "labour of the negative" would take the form of a pathway analogous to the process of education (*Bildung*), or the progress of a "child through school," corresponding to "the history of the cultural development of the world traced, as it were, in outline."[6] Yet, from the standpoint of individual development, it involves "acquiring what thus lies at hand, devouring his inorganic nature, and taking possession of it for himself." From the standpoint of "universal spirit, as substance," in contrast, this is "nothing but its own acquisition of self-consciousness, the bringing about of its own becoming and reflection into self."[7] Central to the movement from natural consciousness to self-consciousness is what Hegel calls the "tremendous" (*ungeheure*) power of the negative; it is the energy of thought, of the pure "I." The nihilism of the Fichtean absolute "I" is none other than death. Yet, crucially, "the life of Spirit is not the life that shrinks from death and keeps itself untouched by devastation, but rather the life that endures it and maintains itself in it. It wins its truth only when, in utter dismemberment, it finds itself."[8]

If what characterizes natural consciousness (or the immediate existence of Spirit) is an apprehension of the antithesis of knowing, on the one hand, and the object known, on the other, then the transition to self-consciousness is made via experience (*Erfahrung*). Science is the process by which that which is taken by natural consciousness as merely a given object that stands in a relation of negativity toward its knowing is now revealed as itself nothing "other" than Spiritual substance. At the same time, consciousness experiences itself as having "othered" itself in the externality of the object. The key passage thus runs as follows:

> . . . experience is the name we give to just this movement, in which the immediate, the unexperienced, i.e. the abstract, whether it be of sensuous [but still unsensed] being, or only thought of as simple, becomes alienated from itself and then returns to itself from this alienation, and is only then revealed for the first time in its actuality and truth, just as it then has become a property of consciousness also.[9]

It is here that Hegel seeks to show that the diremptions that, as he puts it in the so-called *Differenzschrift*, give rise to the need for philosophy are healed in the course of Spirit's consciousness, estrangement from itself, and return to itself in the form of self-consciousness. The pathway that Spirit traverses—what Hegel calls the "pathway of doubt and despair"—crystallizing in modern skepticism, is itself the journey (*Fahrt*) of experience (*Erfahrung*). This is a pathway that leads Spirit back to itself, where it is finally home in and through the other. The pathway is an entirely speculative one.

Perhaps the most influential attempt, other than Marx's, to question this specifically speculative dimension of Hegel's philosophy is that located in Heidegger's early work. In Heidegger's attempt to contest Hegel's culmination of what he calls "ontotheology" or the attempt to determine the Being of beings as God, Heidegger seeks to contest the Hegelian concept of experience as a pathway leading always already home to itself in a way that both plays itself out historically, but yet, at the same time, "pours itself out of history." In so doing, Heidegger draws attention to the "thrownness" (*Geworfenheit*) of *Dasein*, its being stretched between past and the future, that it is *Sein-zum-Tod* and therefore ultimately resists a final totalization. Therefore, for Heidegger, *Dasein* is *unheimlich* (uncanny), or being-not-at-home with itself, insofar as it cannot be reductively understood in terms of enduring presence. For the post-*Kehre* Heidegger, the idea of the *Holzweg*, the path in the woods leading nowhere, a false trail, takes the place of the Hegelian pathway, which is a path home, a path signaling what Robert Pippin calls the "persistence of subjectivity."[10]

While contesting the Hegelian philosophy of history, Arendt and Adorno equally challenge Heidegger's existential glorification of the motifs of homelessness, of ontological homelessness, as a species of what Günther Anders—a thinker close to both, albeit in rather different ways—called "false concreteness." That is to say, their critiques take aim at the very reification of the notion of homelessness itself and the attempt to think what the negation of this condition might look like. In their critique of the Hegelian philosophy of history, Arendt and Adorno no doubt draw upon the writings of their friend Walter Benjamin, in particular, the late writings on history, insofar as, like Benjamin, although without a "weak messianic power," each is concerned with the preserving the memory of the victims of historical progress rather than pressing them into the service of an ever more rational (and therefore rationalized) reality, or what Adorno calls "extorted reconciliation." They also, crucially, draw upon Kant's Third Critique to call into question the possibility of such a reconciliation, as opposed to the tradition of German Idealism, which seeks to carry out the reconciliation which Kant's Third Critique failed to do.

The convergence between Adorno and Arendt becomes even more pronounced if we focus on a key figure in their thinking and this is the chiasmus, in particular, the chiasmus of natural history: the naturalization of history and, at the same time, the historicization of nature. This chiasmus converges in technology, as is fatefully exemplified by the splitting of the atom and the experimentation on the victims of the death camps respectively.[11] As alluded to above, for Adorno, the intertwining of the natural and the historical is the central dynamic of what he calls (with Horkheimer) the "dialectic of enlightenment": history (or progress in the domination of nature) is at the same time a mimetic repetition of nature—the eternal return of the Hobbesian "war of all against all." For Arendt, the concentration camp (*Lager*) exemplifies the eclipse of the political by the social or the reduction of the specifically *human* life to life as such.[12] Far from being a mere coincidence, Adorno's and Arendt's remarkably similar approaches to history can be attributed to two factors: the first, more obvious, factor is Walter Benjamin's critique of historicism; the second, and much less obvious, dimension lies is their respective engagements with the philosophy of Martin Heidegger. I am concerned in this essay primarily with the relation to Heidegger.

Without a doubt, however, to frame the relation between Adorno and Arendt in this way involves us in yet further problems—for their respective relations to Heidegger are perhaps the most profound source of divergence and conflict between them. While Adorno engaged in relentless polemics against Heidegger's philosophy, culminating in the charge that it was "fascist to the core," Arendt—Heidegger's former student and lover—was powerfully influenced by categories of *Existenz* philosophy. Indeed, suspecting Adorno and his Frankfurt associates of conspiring to destroy what was left of Heidegger's reputation in the postwar period, Arendt went so far as to refer to Adorno in a letter to Karl Jaspers as a "half-Jew" and called him "one of the most repugnant people I know."[13] This has led Richard Wolin to claim that, like Heidegger, Arendt "suffered from 'polis envy'—a tendency to view modern political life as a precipitous fall from the glories of a highly mythologized Periclean heyday."[14]

If only things were so simple. Far from sharing Heidegger's "polis envy" and concomitant nostalgia, Arendt derisively characterizes Heidegger, in her important 1946 *Partisan Review* essay as "really (let us hope) the last Romantic."[15] Dana Villa and Seyla Benhabib have sought to show how Arendt criticized Heidegger for remaining within the tradition's tendency to displace praxis by poiesis. While, for Benhabib, Arendt's critical encounter with Heidegger takes the form of a "reluctant modernism," Villa argues that it leads to an "an-archic," postmodern conception of the political.[16] At the same time, as I have argued elsewhere,[17] from his very earliest philosophical statements to his posthumously published *Aesthetic Theory*, Adorno sought to engage in an immanent critique of Heidegger. Were Heidegger's thinking *actually* "fascist to the core," such a critique would simply not be possible; for immanent critique seeks to judge a philosophical position by standards immanent to it—a philosophy that was essentially fascistic would be bereft of such immanent standards, not to mention coherence, and therefore would fail to admit of immanent critique. Indeed, one would have to question the fruitfulness of engaging in a critique of so comprised a philosophy in any case.[18]

But what role could Heidegger have possibly played in the thinking of two German Jewish intellectuals whose most important writings were composed during a period of exile brought about by the very regime Heidegger rather enthusiastically served between 1933 and 1934 as rector of the University of Freiburg and never broke with thereafter?[19] The beginning of an answer to this question can be located in the fact that Heidegger's thinking represents one of the most powerful and influential challenges to the epistemological tradition in Western philosophy. This tradition, inaugurated by Descartes' radical doubt, culminates in Husserl's attempt to heal the rift opened by Cartesian doubt in the phenomenological analysis of intentionality. Heidegger's challenge to the epistemological tradition, whose roots he locates in the Platonic transformation of truth as *alētheia* or disclosure to correctness of representation, can be said to run roughly along two axes. The first is Heidegger's transformation of phenomenology from the pure analysis of the contents of consciousness to a hermeneutics that seeks to show how phenomena disclose themselves through logos or language—hence, the methodological discussion in section 7 of *Being and Time* of "phenomenology" as aiming at the disclosure of "phenomena" through "logos." The second axis is the detailed working out and clarification (through the "existential analytic") of the involvements in the "world" of the existing human being, or *Dasein*. It is through such existential analytic that Heidegger seeks to demonstrate the thoroughly temporal nature of the being (*Sein*) for whom being is at issue, in contradistinction to mere entities (*Seienden*) that are simply present-at-hand (*vorhanden*).

We can gain perspective on Adorno's and Arendt's approaches by briefly juxtaposing them to contemporary "post-foundationalist" interpretations of Heidegger in neopragmatism and poststructuralism. For neopragmatism, Heidegger, like Wittgenstein and Dewey, offers not so much new answers to old questions as a kind of therapy enabling us to liberate ourselves from the old questions as such. Thus, like the pragmatist tradition, Heidegger challenges the detached perspective of the observer or the "knowing that" by appealing to the situated perspective of the participant or the "knowing how." In deconstruction, the temporality of Being, understood in terms of the structuralist account of language as a system of differences, becomes transformed into the differing, deferring movement of differ*a*nce itself. Differ*a*nce always already subverts the binary logic that is constitutive of foundationalism.[20]

In a spirit not unlike that of Rorty and Derrida, in *Against Epistemology*—a text that takes as its epigram the maxim that "Mortals ought to think mortal thoughts"—Adorno calls not for a "first" but for a "last philosophy." That is, he calls for a philosophy that finally relinquishes its drive for solid grounds upon which a system can be constructed.[21] Such a critique of the subject-object paradigm decenters the subject and is therefore a crucial first move in the direction of opening up the possibility of a nonrepressive, nonsubsumptive reconciliation between reason and its other. As Adorno puts it in *Negative Dialectics*: "Reconciliation would be the mindfulness of the many as no longer inimical, which is anathema to subjective reason."[22] Similarly, Arendt's political theory is the result of what she calls a "thinking without banisters" (*Denken ohne Geländer*), that is, thinking without metaphysical supports. In contrast to the "tradition," such thinking would give the political realm—the realm of irreducible plurality—its due by relinquishing the cognitive drive of reducing appearances to essences.

As contributions to political theory and social critique, neopragmatism and deconstruction are inverse images of one another. While Rorty seeks to insulate liberal politics from Heidegger's insight into the world disclosive dimensions of Being by sealing it up within the relatively harmless realm of private ironism, Derrida, in contrast, radicalizes and generalizes world disclosure in a way that blurs the distinction between "interpreting the world" and "changing it." In his more exuberant moments, for instance, Derrida has asserted that there is "nothing beyond the text." It is possible to suggest, therefore, that in neopragmatism, the innovative power of world disclosure is "aestheticized" and hence marginalized; in deconstruction, it is generalized and spins, so to speak, out of control.[23] For Rorty, the breaking free of foundationalism "leaves everything as it is," while for Derrida, the deconstruction of philosophical foundations appears to be, at times, indistinguishable from the material transformation of social practices and institutions.[24] In other words, Rorty and Derrida, while seeking with Heidegger to deflate the claims of the metaphysical tradition, do not view such a deflation as resulting from a reembedding of philosophy into the history of social practices.

In contrast, in this essay I shall argue that, for both Adorno and Arendt, philosophy is not to be understood as a self-contained practice, but rather as determined by its location within the historical practices of society. Both appropriate Heidegger's decentering of the subject by situating it within the tissue of its worldly engagements; at the same time, however, they distance themselves from Heidegger's particular interpretation of temporality. Thus, if the epistemological tradition consistently attempts to establish the subject as transcendental by "bracketing" its a priori embeddedness, Adorno seeks to show how such a subject must be understood as the result of a set of dominant social practices—namely, those geared to self-preservation at all costs. Similarly, Arendt argues that "Heidegger's philosophy is the first *absolutely and uncompromisingly this-worldly philosophy*."[25] She attempts, therefore, to appropriate Heidegger's concept of the "world," that is, the context of significations constituted by what Heidegger calls *Zuhandenheit* (ready-to-hand). However, as we shall see below, Arendt transforms Heidegger's essentially instrumental understanding of the world—a context in which, as already suggested, "knowing how" takes precedence over "knowing that"—in such a way as to emphasize its intersubjective dimensions. In the process, Arendt transforms Heidegger's ambivalent notion of *mit-Sein*—being-with-others-in-the-world—into an understanding of the *political* as the space in which differences between individuals can be disclosed, recognized, and acknowledged *without* being reduced to a more general, unitary identity or essence.[26] In contrast to Rorty and Derrida, then, Adorno's and Arendt's respective *Auseinandersetzungen* or critical engagements with Heidegger involve an appropriation of his decentering and embedding of the subject for a critique of historically situated praxis.

Inextricable from such critical engagements are the experience of and reflections on exile that (as I have already suggested) form the decisive context for Adorno's and Arendt's most important writings.[27] One could say that Adorno and Arendt, like other Jewish and dissident intellectuals—what Martin Jay calls "permanent exiles"[28]—who were forced to flee Europe, lived in an immediate way the very experiences that Heidegger sought to come to grips with in *Sein und Zeit* through words such as *Unheimliche* (uncanny or unhomely), *Geworfenheit* (thrownness), *Befindlichkeit* (sensitivity), and so on. In other words, their experience of exile had a particularly disenchanting effect in their respective receptions of Heidegger. As Benhabib notes, "The events of this century caused the conditions of 'homelessness' and 'worldlessness' that [Arendt] had previously placed at the center of her presentation of Existenz philosophy to become the real life situation of millions upon millions of human beings."[29] As a result of her own experiences, which are not just incidental to the development of her thinking, Arendt could not *but* take a critical stance toward the very *Existenz* philosophy in which she was schooled. Hence, Benhabib argues that the central tension generating her "reluctant modernism," is the tension between *Existenz* philosophy and her experience as a Jewish woman in exile.

By the same token, in what could be taken as a direct rejoinder to Heidegger's understanding of language as the "house of Being," Adorno argues in *Minima Moralia* that "dwelling, in the proper sense, is now impossible."[30] In a way that draws expressly upon his own experience of exile, Adorno argues that

> The returning émigré, who has lost the naïve relationship to what is his own, must unite the most intimate relation to his native language with unflagging vigilance against any fraud it promotes; against the belief that what I should like to call the metaphysical excess of the German language in itself already guarantees the truth of the metaphysics it suggests, or of metaphysics in general.[31]

While sharing with Heidegger the Humboldtian idea of language as a necessary *constituent* of thought, Adorno holds that such an approach carries with it the burden of a higher degree of responsibility, given its tendency to refuse philosophical disputation and, consequently, its tendency to lapse into a "jargon of authenticity."[32]

In Adorno's and Arendt's respective engagements with Heidegger we find, then, a doubling of Heidegger's decentering of the epistemological subject. On the one hand, there is the decentering and reembedding of the epistemological subject whose involvements and concerns are shown to be irreducibly prior to the cognitive relation between subject and object. Yet, at the same time, rather than being grasped as "ontological," such a reembedding is understood historically, or to be more precise, in terms of the intertwining of nature and history—an intertwining that Adorno and Arendt experienced all too directly. If Heidegger's philosophy is a decisive turning away from Novalis's definition of philosophy as "the desire to be at home everywhere in the world," then we might say that Adorno and Arendt can be said to "leave home" twice over: first, as a break with the phenomenological project of recovering the unity of Being and Thought in the intentionality of consciousness; second, as the critique of Heidegger's fundamental ontology. Adorno's and Arendt's respective attempts to understand the twentieth century, then, are, at the same time, inextricable from reflections of their own experiences amid the natural-historical ruins that it has left in its wake. In what follows, I seek to show how in their respective writings, Adorno and Arendt transform the problematic of *Sein und Zeit* into that of natural history, before briefly examining the manner in which such a transformation leads them both, albeit in very different ways, to grapple with Kant's conception of reflective judgment as a way of redeeming transitory phenomena.

Sein und Zeit *as Natural History*

As I have already suggested, while he takes up a deeply polemical stance vis-à-vis Heidegger throughout his career, Adorno seeks nonetheless to develop his own concepts and categories out of an immanent critique of Heideggerian philosophy. Such an immanent critique plays a vitally strategic role, for example, in the structure of *Negative Dialectics*, a text that opens with an account of philosophical experience before moving to a critique of the "ontological need" through to an elaboration of models of "negative dialectics."[33] A much earlier, yet equally strategic, instance of Adorno's engagement with Heidegger emerges in his lecture "The Idea of Natural-History," delivered at the Kant-Gesellschaft in 1932. Taken together with other early writings, according to Rolf Tiedemann, this lecture can be seen as constituting a transition from the neo-Kantian position of his teacher Hans Cornelius to materialism.[34] In the lecture, Adorno argues that Heidegger succeeds in moving beyond the construal of time and being in antithetical terms, and thus overcomes "false stasis and formalism," that is, he pushes beyond the antithesis between the Platonic essences, on the one hand, and life, on the other. This step forward is, however, at the same time, a step backward, in as much as such a *Destruktion* is purchased as the cost of the subordination of history (*Geschichte*) to historicity (*Geschichtlichkeit*). From this, two implications follow: (1) the difference between real historical contingency and the *concept* of historical contingency, namely the concept of *Geschichtlichkeit*, is effaced; and, as a result, (2) ontology becomes tautological.[35] Actual historical events become, then, indistinguishable from Heidegger's own ontology. It is possible to discern here a question that will continue to occupy Adorno throughout his philosophical career, namely: How is it possible to think particularity *conceptually* without at the same time subsuming it? To the two critical points mentioned above—the problem of tautology and the elision of the difference between actual contingency and the concept of contingency—Adorno adds a third: (3) the aspiration not just to the systematic but a structural definition of the encompassing whole (*umfassende Ganzheit*) ultimately grounded in *Dasein*'s grasping its "own most possibility," understood as Being-towards-death.

Despite his far-reaching claims, Adorno insists on the *determinate as opposed to abstract nature* of this critique. Thus, what Heidegger demonstrates is the manner in which natural and historical elements are insuperably interwoven. Yet this insight can only be fully realized by moving away from the "possibilities of Being" (*Möglichkeiten des Seins*) in the direction of really existing entities (*Seienden*). The intentions of Heidegger's approach to the tradition can only be realized inasmuch as it relinquishes the ontological understanding of temporality and moves in the direction of a consideration of actual history itself. Yet such actual history cannot itself be construed exclusively as either the realm of pure freedom or the realm of natural necessity. For the second leads to "false absolutes," while the first leads to "false spiritualism."

Adorno seeks, therefore, to push the engagement with the philosophical "tradition" in a rather different direction than that of Heidegger himself. Drawing on the early Lukács's notion of "second nature" as the "charnel house of long dead interiorities," on the one hand, and the Benjaminian notion of "allegory," on the other, Adorno offers an alternative account of reification as the "forgetting" of what is transitory, or what he will call the "nonidentical." If Lukács, in *Theorie des Romans*, understands history as comprised of cultural forms or conventions that, over time, acquire a certain inertia and therefore come to be experienced as a kind of natural necessity, antithetical to the will of those who produced them, Benjamin detects in Baroque *Trauerspiel* (play of mourning) nature as an allegorical text in which it is possible to read the unfolding of historical events. The setting of the sun, for example, allegorizes the death of a tyrant.[36]

In the process, Adorno transforms the categorial opposition of being and time into the concept of natural history, which enables him to adhere to Heidegger's intentions of undermining this traditional opposition, without allowing either side of the opposition simply to collapse into the other.

Indeed, rather than permitting these oppositions to remain static, Adorno seeks to grasp history at its most *historical* as nature; at the same time, he seeks to grasp nature at its most *natural* as history.[37] The dereifying strategy of undermining the opposition between nature and history aims at releasing the "new" or transience from its reduction to either a naturalized history *or* a historicized nature—Heidegger's *Geschichtlichkeit* or Hegel's *Weltgeschichte*. The critical intention of the idea of *Naturgeschichte* aims at "the new in its newness, not as something that can be translated back into the old existing forms."[38] This problem of addressing the novelty of the "new" leads Adorno, as it does Arendt, to a rethinking of aesthetic judgment. I shall return to this question in the conclusion. Adorno uses the concept of *natural history* as a model in *Dialectic of Enlightenment*, which seeks to lay bare the entwinement of myth (or nature) and enlightenment (or history). While it might seem peculiar to read this text as a response to *Being and Time*, it is worth bearing in mind that Adorno refers in the preface to his 1927 dissertation *Der Begriff des Unbewußtsein in der transzendentalen Seelenlehre* as intending enlightenment in a double sense: first, as the enlightenment of "problematic concepts," and, second, "but also as Enlightenment as the goal in the comprehensive sense, which lends history to the concept."[39]

Natural History as the Intertwining of Enlightenment and Myth

Dialectic of Enlightenment, which Adorno composed with Horkheimer during their years of exile in California, retraces and repeats *Geist's* path of experience, the "Cunning of Reason," as an explicitly sacrificial logic.[40] The historical accomplishments of *Geist*, far from leaving nature behind, are shown to be themselves repetitions of nature. At the same time, the natural (myth) is revealed to be always already historical—that is, as manifesting the logic of disenchantment through rational labor. Adorno and Horkheimer's re-presentation of enlightenment as a sacrificial logic is undertaken with the explicit if, as they admit in the introduction, self-contradictory aim of pushing, by way of reflection, beyond the structure of repetition in which enlightenment seems to be perpetually and irredeemably trapped. Yet at the same time, such a reading cancels out the possibility of conceiving the "new" as the return to an allegedly "primordial experience" that is said by Heidegger to lie beneath the hardened structures of the tradition.

As Adorno puts it, the concept of natural history "does not glorify concern with the original as more primordial than concern with what is mediated, because for it primordiality is itself an object of reflection, something negative."[41] The retracing of enlightenment as myth is therefore undertaken in the service of a transformed concept of enlightenment. Undermining the theodicy of the Hegelian concept—that is to say, the philosophical justification of the rational necessity of human suffering in history—*Dialectic of Enlightenment* shows, in contrast, that the "Cunning of Reason" does not culminate in the plenitude and fullness of a return of *Geist* "home" to itself, but rather in a living death. In other words, the drive to self-preservation at all costs issues in the senseless denial of the very life it seeks to preserve.

Such a dialectic is revealed through an allegorical reading of the *Odyssey* as the "primal history of subjectivity" in which "the self does not constitute the fixed antithesis to adventure, but in its rigidity molds itself only by way of that antithesis: being an entity only in the diversity of that which denies all unity."[42] Like Spirit on its path of doubt (*Zweifels*) and despair (*Verzweiflung*), Odysseus loses himself in order to find himself. However, rather than ultimately finding himself through the progressive subordination of nature to his own purposes, Odysseus obliterates his own sensual nature by repeating blind nature or domination:

> Like the heroes of all true novels later on, Odysseus loses himself in order to find himself; the estrangement from nature that he brings about is realized in the process of the abandonment to nature he contends with in each adventure; and ironically, when he, inexorable, returns home, the inexorable force he commands itself triumphs as the judge and avenger of the legacy of the powers from which he escaped.[43]

The very *inexorability* of the return, the fact of its being determined in advance, confirms, not a break with, but a repetition of the mythological always-the-same (*das Immergleiche*).

The sacrificial logic of enlightenment consists, then, in the repetition of sacrifice, by means of which external nature is mastered through *renunciation* or self-sacrifice. In other words, the nature confronted by the subject is experienced as so frightening that the self is forced to do frightening things to itself in order to survive it; the control of external nature is paid for by an equivalent mastering of the spontaneity of the subject itself. This is exemplified by Odysseus's encounter with the Sirens—who signify the past as the promise of a future happiness. Such a mastery of nature is itself conditional upon the progressive displacement of mimesis as approximation to nature, as manifested in magic, by a deathly form of imitation. The latter is a morbid imitation of, and consequent adaptation to, a nature that, by virtue of the process of rationalization and disenchantment, has become lifeless. The speculative dialectic through which the identity of subject and object is achieved by way of alienation is thereby given an ironic turn: the mirror in which Spirit seeks to catch a glimpse of its own reflection reflects back not the realization and fulfillment of the identity of the knowing subject but, rather, its own destruction. It is here that the full allegorical force of the text reveals itself. The destruction of external nature is, in other words, read as a text in which the fate of the historical subject is written: "For the ego which sinks into the meaningless abyss of itself, objects become allegories of destruction which contain the meaning of its downfall."[44] Read through the allegorical structure of the chiasmus of natural history, Odysseus's journey becomes demythologization as the repetition of myth just as myth is always already enlightenment. Odysseus is compelled to repeat myth at the very moment that he believes himself to have broken with it. In the process, history is revealed as an enchanted "second nature," while nature is understood in terms of a historical process of disenchantment, rationalization, and therefore domination.[45]

Where enlightenment and myth converge most sharply is in Oedipus's anthropomorphic answer to the riddle of the Sphinx. To her riddle, "What goes on four legs in the morning, two legs in the day, and three at night?" the cunning Oedipus answers: "It is man."[46] This answer allegorizes the cost to the subject of its mastery of external nature, inasmuch as the manifold, which not insignificantly manifests itself temporally, is reduced to the unity. Thus, where enlightenment and myth converge is in their logics of sacrifice: while myth involves the external propitiation or appeasement of the gods, enlightenment *internalizes* sacrifice as the renunciation of the self.

I have sought to show how, transformed into the categories of natural history, Adorno seeks to lay bare the intertwining of history and myth as the counterpart of Heidegger's thesis of *Seinsvergessenheit*. We might further be able to clarify the manner in which these processes take place within language itself by way of Nietzsche's early critique of truth. In "On Truth and Lies in a Non-Moral Sense," which forms part of Nietzsche's *Nachlass* writings from the period 1870–72, Nietzsche argues that "Truths are illusions which we have forgotten are illusions; they are metaphors that have become worn out and have been drained of sensuous force, coins which have lost their embossing and are now considered as metal and no longer as coins."[47]

The formation of concepts is constituted out of a certain kind of reification or forgetting. While originally signifying the experience of a particular, the word/concept then is extended to other particulars that bear a similarity to it. However, in the process the *difference* between these particulars is thereby covered over. What is to be included is excluded precisely by this inclusion.

> In particular, let us further consider the formation of concepts. Every word instantly becomes a concept precisely insofar as it is not supposed to serve as a reminder of the unique and entirely individual original experience to which it owes its origin; but rather, a word becomes a concept insofar as it simultaneously has to fit countless more or less similar cases—which means, purely and simply, cases which are never equal and thus altogether unequal. Every concept arises from the equation of unequal things.[48]

Leaving aside, for the moment, the question of the possibility of an entirely original experience (*Urerlebnisse*), Nietzsche's reflections provide a crucial framework for Adorno and Heidegger's own engagements with the philosophical tradition. *Sein und Zeit* can be regarded as seeking to lay bare, as a particular *Holzweg*, the history of Western ontology that perpetuates *Seinsvergessenheit*—a forgetfulness of that which it seeks to grasp, namely, *Sein*. That is to say, while purporting to grasp Being, because it simply reduces it to abstract generality, to what is *vorhanden*, the tradition engages in a forgetting of the experiences that give rise to the thinking of Being in the first place. Namely, the difference between the Being for whom being is, itself a question, on the one hand, and simple entities, on the other.

If Heidegger roots the reification of Being in the context of a tradition that compulsively forgets the question of the meaning of Being, Adorno roots the equation of what is unequal in the very structure of language that is itself inextricable from the social *logic* of exchange in which it is embedded. The increasing emptiness of the signifier is the result of a historical process involving, not the disenchantment of myth, but rather the repetition of mythical sacrifice as rational self-renunciation.[49] In other words, Adorno attempts to understand philosophical concepts as arising out of specific, dominant forms of social practice, namely, those oriented, even after they have long ceased serving this purpose, to self-preservation. Thus, while negative dialectics seeks to root philosophical concepts in the very experience—social suffering—that they themselves mask, *Dialectic of Enlightenment* can be read as seeking to elucidate this logic in solidarity with those who were sacrificed by its unfolding.

Dialectic of Enlightenment can be read as an unfolding of the dialectic of nature and history that emerges, at least in part, as a response to Heidegger's *Being and Time*. Adorno is not unsympathetic to Heidegger's critique of the epistemological tradition that opens up the possibility of understanding the subject-object relation, not as the transcendental, but rather the product of a historical *differentiation*. At the same time, however, Adorno recognizes that it is precisely Heidegger's attempt to undermine the opposition between time and Being that leads to an ontologization of history. As Adorno argues,

> If it is the case that no metaphysical thought was ever created which has not been a constellation of elements of experience, then, in the present instance, the seminal experiences of metaphysics are simply diminished by a habit of thought which sublimate them into metaphysical pain and splits them off from the real pain that gives rise to them.[50]

The implication of such a move is that it freezes contingent, historical social practices into that which is unchanging and unchangeable. In contrast, in *Dialectic of Enlightenment*, Adorno and Horkheimer seek to provide a history of subjectivity in which the elements of experience that have crystallized in concepts are rooted in an account of a process in which nature and history—as a history of suffering—are mutually inextricable.

Arendt and the Fate of the Political

Arendt's account of modernity has typically been read as an attempt to engage in a thoroughgoing critique of Marx's concept of labor by way of a rehabilitation of the categories of Aristotelian political theory.[51] This has, however, begun to give way, since the appearance of Elżbieta Ettinger's book *Hannah Arendt / Martin Heidegger* (1995), to interpretations that pay more attention to Arendt's dialogue with Heidegger. Basing her short account of the relations between Arendt and Heidegger on previously unavailable correspondence between the two, Ettinger shows the extent to which Arendt was intellectually indebted to Heidegger in addition to being emotionally involved with him. This intellectual debt is perhaps nowhere more pronounced than in *The Human Condition*. As Arendt wrote to Heidegger, "You will see that the book has no dedication. If things had ever worked out between us . . . then I would have asked you if I could have dedicated the book to you. It grew right out of the first days in Marburg and so in all respects [is] indebted to you."[52]

Arendt takes Heidegger's decentering of the epistemological subject as her point of departure like Adorno, but reorients it toward the "world," whereas Adorno decenters the subject in relation to a nature from which it has *only apparently* managed to free itself. Moreover, Arendt transforms the Heideggerian concept of the world by emphasizing being-with-others (*mit-Sein*), an aspect that Heidegger viewed with some suspicion. The critical thrust of Arendt's political theory lies in its account of the progressive "de-worlding" of the world or world-alienation, corresponding to a concomitant subjectivism in modern society. Such a loss of the world, at the same time, corresponds to the withdrawal of the political. In contrast, then, to Heidegger, who views the phenomenon of "de-worlding" as immanent in the "tradition," Arendt views it as inextricable from actual history. Indeed, the progressive "de-worlding" of the world is, itself, the result of what Arendt calls the "interpenetration" of nature and history.[53]

While it is beyond the scope of this essay to engage in a detailed discussion of Heidegger's conception of the world, it might be possible to elucidate its basic contours by reference to *Being and Time*'s important discussion of the tool. As a way of undermining the epistemological tradition, specifically the Cartesian resolution of being in the world into subject and object, which, in turn, serves as the basis for the idealist opposition between "spirit" and "nature," Heidegger seeks to show how the relation between the cognitive subject, on the one hand, and its object, on the other, is not prior but rather anterior to the worldly entanglements—characterized by *Dasein*'s *Zuhandenheit* (ready-at-hand). That is to say, it is only when there is a gap, a rift or tear, in the referential context of the *world*, that an object in its isolation presents itself as that which is *vorhanden* (present-at-hand). In Heidegger's famous example, only when a tool, a hammer in this case, breaks down does the object as *zuhanden*, that is, submerged in a web of relations characterized by the "in-order-to," reveal itself as something *vorhanden*, that is, as a naked object.

In contrast to Heidegger's conception of the world, Arendt seeks to show that, while brought into existence via instrumental activity, the world is more than simply a totality of equipment. The world is comprised of those objects, paradigmatically, art works, whose vocation it is to preserve the transitory nature of situated human action.

> Because of their outstanding permanence, works of art are the most intensely worldly of all tangible things; their durability is almost untouched by the corroding effect of natural processes, since they are not subject to the use of living creatures, a use which, indeed, far from actualizing their inherent purpose—as the purpose of a chair is actualized when it is sat upon—can only destroy them. Thus, their durability is of a higher order than that which all things need in order to exist at all; it can attain permanence throughout the ages. In this permanence, the very stability of the human artifice, which, being inhabited and used by mortals can never be absolute, achieves a representation of its own.[54]

The world is constituted by a totality of objects that, in their durability, are able to withstand the endless flux and flow of natural processes. Indeed, it is precisely by being opposed to the circular time of nature that such objects create the possibility of rectilinear time—the past, present, and future—that is the basis for history. Worldly objects transcend both those who make them and the subjects whose memory they preserve. The fate of the political is inextricable from that of the world, for the latter has a doubled relation with praxis. On the one hand, the objects that comprise the world preserve the memory of those forms of action that are specifically political—deeds and speeches—and, at the same time, such works, taken as a whole, form the ongoing context in which political action can take place. The intersubjective nature of the world should, therefore, be clear: the common world forms the horizon against which praxis, understood as exemplary self-disclosure, is possible. Indeed, only by virtue of the "worlding of the world" is it possible for humanity to rise above the pure flow and flux of nature that, in and of itself, is antithetical to meaning and hence ultimately futile.

Arendt argues, therefore, that the experience that has been covered over is not the question of the meaning of Being, as such, but rather the intersubjective experience of praxis.[55] In so doing, she turns her appropriation of Heidegger's philosophy against Heidegger himself, that is, against his own deep-seated suspicion of the public realm, or what he calls *die Öffentlichkeit des Man*—the perennial tendency of *Dasein* to lose itself in inauthentic modes of Being.[56] Arendt argues that, while seeking to engage in a *Destruktion* of the tradition of Western ontology, Heidegger is, himself, unable shake off the anti-political prejudices of this tradition.[57] Such prejudices are manifested paradigmatically in Plato's cave allegory, in which the philosopher takes his leave of the world, disparaged as the realm of *mere* appearance and contingency, and juxtaposed to the eternal realm of the forms. Thus, according to Arendt, if philosophy enters the public realm, it is not to partake of the realm of appearances as appearances, but rather to make such a contingent and indeed dangerous world—a world in which Socrates was put to death—safe for the contemplative practices of philosophy. In other words, Arendt argues that by construing the world as a "totality of equipment," Heidegger remains within the tradition's attempt to subordinate action to work, praxis to poeisis.

If the tradition is constituted, not so much by a forgetting of the meaning of Being, as by a reductive treatment of the *vita activa*, then Arendt seeks a *Destruktion* of the tradition that involves a detailed working out of the basic categories of the *vita activa*: labor, work, and action and the temporal modalities specific to each. Labor has no beginning and no end; it is that form of activity corresponding to the basic biological needs of the human body, hence, "The human condition of labor is life itself."[58] Action, in contrast, is precisely that dimension of the *vita activa* that has managed to transcend the necessity of sustaining biological life. If the condition of labor is life per se (*zōē*), the life that the human species as a species shares with the rest of nature, then action corresponds to that form of individual life (*bios*) differentiated from the species in that it is characterized, not by circularity, but rather by its rectilinear direction, that is, between natality and mortality. In contrast to labor, action has a definite beginning, yet given its contingent, open-ended character, it cannot be said to have a definite end. Action corresponds to the human condition of plurality: "to the fact that men, not Man, live on the earth and inhabit the world."[59]

Standing between labor, on the one hand, and action on the other, is work. As the production of specific objects that, unlike labor, is not consumed in but rather transcends the production process, work is defined by a clearly delineated beginning and end. Work is the specifically *unnatural* aspect of the *vita activa*, inasmuch as it is through work that humanity distinguishes itself from other natural beings by raising itself up out of nature. This it does through fabricating enduring (*vorhanden*) objects that, as it were, create a wall between human beings, on the one hand, and nature on the other. Inasmuch as they arrest the unending flow of natural processes, that is, inasmuch as these objects establish meaning, they participate in opening up a world. While labor and work serve as its necessary conditions, it is through action—liberated from the shackles of external necessity, as in the production of the mere conditions of life, or in the teleocratic activity of fabrication—that individuals are able to disclose themselves through the exemplarity or uniqueness (Arendt calls it "greatness") of their actions and words. "While all aspects of the human condition are somehow related to politics, this plurality is specifically *the* condition—not only the *conditio sine qua non*, but the *conditio per quam*—of all political life."[60]

The critical thrust of Arendt's political theory lies in showing that modernity is constituted by the progressive de-worlding of the world. If the world is that totality of artifacts that constitutes a buffer between finite human life (*bios*), on the one hand, and life as such (*zōē*), on the other, then the phenomenon of world-alienation marks the progressive reduction of the former to the latter. In other words, the phenomenon of "de-worlding of the world" is to be understood as a progressive naturalization of history that is, at the same time, a historicization of nature. Human history comes to be understood as regulated by iron laws of motion, while historically unprecedented events, such as the splitting of the atom, are initiated within nature. The merging of the natural and the historical comes about in the increasing propensity within the historical and natural sciences to understand their respective objects, no longer in terms of different orders of *objects* per se but, rather, as processes. Arendt argues that the connection between nature and history lies

> In the concept of process: both imply that we think and consider everything in terms of processes and are not concerned with single entities or individual occurrences and their special separate causes. The key words of modern historiography—"development" and "progress"—were, in the nineteenth century, also the key words of the then new branches of natural science, particularly biology and geology, one dealing with animal life and the other even with non-organic matter in terms of historical processes.[61]

Arendt understands the phenomenon of world-alienation in terms of two distinct inversions. The first inversion lies in the relationship between the *vita contemplativa* and the *vita activa* as the two fundamental dimensions of the human condition. For the Greeks, contemplation was superior to action, as in Aristotle's characterization of the good life in the *Nicomachean Ethics* as the life dedicated to contemplation. Such an inversion can be seen for example in Marx's privileging of praxis over theory and in Nietzsche's will to power (*Wille zur Macht*). Indeed, while the ancients viewed knowledge as the quiet contemplation of an inherently rational or ordered cosmos, for the moderns, knowledge was that which had to be accomplished through action, namely, through the man-made reconstruction of natural processes. Galileo's decisive proof of the cogency of the heliocentric conception of the universe unleashed an unprecedented questioning of the veracity of the senses: "Nothing could be less trustworthy for acquiring knowledge and approaching truth than passive observation or mere contemplation."[62] In other words, it led to a pervasive skepticism as regards knowledge of those phenomena not *made* by human being themselves.

Within this inversion of the relation between contemplation and action, there is a further inversion that comes about within the *vita activa* itself. The ancient hierarchical conception of the *vita activa*, as quintessentially expressed in Aristotle's political theory, had placed praxis as *ontologically* prior to the production and reproduction of the conditions of life through labor in the *oikos*, or household economy.[63] As Arendt suggests,

> The "good life," as Aristotle called the life of the citizen, therefore was not merely better, more care free or nobler than ordinary life, but of an altogether different quality. It was "good" to the extent that by having mastered the necessities of sheer life, by being freed from labor and work, and by overcoming the innate urge of all living creatures for their own survival, it was no longer bound to the biological life process.[64]

Yet with Galileo's proof by way of the telescope of the heliocentric conception of the universe, the experience of fabrication acquires a dignity that raises it above action. Displacing the traditional questions concerning the "what" and the "why," or final causality, is the question concerning the "how," or efficient causality. Scientists increasingly sought to answer this question by imitating and reproducing natural processes in their experiments. However, while at the very moment that the experience of *homo faber* was establishing its priority within the *vita activa* and, indeed, over the *vita contemplativa*, this experience was, itself, undergoing an important transformation. Traditionally, work was understood as instrumental activity directed to a given end, namely, the production of an object to which such activity was necessarily subordinate. Under modern conditions, the experience of *homo faber* becomes detached from the ends that it might realize; henceforth *process* becomes an end in itself. Under conditions of modernity, work collapses into the process-like quality of labor. The triumph of the most "natural" form of the *vita activa*, namely, labor, represents the final regression of the distinctively human condition into mere life: *bios* is reduced to *zōē*.

The two inversions that, for Arendt, constitute the phenomenon of the "de-worlding of the world" can be seen to crystallize in the interpenetration of nature and history. She seeks to undermine the opposition of nature and history, just as Adorno attempts to grasp history at its most historical as *nature*, and nature at its most natural as *history*. Arendt sees such an interpenetration at work in the putative opposition of Darwin's evolutionary conception of nature and Marx's materialist conception of history—both of which are used and abused in such a way as to form historicist justifications for totalitarian politics. Arendt argues that while Darwin's "nature" is not circular but linear and thus is at bottom historical, Marx's "history" is the expression of a biologistic, metabolic process and, hence, natural. The ideological justification of totalitarianism culminates, therefore, in a joining of nature revealed as historical and a history understood as exhibiting natural "iron laws of historical motion."

The culmination of historicism in totalitarianism, in which society is, as a whole, constantly kept in motion, makes clear that the essence of the joining of the natural and historical consists of a sacrifice of the particular, which, as it were, gets swept away by the torrential flood of the historical process. Where the conceptions of "nature" and "history" meet is in their shared justification of the necessity of a sacrificing of singular individuals— the victims, as it were of historical progress—to suprahuman, "universal" laws of historical motion.[65] Indeed, the attempt to do justice to the specificity of historical events lies at the heart of Arendt's late turn to Kant's theory of reflective judgment, to which I shall return in the conclusion.

The specifically sacrificial dimensions of the eclipse of the political— and thereby the condition of plurality—by the social become especially clear if we read *The Human Condition* in light of Arendt's earlier work. According to Hannah Pitkin, Arendt's central conceptual distinctions arise from her early attempt to work out the relation between "parvenu" and "pariah" in her biography of Rahel Varnhagen, which she completed in exile in France.[66] A central moment in the genealogy of the concept of the social in Arendt's thinking is a characterization of the social as embodying an exclusionary logic. The relation between "parvenu" and "pariah" is to be understood in terms of their differential relations vis-à-vis society. While the pariah is excluded because of her difference—in the case of Varnhagen, because she was a Jewish woman—the parvenu is one who does whatever is required in order to gain acceptance in the very society that excludes those "like" her, including, of course, sacrificing a crucial aspect—what could be called the "nonidentity"—of her own identity. The pariah can only gain entry to the social, that is, become a parvenu, by accepting and internalizing society's exclusionary logic. As against the perspective of the conformism and self-loathing of the parvenu, Arendt advocates the perspective of what she calls that of the "conscious pariah"—the individual who, far from seeking to gain admittance to and acceptance in a society that would exclude the other, takes a stand of solidarity *against* the exclusions that constitute that society with those others similarly excluded. The standpoint of the conscious pariah is what Arendt comes to understand as the political. The political itself embodies the tension comprised of, on the one hand, a recognition of differences between individuals, that is, plurality, and the possibility of sharing and *acting* together in a shared world. The political, then, can be said to involve a kind of nonreductive being-together of difference.[67] Understood in light of her earlier writings completed as she was in flight from the Hitler regime, Arendt's understanding of the inversions of modernity can be now recognized as involving the sacrifice of difference. For if the formation of modernity rests on the progressive eclipse of the political—which is, itself, that space in which differences can appear without being reduced to a common essence, yet on the common horizon of shared world—then modernity is characterized by the increasing subordination of difference to identity. This logic, particularly spelled out in the *Origins of Totalitarianism,* culminates in the concentration camp (*Lager*), in which the spaces between individuals are completely eliminated. With the withdrawal of such spaces, the victims of the camps become squeezed together violently, as by a band of iron, into a single identity.[68]

Writing and Judging

I have sought to argue that Adorno's account of the intertwining of myth and enlightenment can be read as a response to Heidegger's attempt to engage in a deconstruction of the opposition of "time" and "being" by way of the "existential analytic of *Dasein.*" While Adorno is sympathetic to the overall intensions of that strategy, he is deeply suspicious of collapsing the opposition, which he seeks, in contrast, to understand as the relation between nature and history. He seeks to appropriate this opposition as a way of uncovering the hidden convergence of myth and enlightenment in their shared propensity to sacrifice or subsume transitory phenomena or the nonidentical to the universal. I have also sought to show how Hannah Arendt takes up, in parallel fashion, Heidegger's engagement with the tradition in such a way as to diagnose the baleful withdrawal of the political in the face of the overwhelming reach of the increasingly technologically mediated production and reproduction of mere life constitutive of what she calls the social. Yet this line of argumentation should not be permitted to obscure the considerable differences in their critiques of Heidegger. While Arendt takes up Heidegger's decentering of the subject through the "world," which she—in direct opposition to Heidegger—interprets as the space of the political, Adorno turns this decentering in the direction of what he calls the "primacy of the object." If for Adorno what is consigned to oblivion in the dialectic of enlightenment is "the drive for complete, universal and undivided happiness,"[69] then for Arendt it is the possibility of posing the question of the "good life." Thus while Adorno and Arendt seek to understand modernity as a particular intertwining of nature and history, each can be said to accord relative priority to one side of the opposition over the other.

It is not altogether clear, however, how Adorno and Arendt conceive a way beyond the becoming-historical of nature and the naturalization of historical phenomena. While Adorno and Horkheimer discern the utopian content of the Enlightenment in an *Eingedenken* (mindfulness) of suffering nature, it is not clear how such a mindfulness of nature is to transform praxis. By the same token, Arendt's critique of modernity seems to rest, at least in *The Human Condition,* on little more than an evocation of a praxis *irrevocably* lost. Given the apparently irrevocable nature of the withdrawal of such praxis, how is the public space to be reconstituted in the face of the totalitarian tendencies of modern society? A clue to answering this question can be located in the very manner in which both writers characterize modernity's sacrificial logic: they tellingly describe it *literally* as a process of assimilation. That is to say, they understand it as an in-corporation, a subordinating inclusion, of what is particular or nonidentical in the social body. Hence, in *Dialectic of Enlightenment,* as previously suggested, enlightenment's repetition compulsion is understood as a Hobbesian condition of "devouring and being devoured"; identity-thinking is "belly turned mind." Similarly, in an essay entitled "The Concept of Culture," Arendt describes the "entertainment industry" as being "confronted by gargantuan appetites," which must as a consequence constantly pillage the history of culture in order to find suitable material. However, in order for such material to be "entertaining, it must be prepared and easily consumed." Therefore, "mass culture . . . will literally consume the cultural objects, eat them up and destroy them."[70] Thus, Arendt understands the phenomenon of "world-alienation" as, inter alia, the subjection of art objects to a biological process of production and consumption.

Far from being incidental, one could argue that this characterization of the central developmental feature of modernity—the *devouring or swallowing up* of the particular by the universal—might be understood through their respective turns toward reevaluating the significance of aesthetic judgment. In other words, if for Adorno and Arendt, modernity involves the subordination of the "new" to the always-the-same, then it is in aesthetic judgment, that the "new" is specifically posed as a problem. This is because, unlike determinative judgment in which a law, principle, or concept is *already* given and merely awaits application, reflective judgment is characterized by precisely the absence of the former. If cognition involves the subsumption of a particular beneath a universal, then reflective judgment involves a raising or lifting *(erheben)* of the particular to universality. For example, when I judge *this* particular rose to be beautiful, I do not claim: "All roses are beautiful, this flower is a rose, hence this rose is beautiful"; nor do I say: "Beauty is roses, this flower is a rose, this rose is beautiful." Rather, I am judging the object in its *singularity*. The temporal nature of such singularity becomes especially pronounced with the turn of aesthetics away from natural beauty in the late eighteenth century to works of art in the nineteenth, in which the question then becomes, not whether a given object can be judged to be beautiful or not, but rather whether it can be judged *aesthetically* or not, that is to say, as an *art* object. Here, the question that arises is the following: How is it possible to judge a given object as an artwork when there are simply no existing criteria that could orient such a judgment? More specifically, how is it possible to judge an object as an artwork when it represents, not the exemplification of existing forms and/or artistic practices, but rather the often explicit negation of such forms as, for example, in the case of the historical avant-garde? How, in other words, is it possible to judge an object as an artwork when such an object wishes to negate the bourgeois institution, if not the entire history, of art, by sole virtue of which it can announce the *shock of the new*?

Returning specifically to the problem with which we started this section, namely, the propensity in modernity for the universal to *in-corporate* the particular, it is worth noting that central to aesthetic judgment, as Kant had conceived it, is the antinomy of taste, namely, the opposition of two antithetical claims: taste is subjective and thus conceptless, on the one hand, or taste is objective and based on concepts, on the other.[71] The relation between the two forms of taste forms the basis of Arendt's discussion of Kant's Third Critique, which, as she notes, Kant as late as 1787 called the "Critique of Taste."[72] Why, Arendt asks, does Kant seek to base a theory of judgment on "taste," as opposed to the more objective sense of sight? Indeed, how is judgment even possible in the case of senses such as taste and smell, where the taste of a sumptuous meal or the smell of a fragrant rose, admit of no *re-presentation*? In both cases, the object is, as it were, immediately *annihilated* in its being experienced. It is for this reason that questions of taste were held to be beyond dispute: "De gustibus non disputandum est." At the same time, it is *precisely* because taste is inherently discriminatory and addresses the singularity of an object that it becomes the vehicle of reflective judgment. As Arendt puts it:

> taste and smell are the most private of the senses; that is, they sense not an object but a sensation, and this sensation is not object-bound and cannot be recollected. . . . At the same time . . . only taste and smell are discriminatory by their very nature and. . . only these senses relate to the particular *qua* particular, whereas all objects given to the objective senses share their properties with other objects, that is, they are not unique.[73]

Reflective judgment, then, begins with the particular, but does not simply serve as the expression of a subjective preference; rather, it makes a claim to universality. In asserting that this particular rose is beautiful, I am not simply claiming that *I* like it but that *everyone* ought also to consider it beautiful. How, in the absence of a concept under which to subsume this particular object, is it possible to assert the necessity, that is, the binding quality, of this judgment? The judgment of an object as beautiful, in other words, is not simply subjective, but, insofar as such judgments do not simply derive from the *concept* of beauty, neither is it objective. How can a judgment be both nonsubjective and nonobjective?

In Arendt's view, the answer lies in mediation between the imagination and the *sensus communis*—common, or shared communal, sense. The imagination establishes distance between the object and the subject judging it in as much as it enables the subject to re-present the (absent) object. Reflective judgment is premised on what Kant called the "enlargement of thought," the ability to take into account the "possible rather than the actual judgments of others, and by putting ourselves in the place of any other man."[74] The greater the individual's ability to engage in this thought experiment, the more general her thought will be. Such generality, again, must be distinguished from the empty generality of the concept, which works from the universal to particular, for example, from the concept of "table" to the different objects that could be classified under it. The generality that emerges from an "enlarged mentality" is "closely connected with particulars, with the particular conditions of the standpoints one has to go through in order to arrive at one's own 'general standpoint.'"[75] In other words, the generality of reflective judgment entails the ability to view an object from a multiplicity of standpoints or perspectives as a process of arriving at one's own viewpoint rather than simply subsuming a particular object as a species of a genus. Only through its re-presentation by way of the faculty of imagination can an object be reflected upon and thus judged to be beautiful. What is at issue, then, is not the sensually given rose, in relation to which we have managed to establish a certain distance, but rather the act of *judging* it. The pleasure in the judgment of objects, as opposed to the objects themselves, is a pleasure that is only possible in the context of a "world" shared with others, that is, it is possible only in the context of being-in-the-world-with-others (*mit-Sein*). Because aesthetic judgments can never compel in a way that logical proofs can, such judgments necessarily must rely on persuasion, and therefore, in the final instance, on a *sensus communis*.

Arendt's answer to the problem of sacrifice of the particular entailed in the progressive intertwining of nature and history, then, rests upon a rehabilitation of Kant's reflective judgment as the political faculty par excellence. Such rehabilitation hinges, moreover, on the central role played by the *sensus communis*. What makes possible the "nonsubjective" yet, at the same time, "nonobjective" nature of reflective judgment is the ability of the citizen to enlarge his or her mentality in the context of the political community of which he or she is a member. Yet, at the same time, such a reading of Kant is deeply perplexing. It is clearly at odds with Arendt's own account of modernity, in which, as we have seen, with the triumph of the social—and the consequent elimination of spaces between individuals—the conditions for the possibility of a *sensus communis* have all but been destroyed. Central to the process of the de-worlding of the meaningful objects and stories that taken together create a world is a corresponding destruction of tradition that had once provided criteria that oriented judgment. The paradox is that it is precisely the irrevocable erosion of the *sensus communis* in endless, immediate production and consumption that characterizes the "social" that occasions Arendt's turn to the rehabilitation of reflective judgment in the first place. Arendt's attempt to rejuvenate the political by recovering aesthetic judgment ultimately fails, inasmuch as it succumbs to a *petitio principii,* begging its own question by presupposing precisely that which it seeks to effect, namely, the recovery of the common, public world.

For Arendt it is through judging that we make ourselves at "home in the world," Ronald Beiner has suggested.[76] "For a man who no longer has a homeland, writing becomes a place to live," Adorno says in *Minima Moralia.*[77] While Arendt attempts to read Kant's Third Critique as his authentic political philosophy, Adorno appropriates Kant's concept of reflective judgment by transforming it into "writing." It is writing that unfolds the mediation of subject and object *as* intellectual experience. Arguably, Adorno's most sustained reflection on writing can be found in his unpublished piece "Der Essay als Form." In this important essay, Adorno returns to the historical bifurcation of communication and expression, science and art, introduced in *Dialektik der Aufklärung.* While acknowledging that it is simply not possible to reconcile the objectivism of science and the subjectivism of art in the form of an encompassing totality, Adorno argues that it is, indeed, possible, via the essay form, to place communication and expression in a specific relation with each other. While communication makes an object available "for others," expression adheres to the "thing itself." It is precisely this tension, the tension between universal (communicability) and particularity (expression), that the essay form seeks to hold within a productive tension, or *Kraftfeld*. Inasmuch as they embody this tension, essays represent a polemical stance vis-à-vis the priority of cognition within philosophy, by which the particular is either viewed as an exemplification of the universal or is rendered transparent by means of it. At the same time, inasmuch as it is oriented to uncovering truth by the use of concepts, the essay cannot, contrary to the early Lukács, be conceived of as an artwork itself. The essay seeks to realize the intentions of Adorno's conception of philosophy: to give thought the density of experience without, at the same time, losing its stringency.[78] Accordingly, the experiential moment of the essay results from an almost total immersion in the particularity of an object without, at the same time, renouncing the use of concepts and therefore the stringency of thought. At the same time, the essay does not use such concepts to subsume its objects, otherwise the particularity of its object would be sacrificed. The essay, then, embodies the following antinomy: (i) the concept sacrifices the nonidentical; (ii) the essay cannot do without concepts. This antinomy is overcome, that is to say, the nonidentity that is sacrificed, is redeemed by the mimetic unfolding of experience expressed as style.[79] Thus, "The manner of expression is to salvage the precision of the objectified contents sacrificed when definition is omitted, without betraying the subject matter to the arbitrariness of conceptual meanings decreed once and for all."[80] Writing, then, pushes the tension between communication and expression to its limit. On the one hand, it seeks, through its style, to rescue those very moments that are sacrificed by the concept—the rough edges of the object that must, as it were, be smoothed over or "normalized" before it can be grasped conceptually or made commensurable with other objects—but at the same time, writing embodies a conceptuality without which it would relinquish its own claim to universality and truth. In contrast, then, to Arendt who can be criticized for providing what is, ultimately, an *aestheticized* vision of the political—praxis as self-disclosing activity—Adorno argues that aesthetic experience, paradoxically, can only take up its *political* vocation by jealously guarding its own autonomy from politics. By juxtaposing the parallel critiques of modernity in Adorno and Arendt, it becomes possible to recognize in Adorno, not so much a critical theory erected upon shaky normative foundations, as an account of the withdrawal of the political in modernity, which can only be addressed negatively.

Conclusion

We are now in the position to address the question raised at the outset, namely: What do Arendt and Adorno have to say to us today? Edward Said, in his magnificent essay "Reflections on Exile," argues that "our age—with its modern warfare, imperialism, and the quasi-theological ambitions of totalitarian rulers—is indeed the age of the refugee, the displaced person, mass immigration."[81] This is perhaps truer today than when Said first published this essay in 1984. While seeking to avoid a romanticization of this figure, Said argues that the refugee (echoing Arendt's notion of the refugee as the "vanguard of her people") occupies a privileged vantage point: "Most people are principally aware of one culture, one setting, one home; exiles are aware of at least two, and this plurality of vision gives rise to an awareness of simultaneous dimensions, an awareness that—to borrow from music—is *contrapuntal*."[82] It was from such a "contrapuntal" perspective that Arendt and Adorno were able to turn a critical eye on the German philosophical tradition that had nurtured them, albeit, as I indicate, in radically different ways, as well as on the intellectual traditions, culture, and political institutions of the United States—Arendt's permanent home in the postwar period and Adorno's temporary abode until 1949. Moreover, from this contrapuntal perspective, they were able, moreover, to reflect upon the catastrophe that results when men and women are progressively turned into second-class citizens, stripped of citizenship altogether, rendered homeless, and, finally, placed in camps. In a word, when they are made superfluous.[83]

I have sought to argue that Arendt's and Adorno's experience of exile enters deeply and profoundly into their own conceptions of experience, which forms the basis of what I've called a "homeless philosophy." Arendt appropriates Kant's notion of "reflective judgment," which finds its analogue in Adorno's conception of a mimetic relation to the object. In the first, a universal is generated out of the particular as an effect of the imagination, while in the second, the boundary between subject and object is held in tension, simultaneously affirmed and questioned. In both, what is made possible is "new beginning," because such a form of experience, rather than endlessly repeating the affirmation of the structures of dominating subjectivity, opens up the possibility of manifestation of the plurality constitutive of the political (Arendt) or takes as its nonteleological telos a condition of peace, or a genuine, nonreductive communication between subject and object, self and other. Genuine experience, then, is openness to what is different, and is thus steadfastly in opposition to the Hegelian concept of Spirit unburdening itself of otherness on its tortuous journey home to itself, and equally to the Heideggerian topos of ontological uprootedness.

What speaks to us most directly today lies precisely in the force field between Arendt's phenomenological impulse to show the possibility of making a home for human beings amid the depredations of nature, on the one hand, and Adorno's dialectical impulse to show how any conception of home must be limited by the form of its own negation, on the other. This can be understood as the thought that in the face of increasing homelessness both within and, of course, beyond the borders of the nation-state, it is equally important for human beings to have the "right to have rights." At the same time, what must never be forgotten is the cost of such belonging: that membership in community, any community, necessitates and cannot avoid completely the sacrificial logic of identity.

Notes

Chapter 1

1. Georg Lukács, *The Destruction of Reason*, trans. Peter Palmer (London: Merlin, 1980); Theodor W. Adorno, "Extorted Reconciliation: On Georg Lukacs's *Realism in Our Time*," in id., *Notes to Literature*, vol. 1 (New York: Columbia University Press, 1991), 217.
2. See Espen Hammer's Cavellian reading of Adorno's account of the "political" in his *Adorno and the Political* (London: Routledge, 2005).
3. Theodor W. Adorno, *Negative Dialectics* (1966; New York: Continuum, 1973), xx–xxi.
4. Georg Lukács, *Theory of the Novel: A Historico-Philosophical Essay on the Forms of Great Epic Literature*, trans. Anna Bostock (Cambridge, MA: MIT Press, 1974), 22.
5. See John Abromeit, "The Limits of Praxis: The Social Psychological Foundations of Herbert Marcuse and Theodor Adorno's Interpretations of the 1960s Protest Movements," in *Changing the World, Changing Oneself: Political Protest and Collective Identities in West Germany and U.S. in the 1960s and 1970s*, ed. Belinda Davis et al. (Oxford: Berghahn Books, 2010).
6. In *On Revolution* (London: Penguin Books, 1963), for instance, Arendt compares the American Revolution, concerned with the establishment of political space, favorably with the French Revolution, preoccupied with the "social question."
7. See the fascinating discussions between Arendt and her mainly leftist critics such as C. B. Macpherson, Christian Bay, Richard Bernstein, and Albrecht Wellmer in *Hannah Arendt: The Recovery of the Public World,* ed. Melvyn Hill (New York: St. Martin's Press, 1979), 301–39.
8. See Hannah Arendt, *Eichmann in Jerusalem: A Report on the Banality of Evil* (1963), rev. ed. (New York: Penguin Books, 1992).
9. Cited in Michael Ezra, "The Eichmann Polemics: Hannah Arendt and Her Critics," *Democratiya* 9 (Summer 2007): 142. This article provides an excellent overview of this controversy.
10. See Seyla Benhabib, *Another Cosmopolitanism* (New York: Oxford University Press, 2006).

11. Walter Benjamin, "Theses on the Philosophy of History," in *Illuminations*, ed. Hannah Arendt (New York: Schocken Books, 1969), 248.

12. That is not to say that Arendt is close to the Aristotelian, and Adorno close to the Platonic tradition. In spite of her broadly neo-Aristotelian conceptions in *The Human Condition*, Arendt criticizes Aristotle in multiple ways and at multiple junctures. She views Aristotle as very much part of the problematic tradition of Western political thought that is hostile to political freedom, i.e., the publicly constituted in-between space incorporating diverse voices and the plurality of the polis. Rescuing the particular and transient from its obfuscation and destruction by putatively "timeless" absolutes and recognizing the entrenchment of the objective and the subjective, Adorno is likewise decidedly critical of Plato. Adorno's vitriol against Plato and his Idealism at the beginning of his essay "On the Fetish-Character in Music and the Regression of Listening" (1938) is indicative of this general attitude toward Plato. However, there are two very distinct concerns: a concern with the "truth" that is apparent and revealed by appearance, on the one hand, and truth that is concealed by appearance, on the other. These different concerns are already reflected in the different directions of Aristotle and Plato.

13. As we indicate further in this introduction, however, Kant is a key figure for both Adorno and Arendt, though perhaps for different reasons. See contributions to the volume by Bernstein, Gandesha, and Thomä.

14. It is noteworthy that Arendt—against common misperceptions—clearly distances herself from Heidegger both explicitly and in her political theory, although in an essay for the *Festschrift* for Heidegger's eightieth birthday, she eventually rationalizes—and apparently forgives—Heidegger's turn to Hitler. To be sure, Arendt inherits elements of Heidegger's *Existenz* philosophy and fundamental ontology, and some of her central categories are indebted to him. But Arendt simultaneously turns Heidegger's categories, and the implications of his insights, upside down. Heidegger's notion of being-with-others as a constitutive dimension of thereness in the world is the starting point for Arendt's crucial understanding of being-in-the-world; for Arendt, this being-in-the-world points to the all important sphere in-between humans, the commonness of the world shared by equals in which the fundamental human condition of plurality is actualized and in which people articulate their unique "who," the plurality of perspectives that constitute the political. This understanding, however, runs completely counter to Heidegger's disparagement of *Mitsein*, being-in-the-world. Although the world is always shared by others and being-in-the-world, thus, a fundamental condition, he dismisses it as inauthentic, as the fallenness of *Dasein* into the everyday world. This represents exactly the derogatory view of the public, speech, and action Arendt opposes in the tradition of philosophy. For Heidegger, Arendt says, "*Dasein* could be truly itself only if it could pull back from its being-in-the-world into itself, but that is what its nature can never permit it to do, and that is why, by its very nature, it is always falling from itself"; see Hannah Arendt, "What Is Existential Philosophy?" (1946), in *Essays in Understanding, 1930–1954* (New York: Schocken Books,

1994), 179; see also Seyla Benhabib, *The Reluctant Modernism of Hannah Arendt* (Lanham, MD: Rowman & Littlefield, 2003), 51ff.

15. See, for a start, Fred Dallmayr, "Phenomenology and Critical Theory: Adorno," *Philosophy and Social Criticism* 3 (1976): 367–405.

16. On the run from the Nazis before his death, Benjamin had given Arendt a suitcase of manuscripts—among them the "Theses on the Philosophy of History"—and had asked her to forward them to Adorno. Arendt did so when she arrived in New York in June 1941. Told later that one of the manuscripts had been lost, she reacted furiously that "this gang of pigs [i.e., the Institute for Social Research] . . . will simply suppress the manuscript," and that she could "kill all of them" (Arendt to Heinrich Blücher, August 2, 1941, in Hannah Arendt and Heinrich Blücher, *Briefe, 1936–1968* [Munich: Piper, 1996], 127). See also Dirk Auer, Lars Rensmann, and Julia Schulze Wessel, "Affinität und Aversion: Zum theoretischen Dialog zwischen Arendt und Adorno," in *Arendt und Adorno*, ed. id. (Frankfurt: Suhrkamp, 2003), 8ff. Given that the Institute for Social Research did, in fact, provide Benjamin with material support to the very end, Arendt's rancor was scarcely justified.

17. For a discussion of the reverberations of this article, see Hammer, *Adorno and the Political*, 49–53.

18. Arendt to Karl Jaspers," July 4, 1966, in Hannah Arendt and Karl Jaspers, *Briefwechsel, 1926–1969* (Munich: Piper, 1993), 679.

19. Arendt to Karl Jaspers," April 18, 1966, ibid., 670.

20. See Victor Farias, *Heidegger and Nazism* (Philadelphia: Temple University Press, 1989).

21. Arendt to Jaspers, April 18, 1966.

22. For the unpublished letter, see the Walter Benjamin section in the Library of Congress, Manuscript Division. Distance cannot simply be taken for coldness, however, as Adorno shows in *Minima Moralia: Reflections from Damaged Life*, trans. E. F. N. Jephcott (London: Verso, 1974), 126–28.

23. Dagmar Barnouw, "Untröstlich in Amerika: Adorno und die Utopie der Eigentlichkeit," *Merkur: Zeitschrift für europäisches Denken* 53, no. 8 (1999).

24. As Thomas McCarthy indicates, Habermas credits Arendt with having drawn his attention to the crucial Aristotelian distinction between *technē* and poeisis. See his book *The Critical Theory of Jürgen Habermas* (Cambridge, MA: MIT Press, 1985), 387n4.

25. Jürgen Habermas, *Philosophical Discourse of Modernity: Twelve Lectures*, trans. Fredrick Lawrence (Cambridge, MA: MIT Press).

26. In other directions, such reconsiderations have already been initiated, particularly with regard to the relation between Adorno and Heidegger. See, e.g., Hermann Mörchen, *Adorno und Heidegger: Untersuchung einer philosophischen Kommunikationsverweigerung* (Stuttgart: Klett-Cotta, 1981), Fred Dallmayr, *Between Freiburg and Frankfurt: Towards a Critical Ontology* (Amherst, MA: University of Massachusetts Press, 1991), Samir Gandesha, "Leaving Home; On Adorno and Heidegger," in *The Cambridge Companion to Adorno*, ed. Tom Huhn (New

York: Cambridge University Press, 2004), *Adorno and Heidegger: Philosophical Questions,* ed. Iain Macdonald and Krzysztof Ziarek (Stanford: Stanford University Press, 2007), and Nikolas Kompridis, *Critique and Disclosure: Critical Theory Between Past and Future* (Cambridge, MA: MIT Press, 2006).

27. Most prominently, this applies to the work of Seyla Benhabib and her systematic studies of Adorno's critical social theory and philosophy, as well as Arendt's political theory; see Seyla Benhabib, *Critique, Norm, and Utopia: A Study of the Foundations of Critical Theory* (New York: Columbia University Press, 1986), and *Reluctant Modernism of Hannah Arendt* (2003). Dana Villa has also taken important steps in this direction; see Dana Villa, *Public Freedom* (Princeton, NJ: Princeton University Press, 2008). Martin Jay places both thinkers prominently in the history of modern social and political theory; see Martin Jay, *Adorno* (Cambridge, MA: Harvard University Press, 1984), and "The Political Existentialism of Hannah Arendt," in *Permanent Exiles: Essays on the Intellectual Migration from Germany to America* (New York: Columbia University Press, 1985). The broader reception of Adorno's social philosophy in America started in the 1970s, under the influence of Martin Jay's *The Dialectical Imagination: The History of the Frankfurt School and the Institute of Social Research, 1923–1950* (Boston: Little, Brown, 1973), whereas the revived interest in Arendt's political theory really took off in the 1980s. Last but not least, Fred Dallmayr has energetically sought to bridge the divide separating the phenomenological and critical theoretical traditions, taking his inspiration in seemingly equal measures from Heidegger, Arendt, and the Frankfurt School; see, e.g., Dallmayr, *Beyond Dogma and Despair: Toward a Critical Phenomenology of Politics* (Notre Dame, IN: University of Notre Dame Press, 1981), *Critical Encounters: Between Philosophy and Politics* (Notre Dame, IN: University of Notre Dame Press, 1987), and *Between Freiburg and Frankfurt: Toward a Critical Ontology* (Amherst: University of Massachusetts Press, 1991).

28. For an expanded and reflexive understanding of intellectual history, see Martin Jay, *Force Fields: Between Intellectual History and Cultural Critique* (New York: Routledge, 1993).

29. See Alex Demirovic, *Der nonkonformistische Intellektuelle: Die Entwicklung der Kritischen Theorie zur Frankfurter Schule* (Frankfurt: Suhrkamp, 1999) and the review by Max Pensky, "Beyond the Message in a Bottle: The Other Critical Theory," *Constellations* 10, no. 1 (2003): 135–44. This shows definitively the idea that Adorno was a mandarin thinker with an aversion to politics is deeply misleading, and a view perpetuated by Habermas and others such as Rolf Wiggershaus in such a way as to accentuate Habermas's own elaboration of critical theory.

30. Andrew Milner and Jeff Browitt, *Contemporary Cultural Theory: An Introduction* (New York: Routledge), 74.

31. Though skeptical about its realization and actualization, Arendt time and again endorses "the best in the revolutionary tradition—the council system, the always defeated but only authentic outgrowth of every revolution since the eighteenth century" (Hannah Arendt, "On Violence," in id., *Crises of the Republic: Lying in Politics; Civil Disobedience; On Violence: Thoughts on Politics and Revolution*

[New York: Harcourt, Brace & Company, 1972], 124). See also Claude Lefort, "Arendt and the Question of the Political," in *Democracy and Political Theory*, trans. David Macey (Minneapolis: University of Minnesota Press, 1988), 55.

32. Arendt, *On Revolution*, 215ff.

33. Hannah Arendt, "Lying in Politics: Reflections on the Pentagon Papers," in id., *Crises of the Republic*, 1–48.

34. Following Martin Jay's claim that Arendt accepts Carl Schmitt's decisionism and Richard Wolin's suggestion that Arendt's understanding of the political lacks any normative commitment, several authors have recently addressed presumed convergences between Arendt and Schmitt. However, it can be questioned whether those alleged affinities are really conceptually substantive. To be sure, Schmitt and Arendt (and Adorno, for that matter) have in common a Weimar background, criticisms of the modern condition and (modern) liberalism, and share some skepticism toward the primacy of economics and "technicity." Parallel to Arendt, Schmitt also criticizes an age of "depoliticization." Both can be and have been read as theorists who prioritize the political as an existential mode and autonomous realm over, strictly speaking, normative justifications in political thought. Beyond those rather formal parallels, however, we find fundamentally different presuppositions, critiques of modernity, notions of the political, and— despite Arendt's and Adorno's distance toward foundationalism—normative commitments. To begin with, Arendt's and Schmitt's "existential" concept of politics is quite different. For Arendt, politics rests on plurality; she assumes that the fact of human plurality and diversity are the preconditions of political action and agreement. Schmitt, however, sees such plurality as a specific foundational understanding of politics worthy of scathing criticism—and in fact the major political *problem* faced by the state. In Schmitt's view, plurality either needs to be homogenized by the total state or fought against by the ethnic collectivity that is presupposed as the substrate, and ultimately the foundation, of the political, that is, "the most intense and extreme antagonism, and every antagonism becomes that much more political the closer it approaches the most extreme point, that of the friend-enemy grouping" (Carl Schmitt, *The Concept of the Political*, trans. George Schwab [Chicago: University of Chicago Press, 1996], 29). Schmitt hereby presupposes a homogeneous will of a nation "vis-à-vis another nation," as opposed to Arendt's messy Athenian politics and multiplicity of voices. Though there are significant tensions within Schmitt's work, he often praises an extralegal authority and prepolitical foundations of order anchored in a notion of an ethnocultural, homogeneous collectivity. Arendt, to the contrary, rejects such essentialist and extralegal foundations of politics. Among other things, she conceives of politics as acting together based on and through differences, while viewing the construction of the "identical will" of a sovereign as a cardinal sin of Western political thought. Most important, Schmitt conceives of the political in antagonistic terms of friend-enemy relations, a "meaningful antithesis" that entails "the real possibility of physical killing" (33). Arendt, conversely, understands political action as the very opposite of violence. Potential violence against an enemy is entirely at odds with her political thinking.

In fact, Arendt replaces "sovereign will" with "agreed purposes" and the interest of the many; for a "Schmittian" reading of Arendt, see Jay, "Political Existentialism of Hannah Arendt"; for a critique of the notion of a convergence between Schmitt and Arendt, see Dana Villa, *Arendt and Heidegger: The Fate of the Political* (Princeton, NJ: Princeton University Press, 1995).

35. Arendt, "On Violence," in *Crises of the Republic*, 143, 151.

36. Against mainstream interpretations, however, Hammer, *Adorno and the Political*, provides a first strong, but debatable case for conceiving Adorno as a distinctively *political* theorist.

37. Phillip Hansen, *Hannah Arendt: Politics, History and Citizenship* (Stanford: Stanford University Press, 1993), 91.

38. See Wendy Brown, *Edgework: Critical Essays on Knowledge and Politics* (Princeton, NJ: Princeton University Press, 2005).

39. See, among others, Stephen Eric Bronner, *Reclaiming the Enlightenment: Toward a Politics of Radical Engagement* (New York: Columbia University Press, 2004); Dick Howard, *The Specter of Democracy* (New York: Columbia University Press, 2006); Richard Wolin, *The Frankfurt School Revisited* (New York: Routledge, 2006); Lambert Zuidervaart, *Social Philosophy After Adorno* (New York: Cambridge University Press, 2007). In this context, William Sewell's work makes an important contribution. He puts forth the argument that postmodernism has focused too much on the particular and that we now need to bring theories of macrocausation back into consideration (without abandoning some of the best insights of the turn to the particular and to culture in the various "posts"). See William Sewell, *Logics of History: Social Theory and Social Transformation* (Chicago: University of Chicago Press, 2005).

40. Perry Anderson, *The Origins of Post-Modernity* (London: Verso, 2006), 35.

41. On the concept of democratic "non-domination" instead of the notion of self-determination that is, according to Hannah Arendt, tied to the corrupted and obsolete idea of "sovereignty," see James Bohman, *Democracy Across Borders: From Demos to Demoi* (Cambridge, MA: MIT Press, 2007).

42. See Alfred Schmidt, "Adorno: Ein Philosoph des realen Humanismus," *Neue Rundschau* 80, no. 4 (1969): 654–72.

43. Giorgio Agamben has sought to reconcile Foucault's concept of bio-politics with an Arendtian view of the political, focusing on the distinction between *zōē*, life as such, or what Agamben calls "bare life," and *bios*, the distinctively "human" life that is always already inextricable from the tapestry of meaning constitutive of "world." This would seem to be a particularly good bridge to Adorno's diagnosis of late capitalist societies as a societies in which "life has become the ideology of its own absence." See Giorgio Agamben, *Homo Sacer: Sovereign Power and Bare Life* (Stanford: Stanford University Press, 1998), and Jay M. Bernstein, *Adorno: Disenchantment and Ethics* (New York: Cambridge University Press, 2001), an extended analysis of Adorno's claim that "wrong life cannot be lived rightly."

44. Marx's perception that humans have become reduced to abstract labor serves as an implicit starting point for the historical and conceptual critiques of

modern society put forward by Arendt and Adorno. Modern society's economistic tendencies have found their most recent expression in the neoliberal discourse about the ineluctable requirement that the market replace democratic institutions as the site where resources are authoritatively allocated in society. However, both theorists also argue—against Marx—that this is only part of the story. A critical notion of modern society must confront the reduction of the human capacity for action to the category of nonalienated labor—what Marx called "species being"— by pointing to the manner in which the normative weight accorded to human labor tends to sacrifice the "nonidentical," in Adorno's view. In Arendt's words, the modern standpoint of labour—very much the starting point of classical political economy—elides the human capacity to make new beginnings, which is itself a precondition of action. By engendering recognition of difference and the human condition of plurality, a precondition for a universal that does not rule over the particulars, critical rationality and political practice may thus also offer remedies for modernity's malaise, namely, the subjugation of the particular through false universality.

45. Recently, there has been quite a striking reevaluation of Kant's concept of reflective judgment, an excellent example of which is the special double issue devoted to this topic of *Philosophy and Social Criticism* 38, nos. 1–2 (January 2008). It exemplifies recent attempts to apply the insights of aesthetic reflective judgment to the non-aesthetic spheres of politics and morality.

46. G. W. F. Hegel, *The Philosophy of History*, trans. J. Sibree (London: Colonial Press, 1900), 33.

47. Adorno, *Negative Dialectics*, 61ff.

48. Jürgen Habermas, *The Philosophical Discourse of Modernity* (Cambridge, MA: MIT Press, 1990).

49. Believing that crisis not to be irreversible, Francis Fukuyama sought in *The End of History and the Last Man* (New York: Free Press, 1992) to revive the Hegelian thesis of "the end of history" through Alexandre Kojève, but the revival has been short-lived.

50. Johan Fornas, *Cultural Theory and Late Modernity* (London: Sage, 1995), 19, 30.

51. Marshall Berman, *All That Is Solid Melts into Air: The Experience of Modernity* (New York: Penguin Books, 1988). Moishe Postone shows that this "dynamic and contradictory nature" is, in Marx's work, a historically specific characteristic of modern capitalism. In this understanding, Marx was every bit as ambivalent about the developmental dynamic of capitalism as Max Weber; see Moishe Postone, *Time, Labor and Social Domination: A Reinterpretation of Marx's Critical Theory* (New York: Cambridge University Press, 1996).

52. Karl Marx and Friedrich Engels, *The Communist Manifesto*, with an introduction by Eric Hobsbawm (London: Verso, 1998), 38.

53. While Arendt had trouble accepting many of Marx's presuppositions and assumptions, and Adorno challenged any dogmatic appropriation of Marx's insights,

it is the very understanding of modernization and its inherent dynamic that seems to provide bridges between all three authors (and, by the way, Max Weber).

54. See Hannah Arendt, *The Human Condition* (Chicago: University of Chicago Press, 1998), 85.

55. Here one can see interesting parallels with critical theory's critique of the fetishization of labor and productivity, which, perhaps not coincidentally, was also cynically inscribed on the gates to Auschwitz: "Arbeit macht frei."

56. See Agamben, *Homo Sacer*. Moreover, in spite of her criticism of the social question and labor as a mode of activity that has come to undermine political action and plurality, Arendt is concerned with the social question and offers a critique of wealth as capital, "which has taken over the public realm" (Arendt, *Human Condition*, 61–62). She thereby distinguishes between property and wealth. She recognizes that liberation from immediate material need is a precondition of freedom in the public sphere, while criticizing a central feature of the modern age that undermines this precondition of freedom, namely, the modern "expropriation of the poor" (ibid., 68ff.).

57. Immanuel Kant, "An Answer to the Question: What is Enlightenment?" in *What Is Enlightenment: Eighteenth-Century Answers and Twentieth-Century Questions*, ed. James Schmidt (Berkeley: University of California Press, 1996), 58.

58. Adorno, *Negative Dialectics*, 3.

59. Brian O'Connor, *Adorno's Negative Dialectics: Philosophy and the Possibility of Critical Rationality* (Cambridge, MA: MIT Press, 2005).

60. Ibid., 173.

61. Adorno, *Negative Dialectics*, 286.

62. Adorno, *Minima Moralia*, 18.

63. Adorno, *Negative Dialectics*, 284.

64. Benjamin, "Theses on the Philosophy of History," in id., *Illuminations*, 261. To be sure, Adorno recognizes in many places that Hegel takes the particular seriously, even though, in the end, he gives priority to the universal. The concept of "qualitative change" could very well lead to a notion of "reconciliation" that looks more like the "emancipation of dissonance" than *Gleichschaltung*.

65. See Adorno, *Minima Moralia*, 247.

66. Hannah Arendt, "What Is Freedom," in id., *Between Past and Future: Eight Exercises in Political Thought* (New York: Penguin Books, 1977), 143–71, here 148, 170.

67. See Arendt, *On Revolution*.

68. T. J. Clark, *Farewell to an Idea: Episodes from the History of Modernism* (New Haven, CT: Yale University Press, 1999).

69. See Jonathan Schell, "Introduction," in Arendt, *On Revolution*, xx.

70. This is an argument that resonates in some anti-universalistic aspects of postmodern discourse and vulgar Marxism. In a way that anticipates Nietzsche-inflected postmodern criticism—a kind of "hermeneutics of suspicion" gone wild—Adorno argues in the section of *Minima Moralia* entitled "Baby with the Bathwater" that "meaning, as we know, is not independent of genesis, and it is

easy to discern, in everything that cloaks or mediates the material, the trace of insincerity, sentimentality, indeed, precisely a concealed and doubly poisonous interest. But to act radically in accordance with this principle would be to extirpate, with the false, all that was true also, all that, however impotently, strives to escape the confines of universal practice, every chimerical anticipation of a nobler condition, and so to bring about directly the barbarism that culture is reproached with furthering indirectly" (Adorno, *Minima Moralia*, 43–44).

71. In the case of Arendt, such normative ties are often denied; while her theory of judgment distances the (concrete) political from (universal, principled) moral judgment in a Kantian sense, the two forms of judgment are not completely isolated; rather, it can be argued, Arendt's political theory opposes the conflation of political judgment and principled moral judgment and supports notions of aesthetic subjectivity without cutting all ties to normative universalism and cosmopolitanism. For a more normative and universalistic reading of Arendt, conceived as "anthropological universalism," see Benhabib, *Reluctant Modernism*, 195ff.; see also Peg Birmingham, *Hannah Arendt and Human Rights* (Bloomington: University of Indiana Press, 2006).

72. As Lisa Disch points out, Arendt's *inter-est* is neither a bargaining position, as in rational individualism/liberalism or competitive interest-group pluralism, nor a communitarian common good that expresses any authentic needs or pre-political collective identity and harmonizes the wills of disparate participants. See Lisa Disch, "'Please Sit Down, but Don't Make Yourself at Home': Arendtian 'Visiting' and the Prefigurative Politics of Consciousness-Raising," in *Hannah Arendt and the Meaning of Politics*, ed. Craig Calhoun and John McGowan (Minneapolis: University of Minnesota Press), 142.

73. Arendt, "What Is Freedom?" in id., *Between Past and Future*, 165.

74. Ibid., 149.

75. Arendt, "On Violence," in *Crises of the Republic*, 130.

76. Nancy Fraser, "Hannah Arendt in the 21st Century," *Contemporary Political Theory* 3 (2004): 253–61, here 254.

77. To be sure, Axel Honneth has sought to rescue the critical modern concept of reification by recasting it in terms of the philosophy of recognition; see Honneth, *Reification: A New Look at an Old Idea* (New York: Oxford University Press, 2008).

78. See *Jürgen Habermas and the Unfinished Project of Modernity: Critical Essays on "The Philosophical Discourse of Modernity,"* ed. Maurizio Passerin d'Entréves and Seyla Benhabib (Cambridge, MA: MIT Press, 1997).

79. Martin Jay, *Songs of Experience: Modern American and European Variations on a Universal Theme* (Berkeley: University of California Press, 2006).

80. Adorno, *Minima Moralia*, 103.

81. Theodor Adorno, *The Jargon of Authenticity*, trans. Knut Tarnowski and Frederic Will (Evanston, IL: Northwestern University Press, 1973).

82. Immanuel Kant, "Critique of Practical Reason," in Kant, *Practical Philosophy*, ed. by Mary J. Gregor (New York: Cambridge University Press, 1999), 164.

83. Adorno, *Negative Dialectics*, 365.

84. Theodor W. Adorno, "Freudian Theory and the Pattern of Fascist Propaganda," in *The Essential Frankfurt School Reader* (New York: Continuum, 2005), 118–37.

85. See Jay, *Permanent Exiles* and Lars Rensmann, "Returning from Forced Exile: Some Observations on Hannah Arendt's and Theodor Adorno's Experience of Post-War Germany and Their Social and Political Theories on Totalitarianism," *Leo Baeck Institute Yearbook* 49 (2004).

86. Hannah Arendt, *Ich will verstehen: Selbstauskünfte zu Leben und Werk*, ed. Ursula Ludz (Munich: Piper, 1997), 48.

87. Arendt, *Origins of Totalitarianism*, 297.

88. See Seyla Benhabib, *The Rights of Others* (New York: Cambridge University Press, 2004).

89. The related concept of exodus has played a not inconsiderable role in recent contributions to social and political theory. See Giorgio Agamben, *Means Without Ends: Notes on Politics* (Minneapolis: University of Minnesota Press. 2000), and Michael Hardt and Antonio Negri's trilogy *Empire* (2000), *Commonwealth* (2009), and, in particular, *Multitude: War and Democracy in the Age of Empire* (New York: Penguin Press, 2004).

90. An important exception is Susan Buck-Morss's *The Origin of Negative Dialectics: Theodor W. Adorno, Walter Benjamin and the Frankfurt Institute* (New York: Free Press, 1979).

Chapter 2

1. See Detlev Schottker and Erdmut Wizisla, "Hannah Arendt und Walter Benjamin. Konstellationen, Debatten, Vermittlungen," in *Arendt und Benjamin. Texte, Briefe, Dokumente,* ed. id. (Frankfurt: Suhrkamp, 2006), 13ff. (hereafter cited as *Arendt und Benjamin*). See ibid., 153, for Arendt's letter to Gershom Scholem of October 17, 1941, recounting her meeting with "Benji" (Walter Benjamin) in Lourdes after escaping from the Gurs internment camp.

2. See Hannah Arendt, "Walter Benjamin: 1892–1940," introduction to Walter Benjamin, *Illuminations: Essays and Reflections* (New York: Schocken Books, 1968), 21ff., on Benjamin in Paris. On Blücher and herself, see Hannah Arendt to Walter Benjamin, July 16, 1937, reprinted in *Arendt und Benjamin*, 127; Elisabeth Young-Bruehl, *Hannah Arendt: For Love of the World* (New Haven, CT: Yale University Press, 1984), 122.

3. Heinrich Blücher to Arendt from Paris, September 15, 1937, and Arendt to Blücher, September 16, 1937, from Geneva in *Within Four Walls: The Correspondence Between Hannah Arendt and Heinrich Blücher, 1936–1968,* ed. Lotte Kohler (New York: Harcourt, 2000), 39–40. I am grateful to my student Isaiah Wilner for his brilliant seminar paper "Eichmann's Angel: The Holocaust Narrative of Hannah Arendt" (on file with the author) and his playful reconstructions of these chess episodes.

4. Walter Benjamin, "Theses on the Philosophy of History," in id., *Illuminations*, 253.

5. Ibid., 255.

6. See Seyla Benhabib, "Hannah Arendt and the Redemptive Power of Narrative," *Social Research* 57, no. 1 (1990): 167–96. I am indebted for the idea of "redemptive" critique and narrative to Jürgen Habermas's essay "Bewusstmachende oder Rettende Kritik—Die Aktualitat Walter Benjamins," in id., *Philosophisch-Politische Profilen* (Frankfurt: Suhrkamp, 1981), 336–76.

7. See *Arendt und Adorno*, ed. Dirk Auer, Lars Rensmann, and Julia Schulze Wessel (Frankfurt: Suhrkamp, 2003) (hereafter cited as *Arendt und Adorno*), and in particular the introduction by the three editors, "Einleitung: Affinität und Aversion. Zum theoretischen Dialog zwischen Arendt und Adorno," 8ff.

8. For this whole episode, see Young-Bruehl, *Hannah Arendt*, 80.

9. For Arendt's reference to Adorno and Horkheimer as a *Schweinebande* (bunch of pigs) for not wanting to publish Benjamin's "Theses on the Philosophy of History," referred to in this letter as "Über den Begriff der Geschichte," see Hannah Arendt to Heinrich Blücher, August 2, 1941, reprinted in *Arendt und Benjamin*, 146; also *Within Four Walls*, 72–73. For further correspondence on the edition of the "Theses," which Arendt was preparing for English publication in *Illuminations*, see Arendt to Adorno, January 20, 1967, in *Arendt und Benjamin*, 175; Adorno's answer of February 3, 1967, 176–77; and their further exchange in *Arendt und Benjamin*, 178–81. Members of the Institute for Social Research had actually published a version of Benjamin's "Theses" in mimeographed form in 1942 in a volume titled *Walter Benjamin zum Gedächtnis*. Arendt continued to be angry that they had originally not seen fit to publish Benjamin's essay on Baudelaire in the journal of the Institute and had let it appear in 1939 only after it had been cut and edited by Adorno. See Young-Bruehl, *Hannah Arendt*, 167.

10. See Theodor Adorno, *Jargon der Eigentlichkeit* (Frankfurt: Suhrkamp, 1964), trans. Knut Tarnowski and Frederic Will as *The Jargon of Authenticity* (Evanston, IL: Northwestern University Press, 1973). Arendt wrote to Jaspers regarding Alexander Schwan's *Politische Philosophie im Denken Heideggers* (Cologne: Westdeutscher Verlag, 1965) that "the attacks on him [i.e., Heidegger] are coming only from that quarter and no other. . . . Then too, I can't prove it, but I'm quite convinced that the real people behind the scenes are the Wiesengrund-Adorno crowd in Frankfurt. And that is grotesque, all the more so because it has been revealed (students found this out) that Wiesengrund (a half-Jew and one of the most repulsive human beings I know) tried to go along with the Nazis. For years now he and Horkheimer have accused or threatened to accuse anyone in Germany who was against them of being anti-Semitic. A really distinguished bunch, and yet Wiesengrund is not untalented" (Arendt to Jaspers, April 18, 1966, in *Hannan Arendt / Karl Jaspers Correspondence, 1926–1969*, ed. Lotte Köhler and Hans Saner, trans. Robert and Rita Kimber [New York: Harcourt Brace Jovanovich, 1992], 634). As regards the "revelation" by students, Arendt is referring to an article by Adorno in a Frankfurt student newspaper called *Diskus* in 1934, discussing a

poetry collection by the Nazi *Reichsjugendführer* (Reich Youth Leader) Baldur von Schirach. See *Arendt und Adorno*, ed. Auer et al., 8.

Given how extensive Adorno's critique of Jaspers is in *Jargon of Authenticity*, it is unclear to me whether Arendt actually was familiar with this book or was referring to general reviews of it in the German press. Otherwise, it is hard to account for the fact that she leaves Adorno's comments on Jaspers (see e.g., *Jargon of Authenticity*, 22–23, 27–28) uncommented upon. Ironically, Adorno's critique of Heidegger's "jargon" is quite akin to the objections to Heidegger that Jaspers himself had raised in his letter to the Freiburg University Denazification Committee on December 22, 1945: see *The Heidegger Controversy*, ed. Richard Wolin (Cambridge, MA: MIT Press, 1993), 147–51. Jaspers writes of "the torrent" of Heidegger's language and says that his "manner of thinking to me seems in its essence unfree, dictatorial, and incapable of communication, [and it] would today in its pedagogical effects be disastrous" (149).

11. The phrase "primacy of the object" captures multiple epistemological, methodological, and even psychoanalytical dimensions. I shall return to its meaning in Adorno's work. "To use the strength of the subject to break through the fallacy of constitutive subjectivity—this is what the author felt to be his task ever since he came to trust his own mental impulses," he writes in the Preface to *Negative Dialectics*, trans. E. B. Ashton (New York: Seabury Press, 1973), xx (originally published as *Negative Dialektik* [Frankfurt: Suhrkamp, 1973]).

12. See Samir Gandesha's statement: "Mit anderen Worten, wenn für beide die Moderne die Unterordnung des 'Neuen' unter das immergleiche beinhaltet dann wurde das 'Neue' gerade im asthetischen Urteil als Problem behandelt." Gandesha identifies "Das *Auffressen oder Verschlingen* des Partikularen durch das Universelle" (the devouring or swallowing of the particular through the universal) as one of the central features of the development of modernity. Gandesha, "Schreiben und Urteilen. Adorno, Arendt und der Chiasmus der Naturgeschichte," in *Arendt und Adorno*, ed. Auer et al., 227.

13. Theodor W. Adorno, "Zur Aktualität der Philosophie," in *Philosophische Frühschriften. Gesammelte Schriften*, vol. 1 (Frankfurt: Suhrkamp, 1973), 325ff. This lecture was not published until after Adorno's death. Page references in the text are to the English translation by Benjamin Snow of Theodor W. Adorno, "The Actuality of Philosophy," *Telos* 31 (Spring 1977): 120–33.

14. Adorno, "Actuality of Philosophy," 120; emphasis added.

15. See G.W. F. Hegel, *Grundlinien der Philosophie des Rechts* (1821), in *Werke*, ed. Eva Moldenhauer and Karl Markus Michel (Frankfurt: Suhrkamp, 1970), 7: 24; id., *Elements of the Philosophy of Right*, ed. Allen W. Wood (New York: Cambridge University Press, 1991), 20.

16. Adorno, "Actuality of Philosophy," 120.

17. Ibid., 121, also the source of the following quotations in this paragraph.

18. Quotations in this paragraph, ibid., 121–22.

19. See Martin Heidegger, *Sein und Zeit* (1927), 10th ed. (Tubingen: Max Niemeyer, 1963); *Being and Time*, trans. John Macquarrie and Edward Robinson (New York: Harper & Row, 1962).

20. Adorno, "Actuality of Philosophy," 123.
21. Ibid., 123–24, this and the preceding quotation.
22. Ibid., 125, this and the preceding quotation.
23. Georg Lukács, "Reification and the Consciousness of the Proletariat," in id., *History and Class Consciousness,* trans. Rodney Livingstone (Cambridge, MA: MIT Press, 1971), 110–31.
24. Referring to Lukács's solution of the "thing-in-itself problem" through an analysis of the "commodity structure," Adorno writes that "the truth content of a problem is in principle different from the historical and psychological conditions out of which it grows" ("Actuality of Philosophy," 128). This is a reductionist reading of Lukács, for whom "the commodity structure" is not merely a psychological or historical "fact" but a category that shapes the form of a world as well as of consciousness. Adorno does not so much reject the analysis of the commodity structure as much as he substitutes his Benjaminian materialism for Lukács's ontology of social labor. "Like a source of light, the historical figure of commodity and of exchange value may free the form of a reality, the hidden meaning of which remained closed to investigation of the thing-in-itself problem," he writes (ibid., 128). Of course, the Marxian theory of the emancipation of humans from the forces of nature through the transformative activity of labor is subjected to a devastating critique in the *Dialectic of Enlightenment,* according to whose well-known argument the process of social labor is seen as subjecting not only nature but the nature within humans themselves to domination, such that the price of civilization is the repression of the nature within us. See Theodor Adorno and Max Horkheimer, *Dialektik der Aufklärung,* 7th ed. (Frankfurt: Fischer, 1980); *Dialectic of Enlightenment,* trans. John Cumming (New York: Herder & Herder, 1972), and my discussion in Seyla Benhabib, *Critique, Norm and Utopia: A Study of the Foundations of Critical Theory* (New York: Columbia University Press, 1986), 164–71. As Deborah Cook observes, "The affinity between mind and nature should not be understood as positive, it does not authorize a foundational conception of nature because the human mind partially extricated itself from nature in its attempts to dominate it. The mind becomes 'something else,' something other than instinct by virtue of 'reflecting existence' with a view to ensuring its survival. . . . Consequently, reflection on nature in ourselves involves both acknowledging our resemblance to nature as instinctual, embodied beings, *and* respecting nature's heterogeneity." Deborah Cook, "The One and the Many: Revisioning Adorno's Critique of Western Reason," *Studies in Social and Political Thought* 18 (Winter 2010): 74.
25. Adorno, "Actuality of Philosophy," 124–25.
26. Ibid., 126.
27. Ibid., 120.
28. See Walter Benjamin, *The Origin of German Tragic Drama,* trans. John Osbourne (London: New Left Review, 1977). See Susan Buck-Morss's exploration of the terms "configuration" and "crystalization of elements" as methodological dimensions of Benjamin's work in *The Origin of Negative Dialectics: Theodor W.*

Adorno, Walter Benjamin and the Frankfurt Institute (New York: Free Press, 1977), 96–111.

29. This and the preceding quotation are from Adorno, "Actuality of Philosophy," 127; emphasis added.

30. See Max Horkheimer, "Traditional and Critical Theory," in id., *Critical Theory*, trans. M. J. O'Connell et al. (New York: Herder & Herder, 1972), 188–244. "It is easy to imagine Horkheimer also having been irritated by the lecture Adorno gave on the occasion of the *Habilitation*, with the challenging title, 'The Actuality of Philosophy,'" Detlev Claussen writes. "Horkheimer, who according to Adorno thought that people were like animals, tends to derive his thinking from the French materialism of the Enlightenment, while Adorno does the reverse: feeling that animals are like humans, he aspires to go beyond German idealism" (Claussen, *Theodor W. Adorno: One Last Genius*, trans. Rodney Livingstone [Cambridge, MA: Harvard University Press, 2008], 228).

31. Snow, "Introduction to Adorno's 'The Actuality of Philosophy,'" *Telos* 31 (Spring 1977), 116.

32. This and the preceding quotation are from Adorno, "Actuality of Philosophy," 132.

33. Ibid., 133.

34. G. W. F. Hegel, *Die Phanemenologie des Geistes,* ed. J. Hoffmeister, in *Philosophische Bibliothek* (1807; Hamburg: Felix Meiner, 1952), 69; *Hegel's Phenomenology of Spirit*, trans. A. V. Miller, ed. John Findlay (Oxford: Clarendon Press, 1977), 138.

35. Although it has not been much discussed in the literature on Adorno, careful commentators have noted the significance of this early essay in anticipating central themes of Adorno's *Negative Dialectics*; see Claussen, *Theodor W. Adorno*, 321.

36. Hannah Arendt, *The Origins of Totalitarianism* (1951; New York: Harcourt Brace Jovanovich, 1979). Originally published in Britain as *The Burden of Our Time* (London: Secker & Warburg, 1951).

37. See my more extensive discussion in Seyla Benhabib, *The Reluctant Modernism of Hannah Arendt* (1996; new ed., Lanham, MD: Rowman & Littlefield, 2003), 63ff.

38. Arendt, *Origins if Totalitarianism*, viii.

39. Ibid., xv.

40. Hannah Arendt, "A Reply. Rejoinder to Eric Voegelin's Review of *The Origins of Totalitarianism*," *Review of Politics* 15, no. 1 (January 1953): 78.

41. Hannah Arendt, "What Is Existenz Philosophy?" *Partisan Review* 18, no. 1 (1946): 35–56; published in German as "Was ist Existenz Philosophie?" in *Hannah Arendt: Sechs Essays* (Heidelberg: Schneider, 1948); trans. Robert and Rita Kimber as "What Is Existential Philosophy?" in *Arendt: Essays in Understanding, 1930–1954,* ed. Jerome Kohn (New York: Harcourt Brace, 1994), 163–87. As I explain in *Reluctant Modernism of Hannah Arendt*, 56–60n35, I use *Partisan Review*'s title because the German term *Existenzphilosophie* connotes a much wider philosophical

movement—it would include Dilthey's *Lebensphilosophie*, for example—than English "existentialism" or "existential philosophy." All references in the text are, however, to the Kohn edition unless otherwise noted, although I have consulted the original and used my own translations where necessary, as indicated.

42. Arendt, "What Is Existenz Philosophy?" 167.
43. Ibid., 173.
44. Ibid., 168; emphasis added.
45. Ibid., 164.
46. Ibid., 168.
47. See Hannah Arendt, *The Life of the Mind*, ed. Mary McCarthy, vol. 1: *Thinking* (New York: Harcourt Brace Jovanovich, 1978), 14–15, 61.
48. Hannah Arendt, *Between Past and Future: Six Exercises in Political Thought* (New York: Meridian, 1961).
49. Arendt, "What Is Existenz Philosophy?" 171.
50. Ibid., 169.
51. See Adorno, *Negative Dialectics*, 295ff.;see also Benhabib, *Critique, Norm and Utopia*, 209–11, and on Kant and Adorno section VI of this essay.
52. Arendt, "What Is Existenz Philosophy?" 169.
53. Ibid., 171.
54. Ibid., 173.
55. Ibid., 174.
56. This and the preceding quotation are from ibid., 164.
57. Ibid., 165.
58. Ibid., 36 (in the original *Partisan Review* version, used here).
59. Ibid., 165.
60. Ibid., 166.
61. Richard Rorty, "The World Well Lost," originally in *Journal of Philosophy* (1972), reprinted in *Consequences of Pragmatism* (Minneapolis: University of Minnesota Press, 1982), 3–18.
62. See *Hannan Arendt / Karl Jaspers Correspondence, 1926–1969*, ed. Lotte Köhler and Hans Saner, trans. Robert and Rita Kimber, for their exchange concerning the circular issued by the Nazi Ministry of Education, which Heidegger had also signed, letters 40 and 42; on prohibiting Husserl from using the university library, letters 42–49; we find Jaspers's own version of these events and Arendt's insistence that Heidegger could be regarded "as a potential murderer" for having done this to Husserl in letter 48. On Arendt's shyness that Jaspers might not have appreciated what she had to say about his philosophy, letters 42 and 47.
63. See Benhabib, "Appendix: The Personal Is Not the Political," in id., *Reluctant Modernism of Hannah Arendt*, 221–33. Not much of philosophical import has been added in the past decade to understanding the Arendt-Heidegger nexus better, but new biographical accounts of this fascinating story abound. Most recently, see Daniel Maier-Katkin, *Stranger from Abroad: Hannah Arendt, Martin Heidegger, Friendship and Forgiveness* (New York: Norton, 2010).

64. This and the preceding quotation are from Arendt, "What Is Existenz Philosophy?" 177.
65. Ibid., 178.
66. Martin Heidegger, "Letter on Humanism," in id., *Basic Writings*, ed. David Farrell Krell (New York: HarperCollins, 1993), 213–67, here 234; also Heidegger, "Überwindung der Metaphysik," in id., *Vorträge und Aufsätze* (Pfullingen: G. Neske, 1978 [1954]), 67–97; these notes were originally composed between 1936 and 1946.
67. Arendt, "What Is Existenz Philosophy?" 179.
68. Ibid., 180.
69. Again, there are remarkable parallels between Arendt's and Adorno's assessments of these aspects of Heidegger's thought. See Adorno, *Jargon of Authenticity*, 71, 136, and 147ff. "For Heidegger the They become a cloudy mixture of elements which are merely ideological products of the exchange relationship," Adorno writes (151).
70. Arendt, "What Is Existenz Philosophy?" 181–82; emphasis added.
71. Heidegger, *Being and Time*, 55; *Sein und Zeit*, 118; emphasis in the German original.
72. Arendt, "What Is Existenz Philosophy?" 186.
73. Hannah Arendt, *The Human Condition* (1958), 8th ed. (Chicago: University of Chicago Press, 1973), 175ff.
74. Ibid., 178.
75. Ibid., 181–84.
76. See Theodor W. Adorno, Else Frenkel-Brunswik, Daniel J. Levinson, R. Nevitt Sanford et al., *The Authoritarian Personality*, abridged ed., *Studies in Prejudice*, ed. Max Horkheimer and Samuel H. Flowerman (New York: Norton, 1982 [1950]), esp. Adorno's pt. 3, "Qualitative Studies of Ideology," 295ff. Adorno writes of the "mental rigidity" of those who score high on the various scales designated to study prejudice and antisemitism (299), and that "the object must possess features, or at least be capable of being perceived and interpreted in terms of features which harmonize with the destructive tendencies of the prejudiced subject" (300). For further discussion of parallelisms and divergences between Arendt's and Adorno and Horkheimer's analyses of antisemitism, see my essay "From 'the Dialectic of Enlightenment' to 'the Origins of Totalitarianism' and the Genocide Convention: Adorno and Horkheimer in the Company of Arendt and Lemkin," in *The Modernist Imagination: Intellectual History and Critical Theory. Essays in Honor of Martin Jay,* ed. Warren Breckman, Peter E. Gordon, A. Dirk Moses, Samuel Moyn, and Elliot Neaman (New York: Berghahn Books, 2009), 299–331.
77. Theodor Adorno and Max Horkheimer, *Dialektik der Aufklärung*, 7th ed. (Frankfurt: Fischer, 1980), 167; my trans. English translation by John Cumming, *Dialectic of Enlightenment* (New York: Herder & Herder, 1982).
78. Hannah Arendt, "Thinking and Moral Considerations: A Lecture" (1971), reprinted in *Social Research* 50 (Spring–Summer 1984, anniversary issue): 5. I deal extensively with these issues in "From the Problem of Judgment to the Public

Sphere: Rethinking Hannah Arendt's Political Theory," in *Reluctant Modernism of Hannah Arendt*, 172–99.

79. Hannah Arendt, *Eichmann in Jerusalem: A Report on the Banality of Evil: A Report on the Banality of Evil* (1963), rev. ed. (New York: Penguin Books, 1992).

80. Ibid.

81. Hannah Arendt, *Lectures on Kant's Political Philosophy*, ed. Ronald Beiner (Chicago: University of Chicago Press, 1982); id., *Thinking*, "Preface," 3ff.; Immanuel Kant, *Critique of Judgment*, ed. and trans. Werner S. Pluhar (Indianapolis: Hackett, 1987).

82. Richard Bernstein, "Judging—the Actor and the Spectator," in id., *Philosophical Profiles: Essays in a Pragmatic Mode* (Philadelphia: University of Pennsylvania Press, 1986), 232–33. For further discussion of the problem of judgment in Kant's moral philosophy in relation to Arendt's insights, see also Seyla Benhabib, "Judgment and the Moral Foundations of Politics in Hannah Arendt's Thought," *Political Theory* 16, no. 1 (1988): 29–51.

83. Kant, *Critique of Judgment*, 18–19.

84. Arendt, *Thinking*, "Introduction," 5; id., "Thinking and Moral Considerations," 8.

85. Arendt's reflections on judgment continue to fascinate scholars. In an extremely interesting article, David L. Marshall discusses Arendt's view also in the light of her reading of Hegel's doctrine of judgment in his *Logic*. I cannot engage with this argument in this context. See David L. Marshall, "The Origins and Character of Hannah Arendt's Theory of Judgment," *Political Theory*, 38, no. 3 (April 2010): 367–93.

86. Hannah Arendt, "The Crisis in Culture," in id., *Between Past and Future: Six Exercises in Political Thought* (New York: Meridian, 1961), 220–21.

87. Arendt, *Thinking*, 123.

88. Ibid., 103.

89. Kant, *Critique of Judgment*, 228.

90. Adorno, *Negative Dialektik*, 268ff.

91. Ibid., 295ff.

92. I have dealt with these themes in great length in *Critique, Norm and Utopia*; see 70–84 on Hegel's critique of Kant and 205–13 on Adorno's critique of Kant.

93. Adorno, *Negative Dialektik*, 277.

94. Theodor Adorno, *Aesthetische Theorie*, in id., *Gesammelte Schriften*, ed. Rolf Tiedemann (Frankfurt: Suhrkamp, 1970), 7: 111.

95. Ibid., 101–3.

96. This and the preceding quotation ibid., 113. Susan Buck-Morss investigates this search for the "cipher" in relation to Benjamin's method of building constellations in id., *Origins of Negative Dialectics*, 96ff.

97. Albrecht Wellmer, "Truth, Semblance, Reconciliation," in id., *The Persistence of Modernity: Essays on Aesthetics, Ethics and Postmodernism*, trans. David Midgley (Malden, MA: Polity Press, 1991), 7–8.

98. Adorno, *Aesthetische Theorie*, 193.

99. Wellmer, "Truth, Semblance, Reconciliation," 6–7.//
100. Albrecht Wellmer, "Modernism and Postmodernism: The Critique of Reason since Adorno," in id., *Persistence of Modernity*, 71.
101. Arendt, *Human Condition*, 181–85.
102. Jürgen Habermas, "Urgeschichte der Subjektivität und verwilderte Selbstbehauptung," in id., *Philosophisch-Politische Profilen*, 167–79, trans. Frederick Lawrence as "Theodor Adorno—The Primal History of Subjectivity—Self-Affirmation Gone Wild," in *Philosophical-Political Profiles* (Cambridge, MA: MIT Press, 1983), 99–111, here 107.

Chapter 3

Portions of this essay appeared earlier as "Promising and Civil Disobedience (Arendt's Political Modernism)," *Graduate Faculty Philosophy Journal* 28, no. 1 (2007): 47–60.

1. Reinhart Koselleck, *Futures Past: On the Semantics of Historical Time*, trans. Keith Tribe (Cambridge, MA: MIT Press, 1985), 276.
2. Theodor W. Adorno, *Aesthetic Theory*, trans. Robert Hullot-Kentor (Minneapolis: University of Minnesota Press, 1997), 22–23. This version of the paradox of the new converges almost perfectly with the paradox of revolutionary founding.
3. Ibid., 242. For a good discussion of art and praxis, see Espen Hammer, *Adorno and the Political* (London: Routledge, 2006), 131–34.
4. Hammer, *Adorno and the Political*, exemplifies the first strategy, while Lambert Zuidervaart, *Social Philosophy After Adorno* (New York: Cambridge University Press, 2007), exemplifies the second.
5. Sheldon Wolin, "Hannah Arendt: Democracy and the Political," *Salmagundi* 60 (1983): 18.
6. My thought is that this conception of civil disobedience is the political analogue of the notion of fugitive experience and fugitive ethics I developed in my *Adorno: Disenchantment and Ethics* (New York: Cambridge University Press, 2001), chap. 9, § 4.
7. Hannah Arendt, *The Human Condition* (Chicago: Chicago University Press, 1958), 176–78.
8. Hannah Arendt, *On Revolution* (London: Penguin Books, 1963), 145.
9. Ibid., 146.
10. Arendt, *Human Condition*, 237.
11. Ibid., 246.
12. For Adorno, the central usage for promising concerns the *promesse de bonheur*, that is, the promise of happiness, of a life beyond the capitalist present, given by authentic modernist artworks rather than intersubjective relations. In my

Adorno: Disenchantment and Ethics, chap. 9, I extend this notion of the promise of artworks to actions so that it becomes constitutive of the idea ethical possibility.

13. Arendt, *Human Condition*, 237.

14. Stanley Cavell, *A Pitch of Philosophy: Autobiographical Exercises* (Cambridge, MA: Harvard University Press, 1994), 104. My attempt to make sense of the depth of Arendt's understanding of promising has depended on Cavell's elaborate discussions of Austin's treatment of Hippolytus's statement in this work and Stanley Cavell, *Philosophical Passages: Wittgenstein, Emerson, Austin, Derrida* (Oxford: Blackwell, 1994).

15. Cavell, *Philosophical Passages*, 65.

16. Only noninstrumental speaking is like this; but it is at least part of Arendt's thought that there is a stratum or dimension of all speech that contains this noninstrumental aspect, just as there is an aspect of all nonhabitual, nonmechanical human doings that is an action, a beginning. Politics isolates and refines such speaking and acting, giving them the chance of realizing the human potentialities embedded in them.

17. Although Adorno worked through a variety of concepts as an alternative to identity thinking—most stringently, mimesis and freedom toward the object—he never fully worked these concepts up to apply to intersubjective relations (see Zuidervaart, *Social Philosophy After Adorno*, chap. 6). Neither Nietzsche's notion of promising nor Hegel's of recognition tempted Adorno, who remained more concerned with what would promote autonomy rather than what would constitute nondominating social relations this side of utopia (he presumably thought that this side of utopia, nothing would). I understand Arendt's transforming of promising into power as her deepest ethical innovation.

18. Arendt, *On Revolution*, 175.

19. I am abusing the terms "strength" and "force" as Arendt deploys them in "On Violence," in *Crises of the Republic: Lying in Politics; Civil Disobedience; On Violence: Thoughts on Politics and Revolution* (New York: Harcourt Brace Jovanovich, 1972), 143ff., but this seems phenomenologically necessary in order to get at the political character of power.

20. This and the following quotation ibid., 150.

21. Arendt, *On Revolution*, 175.

22. Ibid., 212–13.

23. Ibid., 192; emphasis added.

24. Ibid., 213. My account is close to that of Bonnie Honig, *Political Theory and the Displacement of Politics* (Ithaca, NY: Cornell University Press, 1993), 96–104.

25. Exemplary validity is the only conception of validity compatible with the parameters of Adorno's thought, and, although never directly defended or elaborated by him, is implied by much of what he says; see Hammer, *Adorno and the Political*, 165–66; Bernstein, *Adorno: Disenchantment and Ethics*, chap. 8.

26. Immanuel Kant, *Critique of Judgment*, trans. Werner S. Pluhar (Indianapolis: Hackett, 1987): § 46, 308.

27. Ibid., § 32, 283.

28. My locution here follows Jacques Rancière, *Disagreement: Politics and Philosophy*, trans. Julie Rose (Minneapolis: University of Minnesota Press, 1999), 56–57.

29. Arendt, *On Revolution*, 202.

30. See Sheldon Wolin, "Fugitive Democracy," *Constellations* 1, no. 1 (1994): 16.

31. This and the preceding quotations are from Arendt, *Crises of the Republic*, 88 and 92.

32. Ibid., 74–75.

33. Ibid., 76.

34. Ibid., 56.

35. Rancière, *Disagreement*, 89.

36. Arendt, *Crises of the Republic*, 56; Theodor W. Adorno, *Negative Dialectics*, trans. E. B. Ashton (London: Routledge, 1973), 231; trans. modified.

37. For a nice handling of the relation between praxis and negation in Adorno, see Deborah Cook, *Adorno, Habermas, and the Search for a Rational Society* (London: Routledge, 2004), chap. 5. For a different handling of freedom in Arendt and Adorno, see Alex Demirovic, "Revolution und Freiheit. Zum Problem der radikalen Transformation bei Arendt und Adorno," in *Arendt und Adorno*, ed. Dirk Auer, Lars Rensmann, and Julia Schulze Wessel (Frankfurt: Suhrkamp, 2003), 260–85.

38. The argument of these final paragraphs should be taken as a direct reply to the criticisms of Bernstein, *Adorno: Disenchantment and Ethics*, lodged by Deborah Cook both in *Adorno, Habermas, and the Search for a Rational Society* and in her fine essay "From the Actual to the Possible: Nonidentity Thinking," *Constellations* 12, no. 1 (2005): 21–35.

Chapter 4

A different version of this essay appeared as "A 'Second Coming'? The Return of German Political Theory," *Annual Review of Political Science* 12 (2009): 449–70.

1. Lorenz Jäger, *Adorno: A Political Biography* (New Haven, CT: Yale University Press, 2004); Detlev Claussen, *Theodor W. Adorno: One Last Genius* (Cambridge, MA: Harvard University Press, 2008); Stefan Müller-Doohm, *Adorno: A Biography* (Malden, MA: Polity Press, 2005)

2. Given the current popularity of "identity politics" and theories of identity, I should clarify what I mean by Adorno's "critique of identity philosophies." Obviously, the referent here is not identity politics as currently understood, but philosophies and theories that postulate either a macro-subject or an idea of reason that absorbs everything "other" (as, in fact, the "expression" of the subject—e.g., humanity—or as the by-product of the concept). Fichte is the most obvious example, but the broad tendency of modern, post-Cartesian philosophy is in the direction of "identity" thus understood (the identity of the subject and the object,

to put it in epistemological terms). Adorno is reacting against what he views as a particularly dangerous dimension of the Hegelian-Marxist legacy.

3. This and the preceding quotation are from Theodor Adorno, *Minima Moralia: Reflections from Damaged Life*, trans. E. F. N. Jephcott (London: Verso, 1984), 102.

4. See Jürgen Habermas, "On the German Jewish Heritage," *Telos*, no. 44 (1980).

5. See Jürgen Habermas, "The Classical Doctrine of Politics in Relation to Social Philosophy" and "Labor and Interaction: Remarks on Hegel's Jena *Philosophy of Mind*," both in Habermas, *Theory and Practice*, trans. John Viertel (Boston: Beacon Press, 1974). For the importance of these categorical distinctions, see Seyla Benhabib, *Critique, Norm and Utopia: A Study of the Foundations of Critical Theory* (New York: Columbia University Press, 1986), and id., *The Reluctant Modernism of Hannah Arendt* (Lanham, MD: Rowman & Littlefield, 2003).

6. To avoid confusion: I say this as someone who, on the whole, has tremendous admiration for Adorno's work.

7. See Albrecht Wellmer's important essay "Reason, Utopia, and the *Dialectic of Enlightenment*," in *Habermas and Modernity*, ed. Richard J. Bernstein (Cambridge, MA: MIT Press, 1985), 35–66. In Marx, this lack of concern is obvious in canonical texts like the *Communist Manifesto* (1848), where political differences are reduced to class differences. Eliminate the hierarchal structure of class society and you eliminate the breeding ground of clashing opinions. What is left is set of clear and more or less unanimous general interests of society as such, which means that both the state and the public sphere have been rendered superfluous. The roots of this disinterest in the institutionalization of freedom can be seen as far back as Marx's 1843 *Critique of Hegel's "Philosophy of Right."* In that text, the "political" Marx presents democracy (understood as having its basis in the "will of the people") as the only political constitution that escapes the built-in alienation of the form/content divide that bedevils all other political constitutions (monarchical, republican, etc.). "Alienation" results wherever laws and institutions—the "form" of the constitution—work to overly mediate its "content" (the will of the people). See Karl Marx, *The Critique of Hegel's "Philosophy of Right,"* ed. Joseph O'Malley (New York: Cambridge University Press, 1970), 30–33.

8. See Max Weber, *Economy and Society*, ed. Guenther Roth and Claus Wittich (Berkeley: University of California Press, 1978), 1401–2.

9. Theodor Adorno and Max Horkheimer, *Dialectic of Enlightenment: Philosophical Fragments*, trans. Edmund Jephcott (Stanford: Stanford University Press, 2002), 1.

10. Ibid., *Dialectic of Enlightenment*, 11.

11. Horkheimer quoted in Benhabib, *Critique, Norm and Utopia*, 2.

12. See Jürgen Habermas, "The Public Sphere: An Encyclopedia Article," in *Critical Theory of Society: A Reader*, ed. Stephen Eric Bronner and Douglas MacKay Kellner (New York: Routledge, 1989), 137.

13. Adorno and Horkheimer, *Dialectic of Enlightenment*, 125.

14. This basic analysis recurs in the second half of Jürgen Habermas's *The Structural Transformation of the Public Sphere*, trans. Thomas Burger (Cambridge, MA: MIT Press, 1989). The crucial difference is that Habermas takes the idea and ideal of the "bourgeois public sphere" as it emerged in Enlightenment Europe seriously, whereas Horkheimer and Adorno's analysis tends toward a more traditionally Marxist view: the "public sphere" was always already a scene of ideological manipulation, and essentially so.

15. Adorno, *Minima Moralia*, 55: "The idea that after this war life will continue 'normally' or even that culture might be 'rebuilt'—as if the rebuilding of culture were not already its negation—is idiotic. Millions of Jews have been murdered, and this is seen as an interlude and not the catastrophe itself. What more is this culture waiting for?"

16. Ibid., 26: "We shudder at the brutalization of life, but lacking any objectively binding morality we are forced at every step into actions and words, into calculations that are by humane standards barbaric, and even by the dubious values of good society, tactless. With the dissolution of liberalism, the truly bourgeois principle, that of competition, far from being overcome, has passed from the objectivity of the social process into the composition of colliding and jostling atoms, and therewith as if into anthropology."

17. The impoverishment or "withering" of experience is a constant theme in *Minima Moralia*, as is the end of individual who can actually be said to be a (relatively unique) nodal point of experience: "In many people it is already an impertinence to say 'I'" (ibid., 50).

18. Emphasis added. This and the following quotation, ibid., 15.

19. Ibid., 39.

20. Ibid., 50. This remark is, famously, an inversion of Hegel's dictum "The whole is the true" (G. W. F. Hegel, *The Phenomenology of Spirit*, trans. A. V. Miller [New York: Oxford University Press, 1977], 11).

21. Adorno, *Minima Moralia*, 112–13.

22. This is precisely the temptation Herbert Marcuse succumbed to in his own "up-dating" of *Dialectic of Enlightenment*, the 1960s classic *One-Dimensional Man: Studies in the Ideology of Advanced Industrial Society* (Boston: Beacon Press, 1964).

23. Adorno, *Minima Moralia*, 112; emphasis added.

24. Ibid., 23.

25. In conversation with the author in Berlin, November 2006.

26. Adorno, *Minima Moralia*, 73–74.

27. Theodor W. Adorno, *Negative Dialectics*, trans. E. B. Ashton (New York: Seabury Press, 1973), 408.

28. Adorno and Horkheimer, *Dialectic of Enlightenment*, 9.

29. Ibid., 388.

30. Ibid., 5.

31. Ibid., 156. See Jean Hyppolite's illuminating discussion in his landmark *The Genesis and Structure of Hegel's "Phenomenology of Spirit,"* trans. Samuel Cherniak and John Heckman (Evanston, IL: Northwestern University Press, 1974), 321–33.

32. Adorno and Horkheimer, *Dialectic of Enlightenment*, 148.
33. Ibid., 149.
34. Again, the idea that a certain reductionist violence is (so to speak) "built into" conceptual rationality is found in *Dialectic of Enlightenment*. See ibid., 9–10, 16, 29, 31.
35. Ibid., 149.
36. Ibid., 172: "The circle of identification—which in the end always identifies itself alone—was drawn by a thinking that tolerates nothing outside it; its imprisonment is its own handiwork. Such totalitarian and therefore particular rationality was dictated by the threat of nature. That is its limitation. In fear, bondage to nature is perpetuated by a thinking that identifies, that *equalizes everything unequal*" (emphasis added).
37. Ibid., 149.
38. Ibid., 158.
39. Marcuse's *One-Dimensional Man* was written in order to drive this point home.
40. See Max Weber, "Politics as a Vocation," in *From Max Weber: Essays in Sociology*, ed. H. H. Gerth and C. Wright Mills (New York: Oxford University Press, 1956), 77–80. Of course, the Frankfurt School insists that domination is something that can be *overcome*, either through classical Marxian means (human emancipation through democratization of the economy and the "pacification" of the struggle for existence) or by a more consensus-oriented, deliberative politics. See, in this regard, Herbert Marcuse's essay on Weber in *Negations* (Boston: Beacon Press, 1968), 201–26, and Jürgen Habermas's early essay "Science and Technology as Ideology," in id., *Toward a Rational Society*, trans. Jeremy J. Shapiro (Boston: Beacon Press, 1970), 81–122.
41. On the significance of political struggle as an avenue of freedom, see Dana Villa, *Socratic Citizenship* (Princeton, NJ: Princeton University Press, 2001), chap. 4.
42. See, however, Iris Marion Young's influential *Justice and the Politics of Difference* (Princeton, NJ: Princeton University Press, 1990).
43. See Hannah Arendt, *The Human Condition* (Chicago: University of Chicago Press, 1958), 199–207. Arendt's invocation of Periclean Athens in this section is usually taken as evidence of a bad case of "polis envy." In fact, it points to the importance she attaches to a public realm whose "appearances" take the form of ongoing, open-ended debate, deliberation, and decision by diverse equals ("citizens"). The "public space of freedom" ranks high on Arendt's list of *essentially political* structures and activities because it provides the arena for the expression of discursive difference.
44. Ibid., 57.
45. Ibid., 7.
46. See Hannah Arendt, *On Revolution* (New York: Penguin Books, 1968), 227.
47. See Habermas, *Structural Transformation of the Public Sphere*, esp. 211–22.

48. Adorno, *Negative Dialectics*, 363. In such passages, Adorno is taking the basic Marxian notion of the "fetishism of commodities" and running with it, as Jaeger notes in *Adorno: A Political Biography*, 64–65.

49. See Hannah Arendt, "The Crisis in Culture" in id., *Between Past and Future: Six Exercises in Political Thought* (New York: Penguin Books, 1968), 205–11.

50. Compare Adorno's comments in his 1967 lecture "Education After Auschwitz" to Arendt's response to her critics at a conference held in her honor at York University in 1972. The former—which presumes the need for a teacher/student relationship in the realm of civic education—can be found in Theodor W. Adorno, *Can One Live After Auschwitz? A Philosophical Reader*, ed. Rolf Tiedemann (Stanford: Stanford University Press, 2003), 22–23; the latter in *Hannah Arendt: The Recovery of the Public Realm*, ed. Melvyn Hill (New York: St. Martin's Press, 1979), 309–10. See also Arendt's comments on Aristotle in her essay "What is Authority?" in id., *Between Past and Future*, 118–20.

51. This is the thrust of the argument presented in the oft-misunderstood section entitled "The Rise of the Social" in Arendt's *Human Condition*, 38–49.

52. See my essay "Foucault and the Dystopian Public" in Dana Villa, *Public Freedom* (Princeton, NJ: Princeton University Press, 2008), 255–301.

53. See Arendt, *Human Condition*, §§ 6, 17, 44, and 45.

54. Arendt, *On Revolution*, 30–33.

55. See Arendt, *Human Condition*, § 31, "The Traditional Substitution of Making for Acting," 220–29. For Arendt's critical appropriation of Aristotle's distinction against Plato and himself, see Dana Villa, "Arendt, Aristotle, and Action," in id., *Arendt and Heidegger: The Fate of the Political* (Princeton, NJ: Princeton University Press, 1996), 17–41.

56. Arendt, *Human Condition*, 195.

57. Ibid., 190.

58. Weber, *Economy and Society*, 53.

59. Arendt, *Human Condition*, 180, 220–22. Cf. Arendt, *On Revolution*, 31–32. See also Arendt, *Crises of the Republic: Lying in Politics; Civil Disobedience; On Violence: Thoughts on Politics and Revolution* (New York: Harcourt Brace Jovanovich, 1972), 143.

60. See Arendt's definition in *Crises of the Republic*, 142–43.

61. Arendt, *Between Past and Future*, 165.

62. Arendt, *Human Condition*, 222.

63. For a fuller consideration, see Villa, *Arendt and Heidegger*, chaps. 1 and 2 (17–79).

64. See Arendt, *Human Condition*, 248–68.

65. For Arendt and Adorno, see the essays in this volume. For Heidegger and Adorno, see *Adorno and Heidegger: Philosophical Questions,* ed. Iain Macdonald and Krzysztof Ziarek (Stanford: Stanford University Press, 2007), especially Fred Dallmayr's essay on "Adorno and Heidegger on Modernity" (167–82); also Hermann Mörchen, *Adorno und Heidegger: Untersuchung einer philosophischen Kommunikationsverweigerung* (Stuttgart: Klett-Cotta, 1998).

66. Hannah Arendt, *The Origins of Totalitarianism* (New York: Harcourt Brace Jovanovich, 1979), esp. 392–419.

67. Arendt, *On Revolution*, 141–78. I should note that this constitutional emphasis is not appreciated by all "Arendtians." See, e.g., Sheldon Wolin's *The Presence of the Past* (Baltimore: Johns Hopkins University Press, 1990), 8–31, where Wolin bemoans the "constitutionalization" of democracy, equated this with democracy's dis-essencing.

68. No matter what one thinks of Hegel's political philosophy, such a view—like the many postwar liberal caricatures presented in the Anglo-American world—is clearly untenable. For a corrective, see the judicious account presented in Shlomo Avineri's *Hegel's Theory of the Modern State* (New York: Cambridge University Press, 1972).

69. As Habermas has succinctly put it, "The old Frankfurt School never took bourgeois democracy very seriously." See Habermas, *Autonomy and Solidarity: Interviews with Jürgen Habermas*, ed. Peter Dews (London: Verso, 1986), 98.

70. This is not to say her reading of these revolutions is entirely unproblematic. For a sympathetic yet critical view, see Albrecht Wellmer's essay "Hannah Arendt on Revolution," in *The Cambridge Companion to Hannah Arendt*, ed. Dana Villa (New York: Cambridge University Press, 2001).

71. Jäger, *Adorno: A Political Biography*.

72. One does well to remember that Bernard-Henri Lévy, the most visible of the so-called *nouveaux philosophes*, started out as the most militant of Maoists. See Michel Foucault, "On Popular Justice: A Discussion with Maoists" in id., *Power/Knowledge*, ed. Colin Gordon (New York: Pantheon Books, 1980), 1–36 (Henri-Levy is "Victor").

Chapter 5

1. See Arendt to Jaspers, August 6, 1955, in *Hannah Arendt / Karl Jaspers Correspondence, 1926–1969*, ed. Lotte Köhler and Hans Saner, trans. Robert and Rita Kimber (New York: Harcourt Brace Jovanovich, 1992), 264; id. to Blücher, May 25, 1955, in *Hannah Arendt / Heinrich Blücher: Briefe, 1936–1968*, ed. Lotte Köhler (Munich: Piper, 1996), 384.

2. Elisabeth Young-Bruehl, *Hannah Arendt: For Love of the World* (New Haven, CT: Yale University Press, 1982), 324, says that Arendt wanted the title *Amor mundi* for what became *The Human Condition* (Chicago: Chicago University Press, 1958). Arendt refers to it by the latter title in a letter to Mary McCarthy on June 7, 1957; see *Between Friends: The Correspondence of Hannah Arendt and Mary McCarthy, 1949–1975*, ed. Carol Brightman (London: Secker & Warburg, 1995), 50.

3. Ursula Ludz and Ingeborg Nordmann say that *Amor mundi* was a provisional title for a work in progress, which was realized only partly and in sections; see their notes and comments in their edition of Arendt's *Denktagebuch, 1950–1973* (Munich: Piper, 2002), 1050–51; see also Ludz's comments in her edition of

Arendt's *Was ist Politik?* (Munich: Piper, 1993), 148. *The Human Condition* is the most significant of the completed publications that resulted. As we shall see, however, it was not just because she organized the material in a particular way that Arendt dropped the title *Amor mundi*.

4. Ralph Waldo Emerson, *Essays and Lectures*, ed. Joel Porte (New York: Library of America, 1983), 272.

5. Hannah Arendt, *Love and Saint Augustine*, ed. Joanna Vecchiarelli Scott and Judith Chelius Stark (Chicago: Chicago University Press, 1996), 23. This is an English version of the original text, partly revised and rewritten by Arendt around 1960. The quotations given here are, however, in line with Arendt's earliest reflections on the subject of love; see Arendt, *Der Liebesbegriff bei Augustin: Versuch einer philosophischen Interpretation* (Berlin: Springer, 1929).

6. Arendt, *Love and Saint Augustine*, 23, 20, 84.

7. Ibid., 21.

8. Ibid., 24; cf. Arendt, *Human Condition*, 10.

9. Arendt, *Love and Saint Augustine*, 50.

10. Ibid., 108.

11. Ibid., 66–68, 77, 81.

12. Ibid., 77–78.

13. See Dieter Thomä, "Heidegger und Arendt: Liebe zur Welt," in *Heidegger Handbuch*, ed. id. (Stuttgart: Metzler, 2003), 397–402.

14. Arendt, *Human Condition*, 53.

15. Ibid., 53–54, 242.

16. Hannah Arendt, *Rahel Varnhagen: The Life of a Jewess*, ed. Liliane Weissberg (Baltimore: Johns Hopkins University Press, 1997), 113; cf. 88.

17. Arendt to Heidegger, April 1925, in Hannah Arendt and Martin Heidegger, *Letters, 1925–1975*, ed. Ursula Ludz, trans. Andrew Shields (Orlando, FL.: Harcourt, 2004), 15.

18. See Hannah Arendt, *On Revolution* (New York: Viking, 1963), 135–37.

19. Whereas the German version uses the philosophical term *Weltlosigkeit*, the English version speaks of a totalitarian "threat" to the world; see Hannah Arendt, *The Origins of Totalitarianism* (New York: Harcourt Brace Jovanovich, 1979), 302; Hannah Arendt, *Elemente und Ursprünge totalitärer Herrschaft*, (Munich: Piper, 1986), 470.

20. Arendt, *Origins of Totalitarianism*, 477.

21. Arendt, *Human Condition*, 175.

22. Ibid., 242.

23. Emerson, *Essays and Lectures*, 242.

24. Arendt, *Human Condition*, 242; cf. id., *Denktagebuch*, 214–15.

25. Arendt, *Denktagebuch*, 289.

26. For a brief discussion of these findings see Dieter Thomä, "Passion und Aktion: Eine Schatzsuche in Hannah Arendts 'Denktagebuch 1950–1973,'" *Literaturen* 9 (2002): 5–9.

27. Arendt, *Denktagebuch*, 289.

28. Ibid., 203.
29. Ibid., 203–4.
30. Ibid., 203.
31. Ibid., 204. The German original reads as follows: "Als *Handelnde*, die nur innerhalb der gemeinsam bewohnten Welt und nur durch ausdrückliche Realisierung dieses Gemeinsam-seins handeln können, sind Menschen wirklich Menschen im Sinne einer spezifischen Menschlichkeit.—Und als *Liebende*, die als Eine die Zwei brauchen, um sich von der Natur die Drei usw. schenken zu lassen, nämlich aus der Einzigkeit sofort in die Mehrheit, aus dem Singular in den Plural müssen, [sind die Menschen], ist jeder Mensch—auf eine nicht auszudenkende ironische Weise—auch *der* Mensch."
32. Ibid., 459; cf. 365.
33. Ibid., 459; cf. 373.
34. Ibid., 471.
35. Ibid., 482.
36. Arendt to Heidegger, May 8, 1954, in Arendt and Heidegger, *Letters, 1925–1975*, 120.
37. Arendt, *Denktagebuch*, 523, 539.
38. Arendt, *Human Condition*, 10.
39. Arendt, *Denktagebuch*, 334.
40. This discovery complements Plato's "discovery of the soul"; see Arendt, *Denktagebuch*, 526. The traditional translation of *thymos* is of course "heart"; see the extended discussion in Pietro Pucci, *Odysseus Polutropos: Intertextual Readings of the Odyssey and the Iliad* (Ithaca, NY: Cornell University Press, 1987), 157–87.
41. Arendt, *Denktagebuch*, 334.
42. Ibid., 525.
43. Arendt, *Human Condition*, 39, 58–59.
44. Arendt, *Denktagebuch*, 7.
45. Hannah Arendt, *Between Past and Future: Eight Exercises in Political Thought* (London: Penguin Books, 2006), 164.
46. Augustine, *The City of God* 12.20, trans. Henry Bettenson (London: Penguin Books, 2003), 502; Arendt's translation in *Origins of Totalitarianism*, 473.
47. Immanuel Kant, *Critique of Pure Reason*, trans. and ed. Paul Guyer and Allen W. Wood (New York: Cambridge University Press, 1998), A445/B473.
48. Arendt, *Zwischen Vergangenheit und Zukunft* (Munich: Piper, 1994), 220; the passage on Augustine and Kant is missing from the English version of Arendt's essay, "What Is Freedom?" in id., *Between Past and Future*, 166–67. For a more extensive discussion of Kant's notion of "beginning" in relation to Augustine's *initium*, see Hannah Arendt, *The Life of the Mind*, ed. Mary McCarthy, vol. 2: *Willing* (London: Secker & Warburg, 1978), 108.
49. Arendt, *Elemente und Ursprünge totalitärer Herrschaft*, 723; id., *Origins of Totalitarianism*, 473.
50. Arendt, *Life of the Mind*, 2: 60.

51. Charles Taylor, *Human Agency and Language: Philosophical Papers I* (New York: Cambridge University Press, 1985), 18.

52. Arendt, *Denktagebuch*, 303. This is in line with Schiller's remarks on the resemblance between the "savage" *dominated* by instincts and the "barbarian" fiercely *dominating* his instincts; see Friedrich Schiller, *On the Aesthetic Education of Man, in a Series of Letters*, trans. Elizabeth Wilkinson and Leonard Ashley Willoughby (Oxford: Clarendon Press, 1967), 21.

53. Arendt, *Human Condition*, 181–88.

54. See, e.g. Hannah Arendt, *Essays in Understanding, 1930–1954*, ed. Jerome Kohn (New York: Harcourt Brace, 1994), 321; Arendt, *Human Condition*, 177–80; Arendt, *On Revolution*, 212; Arendt, *Origins of Totalitarianism*, 479; Arendt, *Life of the Mind*, 2: 217. The concept of "natality" is not explicitly mentioned in the early German version of *Love and Saint Augustine*, but in her later amendments, Arendt draws a line from her earlier remarks on *fieri* and *initium*, "becoming" and beginning," to "natality"; Arendt, *Der Liebesbegriff bei Augustin*, 37; id., *Love and Saint Augustine*, 51, 55, 132, 147.

55. "Natality" is often praised as being a complement or corrective to Heidegger's focus on "mortality"; see, e.g., Dana Villa, *Arendt and Heidegger: The Fate of the Political* (Princeton, NJ: Princeton University Press, 1996), 141. Julia Kristeva celebrates Arendt's courage in raising the question of natality in the aftermath of the Shoah; see Kristeva, *Hannah Arendt* (New York: Columbia University Press, 2001), 47. Seyla Benhabib is much more reluctant to do so and seeks to think "with Arendt contra Arendt": instead of linking natality and spontaneity to public freedom, Benhabib highlights the role of education in the private sphere as well; see Benhabib, *Reluctant Modernism of Hannah Arendt* (Thousand Oaks, CA: Sage, 1996), 134–37.

56. Arendt, *Human Condition*, 178.

57. Ibid., 177–78; Hannah Arendt, *Vita activa oder vom tätigen Leben* (Stuttgart: Kohlhammer, 1960), 166–67, 242.

58. Ibid., 167.

59. Arendt, *Human Condition*, 246; id., *Vita activa*, 242.

60. Arendt, *Human Condition*, 178; id., *Vita activa*, 167.

61. Arendt, *Human Condition*, 178.

62. Arendt, *Life of the Mind*, 2: 217.

63. Arendt, *Human Condition*, 245.

64. On the "discovery of childhood" as a cultural achievement, see Philippe Ariès, *Centuries of Childhood: A Social History of Family Life* (New York: Vintage Books, 1962), 33–49.

65. This and the preceding two quotations are from Arendt, *Love and Saint Augustine*, 56.

66. Arendt, *Life of the Mind*, 2: 110; cf. Kristeva, *Hannah Arendt*, 202–19.

67. Arendt, *Human Condition*, 208.

68. Ibid., 159–67.

69. Ibid., 190.

70. Ibid., 23–28, 220.
71. Ibid., 15.
72. Amélie Oksenberg Rorty, "The Historicity of Psychological Attitudes: Love Is Not Love Which Alters Not When It Alteration Finds," in id., *Mind in Action: Essays in the Philosophy of Mind* (Boston: Beacon Press, 1988), 121–34, 359–60.
73. Arendt, *Life of the Mind*, 2: 123.
74. Ibid., 144–45.
75. Arendt, *Denktagebuch*, 372–74; for an abridged and less dramatic version of these considerations, see Arendt, *Human Condition*, 242.
76. In the sense of Emerson's "The soul *becomes*" (Emerson, *Essays and Lectures*, 271). See Dieter Thomä, "Zur Rehabilitierung der Selbstliebe," in id., *Vom Glück in der Moderne* (Frankfurt: Suhrkamp, 2003), 270–91; id., "Das werdende Selbst: Identität, Alterität und Interaktion nach Emerson, Nietzsche und Cavell," in *Happy Days. Lebenswissen nach Cavell*, ed. Kathrin Thiele and Katrin Trüstedt (Munich: Fink, 2010), 171–86.
77. Heidegger to Arendt, May 13, 1925, in Arendt and Heidegger, *Letters, 1925–1975*, 21; Arendt, *Denktagebuch*, 284; Arendt, *Life of the Mind*, 2: 136, 144.
78. Arendt, *Human Condition*, 242.
79. In a moving response to Heidegger's condolences after the death of Heinrich Blücher, Arendt concedes that a "world" sometimes does emerge and exist for lovers: as the only "homeland" (*Heimat*) that she and Blücher recognized (Arendt to Heidegger, November 27, 1970, in Arendt and Heidegger, *Letters, 1925–1975*, 173).
80. See Dieter Thomä, "Keine Energie ohne Individualität: Kontext und Aktualität der Bildungstheorie Wilhelm von Humboldts," *Studia Philosophica* 65 (2006): 199–220.
81. Theodor W. Adorno, *Critical Models: Interventions and Catchwords*, trans. Henry W. Pickford (New York: Columbia University Press, 1998), 164.
82. Ibid., 165.
83. Arendt, *Life of the Mind*, 75.
84. Max Horkheimer and Theodor W. Adorno, *Dialectic of Enlightenment*, trans. John Cumming (New York: Continuum, 1988), 33; translation amended by the editors.
85. Ibid., 54–55.
86. Theodor W. Adorno, *Negative Dialectics* (London: Routledge, 2000), 260; see Christoph Menke, *Reflections of Equality*, trans. Howard Rouse and Andrei Denejkine (Stanford: Stanford University Press, 2006), 58.
87. Adorno, *Negative Dialectics*, 261 ("the heteronomous admixture in the inner composition of autonomy").
88. Arendt, *Human Condition*, 181.
89. Adorno, *Critical Models*, 165.
90. Theodor W. Adorno, *Minima Moralia: Reflections from Damaged Life*, trans. E. F. N. Jephcott (London: Verso, 2005), 195.
91. Arendt, *Denktagebuch*, 491.

92. Arendt, *On Revolution*, 136.
93. See Claus Offe, *Reflections on America: Tocqueville, Weber, and Adorno in the States*, trans. Patrick Camiller (Malden, MA: Polity Press, 2005).
94. Adorno, *Negative Dialectics*, 202.
95. Ibid., 228; see Christoph Menke, *Spiegelungen der Gleichheit: Politische Philosophie nach Adorno und Derrida* (2000; Frankfurt: Suhrkamp, 2004), 154. The chapter from which this passage is taken appears only in the 2nd German edition of Menke's book and is not included in Howard Rouse's and Andrei Denejkine's English translation, *Reflections of Equality* (Stanford: Stanford University Press, 2006).
96. Adorno, *Negative Dialectics*, 228–29.
97. Spinoza, *Ethics*, ed. G. H. R. Parkinson (New York: Oxford University Press, 2000), IV, App. § 13, 283.
98. Menke, *Spiegelungen der Gleichheit*, 156; John McDowell, *Mind, Value, and Reality* (Cambridge, MA: Harvard University Press, 1998), 53.
99. Adorno, *Negative Dialectics*, 299; cf. Josef Früchtl, "'Leben wie ein gutes Tier.' Ethik zwischen Mitleid und Diskurs," *Deutsche Zeitschrift für Philosophie* 41 (1993): 986, 993–94.
100. Adorno, *Minima Moralia*, 156.
101. Adorno, *Negative Dialectics*, 203.
102. Horkheimer and Adorno, *Dialectic of Enlightenment*, 116.
103. Adorno, *Negative Dialectics*, 260.
104. Theodor W. Adorno, *Erziehung zur Mündigkeit* (Frankfurt: Suhrkamp, 1970), 118.
105. Jürgen Habermas, *Philosophical-Political Profiles*, trans. Frederick G. Lawrence (Cambridge, MA: MIT Press, 1983), 106–10.
106. Adorno, *Minima Moralia*, 157. The quotation within this quotation—"being, nothing else . . ."—obviously refers to the opening lines of Hegel's *Logic*. In *Rêveries du promeneur solitaire*, Rousseau describes the archetype of an almost symbiotic situation and allows "l'agitation" of the soul to merge with "l'agitation de l'eau." The lake's "mouvement continu . . . me berçait" making the solitary walker "faire sentir avec plaisir mon existence" ("the continual movement . . . lulled me" and made "me feel my existence with pleasure"); Jean-Jacques Rousseau, "Les rêveries du promeneur solitaire," in *Œuvres complètes*, vol. 1, ed. Bernard Gagnebin and Marcel Raymond (Paris: Gallimard, 1959), 1045; Rousseau, "Reveries of the Solitary Walker," trans. Charles E. Butterworth, in *Collected Writings*, vol. 8, ed. Christopher Kelly (Hanover, NH: Dartmouth University Press, 2000), 45. The English translation does not render the precious correspondence between internal and external processes properly; the French word *agitation* is rendered as both "tossing" and "disturbance." See Dieter Thomä, "Das 'Gefühl der Existenz' und die Situation des Subjekts: Mit Rousseau gegen Derrida und de Man denken," in *Philosophie der Dekonstruktion*, ed. Andrea Kern and Christoph Menke (Frankfurt: Suhrkamp, 2002), 311–30.
107. Horkheimer and Adorno, *Dialectic of Enlightenment*, 255.

108. Charles Taylor, *Sources of the Self: The Making of the Modern Identity* (New York: Cambridge University Press, 1989), 159–76.
109. Horkheimer and Adorno, *Dialectic of Enlightenment*, 254.
110. Ibid., 93–94.

Chapter 6

1. Hannah Arendt and Hans Jürgen Benedict, "Revolution, Violence, and Power: A Correspondence," *Constellations* 16, no. 2 (2009): 302–6, here 304. Arendt does not restrict one's "own world" or specific context to the political realm of the nation-state or deduce its boundaries on the basis of theoretical justifications: "How broadly the lines are drawn cannot be concluded in theory but in most cases it can be easily deduced in practice."
2. Human action can create new spaces and institutions beyond territorial confines: "The *polis*, properly speaking, is not the city-state in its physical appearance; it is the organization of the people as it arises out of acting and speaking together, and its true space lies between people living together for this purpose, no matter where they happen to be: 'Where you go, you will be a *polis*.': these famous words . . . expressed the conviction that action and speech create a space between the participants which can find its proper location almost any time and anywhere." Hannah Arendt, *The Human Condition* (1958; Chicago: University of Chicago Press, 1998), 190, 198–99.
3. Hannah Arendt, "Karl Jaspers: Citizen of the World?" (1957), in id., *Men in Dark Times* (New York: Harcourt, Brace & World, 1968), 81–82. See also Arendt and Benedict, "Revolution, Violence, and Power," 304.
4. Arendt, "Karl Jaspers," 82.
5. Theodor W. Adorno, *Minima Moralia: Reflections from Damaged Life,* trans. E. F. N. Jephcott (London: Verso, 1974), 103.
6. Theodor W. Adorno, "Progress," in id., *Critical Models: Interventions and Catchwords* (New York: Columbia University Press, 1998), 144.
7. On more optimistic prospects of legal cosmopolitanism and international law's capacity to tame power politics, see Jürgen Habermas, "Does the Constitutionalization of International Law Still Have a Chance?" in id., *The Divided West* (Malden, MA: Polity Press, 2006), 115–93; Daniele Archibugi, *The Global Commonwealth of Citizens: Toward Cosmopolitan Democracy* (Princeton, NJ: Princeton University Press, 2008); David Held, *Democracy and the Global Order* (Stanford: Stanford University Press, 1996). For recent advanced discussions of the nuclei of global democratization, see Robert E. Goodin, "Global Democracy: In the Beginning," *International Theory* 2, no. 2 (2010), and the essays in *Global Democracy: Normative and Empirical Perspectives*, ed. Daniele Archibugi, Mathias Koenig-Archibugi, and Raffaele Marchetti (New York: Cambridge University Press, 2011).
8. There is, to be sure, renewed interest in Arendt and international political theory; see, e.g., *Hannah Arendt and International Relations*, ed. Anthony F. Lang

and John Williams (New York: Palgrave, 2005); Ronald Axtmann, "Globality, Plurality, and Freedom: The Arendtian Perspective," *Review of International Studies* 32, no. 1 (2006); Patrick Hayden, *Political Evil in a Global Age: An Arendtian Perspective* (New York: Routledge, 2009); and Lars Rensmann, "Europeanism and Americanism in the Age of Globalization: Hannah Arendt on Europe and America and Implications for a Post-National Identity of the EU Polity," *European Journal of Political Theory* 5, no. 2 (2006). There are two notable cosmopolitan readings of Arendt: Hayden's *Political Evil* sees Arendt as a "cosmopolitan realist" (22), and Robert Fine's *Cosmopolitanism* (New York: Routledge, 2007) alludes to her "worldly cosmopolitanism" (96–132). On the claim that Arendt promotes a modest, "realist" cosmopolitanism, see also Patricia Owens, *Between War and Politics: International Relations and the Thought of Hannah Arendt* (New York: Oxford University Press, 2007), 145–46.

9. Chamsy El-Ojeili and Patrick Hayden, *Critical Theories of Globalization* (New York: Palgrave, 2006), 132; Lambert Zuidervaart, *Social Philosophy After Adorno* (New York: Cambridge University Press, 2007); Matthias Benzer, *The Sociology of Theodor Adorno* (New York: Cambridge University Press, 2011).

10. Hannah Arendt, *The Origins of Totalitarianism* (1951; 3rd ed., New York: Harcourt, Brace & World, 1968), 297.

11. For an initial conceptualization of "cosmopolitanism from below," see Fuyuki Kurasawa, "A Cosmopolitanism from Below: Alternative Globalization and the Creation of a Solidarity Without Bonds," *European Journal of Sociology* 45, no. 2 (2004): 233–55. Such political vernacularizations are not limited to *national* "sovereign" constitutional contexts. My use of the term "vernacularization" as a way to conceptualize an important element of Arendt's and Adorno's cosmopolitanism overlaps with Seyla Benhabib's understanding of vernacularized cosmopolitan norms through "democratic iterations," according to which cosmopolitan legal norms and principles are adopted to national contexts. Following Benhabib, this happens through permanent, open processes of democratic (re)interpretation within particular political communities that transform existing laws and self-understandings. Benhabib's primary focus, however, is on "jurisgenerative politics" and the changing understanding of *legal* norms. See Seyla Benhabib, "Claiming Rights Across Borders: International Human Rights and Democratic Sovereignty," *American Political Science Review* 103, no. 4 (2009): 691–704; id., *Another Cosmopolitanism* (New York: Oxford University Press, 2006).

12. Arendt's and Adorno's theorizing, proficient in thinking without banisters, is "groundless" in its criticism of any deceptively secure foundation anchored in philosophical systems or, for that matter, false universals of law and morality; both theorists oppose the metaphysical foundationalism underlying abstract moral universalism, just as they both aim at subverting false particulars and essentialized identity constructs that seek to ground politics in fixed cultural particularisms or other natural and ethnic substrates. Adorno views the latter as an especially regressive form of "identitarian thinking." Neither Arendt nor Adorno denies the significance of historically generated cultural identities. But they do object to the

uncontested affirmation of such identity constructs—in that, Arendt and Adorno are clearly post-traditional theorists. On the notion of "groundless cosmopolitics," see Ayten Gundogdu, "'A Right to Have Rights': Hannah Arendt and the Outlines of a Groundless Cosmopolitics" (paper presented at the Western Political Science Association Annual Meeting, San Antonio, April 21–24, 2011).

13. A broader exploration of their contributions and their relevance for contemporary cosmopolitan theory is the subject of my forthcoming book *The Constitution of Humanity: Global Politics After Arendt and Adorno*.

14. For Arendt's critique of the very concept of sovereignty in political thought, see Hannah Arendt, "What Is Freedom?" in id., *Between Past and Future: Eight Exercises in Political Thought* (1961; rev. ed., New York: Penguin Books, 1977), 143–71. On the discussion of "sovereignty" in conventional international law and contemporary realist international relations theory, see Stephen Krasner, *Sovereignty: Organized Hypocrisy* (Princeton, NJ: Princeton University Press, 1999), and Joanne Pemberton, *Sovereignty: Interpretations* (London: Palgrave, 2009); for an earlier critique of absolute sovereignty in Carl Schmitt and beyond, see Jürgen Habermas, *The Inclusion of the Other* (Cambridge, MA: MIT Press, 1996).

15. Rolando Vázquez rightly argues that Arendt thinks about politics with and through events, which keeps at bay the thought of abstract universal pretensions "that has dominated the panorama of modernity," and preconceived "determinate judgments," i.e., the application of established universal principles to particulars. However, for Arendt—just as for Adorno—particular events can have universal implications, which is why I argue that it is inadequate to claim that Arendt's concern with the particular and particular experiences a priori excludes elements of universal validity. See Rolando Vázquez, "Thinking the Event with Hannah Arendt," *European Journal of Social Theory* 9, no. 1 (2006): 46ff.

16. Arendt, "On Violence," in *Crises of the Republic: Lying in Politics; Civil Disobedience; On Violence: Thoughts on Politics and Revolution* (New York: Harcourt Brace Jovanovich, 1972), 108.

17. Seyla Benhabib, *The Rights of Others* (New York: Cambridge University Press, 2004), 60.

18. Arendt, *Origins of Totalitarianism*, 231.

19. Ibid., 287.

20. Ibid., 283.

21. Hannah Arendt, *Eichmann in Jerusalem* (New York: Penguin Books, 1963), 268.

22. Arendt, *Origins of Totalitarianism*, 293: "The Rights of Man, supposedly inalienable, proved to be unenforceable—even in countries whose constitutions were based upon them—whenever people appeared who were no longer citizens of any sovereign state." Arendt concedes, however, that several of those constitutional democracies provide the right to asylum "as a genuine substitute for national law" (295).

23. Ibid., 296.

24. Ibid., 280ff.

25. Hannah Arendt, "The Seeds of a Fascist International" (1945), in id., *Essays in Understanding, 1930–1954: Formation, Exile, and Totalitarianism* (New York: Schocken Books, 1994), 143.

26. Arendt, *Origins of Totalitarianism*, 299.

27. Ibid., 466. See also Dana Villa, *Public Freedom* (Princeton, NJ: Princeton University Press, 2008).

28. Arendt, *Origins of Totalitarianism*, 298–99. On her constitutionalism, see, e.g., Hannah Arendt, *On Revolution* ([1963; New York: Penguin Books, 1991), 139ff. See also Villa, *Public Freedom*, esp. 85–107; George Kateb, "Death and Politics: Hannah Arendt's Reflections on the American Constitution," *Social Research* 54, no. 3 (1987): 605–16; Jeremy Waldron, "Arendt's Constitutional Politics," in *The Cambridge Companion to Hannah Arendt*, ed. Dana Villa (New York: Cambridge University Press, 2000), 201–19; and Verity Smith, "Dissent in Dark Times: Hannah Arendt on Civil Disobedience and Constitutional Patriotism," in *Thinking in Dark Times: Hannah Arendt on Ethics and Politics,* ed. Roger Berkowitz, Jeffrey Katz, and Thomas Keenan (New York: Fordham University Press, 2010), 105–14.

29. Seyla Benhabib, "International Law and Human Plurality in the Shadow of Totalitarianism," in *Politics in Dark Times: Encounters with Hannah Arendt*, ed. id. (New York: Cambridge University Press, 2010), 222, 232. A more complex relationship between circumscribed republican freedom and international law, especially as it pertains to the question of genocide, is one of the subtexts of *Eichmann in Jerusalem*. On the jurisprudential issues behind the Eichmann trial in Arendt's perspective, see also Leora Bilsky, "The Eichmann Trial and the Legacy of Jurisdiction," in *Politics in Dark Times*, ed. Benhabib, 198–218.

30. Arendt, *Eichmann in Jerusalem*, 257, 268. This new crime of genocide goes beyond legalized discrimination and mass expulsion. It is characterized by the wish "to make the entire Jewish people disappear from the face of the earth," and is thus a crime against "the human status." On Arendt and crimes against humanity, as well as the implications for international law, see Benhabib, "International Law and Human Plurality," 219–43; Fine, *Cosmopolitanism*, 96–114; Lars Rensmann, "Genocidal Politics: Crimes Against Humanity in Global Perspective," *Journal of Contemporary History* 44, no. 4 (2009): 753ff.

31. Arendt, *Eichmann in Jerusalem*, 262, 272.

32. Ibid., 290ff.

33. Ibid., 272.

34. See Robert Fine, "Debating Human Rights, Law, and Subjectivity: Arendt, Adorno, and Critical Theory," chapter 7 in this volume.

35. Arendt, *Eichmann in Jerusalem*, 267.

36. Ibid., 275.

37. Arendt, "Karl Jaspers," 91.

38. Arendt, *Origins of Totalitarianism*, 298.

39. Ibid., 298.

40. Arendt, *Eichmann in Jerusalem*, 271.

41. See Fine, *Cosmopolitanism*, 96–114.

42. Arendt and Benedict, "Revolution, Violence, and Power," 304.
43. Arendt, *Origins of Totalitarianism*, 297.
44. Arendt, *Eichmann in Jerusalem*, 259.
45. See James Ingram, "What Is a 'Right to Have Rights'? Three Images of the Politics of Human Rights," *American Political Science Review* 102, no. 3 (2008): 401–16.
46. Fine, *Cosmopolitanism*, 111.
47. Ibid., 117.
48. Habermas, "Does the Constitutionalization of International Law Still Have a Chance?" 174.
49. Adorno, "Progress," 145. In *Problems of Moral Philosophy* (Stanford: Stanford University Press, 2001), based on lectures he had given in 1963, Adorno even hesitates to use the term "humanity," because it is "one of the expressions that reify and hence falsify crucial issues by merely speaking of them" (169).
50. Theodor W. Adorno and Max Horkheimer, *Dialectic of Enlightenment: Philosophical Fragments* (Stanford: Stanford University Press, 2002), 138.
51. Theodor W. Adorno, *History and Freedom: Lectures, 1964–1965* (Malden, MA: Polity Press, 2006), 104. Adorno argues that the more hopeless and irrational nationalism's cause, the fiercer it may in fact become. In the age of international communication and cosmopolitan exchange, Adorno claims, "nationalism cannot really believe in itself anymore and must exaggerate itself to the extreme in order to persuade itself and others that it is still substantial." See Theodor W. Adorno, "Education after Auschwitz," in id., *Critical Models: Interventions and Catchwords* (New York: Columbia University Press, 1998), 203. This is reminiscent of Arendt's image of national sovereignty as a "walking corpse."
52. See Craig Reeves, "Exploding the Limits of Law: Judgment and Freedom in Arendt and Adorno," *Res Publica* 15, no. 2 (2009): 137–64.
53. See Karl Marx, "Contribution to a Critique of Hegel's Philosophy of Law," in *Marx's Early Writings*, ed. Lucio Coletti (London: Penguin Books, 1975). On Marx and jurisprudence, see Robert Fine, *Democracy and the Rule of Law: Marx's Critique of the Legal Form* (Caldwell, NJ: Blackburn Press, 2002).
54. Adorno, *History and Freedom*, 140.
55. "A legally unrestricted majority rule, that is, a democracy without a constitution, can be very formidable in the suppression of the rights of minorities and very effective in the suffocation of dissent without any use of violence" (Arendt, "On Violence," 141). This concept is further explored in many places of Arendt's work, especially in *On Revolution*.
56. Theodor W. Adorno, "Critique," in id., *Critical Models*, 281.
57. Adorno, *Minima Moralia*, 43.
58. See Adorno and Horkheimer, *Dialectic of Enlightenment*, 12.
59. Ibid., 141.
60. Ibid., 138.
61. On international tribunals and the Nuremberg trial in particular, see Theodor W. Adorno, *Guilt and Defense: On the Legacies of National Socialism in Postwar Germany* (Cambridge, MA: Harvard University Press, 2010).

62. Theodor W. Adorno, *Negative Dialectics* (1966; New York: Continuum, 1973), 309.

63. Ibid., 309.

64. Adorno, *Problems of Moral Philosophy*, 122.

65. Adorno, *Negative Dialectics*, 309.

66. It is Aristotle's "imperishable glory," Adorno argues, to have proclaimed this in his doctrine of equity. Through equity, Aristotle recognizes that the more consistent and universal legal systems are worked out, the greater their inability to find just ways to deal with what defies absorption—a deficiency that requires rectification. See Adorno, *Negative Dialectics*, 311. See also Adorno, *Problems of Moral Philosophy*, 124: Aristotelian fairness requires that "we should not just act in accordance with the law, but that we should also take account of the person we are dealing with and his particular circumstances." According to Aristotle, every action needs to be judged according to all the relevant situative circumstances; it is not possible to judge the "raw material" of human behavior only in general terms. The doctrine of *epieikeia* (considerateness) makes equity superior to the general law. The former is the rectification of legal justice and the virtue that corrects the law. Since all law is universal, and it is often deficient when dealing with the particular, it needs equity, that is, the "correction of law, where it is deficient on account of its universality." Aristotle, *Nichomachean Ethics*, ed. Roger Crisp (New York: Cambridge University Press, 2000) 100, 1137b. Of course, for Aristotle, the rule of law is also better than the unmediated rule of particulars equipped with power; the rule of law is "preferable to that of any individual." See Aristotle, *The Politics and the Constitution of Athens*, trans. Stephen Everson (New York Cambridge University Press, 1996), *Politics* III.16, p. 88

67. Laws may be incapable of establishing justice in the face of unspeakable atrocities. But Adorno boldly claims that once the "judicial machinery" is mobilized against genocidal killers, "with codes of procedure, black robes, and understanding defense lawyers . . . justice—incapable anyway of imposing sanctions that would fit the crime—is falsified already" (Adorno, *Negative Dialectics*, 286–87). But would it really be more justified to "execute mass murderers on the spot," as Adorno suggests, rather than putting them on trial, however deficient such judicial procedures may be?

68. Habermas conceives a "political constitution of a decentered world society as a multilevel system." The constitutionalization of international law is hereby reserved to limited functions and based on less demanding legitimacy requirements than in constitutional democracies: "If the international community limits itself to securing peace and protecting human rights, the requisite solidarity among world citizens need not reach the level of the implicit consensus on thick political value-orientations that is necessary for the familiar kind of civic solidarity among fellow-nationals." Habermas hereby also suggests "judicial oversight" as the mechanism that presumably sufficiently legitimizes the global enforcement of human rights, i.e., "humanitarian interventions": "We can take it for granted that these basic rights are accepted worldwide and that the judicial oversight of

the enforcement of law for its part follows rules that are recognized as legitimate." See Habermas, "Does the Constitutionalization of International Law Still Have a Chance?" 135, 143, 174.

69. Adorno, *Negative Dialectics*, 337. See also Reeves, "Exploding the Limits of Law," 162.

70. Adorno, *Negative Dialectics*, 286.

71. Ibid., 286.

72. "No man should be tortured; there should be no concentration camps—while all of this continues in Asia and Africa and is repressed merely because, as ever, the humanity of civilization is inhuman toward the people it shamelessly brands as uncivilized" (Adorno, *Negative Dialectics*, 285).

73. J. M. Bernstein, "Suffering Injustice: Misrecognition as Moral Injury in Critical Theory," in *Language Without Soil: Adorno and Late Philosophical Modernity*, ed. Gerhard Richter (New York: Fordham University Press, 2010), 51.

74. Adorno, *Negative Dialectics*, 286.

75. "Categorical" refers to an "absolutely universal and necessary rule"; it means "absolutely valid, in contrast to 'hypothetical', only conditionally valid" (Adorno, *History and Freedom,* 125).

76. Danilo Zolo, "The Political and Legal Dilemmas of Globalization," *Theoria* 51 (2004): 40. In a similar vein, according to Chantal Mouffe, all cosmopolitanism and universal human rights claims are necessarily "the world hegemony of a dominant power [imposing] its conception of the world on the entire planet." Mouffe, *On the Political: Thinking in Action* (New York: Routledge, 2005), 110.

77. A recent case in point is the case of Syria's almost successful bid for a seat in the UN Human Rights Council at a time when its government was slaughtering peacefully demonstrating citizens at home. Local activists, transnational NGOs, dozens of Arab human rights groups, and Western governments ultimately succeeded in opposing Syria's bid for a seat, which was long endorsed by the fifty-three-member Asian Group. See Edith M. Lederer, "Campaign to Bar Syria from UN Human Rights Body," http://arabnews.com/middleeast/article373423.ece (accessed September 21, 2011). A "sovereignist" view is neither able to grasp these complexities nor understands the relevance of universal human rights claims articulated by the victims of "sovereign" governments across the globe.

78. Many horrors today, Adorno states, are nothing more than the extension of "popular customs that have taken on . . . violent and irrational features precisely because they have become detached from reason" (Adorno, *Problems of Moral Philosophy,* 18).

79. Adorno, "Progress," 144.

80. On the concept of "political modernity" and its antinomies, see Samir Gandesha and Lars Rensmann, "Understanding Political Modernity: Rereading Arendt and Adorno in Comparative Perspective," chapter 1 in this volume. Political modernity can be differentiated into all-pervasive *modernization* dynamics, which entail technological progress but are dominated by an instrumental economic rationality and glorification of labor society that is "de-worlding the world" and also

creates material conditions of superfluousness; emancipatory aspects of *modernity*, embodied in universal claims to freedom, individual rights, and nondomination that are in part actualized in democratic constitutions and institutions; and *modernism*, i.e., critical and aesthetic self-reflections of political modernity. Early on, both Arendt and Adorno diagnose that many constitutive features—and contradictions—of political modernity have become globalized, or part of the new "global condition" of politics and society.

81. Moreover, for Adorno, there is a flip side to the "actually existing" cosmopolitanization of societies. It does not only replace national bonds of society but also tends to eradicate diversity. "[I]t is no longer the case that so-called cosmopolitanism is the more abstract thing in contrast to the individual nations; cosmopolitanism now possesses the greater reality. We can now see a convergence of countless spheres of life and forms of production. . . . . Compared with this, the differences between nations are merely rudimentary vestiges" (Adorno, *History and Freedom*, 109–11). In strikingly similar terms, Arendt fears a global "leveling down" of differences. For Arendt, new global integration may well render the historical pasts of nations, in their "utter diversity and disparity . . . nothing but obstacles on the road to a horridly shallow unity" (Arendt, "Karl Jaspers," 87).

82. Liberal theory's notion of negative freedom (in its classical Benthamite version), where the function of the state's law is only to secure individual liberty, is incapable of recognizing, let alone addressing, these issues.

83. Arendt, *Origins of Totalitarianism*, p. vii. On Arendt and "superfluous humanity," see Hayden, *Political Evil*, 32–54.

84. Both Arendt and Adorno insist that the Nazi genocide was a distinct, unprecedented phenomenon; but they also view totalitarianism as shaped by inner tensions of political modernity. The ideas and institutions of political modernity have created new opportunities for human freedom. Yet global political modernity also provides enabling conditions for new forms of subjugation and societal regress. But this does not mean that we should "exaggerate the systemacity and totalizing character" of domination in the twenty-first century, as Nancy Fraser reminds us in *Scales of Justice: Reimagining Political Space in a Globalizing World* (New York: Columbia University Press, 2007), 139.

85. Hannah Arendt, "On Humanity in Dark Times," in id., *Men in Dark Times*, 11.

86. Walter Benjamin, "The Task of the Translator," in id., *Illuminations: Essays and Reflections*, ed. Hannah Arendt, trans. Harry Zohn (New York: Schocken Books, 1968).

87. The vernacularization of cosmopolitan norms and the emergence of transformative "authentic" claims to human dignity and rights needs to be distinguished from William Kymlicka's "politics in the vernacular." The latter points in a very different direction: it calls such engagement with universality—that is, ethnocultural groups' appropriation of inclusive, universalistic claims to human dignity—into question. See Will Kymlicka, *Politics in the Vernacular: Nationalism, Multiculturalism and Citizenship* (New York: Oxford University Press, 2001).

88. Since such vernacularization entails cultural dialogue and defamiliarizing that is reflective of false universals, it challenges particularism that seeks to justify violence against humans and the violation of human dignity—epitomized, for instance, by the "legal" and "constitutional" death penalty for blasphemy.

89. Michael Ignatieff calls this the "advocacy revolution." See Ignatieff, *Human Rights as Politics and Idolatry* (Princeton, NJ: Princeton University Press, 2000). For a recent example, think of the grassroots democratic uprising in Iran, which interlinked local activists and transnational support groups.

90. Adorno, *Problems of Moral Philosophy*, 124.

91. Ibid., 123.

92. Ibid., 19.

93. Hannah Arendt, *The Life of Mind*, vol. 1: *Thinking* (New York: Harcourt Brace Jovanovich, 1978), 193 (§ 1).

94. See Fine, *Cosmopolitanism*, 126. On Arendt's concepts of solidarity, see also Ken Reshaur, "Concepts of Solidarity in the Political Theory of Hannah Arendt," *Canadian Journal of Political Science* 25, no. 4 (1992): 723–26. In contrast to Adorno, Arendt separates such solidarity from emotions and passions she associates with "pity." For Arendt, such separation enables global solidarity based on the common interest of human dignity. For "solidarity, because it partakes of reason, and hence of generality, is able to comprehend a multitude conceptually, not only the multitude of a class or a nation or a people, but eventually all mankind. But this solidarity, though it may be aroused by suffering, is not guided by it" (Arendt, *On Revolution*, 79).

95. Hannah Arendt, "Rosa Luxemburg," in id., *Men in Dark Times*, 52.

96. Hannah Arendt, "Thoughts on Politics and Revolution," in Arendt, *Crises of the Republic* (1972), 232.

97. Arendt, "Karl Jaspers," 83.

98. Benhabib, "Claiming Rights Across Borders"; see also Andrei S. Markovits and Lars Rensmann, *Gaming the World: How Sports Are Reshaping Global Politics and Culture* (Princeton, NJ: Princeton University Press, 2010), 49.

99. See Jeffrey Flynn, "Human Rights, Transnational Solidarity, and Duties to the Global Poor," *Constellations* 16, no. 1 (2009).

100. Arendt, *Human Condition*, 198–99.

101. Ibid., 190. See also Lars Rensmann, "Cosmopolitan Republics: Rethinking Global Democracy with Hannah Arendt" (paper presented at the 105th Annual Meeting of the American Political Science Association, Toronto, September 3–6, 2009), http://papers.ssrn.com/sol3/papers.cfm?abstract_id=1449779 (accessed September 21, 2011).

102. Jeffrey C. Isaac, "A New Guarantee on Earth: Hannah Arendt on Human Dignity and the Politics of Human Rights," *American Political Science Review* 90, no. 1 (1996): 71. Such transnational social movements struggling for political change by engaging in local and transnational public actions and public spaces have also been conceived as "globalization from below." See Jeremy Brecher, Tim Costello, and Brendan Smith, *Globalization from Below: The Power of Solidarity*

(Cambridge, MA: South End Press, 2000); Sidney G. Tarrow, *The New Transnational Activism* (New York Cambridge University Press, 2005); Jackie Smith, *Social Movements for Global Democracy* (Baltimore: Johns Hopkins University Press, 2008); and Charles Lindholm and José Pedro Zúquete, *The Struggle for the World: Liberation Movements for the 21st Century* (Stanford: Stanford University Press, 2011), 83–121. Rainer Forst's recent work on human rights engages in decentering cosmopolitics by conceiving of human rights claims as derived from those autonomous political participants who claim them in their struggle against the domination and oppression from which they suffer; see Rainer Forst, "The Justification of Human Rights and the Basic Right to Justification: A Reflexive Approach," *Ethics* 120, no. 4 (2010): 711–40.

103. Adorno, "Progress," 144.

104. Theodor W. Adorno, "Die auferstandene Kultur," in id., *Gesammelte Schriften,* vol. 20.2 (Frankfurt: Suhrkamp, 1986), 454.

105. Adorno, *Problems of Moral Philosophy,* 176.

106. Adorno, "Progress," 145.

107. Theodor W. Adorno, "Heine the Wound," in id., *Notes to Literature,* vol. 1 (New York: Columbia University Press, 1991), 85.

108. Adorno, *Minima Moralia,* 156.

109. Seyla Benhabib suggests that Arendt "underestimates the potentialities of planetary politics" (Benhabib, *Rights of Others,* 60). As has been shown in this essay, I do not think that this is entirely true. Arendt rethinks the problem starting with the aporia that the nation-state system has failed us. Arendt laments the "intolerable situation of global responsibility" and unequivocally views a global empire as a dangerous remedy. Yet she engages with forms of cosmopolitan politics—and elements of global political theory, for that matter.

110. Arendt, *Origins of Totalitarianism,* ix.

111. Arendt, "Karl Jaspers," 93.

112. Adorno, *Problems of Moral Philosophy,* 142.

113. Ibid., 144.

114. Ibid., 176.

115. See Adorno, "Progress," 145, on "forced unity."

116. Adorno, *Minima Moralia,* 103.

117. Arendt, "Karl Jaspers," 90.

118. Adorno, *History and Freedom,* 111.

119. Arendt, "Karl Jaspers," 89.

120. Adorno, *History and Freedom,* 111.

121. Adorno and Horkheimer, *Dialectic of Enlightenment,* 165.

122. Adorno, *History and Freedom,* 111. One of the very few critical theorists who have explored and further developed the Frankfurt School's dialectical theory of technology is Andrew Feenberg; see his *Critical Theory of Technology* (New York: Oxford University Press, 1991).

123. Arendt, "Karl Jaspers," 83.

124. Ibid., 83.

125. In our current age, new information technologies and social media have indeed enabled citizens to create new transnational movements, alliances and bonds. The former have also played a key role as oppositional networking tools in the democratic uprisings in the Middle East, engendering the vernacularization of demands for human dignity and rights. This "cosmopolitan" power is, to be sure, among the unintended consequences of technological developments, which can also serve as means of violence. Technology, "having provided the unity of the world, can just as easily destroy it[,] and the means of global communication were designed side by side with means of possible global destruction," Arendt writes. Moreover, it is far from clear that humanity's common factual present, which is not based on a common past, also guarantees a common future (Arendt, "Karl Jaspers," 83).

126. Adorno, *Problems of Moral Philosophy*, 167.

127. Hannah Arendt, *The Life of the Mind*, ed. Mary McCarthy, vol. 1: *Thinking* (New York: Harcourt, Brace Jovanovich, 1978), 196 (§ 2). See also Fine, *Cosmopolitanism*, 128.

128. For different interpretations of Arendt's "right to have rights," see Peg Birmingham, *Hannah Arendt and Human Rights* (Bloomington: Indiana University Press, 2006); see also Serena Parekh, *Hannah Arendt and the Challenge of Modernity: A Phenomenology of Human Rights* (New York: Routledge, 2008).

129. Albert Weale, *Democracy* (New York: St. Martin's Press, 1999), 8–13.

130. In this view, any theory that does not reflect on the actual conditions of human life remains formalistic. Arendt rejected "empirical sociology" as a behavioral science that is incapable of understanding human affairs, and Adorno levels a similar criticism at "positivist" sociologists. Yet they both deem an inquiry into the specific historical circumstances of social and political life necessary. See Peter Baehr, *Hannah Arendt, Totalitarianism, and the Social Sciences* (Stanford: Stanford University Press, 2010); Theodor Adorno et al., *The Positivist Dispute in German Sociology* (1976; Aldershot, UK: Ashgate, 1981). Cosmopolitan theorizing, too, turns into abstract idealistic proposals—Arendt would say it mimics the "declarations . . . by philanthropists supported by . . . professional idealists"—if it is not empirically and politically grounded "in this world." Arendt, *The Origins of Totalitarianism* (1951; 3rd ed., New York: Harcourt, Brace & World, 1968), 292.

131. This, of course, implies a critique of "realist" theories of international relations.

132. Arendt and Benedict, "Revolution, Violence, and Power," 304. In the words of Adorno, "true injustice is always to be found at the precise point where you put yourself in the right and other people in the wrong. . . . In other words, if you were to press me to follow the example of the Ancients and make a list of the cardinal virtues, I would probably respond cryptically by saying that I could think of nothing except for modesty" (Adorno, *Problems of Moral Philosophy*, 169).

133. David Harvey, *Cosmopolitanism and the Geographies of Freedom* (New York: Columbia University Press, 2009), 283.

134. Arendt, *Origins of Totalitarianism*, vii.

135. Adorno, *Minima Moralia*, 103.

136. I owe special thanks to Robert Fine, Samir Gandesha, Adam Gannaway, Suzanne Hawkins, Jennet Kirkpatrick, Thomas Murphey, and Mark Rigstad for helpful comments, insights, and suggestions.

Chapter 7

1. See Hannah Arendt, *Between Past and Future: Six Exercises in Political Thought* (New York: Penguin Books, 1977), 26–28.
2. Friedrich Nietzsche, *The Will to Power* (New York: Vintage Books, 1969), 9.
3. Friedrich Nietzsche, *Untimely Meditations* (New York Cambridge University Press, 1983), 148–49.
4. Hannah Arendt, *Essays in Understanding, 1930–1954* (New York: Harcourt Brace, 1994), 233.
5. Theodor W. Adorno, *Minima Moralia: Reflections from Damaged Life*, trans. E. F. N. Jephcott (London: NLB, 1974), 55.
6. Ibid., 54.
7. Theodor W. Adorno, "After Auschwitz," in id. *Negative Dialectics* (London: Routledge, 1973), 361–62.
8. Hannah Arendt, *The Origins of Totalitarianism* (1951; 3rd ed., New York: Harcourt Brace Jovanovich, 1973), 275.
9. Ibid., 299.
10. Ibid., 272.
11. Giorgio Agamben, *Homo Sacer: Sovereign Power and Bare Life* (Stanford: Stanford University Press, 1998), 127.
12. Arendt, *Origins of Totalitarianism*, 127–31.
13. Ibid., 130. The distinction between imperialism and empire building was important for Arendt's analysis of the decline of legality and the rights of man.
14. Ibid., 176. Arendt argued with reference to Disraeli that the heirs of Burke in England prefigured "the menacing transformation of the people from a nation into an 'unmixed race of first-rate organisation' that felt itself to be 'the aristocracy of nature'" (ibid., 183).
15. Zygmunt Bauman offers a compelling version of this perspective in *Modernity and the Holocaust* (Malden, MA: Polity Press, 1990).
16. Arendt, *Origins of Totalitarianism*, 462.
17. Ibid., 462.
18. Ibid., 464.
19. Ibid., 462.
20. Agamben, *Homo Sacer*, 126. See also Giorgio Agamben "Beyond Human Rights," in *Means Without End: Notes on Politics* (Minneapolis: University of Minnesota Press, 2000), 15–26. This reading of Arendt also enters into the work of writers who share no such hostility to human rights. See, e.g., Jean Cohen, "Rights, Citizenship and the Modern Form of the Social: Dilemmas of Arendtian

Republicanism," *Constellations* 3, no. 2 (1996): 164–89, and Christoph Menke, "The 'Aporias of Human Rights' and the 'One Human Right': Regarding the Coherence of Hannah Arendt's Argument," *Social Research* 74, no. 3 (Fall 2007): 739–62. Paul Gilroy summarizes the new orthodoxy thus: "Arendt and Agamben are linked by their apparent distaste for analyzing racism, but also for their complex and critical relations to the idea of the human. This combination of positions can facilitate hostility to the project of human rights, which is dismissed for its inability to face the political and strategic processes from which all rights derive and for a related refusal to address the analytical shortcomings that arise from the dependence of human rights on an expansion of the rule of law—which incidentally can be shown to be fully compatible with colonial crimes" (Gilroy, *Darker than Blue: On the Moral Economies of Black Atlantic Culture* [Cambridge, MA: Harvard University Press, 2010], 85). Agamben encourages this interpretation of Arendt's work, but we should not assume he is right.

21. Arendt, *Origins of Totalitarianism,* ix.
22. Hannah Arendt, "'The Rights of Man': What Are They?" *Modern Review* 3, no. 1 (1949): 24–36.
23. Arendt, *Origins of Totalitarianism*, 298.
24. Ibid.
25. Immanuel Kant, *Political Writings* (New York: Cambridge University Press, 1991), 106, 172–73.
26. Arendt, *Origins of Totalitarianism*, 299.
27. Ibid., 297.
28. Kant, *Political Writings,* 107–8.
29. Ibid., 132.
30. Ibid., 26.
31. Ibid., 298.
32. Theodor W. Adorno, *History and Freedom: Lectures, 1964–65* (Malden, MA: Polity Press, 2006), 180. Craig Reeves, "Exploding the Limits of the Law" (MS, King's College, London, 2009), provides an interesting discussion.
33. Adorno, *History and Freedom,* 180–81.
34. See, e.g., Franz Neumann, *The Rule of Law* (Oxford: Berg, 1986).
35. Theodor W. Adorno, *Negative Dialectics* (New York: Continuum, 1981), 309.
36. Ibid., 345.
37. Ibid., 334.
38. Ibid., 329.
39. See Robert Fine, *Political Investigations: Hegel, Marx and Arendt* (New York: Routledge, 2001), chap. 1.
40. Adorno, *History and Freedom*, 63.
41. Ibid., 207.
42. Adorno *Minima Moralia*, 247.
43. Herbert Marcuse *Reason and Revolution: Hegel and the Rise of Social Theory* (Boston: Beacon Press, 1979), 294.

44. Simon Jarvis, *Adorno: A Critical Introduction* (Malden, MA: Polity Press, 1998), 169

45. Adorno, *Minima Moralia*, 17.

46. Adorno, *History and Freedom*, 252–3.

47. G. W. F. Hegel, *Elements of the Philosophy of Right* (New York: Cambridge University Press, 1991), § 2.

48. Ibid., § 32.

49. Ibid., § 31.

50. Ibid., § 21.

51. *History and Freedom*, 140, cited in Marianne Tettlebaum, "Political Philosophy," in *Theodor Adorno: Key Concepts,* ed. Deborah Cook (Stocksfield, UK: Acumen, 2008), 131.

52. Adorno *Negative Dialectics*, 237.

53. Ibid., 236.

54. Ibid.

55. Theodor Adorno, *Critical Models: Interventions and Catchwords* (New York: Columbia University Press, 1998), 281.

56. Hannah Arendt, "Thoughts on Politics and Revolution," in *Crises of the Republic: Lying in Politics; Civil Disobedience; On Violence: Thoughts on Politics and Revolution* (New York: Harcourt Brace Jovanovich, 1972), 214–15.

57. Arendt, *Origins of Totalitarianism*, xiv.

58. Arendt, *Eichmann in Jerusalem*, 233.

59. Ibid., 294.

60. Ibid., 295.

61. Ibid., 230.

62. Adorno, *History and Freedom*, 240.

63. Ibid.

64. Theodor W. Adorno, *Problems of Moral Philosophy* (Malden, MA: Polity Press, 2001), 8. My gratitude to Craig Reeves, "Exploding the Limits of the Law," for alerting me to these connections.

65. Hannah Arendt, *Lectures on Kant's Political Philosophy* (Chicago: University of Chicago Press, 1989), 75–76.

66. I am particularly grateful to Lars Rensmann, Samir Gandesha, Glyn Cousin, David Seymour, and Lydia Morris for their hugely valuable help in writing this paper.

Chapter 8

1. See Martin Jay, *Adorno* (Cambridge, MA: Harvard University Press, 1984), 39.

2. Like so many other Jewish critics, Arendt objected in particular to Sartre's contention that the Jew was a product of the antisemitic gaze. See Hannah Arendt, *The Origins of Totalitarianism* (1951; 3rd ed., New York: Harcourt Brace

Jovanovich, 1973), xv. For a more complicated appreciation of the overlaps between Arendt's and Sartre's analyses, see Richard J. Bernstein, *Hannah Arendt and the Jewish Question* (Cambridge, MA: MIT Press, 196), 47–48 and n. 2, 195–97. For other Jewish critics of Sartre, see Jonathan Judaken, *Jean-Paul Sartre and the Jewish Question: Anti-antisemitism and the Politics of the French Intellectual* (Lincoln: University of Nebraska Press, 2006), chap. 8.

3. On Arendt's somewhat fractious relations with the Frankfurt School and specifically Adorno, see Elisabeth Young-Bruehl, *Hannah Arendt: For Love of the World* (New Haven, CT: Yale University Press, 1982), esp. 166–68.

4. See Julie Kalman, *Rethinking Anti-Semitism in Nineteenth-Century France* (New York: Cambridge University Press, 2010), 128–54.

5. Hannah Arendt, "A Reply. Rejoinder to Eric Voegelin's Review of *The Origins of Totalitarianism*," *Review of Politics* 15, no. 1 (January 1953): 68–85, 77.

6. On this point, see Arendt's comments in *The Origins of Totalitarianism*, "Preface to Part One," xii–xiii.

7. Ibid., xiv.

8. Lisa Jane Disch, "More Truth than Fact: Storytelling as Critical Understanding in the Writings of Hannah Arendt," *Political Theory* 21, no. 4 (November 1993): 665–95, 677.

9. Jean-François Lyotard, *Heidegger and "the Jews,"* trans. Andreas Michel and Mark Roberts (Minneapolis: University of Minnesota Press, 1990).

10. Seyla Benhabib, "Hannah Arendt and the Redemptive Power of Narrative," *Social Research* 57, no. 1 (Spring 1990): 167–96, 180.

11. Ibid., 180.

12. This and the preceding quotation are from Disch, "More Truth than Fact," 667.

13. Eric Voegelin, review of *The Origins of Totalitarianism* by Hannah Arendt, *Review of Politics* 15, no. 1 (January 1953): 68–85. The reason for turning to this review as an introduction to Arendt's text is precisely because Arendt vehemently accused Voegelin of misreading her work on methodological grounds. In so doing, Arendt offered a distilled statement on her methodology. Voegelin and Arendt differed not only on the understanding of causality but also on the question of human nature. For the latter point, see Young-Bruehl, *Hannah Arendt*, 253–54.

14. This and the preceding quotation are from Voegelin's review, cited in the preceding note, 69.

15. For a sophisticated account of antisemitism in term of scapegoat theories, see Yves Chevalier, *L'antisémitisme: Le Juif comme bouc émissaire* (Paris: Cerf, 1988).

16. Arendt, *Origins of Totalitarianism*, 5.

17. This and the preceding quotation ibid., 6.

18. Ibid., 8.

19. For the elaboration of this argument, see Dan Cohn-Sherbok, *The Paradox of Anti-Semitism* (New York: Continuum, 2006). For an amplification of what I take to be the more sophisticated views on this paradox by Léon Poliakov and

Jean-Paul Sartre, see Jonathan Judaken, "Homo Anti-Semiticus: Lessons and Legacies," *Holocaust and Genocide Studies* 23, no. 3 (Winter 2009): 461–77, 463–64.

20. Zygmunt Bauman, "Allosemitism: Premodern, Modern, Postmodern," in *Modernity, Culture and 'the Jew,'* ed. Bryan Cheyette and Laura Marcus (Stanford: Stanford University Press, 1998), 153.

21. Arendt, *Origins of Totalitarianism*, 12.

22. Ibid., 53.

23. Ibid., 15.

24. Ibid., 66.

25. Ibid.

26. See Hannah Arendt, *Rahel Varnhagen: The Life of a Jewess*, ed. Liliane Weissberg, trans. Richard and Clara Winston (Baltimore: Johns Hopkins University Press, 1997). On the ways that Varnhagen was a ghost for Arendt, see Pierre Birnbaum's chapter "Hannah Arendt: Hanna and Rahel, "Fugitives from Palestine," in id., *Geography of Hope: Exile, the Enlightenment, Disassimilation*, trans. Charlotte Mandell (Stanford: Stanford University Press, 2008), 203–41.

27. Hannah Arendt, "The Jew as Pariah: A Hidden Tradition," *Jewish Social Studies* 6, no. 2 (April 1944): 99–122, reprinted in id., *The Jew as Pariah: Jewish Identity and Politics in the Modern Age*, ed. Ron H. Feldman (New York: Grove Press, 1978), 67–90.

28. Arendt, *Origins of Totalitarianism*, 57.

29. Ibid., 56.

30. Ibid., 60.

31. Ibid., 66. For a wonderfully nuanced version of such a conception of Jewishness, see Yosef Hayim Yerushalmi, *Freud's Moses: Judaism Terminable and Interminable* (New Haven, CT: Yale University Press, 1991), 10ff.

32. Arendt, *Origins of Totalitarianism*, 68.

33. Julia Kristeva, *Hannah Arendt*, trans. Ross Guberman (New York: Columbia University Press. 2001), 145.

34. Bauman makes this point about Jews in "Allosemitism," in *Modernity, Culture, and 'the Jew,'* ed. Cheyette and Marcus, 146.

35. Arendt, *Origins of Totalitarianism*, 87.

36. On these interconnections at the end of the nineteenth century, see Richie Roberts, "Historicizing Weininger: The Nineteenth-Century German Image of the Feminized Jew," in *Modernity, Culture, and 'the Jew,'* ed. Cheyette and Marcus; Daniel Boyarin, *Unheroic Conduct: The Rise of Heterosexuality and the Invention of the Jewish Man*, pt. 2; George Mosse, *The Image of Man: The Creation of Modern Masculinity* (New York: Oxford University Press, 1996), chaps. 4–5; and Chris Forth, *The Dreyfus Affair and the Crisis of French Manhood* (Baltimore: Johns Hopkins University Press, 2004).

37. Arendt, *Origins of Totalitarianism*, 80.

38. Eve Kosofsky Sedgwick, *Epistemology of the Closet* (1990; Berkeley: University of California Press, 2008), also compares the Jew to the homosexual, arguing

for their differences, but is wrong to emphasize these so much, just as Arendt is wrong to emphasize their sameness.

39. Arendt, *Origins of Totalitarianism*, 82.
40. Ibid., 84.
41. Ibid., 20.
42. Ibid., 40.
43. On Arendt and Zionism, see her *Jew as Pariah*, ed. Feldman, pt. 2. See also Bernstein, *Hannah Arendt and the Jewish Question*, chap. 5, and Dagmar Barnouw, *Visible Spaces: Hannah Arendt and the German-Jewish Question* (Baltimore: Johns Hopkins University Press, 1990), chap. 3, as well as the chapters by Amnon Raz-Krakotzkin, Moshe Zimmermann, and Richard Bernstein in *Hannah Arendt in Jerusalem*, ed. Steven E. Aschheim (Berkeley: University of California Press, 1999).
44. Arendt, *Origins of Totalitarianism*, 20.
45. Pierre Birnbaum, *Anti-Semitism in France: A Political History from Leon Blum to the Present*, trans. Miriam Kochan (Oxford: Blackwell, 1992), 7.
46. On Arendt's relation to Marx on these points, see Ron Feldman, introduction to Arendt, *Jew as Pariah*, 40.
47. Arendt, "Tradition and the Modern Age," in id., *Between Past and Future: Six Exercises in Political Thought* (New York: Penguin Books, 1968), 25.
48. Martin Jay, *The Dialectical Imagination* (Boston: Little, Brown, 1973), 133. Jay paraphrases Pollock in this quotation. Rolf Wiggershaus makes the same point in the conclusion of his biographical sketch of the circle around Horkheimer: "This biographical panorama shows that none of those belonging to the Horkheimer circle was politically active; none of them had his origins either in the labour movement or in Marxism; all were from Jewish families, although the relation of their families to Judaism was extremely varied, extending from complete assimilation to Jewish orthodoxy. For all of them, awareness of the problem of anti-Semitism seemed to have lost its relevance in view of their intellectual activities, which were directed against capitalism" (Wiggershaus, *The Frankfurt School: Its History, Theories, and Political Significance*, trans. Michael Robertson [Cambridge, MA: MIT Press, 1995], 104).
49. Wiggershaus, *Frankfurt School*, 275. See also Jack Jacobs, "Max Horkheimer's *Die Juden und Europa* Appears," in *Yale Companion to Jewish Writing and Thought in German Culture 1096–1996*, ed. Sander L. Gilman and Jack Zipes (New Haven, CT: Yale University Press, 1997), 573.
50. Max Horkheimer, "The Jews in Europe," in *Critical Theory and Society: A Reader*, ed. Stephen Eric Bronner and Douglas Mackay Kellner (New York: Routledge, 1989), 77–94.
51. Theodor Adorno, "Research Project on Anti-Semitism," *Studies in Philosophy and Social Science* 9 (1941): 124–43.
52. This and the following quotations cited in Wiggershaus, *Frankfurt School*, 276–77.
53. Max Horkheimer, "Preface," in Theodor W. Adorno, Else Frenkel-Brunswik, Daniel J. Levinson, R. Nevitt Sandford et al., *The Authoritarian Personality* (New York: Harper & Row, 1950), xi.

54. Ernst Simmel, *Anti-Semitism: A Social Disease*, ed. id. (New York: International Universities Press, 1946), "Introduction."
55. Ibid., xxv.
56. Max Horkheimer, "Sociological Background of the Psychoanalytic Approach," ibid., 2–6.
57. Theodor W. Adorno, "Anti-Semitism and Fascist Propaganda," ibid., 126–27.
58. Ibid., 129.
59. Ibid., 132–33.
60. Ibid., 137.
61. Max Horkheimer and Samuel Flowerman, "Foreword to *Studies in Prejudice*," in Adorno et al., *Authoritarian Personality*, vi–vii.
62. Horkheimer, "Preface," in Adorno et al., *Authoritarian Personality*, xi.
63. Ibid., xii.
64. Adorno et al., *Authoritarian Personality*, 744.
65. Ibid., 747.
66. Ibid., 608.
67. Ibid., 617.
68. Ibid., 622–23.
69. Ibid., 638.
70. Max Horkheimer and Theodor Adorno, *Dialectic of Enlightenment*, trans. John Cumming (New York: Continuum, 2000), 168.
71. Horkheimer and Adorno, *Dialectic of Enlightenment*, 169.
72. Max Weber, *Ancient Judaism*, trans. and ed. Hans H. Gerth and Don Martindale (Glencoe, IL: Free Press, 1952). For some of the critical literature on Weber, see Ephraim Schmeuli, "The 'Pariah People' and Its 'Charismatic Leadership: A Reevalution of Max Weber's 'Ancient Judaism,'" *American Academy of Jewish Research Proceedings* 36 (1968): 167–247; Freddy Raphaël, "Max Weber et le judaïsme antique," *Archives Européennes de Sociologie* 11 (1970): 297–336; and David Ellenson, "Max Weber on Judaism and the Jews," in *After Emancipation: Jewish Religious Responses to Modernity* (Cincinnati: Hebrew Union College Press, 2004), 80–95.
73. Horkheimer and Adorno, *Dialectic of Enlightenment*, 178.
74. Ibid., 181.
75. Ibid., 184–85.
76. Ibid., 186.
77. Ibid., 184.
78. Ibid., 185.
79. This and the preceding quotation ibid., 186.
80. Ibid., 175.
81. On this point, see Stephen Haynes, *Reluctant Witnesses: Jews and the Christian Imagination* (Louisville, KY: Westminster John Knox Press, 1995), 10–11. Along Barthesian lines, Haynes suggests that "myth transforms a previously established *sign* into an empty *signifier* that has been 'drained.' Thus the *sign* in

a language system becomes a signifier in a myth system, a system with its own signified. In the myth I am analyzing in this book, the *sign* of a language system (actually the identity of the *signifier* 'Jew' with a group of people believed to share common characteristics, history and origins) is taken over to form the empty signifier that is the basis of the myth. In the metalanguage of myth, this *sign* which identifies 'Jews' with real Jews and 'Jewish history' with an accepted version of their story becomes the signifier for a new signified . . . this mythical sign takes many forms—including associations of Jewish exile and divine punishment, Jewish preservation and divine providence, Jewish restoration and divine guidance, Jewish conversion and divine love."

Chapter 9

Parts of this essay were translated by Lewis P. Hinchman.

1. See Jeffrey C. Isaac, *Democracy in Dark Times* (Ithaca, NY: Cornell University Press, 1998), 23. As Isaac argues, for Arendt and Adorno the Nazi atrocities signified an "apotheosis of the destructive impulses at the heart of modern civilization."
2. Ira Katznelson, *Desolation and Enlightenment: Political Knowledge After Total War, Totalitarianism, and the Holocaust* (New York: Columbia University Press, 2003), 44.
3. Hannah Arendt, *The Origins of Totalitarianism* (1951; 3rd ed., New York: Harcourt, Brace & World, 1968), ix.
4. Referring to the precarious position of Arendt and Adorno in the canon of political theory, and especially to the marginalization of Arendt and Adorno as thinkers who take Auschwitz and its implications for political theory seriously, Jeffrey Isaac points out that the "academic discipline of political theory has found it possible to produce thousands upon thousands of pages about justice and morality as if Auschwitz had never existed and the complex events preceding and following it had never occurred" (Jeffrey C. Isaac, *Arendt, Camus, and Modern Rebellion* [New Haven, CT: Yale University Press, 2009], 12).
5. Arendt used "antisemitism," not "anti-Semitism" throughout her work, for the good reason that, as she observes in *Origins of Totalitarianism*, antisemites do not oppose any "Semitism," as the more popular term "anti-Semitism" suggests. As Arendt points out, and as elaborated in this chapter, "antisemitism" is an ideology that constructs a Jewish enemy but has nothing to do with any opposition to "Semitic" ethnic origins or language communities. In the original German usage, *Antisemitismus* is never hyphenated. We have adopted the use of "antisemitism" throughout this volume. See also *Thinking in Dark Times: Hannah Arendt on Ethics and Politics*, ed. Roger Berkowitz, Jeffrey Katz, and Thomas Keenan (New York: Fordham University Press, 2010), xi; *Politics and Resentment: Antisemitism and Counter-Cosmopolitanism in the European Union*, ed. Lars Rensmann and Julius H. Schoeps (Leiden: Brill, 2011).

6. Dana Villa, "Genealogies of Total Domination: Arendt, Adorno, and Auschwitz," in id., *Public Freedom* (Princeton, NJ: Princeton University Press, 2008); Isaac, *Democracy in Dark Times*.

7. Lambert Zuidervaart, *Social Philosophy After Adorno* (New York: Cambridge University Press, 2007), 107ff.

8. Adorno also emphasizes the "belated . . . process of nation-building linked to the principle of the bourgeois revolution" in Germany. This "belated arrival was no less fatal for National Socialism since it endowed that movement with the particular and terrible qualities that occur in history whenever, as Hegel puts it, something is abandoned by the world spirit. . . . I believe then that you must think of the specific case of German nationalism, and no doubt also its virulent nature, as the product of a failed process of nation-building and of its productive function, both matters associated with its belated arrival on the world stage" (Theodor W. Adorno, *History and Freedom: Lectures, 1964–1965* [Malden, MA: Polity Press, 2006], 112).

9. On this argument, see Lars Rensmann and Julia Schulze Wessel, "Radikalisierung oder 'Verschwinden' der Judenfeindschaft? Arendts und Adornos Theorien zum modernen Antisemitismus," in *Arendt und Adorno*, ed. Dirk Auer, Lars Rensmann, and Julia Schuze Wessel (Frankfurt: Suhrkamp, 2003), 97–129.

10. Hannah Arendt, *Eichmann in Jerusalem: A Report on the Banality of Evil* (1963; rev. ed., London: Penguin Books, 1965), 21–55.

11. See Theodor W. Adorno, Else Frenkel-Brunswik, Daniel J. Levinson, R. Nevitt Sanford et al., *The Authoritarian Personality* (1950; New York: Norton, 1982), 355ff.

12. See, e.g., Arendt's notes on psychology in her diary: "The Freudian mistake, and the mistake of all modern psychology is that they claim to know what they almost certainly cannot know, not just the nonsense about 'the unconscious,' but the oldest prejudice: what is hidden . . . is what I am ashamed of, and therefore what is *bad*" (Hannah Arendt, *Denktagebuch, 1950–1973*, ed. Ursula Ludz [Munich: Piper, 2002], 2: 659; our trans., Arendt's emphasis).

13. Theodor Adorno and Max Horkheimer, *Dialectic of Enlightenment: Philosophical Fragments*, trans. Edmund Jephcott (Stanford: Stanford University Press, 2002), xix; on the "Elements of Anti-Semitism," see Lars Rensmann, *Kritische Theorie über den Antisemitismus: Studien zu Struktur, Erklärungspotenzial und Aktualität* (Hamburg: Argument, 1998).

14. Theodor W. Adorno, "Zur Bekämpfung des Antisemitismus heute," in id., *Kritik: Kleine Schriften zur Gesellschaft* (Frankfurt: Suhrkamp, 1971), 105–33, here 120.

15. Seyla Benhabib, *The Reluctant Modernism of Hannah Arendt* (Lanham, MD: Rowman & Littlefield, 2003), 64.

16. Arendt, *Origins of Totalitarianism*, viii.

17. Seyla Benhabib, "Hannah Arendt and the Redemptive Power of Narrative," *Social Research* 57, no. 1 (1990): 167–96, reprinted in *Hannah Arendt: Critical Essays*, ed. Lewis P. Hinchman and Sandra Hinchman (Albany: State University of

New York Press, 1994), 111–40. On storytelling in Arendt's political theorizing, see also Lisa Jane Disch, *Hannah Arendt and the Limits of Philosophy* (Ithaca, NY: Cornell University Press, 1996).

18. Of Benjamin's characteristic way of thinking Arendt writes: This "thinking, fed by the present, works with the 'thought fragments' it can wrest from the past and gather about itself. Like a pearl diver who descends to the bottom of the sea, not to excavate the bottom and bring it to light but to pry loose the rich and the strange, the pearls and the corals in the depths and to carry them to the surface, this thinking delves into the depths of the past—but not in order to resuscitate it the way it was and to contribute to the renewal of extinct ages" (Hannah Arendt, "Walter Benjamin, 1892–1940," in id., *Men in Dark Times* [New York: Harcourt, Brace & World, 1968], 153–206, here 205).

19. Benhabib, "Hannah Arendt and the Redemptive Power of Narrative," 113.

20. Benhabib, *Reluctant Modernism of Hannah Arendt*, 64.

21. Theodor W. Adorno and Max Horkheimer, "Vorwort zu Paul W. Massings 'Vorgeschichte des politischen Antisemitismus,'" in Max Horkheimer, *Gesammelte Schriften* (Frankfurt: Fischer, 1985), 8: 128. On this argument in the Frankfurt School's theorizing of antisemitism, see Anson Rabinbach, "Why Were the Jews Sacrificed? The Place of Anti-Semitism in the *Dialectic of Enlightenment*," *New German Critique* 81 (Autumn 2000): 49–64; Rensmann, *Kritische Theorie über den Antisemitismus*; Jonathan Judaken, "Between Philosemitism and Antisemitism: The Frankfurt School's Anti-Antisemitism," in *Antisemitism and Philosemitism in the Twentieth and Twenty-First Centuries: Representing Jews, Jewishness and Modern Culture*, ed. Phyllis Lassner and Lara Trubowitz (Newark: University of Delaware Press, 2008), 23–46; and Jan Plug, "Idiosyncrasies: Of Anti-Semitism," in *Language Without Soil: Adorno and Late Philosophical Modernity*, ed. Gerhard Richter (New York: Fordham University Press, 2010), 52–75. For a rather undifferentiated earlier general criticism of the Frankfurt School that ignores the richness of critical theory's account of antisemitism see Erhard Bahr, "The Anti-Semitism Studies of the Frankfurt School: The Failure of Critical Theory," in *Foundations of the Frankfurt School of Social Research*, ed. Judith Marcus and Zoltan Tar (New Brunswick, NJ: Transaction Books, 1984), 311–21.

22. Adorno indicated that he might someday offer a more comprehensive theory of antisemitism in his essay "Zur Bekämpfung des Antisemitismus heute," 120.

23. It is noteworthy that virtually all research on antisemitism contradicts Arendt's historical claim about the radical disjuncture of anti-Judaism or early antisemitism, on the one hand, and modern antisemitism, on the other; for an overview on historical research on antisemitism, see, e.g., Saul Friedlander, *Nazi Germany and the Jews: The Years of Persecution, 1933–39* (New York: HarperCollins, 1997); on the history of antisemitism from ancient times to the present, see Robert Wistrich, *A Lethal Obsession: Antisemitism—from Antiquity to Global Jihad* (New York: Random House, 2010); for contemporary hypotheses and findings, see also *Politics and Resentment*, ed. Rensmann and Schoeps.

24. As used by Nietzsche, the term *ressentiment* is more apt than "resentment," because it equates hostility to a person or group, not just with the latter's supposed culpability for grievances, but also with a feeling of inferiority, paired with claims to superior morality to the resented on the part of the resenter.

25. Adorno and Horkheimer, *Dialectic of Enlightenment*, 144. If one reviews the history of antisemitism, it can scarcely be denied that there is some relation between traditional and modern forms of anti-Jewish prejudice. However, Arendt's dogged refusal to derive antisemitism from any familiar phenomena may be ascribed more plausibly to her approach to the philosophy of history than to historical realities themselves. Arendt herself devoted an entire chapter of an unpublished treatise on modern antisemitism to the religious and secularized forms of anti-Jewish attitudes—although this essay was written before she realized what had happened in Auschwitz. See the Hannah Arendt Archives at Oldenburg, Germany, Antisemitism, 61.8.

26. Adorno and Horkheimer, *Dialectic of Enlightenment*, 140.

27. For a more detailed account of this argument see Julia Schulze Wessel, *Ideologie der Sachlichkeit: Hannah Arendts politische Theorie des Antisemitismus* (Frankfurt: Suhrkamp, 2006), 36ff.

28. Theodor W. Adorno, *Negative Dialectics* (New York: Continuum, 1970), 365.

29. Hannah Arendt, *Rahel Varnhagen: The Life of a Jewess* (Baltimore, MD: Johns Hopkins University Press, 2000), and "The Jew as Pariah: A Hidden Tradition," in Arendt, *The Jewish Writings*, ed. Jerome Cohen and Ron H. Feldman (New York: Schocken Books, 2007), 275–97.

30. Adorno and Horkheimer, *Dialectic of Enlightenment*, 138. In theoretical terms, Adorno also develops the critique of assimilation in the context of his general critique of the "melting pot" ideal of modern capitalist society, which seems to be progressive and democratic but actually mirrors powerful societal imperatives that force citizens to give up their differences and individuality. "The melting-pot was introduced by unbridled industrial capitalism. The thought of being cast into it conjures up martyrdom, not democracy" (Theodor W. Adorno, *Minima Moralia: Reflections from Damaged Life*, trans. E. F. N. Jephcott [London: Verso, 1994], 102–3).

31. Adorno and Horkheimer, *Dialectic of Enlightenment*, 9.

32. Arendt, *Origins of Totalitarianism*, 54ff.

33. Adorno and Horkheimer, *Dialectic of Enlightenment*,147.

34. Ibid., 148.

35. Ibid., 9.

36. Ibid., 139.

37. Arendt, *Origins of Totalitarianism*, 7.

38. For Adorno, antisemitism is fundamentally distinct from other (racist) resentments in that it identifies Jews with all negative aspects and universalistic claims of *modernity*. Although Jews are not only "scapegoats," and antisemitism cannot be explained by any simple scapegoat theory (for Arendt, any "scapegoat

explanation" escapes the seriousness of antisemitism), they are, among other things, "indeed the scapegoat," not only for individual maneuvers and machinations, but "in the wider sense" that the economic injustices of capitalism are attributed to them. For Adorno, this identification of Jews with modern capitalism can be traced back to the circumstance that it is a "socially necessary illusion" to make the "circulation sphere," the world of merchants and finance, responsible for capitalist exploitation: the merchant is the "bailiff for the whole system." And Jews, while not the only agents in the circulation sphere, "had been locked up in it too long not to reflect in their makeup something of the hatred so long directed at that sphere. Unlike their Aryan colleagues, they were largely denied access to the source of added value," that is the production sphere. See Adorno and Horkheimer, *Dialectic of Enlightenment*, 142–43.

39. Adorno and Horkheimer, *Dialectic of Enlightenment*, 165.

40. Ibid., 141.

41. Ibid., 138. It is part of the contradictory antisemitic perception that Jews are seen as ultimately powerless, just as they are simultaneously perceived as a secret, omnipresent power controlling and dominating the world.

42. Adorno and Horkheimer, *Dialectic of Enlightenment*, 143.

43. Arendt, *Origins of Totalitarianism*, 20ff.

44. Ibid., 7.

45. Ibid., 54ff.

46. Adorno and Horkheimer, *Dialectic of Enlightenment*, 138.

47. Arendt, *Origins of Totalitarianism*, 8.

48. Adorno, to be sure, also questions the deterministic model that seeks to explore "causalities" in human affairs (*Negative Dialectics*, 214ff.). See also Brian O'Connor, *Adorno's Negative Dialectic: Philosophy and the Possibility of Critical Rationality* (Cambridge, MA: MIT Press, 2004), 76.

49. Adorno and Horkheimer, *Dialectic of Enlightenment*, 140.

50. Ibid., 142–43.

51. On this point, see esp. Arendt, *Origins of Totalitarianism*, 89–120, the chapter on Dreyfus.

52. The distinction may be traced back to Otto Glagau, a journalist for the widely read weekly *Die Gartenlaube*, in which he published a series of antisemitic articles in 1874. He originally made the distinction to attack "demagogic" antisemites. In her study of antisemitism in nineteenth-century Germany, *Germans, Jews, and Antisemites: Trials in Emancipation* (New York: Cambridge University Press, 2006), Shulamit Volkov examines Glagau, yet she does not attribute much significance to the dichotomy, since with antisemitic groups, strategic motives and passionate hatred of Jews always intermingled.

53. Adorno and Horkheimer, *Dialectic of Enlightenment*, 140.

54. For a more detailed account of this distinction in Arendt, see Schulze Wessel, *Ideologie der Sachlichkeit*, 97ff.

55. See, e.g., the historical account by Peter Longerich, *Holocaust: The Nazi Persecution and Murder of the Jews* (New York: Cambridge University Press, 2010).

56. Adorno and Horkheimer, *Dialectic of Enlightenment*, 157.
57. Arendt, *Origins of Totalitarianism*, 99.
58. Ibid., 106ff.
59. Ibid., 107.
60. Ibid., 108.
61. Adorno and Horkheimer, *Dialectic of Enlightenment*, 156.
62. Ibid., 154.
63. Ibid., 157.
64. Rensmann, *Kritische Theorie über den Antisemitismus*, 96.
65. Adorno and Horkheimer, *Dialectic of Enlightenment*, 154.
66. Ibid., 153. This projection mechanism attributing socially tabooed impulses to Jews also points to the structuring ambivalences in the antisemitic image of Jews: the dialectic of collective admiration and denigration, as Zygmunt Bauman argues in *Modernity and Ambivalence* (Malden, MA: Polity Press, 1993).
67. Christopher Hitchens, "Reflections on Antisemitism," in *Thinking in Dark Times: Hannah Arendt on Ethics and Politics*, ed. Roger Berkowitz, Jeffrey Katz, and Thomas Keenan (New York: Fordham University Press, 2010), 22.
68. Arendt, *Eichmann in Jerusalem*, 30.
69. Ibid., 48–49. See also Peter Baehr, "Banality and Cleverness: *Eichmann in Jerusalem* Revisited," in *Thinking in Dark Times*, ed. Berkowitz et al., 139–44.
70. Hannah Arendt, *The Life of the Mind*, ed. Mary McCarthy, vol. 1: *Thinking* (New York: Harcourt Brace Jovanovich, 1978), 5.
71. Adorno does so only in the seventh thesis of the "Elements of Antisemitism"; see Adorno and Horkheimer, *Dialectic of Enlightenment*, 165–72.
72. On critical rationality, according to which "freedom is inseparable from enlightenment thinking" (Adorno and Horkheimer, *Dialectic of Enlightenment*, xvi) in the work of Arendt and Adorno, see the introduction to this volume as well as Benhabib, *Reluctant Modernism of Hannah Arendt*; and O'Connor, *Adorno's Negative Dialectic*.
73. Adorno and Horkheimer, *Dialectic of Enlightenment*, 130. The German original ("Gesellschaft" in Adorno, *Soziologische Schriften*, vol. 1 [Frankfurt: Suhrkamp, 1973]) has *barbarische Beziehungslosigkeit* (barbaric unrelatedness); in Edmund Jephcott's otherwise persuasive translation, this is rather inappropriately translated as "barbaric incoherence."
74. Arendt, *Origins of Totalitarianism*, 322; see also Herbert Marcuse, *Feindanalysen: Über die Deutschen* (Lüneburg: zu Klampen, 1998), 103.
75. Arendt, *Origins of Totalitarianism*, 350.
76. See Schulze Wessel, *Ideologie der Sachlichkeit*, 127–28.
77. See also Rensmann, *Kritische Theorie über den Antisemitismus*, 104.
78. On this point, see especially the chapter on continental imperialism and populist nationalism in Arendt, *Origins of Totalitarianism*, 227–49.
79. Hitchens, "Reflections on Antisemitism," 22.
80. Adorno and Horkheimer, *Dialectic of Enlightenment*, 157.
81. Ibid., 140–41.

82. On Arendt's concept of ideology, see her "Ideologie und Terror," in *Offener Horizont: Festschrift für Karl Jaspers*, ed. Klaus Piper (Munich: Piper, 1953), 229–54; also Hannah Arendt, "On the Nature of Totalitarianism: An Essay in Understanding," in id., *Essays in Understanding, 1930–1954: Formation, Exile, and Totalitarianism* (New York: Schocken Books, 1994), 328–60.
83. Adorno and Horkheimer, *Dialectic of Enlightenment*, 153.
84. Hannah Arendt, "The Concept of History: Ancient and Modern," in id., *Between Past and Future: Six Exercises in Political Thought* (New York: Penguin Books, 1968), 87.
85. Arendt, *Denktagebuch*, 193.
86. Arendt, "Concept of History," 87–88.
87. Adorno, *Negative Dialectics*, 309.
88. Theodor W. Adorno, "The Meaning of Working Through the Past," in id., *Critical Models: Interventions and Catchwords* (New York: Columbia University Press, 1998), 101.
89. Adorno and Horkheimer, *Dialectic of Enlightenment*, 140.
90. Theodor W. Adorno, "Education After Auschwitz," in id., *Critical Models*, 198.
91. Theodor W. Adorno, "Studies in the Authoritarian Personality," in id., *Gesammelte Schriften*, vol. 9.1 (Frankfurt: Suhrkamp, 1973), 486.
92. Ibid.
93. Reflective judgment, according to Kant's *Critique of Judgment*, is the ability to tell right from wrong without the guidance of abstract or fixed rules. It is the capacity for independent judgment, which persists even if the world around us goes mad. It can be distinguished from determinate judgment, which is the capacity to apply given, socially established principles to any set of particulars. See Robert Fine, *Cosmopolitanism* (New York: Routledge, 2007), 125.
94. See Schulze Wessel, *Ideologie der Sachlichkeit*, 196ff.
95. Arendt describes Eichmann as somebody who was fed up with his "humdrum life without significance and consequence" (*Eichmann in Jerusalem*, 61).
96. Adorno, "Education After Auschwitz," 198.
97. Arendt, *Eichmann in Jerusalem*, 151.
98. Adorno and Horkheimer, *Dialectic of Enlightenment*, 140.
99. Ibid., 150ff.
100. Adorno, "Studies in the Authoritarian Personality," 486.
101. Hannah Arendt, "Auschwitz on Trial," in *Responsibility and Judgment*, ed. Jerome Kohn (New York: Schocken Books, 2003). It is noteworthy that for both Arendt and Adorno the Nazi "bureaucracy" also somewhat disguised the total disintegration of totalitarian society. As Robert Fine points out, behind the "simulacrum of bureaucracy," we find no hierarchy of command or system of rules recognizable to students of Max Weber. Officials in authority positions could be replaced and denounced by juniors in the competition of rackets, and "one apparatus was liable to be liquidated in favor of another"; the stability and hierarchy that Arendt identified with the "state" and its genuine administration was utterly

absent in the totalitarian movement-state or "anti-state"; see Fine, *Cosmopolitanism*, 107; see also Lars Rensmann, "Der totale Staat als Un-Staat: Hannah Arendts und Franz Neumanns politische Theorien totalitärer Herrschaft," in *Kritische Theorie des Staates*, ed. Samuel Salzborn (Baden-Baden: Nomos, 2009).

102. For an elaboration of this mode, see Hannah Arendt, *The Human Condition* (Chicago: University of Chicago Press, 1958), 38ff.
103. Adorno and Horkheimer, *Dialectic of Enlightenment*, 140.
104. Arendt, *Eichmann in Jerusalem*, 36–55, 69ff.
105. Ibid., 69.
106. Adorno, "Studies in the Authoritarian Personality," 486.
107. Adorno and Horkheimer, *Dialectic of Enlightenment*, 165ff.
108. Adorno, "Studies in the Authoritarian Personality, 486–87.
109. Rensmann, *Kritische Theorie des Antisemitismus*, 140.
110. Arendt, *Eichmann in Jerusalem*, 48.
111. Benhabib, "Hannah Arendt and the Redemptive Power of Narrative," 116.
112. Adorno and Horkheimer, *Dialectic of Enlightenment*, 139.
113. Hitchens, "Reflections on Antisemitism," 20ff.
114. Quoted in Elisabeth Young-Bruehl, *Hannah Arendt: For Love of the World* (New Haven, CT: Yale University Press, 2004), 391.
115. Hannah Arendt in a long-distance conversation with Thilo Koch, in Hannah Arendt, *Ich will verstehen: Selbstauskünfte zu Leben und Werk*, ed. Ursula Ludz (Munich: Piper, 1997), 37.
116. On equality in Arendt, see Jeremy Waldron, "Arendt and the Foundation of Equality," in *Politics in Dark Times: Encounters with Hannah Arendt*, ed. Seyla Benhabib (New York: Cambridge University Press, 2010), 17–38.
117. Arendt, *Eichmann in Jerusalem*, 268–69.

Chapter 10

Parts of this essay have previously appeared in German under the title "Paria wider Willen," in *Arendt und Adorno*, ed. Dirk Auer, Lars Rensmann, and Julia Schulze Wessel (Frankfurt: Suhrkamp, 2003), 35–56, © Suhrkamp Verlag. Reprinted with the permission of the publisher.

1. See Theodor W. Adorno, "Über die geschichtliche Angemessenheit des Bewußtseins. Gespräch mit Peter Hasselberg," *Akzente* 12, no. 6 (1965). Here Adorno goes on to say that "consciousness generally means experience, namely, the ability to acquire experiences, even in the knowledge of scars" (492). Hannah Arendt puts it in a similar way: "I do not believe that there is any thought process possible without personal experience. Every thought is an afterthought, that is a reflection on some matter or event." Hannah Arendt, "'What Remains? The Language Remains': A Conversation with Günter Gaus" (1964), in id., *Essays in Understanding, 1930–1954: Formation, Exile, and Totalitarianism* (New York: Schocken Books,

1994), 20. And in response to the question of what the subject of our thinking is, she answers: "Experience! Nothing else!"; see Hannah Arendt, *Ich will verstehen: Selbstauskünfte zu Leben und Werk*, ed. Ursula Ludz (Munich: Piper, 1996), 79.

2. On the relationship between thinking and experience in Arendt, see Claudia Althaus, *Erfahrung denken. Hannah Arendts Weg von der Zeitgeschichte zur politischen Theorie* (Göttingen: Vandenhoeck & Ruprecht, 2000); and on theory and the experience of forced exile, Lars Rensmann, "Returning from Forced Exile: Some Observations on Hannah Arendt's and Theodor W. Adorno's Experience of Post-War Germany and Their Social and Political Theories on Totalitarianism," *Leo Baeck Institute Yearbook* 49 (2004): 380–406.

3. In relation to Adorno, see Gunzelin Schmid Noerr, *Gesten aus Begriffen* (Frankfurt: Suhrkamp, 1997), 117, and Martin Jay, "Adorno in America," in id., *Permanent Exiles: On the Intellectual Migration from Germany to America* (New York: Columbia University Press, 1985), 120–37, showing how Adorno's "thinking was radicalized by his emigration." In relation to Arendt, see Richard Bernstein, *Hannah Arendt and the Jewish Question* (Cambridge, MA: MIT Press, 1996). On exiled German intellectuals in general, see *Exile, Science, and Bildung: The Contested Legacies of German Émigré Intellectuals*, ed. David Kettler and Gerhard Lauer (New York: Palgrave Macmillan, 2005).

4. See Wolf Lepenies, "Das Ende der Utopie und die Rückkehr der Melancholie. Blick auf die Intellektuellen eines alten Kontinents," in *Intellektuellendämmerung?* ed. Martin Meyer (Munich: Carl Hanser, 1992).

5. We can disregard the fact that the nearly identical diagnosis of their epoch conceals different contexts for their respective critiques of modernity, since we are less concerned with a general comparison of their theories here than with a discussion of those positions of Adorno and Arendt that are relevant to the problem.

6. Arendt, "'What Remains?'" 4.

7. Ibid., 5.

8. This and the preceding quotation are from Arendt, "'What Remains?'" 11. "I thought that it had to do with this profession, with being an intellectual. I am speaking in the past tense," she writes. "Today I know more about it." Later Arendt rails against the "feebleminded reflectivity or reflective feeblemindedness of intellectuals" (Hanna Arendt and Mary McCarthy, *Im Vertrauen. Briefwechsel, 1949–1975* [Munich: Piper, 1995], 73) and says "they are, after all, intellectuals, which is considerably worse than representatives of particular interests" (Hannah Arendt and Karl Jaspers, *Briefwechsel, 1926–1969* [Munich: Piper, 1985], 670).

9. Hannah Arendt, "We Refugees," in id., *The Jewish Writings*, ed. Jerome Kohn and Ron H. Feldman (New York: Schocken Books, 2007), 264–65.

10. That in doing so Arendt and Adorno come up against the same central problem is no coincidence, however. Jews and intellectuals occupy very similar positions in the modernist epistemology: they are the symbolic representation of difference, i.e., of that which can never be entirely integrated into the existing order. Accordingly, ever since the Dreyfus Affair, anti-intellectualism has been connected with antisemitism: both ideologies portray Jews and intellectuals as

rootless, decadent, unpatriotic, and pernicious. See Dietz Bering, *Die Intellektuellen: Geschichte eines Schimpfwortes* (Stuttgart: Ullstein, 1987).

11. Theodor W. Adorno, "On the Question: What is German?" in Adorno, *Critical Models: Interventions and Catchwords*, trans. Henry W. Pickford (New York: Columbia University Press, 1998), 212.

12. Theodor W. Adorno to Siegfried Kracauer, September 1, 1955, Deutsches Literaturarchiv, Marbach am Neckar; reprinted in Theodor W. Adorno and Siegfried Kracauer, *Briefwechsel* (Frankfurt: Suhrkamp, 2008).

13. Arendt, "'What Remains?'" 13. For Arendt, it followed that the "temptation to be permitted to write in one's own language once more ... is the only return from exile ... which one can never entirely banish from one's dreams" (Arendt, *Die verborgene Tradition* [Frankfurt: Suhrkamp, 1976], 7).

14. Theodor W. Adorno, *Minima Moralia: Reflections from Damaged Life,* trans. E. F. N. Jephcott (1951; London: Verso, 1974), 46–47. For a detailed analysis of Adorno's view of America, which despite all criticism was quite ambivalent, see Jay, "Adorno in America." An even more extensive analysis, which draws similar conclusions about Adorno's ambivalence, is David Jenemann, *Adorno in America* (Minneapolis: University of Minnesota Press, 2007).

15. Hannah Arendt, *The Origins of Totalitarianism* (1951; 3rd ed., New York: Harcourt, Brace & World, 1968), 293.

16. See *Displacements: Cultural Identities in Question*, ed. Angelika Bammer (Bloomington: Indiana University Press, 1994). Here displacement is understood as separation "of people from their native culture either through physical dislocation (as refugees, immigrants, migrants, exiles, or expatriates) or the colonializing imposition of a foreign culture."

17. Adorno, *Minima Moralia*, 33.

18. See Adrienne Rich, "Notes Toward a Politics of Location," in id., *Blood, Bread, and Poetry: Selected Prose, 1979–1985* (New York: Norton, 1986), 210–31; also David Simpson, *Situatedness, or, Why We Keep Saying Where We're Coming From* (Durham, NC: Duke University Press, 2002); Lars Rensmann, chapter 6 of this book.

19. See Homi K. Bhaba, "The Third Space," in *Identity, Community, Culture, Difference*, ed. Jonathan Rutherford (London: Lawrence & Wishart, 1990).

20. Arendt, "We Refugees," 265.

21. Theodor W. Adorno and Max Horkheimer, *Dialectic of Enlightenment*, trans. Edmund Jephcott (Stanford: Stanford University Press, 2002), 179. Elsewhere, Adorno states somewhat more drastically: "It is made unmistakably clear to the intellectual from abroad that he will have to eradicate himself as an autonomous being if he hopes to achieve anything or be accepted as an employee of the super-trust into which life has been condensed" (Adorno, "Aldous Huxley and Utopia," in *Prisms*, trans. Samuel and Shierry Weber [Cambridge, MA: MIT Press, 1988], 98).

22. "A glance at the literary output of those émigrés who, by discipline and a sharp separation of spheres of influence, performed the feat of representing the

German mind, shows what is to be expected of a happy reconstruction: the introduction of Broadway methods on the Kurfürstendamm, which differed from the former in the Twenties only through its lesser means, not its better intentions" (Adorno, *Minima Moralia*, 57–58).

23. Ibid., 33.

24. Theodor W. Adorno, "Theorie der Halbbildung" (1959), in id., *Gesammelte Schriften* (Frankfurt: Suhrkamp, 1997), 8: 101.

25. Adorno, *Minima Moralia*, 33.

26. Hannah Arendt, *Rahel Varnhagen: The Life of a Jewess*, trans. Richard and Clara Winston (Baltimore: Johns Hopkins University Press, 1997). Besides associated feelings of guilt and shame, which, as further studies of the history of Jewish assimilation have shown, can become amplified to the point of self-hatred, another fatal aspect of compulsive assimilation, according to Arendt, consists in the fact that the search for individual routes of escape may facilitate a refusal of solidarity by other Jews.

27. Hannah Arendt, "On Hannah Arendt," in *Hannah Arendt: The Recovery of the Public World*, ed. Melvyn A. Hill (New York: St. Martin's Press, 1979), 336–37.

28. Jewish identity can, of course, become a political topic, for example, when action is being taken against antisemitism. In that case, however, it will have changed from a "natural" fact, acquired by birth, to a political one.

29. Theodor W. Adorno, "Die auferstandene Kultur" (1949), in id., *Gesammelte Schriften*, vol. 20.2 (Frankfurt: Suhrkamp, 1997), 456.

30. Adorno, *Gesammelte Schriften*, 20.2: 459.

31. The search for such a place is analogous to Kafka's dream of escaping from a struggle between two opponents, one of whom is always supporting him against the other. On account of his experience in fighting, he is to be instituted as the judge over his two fighting opponents.

32. See Arendt, *Rahel Varnhagen*.

33. Theodor W. Adorno to Thomas Mann, December 28, 1949, in Theodor W. Adorno and Thomas Mann, *Briefwechsel, 1943–1955* (Frankfurt: Fischer, 2002), 49.

34. Adorno, *Minima Moralia*, 126.

35. Theodor W. Adorno, "Fragen an die intellektuelle Emigration," in id., *Gesammelte Schriften*, 20.1: 353.

36. Adorno, *Minima Moralia*, 129.

37. Adorno, "Fragen an die intellektuelle Emigration," 353.

38. Adorno, *Minima Moralia*, 68.

39. Ibid., 26.

40. Hannah Arendt, *Das Urteilen: Texte zu Kants kritischer Philosophie* (Munich: Piper, 1985); see also Hannah Arendt, *Lectures on Kant's Political Philosophy*, ed. Ronald Beiner (Chicago: University of Chicago Press, 1992).

41. "Do I imagine myself being influential? No. I want to understand. And if others understand—in the same sense that I have understood—that gives me a sense of satisfaction, like feeling at home" (Arendt, "'What Remains?'" 3).

42. Hannah Arendt, speech on the occasion of being awarded the Danish government's Sonning Prize for Contributions to European Civilization in 1975,

quoted from Elisabeth Young-Bruehl, *Hannah Arendt: For Love of the World* (New Haven, CT: Yale University Press, 2004), xi.

43. Adorno, *Minima Moralia*, 38.

44. See Anne Kuhlmann, "Das Exil als Heimat. Über jüdische Schreibweisen und Metaphern," *Exilforschung. Ein Internationales Jahrbuch* 17 (1999).

45. Adorno to Thomas Mann, June 3, 1950, in Theodor W. Adorno and Thomas Mann, *Correspondence, 1943–55*, trans. Nicholas Walker, ed. Christopher Gödde and Thoma Sprecher (Malden, MA: Polity Press, 2006), 46.

46. Cf., e.g., Vilém Flusser, according to whom "human dignity consists precisely in having no roots," which is to say, "to remain displaced, and that means: to let oneself be displaced again and again" (Flusser, *Von der Freiheit des Migranten. Einsprüche gegen den Nationalismus* [Berlin: EVA, 2000], 107).

47. Edward Said, *Culture and Imperialism* (New York: Knopf, 1993), 332. Said adds, to be sure: "Yet it is no exaggeration to say that liberation . . . has now shifted from the settled . . . to its unhoused, decentered, and exilic energies, energies whose incarnation today is the migrant, and whose consciousness is that of the intellectual and artist in exile, the political figure between domains, between forms, between homes, and between languages."

48. Adorno, *Minima Moralia*, 103.

49. Arendt, *The Human Condition* (Chicago: University of Chicago Press, 1958), 7.

50. Arendt, *Origins of Totalitarianism*, 277.

51. Arendt, *Die verborgene Tradition*, 73.

52. Arendt, *Origins of Totalitarianism*, 279.

53. Ibid., 296–97.

54. Arendt, *Die verborgene Tradition*, 73.

55. Adorno, *Minima Moralia*, 149.

56. Ibid., 149.

57. Ibid., 150.

58. Arendt, *Human Condition*, 38ff.

59. Ibid., 39.

60. Ibid., 322.

61. Ibid., 332.

62. Theodor W. Adorno, "Reflexionen zur Klassentheorie" (1942), in id., *Gesammelte Schriften* (Frankfurt: Suhrkamp, 1997), 8: 377.

63. Arendt, *Human Condition*, 58.

64. Theodor W. Adorno, "On Subject and Object," in id., *Critical Models*, 247.

65. Adorno, *Minima Moralia*, 102–3.

66. Arendt, *Origins of Totalitarianism*, 109.

67. Adorno, *Minima Moralia*, 103.

68. Hannah Arendt, *Elemente und Ursprünge totaler Herrschaft* (1955; Munich: Piper, 1986), 109.

69. Arendt and Jaspers, *Briefwechsel*, 65.

70. Adorno, "On Subject and Object," 247.

71. Adorno, *Minima Moralia*, 88–89.

72. Theodor W. Adorno, *Against Epistemology: A Metacritique. Studies in Husserl and the Phenomenological Antinomies*, trans. W. Domingo (Oxford: Blackwell, 1982), 83.

73. On the notion and meaning of the "free-floating intellectual," see Karl Mannheim, *Sociology as Political Education,* ed. David Kettler and Colin Loader (New Brunswick, NJ: Transaction), 21, and its critique in Theodor W. Adorno, *Introduction to Sociology* (Stanford: Stanford University Press, 2000), 130. All this only seemingly stands in contradiction to the concept of the intellectual as exile, standing site-less, so to speak, between, above, and adjacent to tradition. The validity of this conception of the intellectual is not universal, but based on a decision grounded in the politics of theory, i.e., a contingent decision that has been made against the background of a specific historical constellation. According to Adorno (*Minima Moralia*, 150), "today the trace of the human seems to be solely attached to the individual in his decline"; according to Arendt (Arendt and Jaspers, *Briefwechsel*, 65), " today one can create an existence of some human dignity only at the fringes of society." This illustrates the temporal index of claims to validity with regard to the position of the intellectual, and how Arendt and Adorno reflect on their own particular historical location. Adorno and Arendt are pariahs against their will. As such, they don't speak from a neutral, common point of view, but from a particular perspective that is theirs alone.

74. Zygmunt Bauman, "Legislators and Interpreters: Culture as the Ideology of Intellectuals," in id., *Intimations of Postmodernity* (London: Routledge, 1992), 1.

75. Michael Walzer, *Interpretation and Social Criticism* (Cambridge, MA: Harvard University Press, 1987), 61.

76. Walzer does, however, believe that critics require a certain distance or position at the margins.

77. In a similar fashion, Michel Foucault describes the activity of the critic "as a certain way of thinking, of speaking, of acting, too, a certain relationship to that which exists, to that which one knows, to that which one does, a relationship to society, to culture, to others as well." Thus "critique exists only in relationship to something other than itself." Michel Foucault, "What Is Critique," in id., *The Politics of Truth* (New York: Semiotext(e), 1997).

78. Even in the "innermost recesses of humanism," according to Adorno, "as its very soul, there rages a frantic prisoner who, as a Fascist, turns the world into a prison" (*Minima Moralia*, 89).

79. Hannah Arendt, *The Life of the Mind*, ed. Mary McCarthy, vol. 1: *Thinking* (New York: Harcourt Brace Jovanovich, 1978), 70.

80. Hannah Arendt, "A Letter to Gershom Scholem," in id., *Jewish Writings*, 466.

81. Adorno, *Minima Moralia*, 68. Translation slightly modified.

82. Hannah Arendt, "On Humanity in Dark Times: Thoughts About Lessing," in id., *Men in Dark Times* (New York: Harcourt, Brace & World, 1968), 13.

83. Ibid., 23. Arendt continues: "Thus, in the case of a friendship between a German and a Jew under the conditions of the Third Reich it would scarcely have

been a sign of humaneness for the friends to have said: Are we not both human beings? It would have been mere evasion of reality and of the world common to both at the time; they would not have been resisting the world as it was."

84. Ibid., 22.

85. Adorno, *Minima Moralia*, 26.

86. Ibid., 132.

87. Thorsten Bonacker, *Die Normative Kraft der Kontingenz. Nichtessentialistische Gesellschaftskritik nach Weber und Adorno* (Frankfurt: Campus, 2000), 30.

88. See Zygmunt Bauman, *Modernity and Ambivalence* (Ithaca, NY: Cornell University Press, 1991), 90–94.

89. Richard Rorty, *Philosophy and the Mirror of Nature* (Princeton, NJ: Princeton University Press, 2009), 389.

Chapter 11

This chapter is a much revised version of my essay "Writing and Judging: Adorno, Arendt and the Chiasmus of Natural History," *Philosophy Social Criticism* 30, no. 4 (June 2004): 445–75.

1. Hannah Arendt, *Reflections on Literature and Culture*, ed. Susannah Young-ah Gottlieb (Stanford: Stanford University Press, 2007).

2. See Alex Demirovic, *Der nonkonformistiche Intellecktuelle. Die Entwicklung der Kritische Theorie zur Frankfurter Schule* (Frankfurt: Suhrkamp, 1999), and Max Pensky, "Beyond the Message in the Bottle: The Other Critical Theory," *Constellations* 10, no. 1 (March 2003): 135–44.

3. Elisabeth Young-Bruehl, *Hannah Arendt: For Love of the World* (New Haven, CT: Yale University Press, 1982), 104.

4. Theodor W. Adorno, *Lectures on Negative Dialectics*, trans. Rodney Livingstone (Malden, MA: Polity Press, 2008): 17.

5. Hannah Arendt, "We Refugees," in id., *The Jewish Writings*, ed. Jerome Kohn and Ron H. Feldman (New York: Schocken Books, 2007), 274.

6. Hegel, *Phenomenology of Spirit,* trans. A. V. Miller (Oxford: Oxford University Press, 1977), § 28.

7. Ibid., § 28.

8. Ibid., § 32.

9. Ibid., § 36.

10. Robert B. Pippin, *The Persistence of Subjectivity: On the Kantian Aftermath* (New York: Cambridge University Press, 2005).

11. "Every progress in science in the last decades, from the moment it was absorbed into technology and thus introduced into the factual world where we live our everyday lives, has brought with it a veritable avalanche of fabulous instruments and ever more ingenious machinery," Arendt writes. "All of this makes it more unlikely every day that man will encounter anything in the world around

him that is not man-made and hence is not, in the last analysis, he himself in a different disguise" ("The Conquest of Space and the Stature of Man," in id., *Between Past and Future: Six Exercises in Political Thought* [1968; London: Penguin Books, 1993], 277).

12. Hannah Arendt, "The Concept of History," in *Between Past and Future: Six Exercises in Political Thought* (New York: Penguin Books, 1961), 42.

13. Cited in Eżbieta Ettinger, *Hannah Arendt / Martin Heidegger* (New Haven, CT: Yale University Press), 119.

14. Richard Wolin, *Heidegger's Children: Hannah Arendt, Karl Löwith, Hans Jonas and Herbert Marcuse* (Princeton, NJ: Princeton University Press, 2001), 69.

15. Hannah Arendt, "What Is Existential Philosophy?" in id., *Essays in Understanding, 1930–1954: Formation, Exile and Totalitarianism*, trans. Jerome Kohn (New York: Schocken Books, 1994): 187n.

16. See Seyla Benhabib, *The Reluctant Modernism of Hannah Arendt* (London: Sage, 1994), and Dana Villa, *Arendt and Heidegger: The Fate of the Political* (Princeton, NJ: Princeton University Press, 1996).

17. See Samir Gandesha, "Leaving Home: On Adorno and Heidegger," in *The Cambridge Companion to Adorno*, ed. Tom Huhn (New York: Cambridge University Press, 2004), 101–28.

18. In his *Heidegger and "the Jews,"* trans. Andreas Michel and Mark Roberts (Minneapolis: University of Minnesota Press, 1990), Jean-Francois Lyotard seeks to read the implication of Heidegger's philosophy in fascism as itself symptomatic of certain features of philosophy per se, and disputes the either/or logic of the argument that if Heidegger's philosophy was great, it could not have been fascist; and if it was fascist, it could not have been great.

19. Perhaps the most infamous example of this is Heidegger's refusal to alter his references to the "inner strength and greatness of National Socialism" in the 1953 reprint of *Introduction to Metaphysics* (originally published in 1935). This played a crucial role in Habermas's break with his youthful Heideggerianism. See Jürgen Habermas, "Martin Heidegger: Zur Veröffentlichung von Vorlesungen aus dem Jahre 1935," in id., *Philosophisch-politische Profile* (Frankfurt: Suhrkamp, 1981), 65–71.

20. See for representative examples of each, Richard Rorty, "Overcoming the Tradition: Heidegger and Dewey," in *Heidegger and Modern Philosophy*, ed. Michael Murray (New Haven, CT: Yale University Press, 1978), 239–58, and Jacques Derrida, "Différance" in *Margins of Philosophy*, trans. Alan Bass (Chicago: University of Chicago Press, 1982), 1–28. According to Rolf Wiggershaus, *Wittgenstein und Adorno. Zwei Spielarten modernen Philosophierens* (Göttingen: Wallstein, 2000), Adorno attempts, like Wittgenstein, to move beyond the perspective of the objective observer.

21. One could argue, however, that inasmuch as Adorno's thinking takes as its point of departure Hegel's dialectic, with its own eschewal of foundations, he has no need for an appropriation of Heidegger's critique of foundationalism. While it is true that Adorno often draws on Hegelian arguments in his critique of Husserl,

Adorno's immanent critique of Heidegger forms the basis for his attempt to develop what Susan Buck-Morss calls "dialectics without identity" (Buck-Morss, *The Origins of Negative Dialectics: Theodor W. Adorno, Walter Benjamin and the Frankfurt Institute* [New York: Free Press, 1977], chap. 4).

22. Adorno, *Negative Dialectics*, 6; trans. modified. For Adorno's argument for the necessity of engaging with the tradition, and his understanding of philosophy as hermeneutic, see also id., "Tradition and Knowledge," ibid., 53–55.

23. See Christoph Menke, *The Sovereignty of Art: Aesthetic Negativity in Adorno and Derrida* (Cambridge, MA: MIT Press, 1998), for an illuminating comparison of deconstruction and negative dialectics.

24. See Michel Foucault, *Discipline and Punish*, trans. Alan Sheridan (New York: Vintage Books, 1979).

25. Arendt, "What Is Existential Philosophy?" 49; emphasis added.

26. The difficulties of so doing are made clear in Michael Theunissen's *Das Andere* (1965), trans. Christopher Macann as *The Other: Studies in the Social Ontology of Husserl, Heidegger, Sartre, and Buber* (Cambridge, MA: MIT Press, 1984), in which he argues that *mit-Sein* is hardly intersubjective, but rather involves the reduction of the other in a monological way to the worldliness of *Dasein*'s "world."

27. Adorno's period of exile falls between 1933 and his return to Germany in 1949 and includes *Dialectic of Enlightenment, Philosophy of Modern Music, The Authoritarian Personality*, and *Minima Moralia*, in addition to having played a more than just an advisory role in Thomas Mann's composition of *Dr. Faustus* (see the recently published exchange of letters between Adorno and Mann). I consider Arendt's period of exile to be from the time of her fleeing Germany until she became an American citizen, for, until that time, she was essentially stateless.

28. Martin Jay, *Permanent Exiles* (New York: Columbia University Press, 1985).

29. Benhabib, *Reluctant Modernism of Hannah Arendt*, 62–63.

30. Theodor W. Adorno, *Minima Moralia: Reflections from Damaged Life*, trans. E. F. N. Jephcott (London: Verso, 1974), 38.

31. Theodor W. Adorno, "On the Question: 'What is German?'" in id., *Critical Models: Interventions and Catchwords*, trans. Henry W. Pickford (New York: Columbia University Press, 1998), 213.

32. Adorno is thus in agreement with Rorty's critique in "Overcoming the Tradition."

33. See Adorno, *Negative Dialektik* (Frankfurt: Suhrkamp, 1973), "Vorrede," 10.

34. See Rolf Tiedemann, "Editorische Nachbemerkung," in Theodor W. Adorno, *Gesammelte Schriften* (Frankfurt: Suhrkamp, 1997), 1: 381–84.

35. Rorty's critique in "Overcoming the Tradition" is articulated along similar lines.

36. Walter Benjamin, *The Origin of German Tragic Drama*, trans. John Osborne (London: Verso, 1977).

37. As Adorno puts it in *Negative Dialektik*, "Die herkömmliche Antithesis von Natur und Geschichte ist wahr und falsch; wahr, soweit sie ausspricht, was dem Naturmoment widerfuhr; falsch, soweit sie die Verdeckung der Naturwüchsigkeit

der Geschichte durch diese selber vermöge ihrer begrifflichen Nachkonstruktion apologetisch widerholt" (351).

38. Theodor W. Adorno, "The Essay as Form," in id., *Notes to Literature*, trans. Shierry Weber Nicholsen (New York: Columbia University Press, 1991), 1: 21.

39. Adorno, *Gesammelte Schriften*, 1: 81. My translation.

40. In the following eight paragraphs I draw substantially upon the argument of Gandesha, "Leaving Home: On Adorno and Heidegger."

41. Adorno, "Essay as Form," in id., *Notes to Literature*, 1: 19.

42. Adorno and Horkheimer, *Dialectic of Enlightenment*, 47.

43. Ibid., 47–48.

44. Ibid., 192.

45. See also Adorno, "Die Idee der Naturgeschichte," in id., *Gesammelte Schriften*, 1: 345–65.

46. See Robert Hullot-Kentor, "Back to Adorno," *Telos* 81 (Fall 1989): 5–29, on the importance of Oedipus in the original conception of the text. See also Samir Gandesha, "Enlightenment as Tragedy: Reflections on Adorno's Ethics," *Thesis Eleven* 65 (May 2001): 109–30.

47. Friedrich Nietzsche, "On Truth and Lies in a Nonmoral Sense," in *Philosophy and Truth: Selections from Nietzsche's Notebooks of the Early 1870's*, trans. and ed. David Breazeale (Atlantic Highlands, NJ: Humanities Press, 1979), 84.

48. Ibid., 83.

49. See *Quasi una Fantasia: Essays on Modern Music*, trans. Rodney Livingstone (London: Verso, 1998), 2, where Adorno argues that the new music dissociates itself from the reified form of language, "which degrades the particular into a token, into the superannuated signifier of fossilized subjective meanings."

50. Theodor Adorno, *The Jargon of Authenticity*, trans. Knut Tarnowski and Frederic Will (Evanston, IL: Northwestern University Press, 1973), 38.

51. See, e.g., Mildred Bakan, "Hannah Arendt's Concepts of Labor and Work."

52. Ettinger, *Hannah Arendt / Martin Heidegger*, 114.

53. Arendt, "Concept of History," 61.

54. Arendt, *Human Condition*, 167–68.

55. See Villa, *Arendt and Heidegger*, xi. Arendt can therefore be regarded as an important, if at times little acknowledged, source of Habermas's attempt to provide an alternative account of rationalization to the Weber-inspired critique of rationalization from Lukács to Horkheimer and Adorno. Such an account seeks to differentiate between instrumental and strategic forms of rationality, on the one side, and the communicative or intersubjective form, on the other. See Jürgen Habermas, *The Theory of Communicative Action,* trans. Thomas McCarthy (Boston: Beacon Press, 1984).

56. Martin Heidegger, *Sein und Zeit*, 10th ed. (Tubingen: Max Niemeyer, 1963); *Being and Time*, trans. John Macquarrie and Edward Robinson (New York: Harper & Row, 1962), § 38.

57. See Benhabib, *Reluctant Modernism of Hannah Arendt*, and Villa, *Arendt and Heidegger*.

58. Arendt, *Human Condition*, 7.
59. Ibid., 7.
60. Ibid., 7.
61. Arendt, "Concept of History," 61.
62. Arendt, *Human Condition*, 290.
63. See Aristotle, *The Politics*, trans. Ernest Barker (Oxford: Oxford University Press, 1958), esp. bk. 1.
64. Arendt, *Human Condition*, 37.
65. See Hannah Arendt, *Lectures on Kant's Political Philosophy*, ed. Ronald Beiner (Chicago: Chicago University Press, 1992), 66.
66. Hanna Fenichel Pitkin, *The Attack of the Blob: Hannah Arendt's Concept of the Social* (Chicago: University of Chicago Press, 1998).
67. Ibid., esp. chap. 4.
68. Arendt, *Origins of Totalitarianism*, 465–66.
69. Adorno and Horkheimer, *Dialectic of Enlightenment*, 57; trans modified.
70. Hannah Arendt, "The Crisis in Culture," in id., *Between Past and Future: Six Exercises in Political Thought* (New York: Meridian, 1961), 207.
71. See Immanuel Kant, *Critique of Judgment*, trans. W. Pluhar, (Indianapolis: Hackett, 1987), § 55–57.
72. Arendt, *Lectures on Kant's Political Philosophy*, ed. Beiner, 66.
73. Ibid., 66.
74. Ibid., 43.
75. Ibid., 44.
76. Ronald Beiner, "Interpretive Essay," in Arendt, *Lectures on Kant's Political Philosophy*, 93.
77. Theodor W. Adorno, *Minima Moralia*, trans. E. F. N. Jephcott (London: Verso, 1978), 87.
78. See Theodor W. Adorno, *Prisms*, trans. Samuel and Shierry Weber (Cambridge MA: MIT Press, 1988), 240.
79. See Shierry Weber Nicholsen's extremely suggestive interpretation, *Exact Imagination, Late Work: On Adorno's Aesthetics* (Cambridge, MA: MIT Press, 1997).
80. Theodor W. Adorno, "The Essay as Form," in id., *Notes to Literature, Volume I*, trans. S. W. Nicholsen (New York: Columbia University Press, 1992), 12.
81. Edward Said, *Reflections on Exile and Other Essays* (Cambridge, MA: Harvard University Press, 2002), 174.
82. Ibid., 186.
83. See Giorgio Agamben, *Homo Sacer: Sovereign Power and Bare Life*, trans. Daniel Heller-Roazen (Stanford: Stanford University Press, 1998), id., *Remnants of Auschwitz: The Witness and the Archive*, trans. Daniel Heller-Roazen (New York: Zone Books, 1999), and Primo Levi, *Survival in Auschwitz: The Nazi Assault on Humanity* (New York: Simon & Schuster, 1996), which discuss this logic in detail.

Index

administered society, 8, 80–84, 90, 165, 192, 240
administration, 8, 155–56, 219–22, 335
administrative despotism, 98
Adorno, Theodor W., "The Actuality of Philosophy," 20, 34, 38, 41; *Against Epistemology*, 256; *The Authoritarian Personality*, 187–91, 199; *Critical Models*, 170; "*Der Essay als Form*," 277; *Dialectic of Enlightenment* (with Max Horkheimer), 6, 48, 80–102, 120, 125, 188, 192–201, 221, 235, 248, 254, 261–65, 273; *History and Freedom*, 149, 165, 169, 171; *The Jargon of Authenticity*, 33; *Minima Moralia: Reflections from Damaged Life*, 15, 80, 86, 89–91, 123, 124, 234, 246, 258, 277; *Negative Dialectics*, 2, 13, 19, 79–81, 91–93, 104, 165, 250, 256, 260; *Problems of Moral Philosophy*, 171; *Studies in Philosophy and Social Science*, 186
Adorno and Horkheimer, 2, 6, 23, 48, 80–90, 120, 125, 188, 192–99, 209, 214, 261, 265, 273; *Dialectic of Enlightenment*, 6, 48, 80–102, 120, 125, 188, 192–201, 221, 235, 248, 254, 261–65, 273
Adorno-Jahre, 78, 81, 89
Agamben, Giorgio, 177
American Revolution, 32, 70–71, 122
Anders, Günther, 32–33, 253

Anderson, Perry, 10
antisemitism, 3, 5, 23–25, 32, 40, 48, 127, 147, 173–225, 298, 325, 329, 331, 332, 333, 337, 339; modern antisemitism, 174, 179, 198, 199, 202–6, 208, 211, 212, 214, 216, 217, 219–25; Nazi antisemitism, 40, 198; philosophical antisemitism, 188; political antisemitism, 180, 183; religious antisemitism, 188, 202; social antisemitism, 181; totalitarian antisemitism, 25, 199, 201, 206, 217, 222–24
Arendt, Hannah: *Between Past and Future: Six Exercises in Political Thought*, 42, 80; "The Crisis in Culture," 50; *Crisis of the Republic*, 80; *Eichmann in Jerusalem*, 3, 32, 250; *The Human Condition*, 21, 105–10, 120; *The Life of the Mind*, 42, 110, 112–13, 116–17; *Love and Saint Augustine*, 106–7, 115; *On Revolution* 32, 64, 69, 71, 72, 80, 96, 102–3, 107; *The Origins of Totalitarianism*, 108, 176, 200, 272; *Rahel Varnhagen: The Life of a Jewess*, 107, 203, 236; "We Refugees," 232, 246, 251; "What is Existenz Philosophy?," 20, 34, 36, 40, 50; "What is Freedom?," 67, 100
Aristotle, 4, 98–101, 110, 112, 119, 249, 269, 270, 282, 304, 316
Auschwitz, 3–4, 13, 19, 93, 142, 155, 198, 200, 202, 229

authoritarian personality, 22, 48, 190, 217, 248
authoritarianism, 23, 190
autonomy, 12–16, 21, 22, 50, 52, 76, 87, 106, 111–16, 121, 122, 126, 145, 165, 216, 225, 278, 299, 309

Bauman, Zgymunt, 179
Benedict, Hans Jürgen, 129
Benjamin, Walter, 2–5, 15, 31–53, 144–46, 175–76, 200, 250–54, 260; *Gesammelte Schriften*, 2; *Illuminations: Essays and Reflections*, 2, 32, 40; *Origin of German Tragic Drama*, 37; "The Task of the Translator," 145; "Theses on the Philosophy of History," 31–32
Berman, Russell A., 7
Birnbaum, Pierre, 184
Blücher, Heinrich, 31, 32, 105
Bonacker, Thorsten, 244
bureaucracy, 40, 71–72, 177, 240, 335
bureaucratic rationality, 72, 82, 160
bureaucratization, 214
Burke, Edmund, 160

capitalism, 10, 12, 157, 170, 183, 193, 207, 214, 287, 327, 333; financial capitalism, 24, 174, 180, 184, 196; global capitalism, 191; industrial capitalism, 332; late capitalism, 80–81, 84, 88; modern capitalism, 205, 207, 217, 287, 333; monopoly capitalism, 90, 186, 192; postliberal capitalism, 86
categorical imperative, 19, 52, 135, 137, 141–42
Cavell, Stanley, 63, 64
civil disobedience, 21, 56, 59, 67, 73–75
civil rights, 101, 132, 138, 141, 170
civil rights movement, 65, 74
civil society, 7, 82, 98, 155, 165–68
Clark, T.J., 15, 16
commodification, 24

communicative action, 6, 80
communicative rationality, 54
communicative reason, 18
constitutionalism, 15, 103, 135, 314
Constitution of the United States (*or* American Constitution), 60, 61, 67–72
cosmopolitanism, 15, 129–63, 172, 184, 205, 251
cosmopolitics, 129–63, 313, 320
crimes against humanity, 23, 129–32, 135, 136, 141, 142, 144, 147, 151, 152, 314
critical political theory, 9, 269
critical theory, 4, 15, 24, 38–39, 54, 57–58, 88, 154–57, 166, 185, 196, 213, 248, 278

Dasein, 35–36, 43–48, 253, 260, 266–267, 272
Demirovic, Alex, 7
democracy, 7–8, 17, 59–61, 73, 139, 150, 170, 249, 301, 305, 315, 332; American democracy, 8; Athenian democracy, 99; constitutional democracy, 61, 76, 205, 305; Greek democracy, 59, 99; liberal democracy, 94, 95; radical democracy, 60; representative democracy, 7, 71–73; republican democracy, 95
democratic constitutions, 318
democratic deficit, 15
democratic institutions, 287, 318
democratic public sphere, 8
determinate critique, 260
determinate judgment, 172, 313, 335
determinate negation, 55, 60, 75
Derrida, Jacques, 91, 94, 256, 257; *Writing and Difference*, 91, 94, 256, 257
Descartes, René, 37, 255
disenchantment, 56, 261, 263–64
domination, 8, 9, 13, 22, 24, 40, 56, 76, 83, 86, 94–95, 100, 120, 124, 139–40, 142, 144, 151, 154, 180, 198, 206, 207,

223, 249, 254, 262, 263, 293, 303; capitalist domination, 9; fascist domination, 192; human domination, 200; political domination, 157; social domination, 251; system of domination, 139, 193, 239; total domination, 192, 202, 215, 217, 240, 242; totalitarian domination, 169, 222
Dreyfus Affair, 26, 176, 182, 208, 241

Eichmann, Adolf, 49, 176, 199, 212, 217–24
Eichmann trial, 3, 50, 231
Enlightenment, 8, 18, 22, 78, 82, 84, 160, 180, 181, 192, 247, 261, 273
Ettinger, Elizbieta, 265; *Hannah Arendt/Martin Heidegger*, 265
equality, 8, 67, 74, 76, 77, 139, 146, 158, 168, 180, 194, 238, 240–41, 336; formal equality, 17, 141; political equality, 140, 147, 180, 206, 224, 238
European Jewry, 82, 90, 174, 179, 180, 195, 219

false universals, 9, 14, 15, 20, 33–34, 44, 48, 50, 52, 55, 150, 312, 319
fascism, 22–23, 33, 48, 80, 166–69, 187–94, 215, 222, 239, 254–55
Fenichel, Otto, 188; "Elements of a Psychoanalytic Theory of Anti-Semitism," 188
Feuerbach, Ludwig, 34
Fichte, Johann Gottlieb, 91
formalism, 11, 23, 147, 152, 259; legal formalism, 137–40, 143, 152
Foucault, Michel, 98, 104
Frankfurt School, 5–6, 54, 80–85, 94, 98, 104, 174, 185, 192, 195
French Revolution, 32, 179
Freud, Sigmund, 4, 81, 102, 186, 189; *Moses and Monotheism*, 186

genocide, 14, 22–23, 130–37, 140–43, 150–53, 156, 197, 208, 222–23, 231

German Idealism, 3, 14, 20, 41, 253
Gleichschaltung, 5, 231, 232, 288
globality, 137, 144, 312
globalization, 10, 13, 130, 238, 319
global political modernity, 23, 144, 153, 318
global political theory, 130
Glucksmann, André, 104
Gunterman, Norman, 190; *Prophets of Deceit* (with Leo Löwenthal), 190

Habermas, Jürgen, 6, 11, 18, 54, 80–82, 97, 124, 141, 248; *Philosophical Discourse of Modernity*, 89; *Reason and the Rationalization of Society*, 82; "Urgeschichte der Subjektivitat und verwilderte Selbstbehauptung," 54
Hegel, G. W. F., 3–4, 6, 8, 11–13, 15, 19–22, 39–45, 52–53, 81, 85, 88, 101–03, 124, 138, 141, 148, 157, 164–70, 181, 250–53, 260–62, 279; *The Phenomenology of Spirit*, 251; *Philosophy of Right*, 103, 141, 164–68; *Science of Logic*, 92
Heidegger, Martin, 3–5, 19, 33–36, 43–49, 91, 92, 97, 101–10, 115, 119, 175, 250–73, 279; *Being and Time*, 107, 255, 261, 265–66; "The Idea of Natural History," 259
hermeneutics, 18, 255, 288
heteronomy, 10, 121, 126, 138, 151, 224; global heteronomy, 149
Hitler-Stalin pact, 32
Hofmannstahl, Hugo von, 2
Holocaust, 2–3, 22–25, 33, 79, 130, 137, 150, 197–98, 202, 213, 223–25
Homer, 83; *Odyssey*, 82, 262
Honneth, Axel, 6, 18, 248
Horkheimer, Max, 38, 80–90, 123, 185–88, 194–99, 221, 231, 254, 261; *Dialectic of Enlightenment* (with Theodor W. Adorno), 6, 48, 80–102, 120, 125, 188, 192–201, 221, 235, 248, 254, 261–265, 273; *Eclipse of*

Reason, 82; "Traditional and Critical Theory," 38
human dignity, 42, 131, 133, 135–37, 144–53, 162, 318, 319, 321, 340, 341
human rights, 23, 25, 131–137, 139, 140, 142–47, 151–53, 154, 157, 159–64, 172, 179, 317, 318, 320, 321, 322, 323
humanity, 9, 23, 25, 42, 47, 53, 60, 109, 110, 118, 123, 130–50, 153, 155, 160, 162, 163, 168, 181, 193, 194, 218, 225, 232, 244–45, 267, 268, 300, 315, 317, 321
Hume, David, 37
Husserl, Edmund, 9, 35–37, 44, 255; *The Crisis of European Sciences*, 9

idealism, 35, 91, 159, 239, 242, 282; transcendental idealism, 35
indeterminate negation, 138
Institute for Social Research, 5, 85, 231
instrumental rationality, 13, 24, 83, 92, 154, 156, 193, 345
interactionism, 174
international law, 3, 131–43, 146, 150–53, 162, 311, 313, 314
internationalism, 184
intersubjectivity, 6, 36, 124
Isaac, Jeffrey, 146

Jaspers, Karl, 5, 105, 129, 136, 254
Jewish Question, 174, 181, 184–85
Jewishness, 182–185, 234
Judaism, 24, 173, 178, 181, 194–95

Kant, Immanuel, 2–4, 8, 11, 13, 19–23, 26, 34, 37, 41–45, 48–55, 60, 69–70, 73, 79, 81, 91–93, 112–16, 121, 123, 129, 135–38, 141–42, 147–48, 150–52, 157, 159–72, 240, 247, 251–53, 259, 271, 275–79; *The Critique of Judgement*, 20, 34, 49, 50; *The Critique of Practical Reason*, 92; *Groundwork of the Metaphysics of Morals*, 92; "Idea for a Universal History from a Cosmopolitan Point of View," 251; *Metaphysics of Justice*, 169
Kierkegaard, Soren, 35, 36, 41, 43
Kracauer, Siegfried, 231
Kristeva, Julia, 182

Lazare, Bernard, 251; and Max Weber, 180
Lefort, Claude, 7
legalism, 23, 134, 136, 139
Levinas, Emmanuel, 91, 94; *Totality and Infinity*, 91, 94
liberalism, 17, 68, 75, 81, 139, 285, 289, 302
liberty, 101, 138, 141, 160, 318
Locke, John, 37, 72, 81, 139, 170
Löwenthal, Leo, 22, 188, 190, 199; *Prophets of Deceit* (with Norman Gunterman), 190
Lukács, Georg, 2, 36, 38, 104, 260, 277; *The Destruction of Reason*, 2; *History and Class Consciousness*, 36
Luxemburg, Rosa, 32, 146, 176
Lyotard, Jean-François, 7, 10, 175

McDowell, John, 122
Mann, Thomas, 7, 237, 278
Mannheim, Karl, 230, 242
Marburg School, 35, 37
Marx, Karl, 3–8, 12–13, 19, 34, 38, 81, 86, 89–95, 101, 138, 165, 184, 196, 250, 253, 265, 269, 271; *Communist Manifesto* (with Friedrich Engels), 12, 86; *Contribution to a Critique of Hegel's "Philosophy of Right,"* 138; *The German Ideology*, 90; *On the Jewish Question*, 90
Marx and Engels, 12, 85, 90
Marxism, 57, 75, 81, 91, 98
Marxist, 75, 80, 84–88, 104, 161, 190, 249
Massing, Paul, 188; *Rehearsal for Destruction*, 190
Maupassant, Guy de, 124; *Sur l'eau*, 124
Menke, Christoph, 122, 310

Milton, John, 116; *Paradise Lost,* 116; *Paradise Regained,* 116
Mitsein, 46–48, 282
modernism, 2, 10, 12, 15, 16, 21, 56, 58, 69, 71, 76, 337; artistic modernism, 56, 57; philosophical modernism, 57; "reluctant modernism," 254, 258
modernity, 9, 10, 12–15, 18, 19, 21, 22, 24, 56–58, 69, 70, 76, 77, 82, 130, 155, 169, 174, 177, 179, 181, 183, 184, 187, 190–93, 195–96, 198, 199, 202, 205, 207, 208, 211, 212, 213, 223, 224, 238, 248, 265, 272–74, 276, 278, 285, 287, 292, 313, 332; political modernity, 1, 9, 11–21, 23, 26, 144, 150, 153, 198, 225, 317, 318
modernization, 12–15, 18, 21, 204, 211, 214, 288, 317
Montesquieu, 81, 102, 139 170

nation-state, 10, 16, 23, 40, 131, 132, 133, 137, 139, 142, 147, 158, 177–84, 247, 279
national socialism, 2, 165, 169, 192, 200, 208, 231
natural history, 259, 261–63, 271, 273
natural law, 163–64, 249
Naturgeschichte, 38, 261
Nazi Germany, 26, 49, 185, 225, 250
Nazi regime, 1, 24, 49
Nazism, 33, 48, 156, 224, 249
Nazizeit, 79, 103–4
neo-Kantian, 35, 37, 259
neo-marxist, 75, 79, 85
Nietzsche, Friedrich, 59, 62, 64, 81–82, 91, 101–2, 108, 155, 263–64, 269, 288; *The Gay Science,* 108; *On the Genealogy of Morals,* 83; "On Truth and Lies in a Non-Moral Sense," 263
nondomination, 10, 12, 14–15, 286, 318
nonidentity, 93, 21, 22, 52–54, 57, 59, 92, 94, 195, 251, 272, 278
Nuremberg Laws, 133

O'Connor, Brian, 91

Odysseus, 83, 125, 249, 262–63
ontology, 35–37, 43, 45, 59, 81, 147, 259–60, 264, 267

particularism, 9, 11, 15, 241, 312, 319
Pensky, Max, 248
phenomenology, 4, 18, 35–37, 44, 62, 71, 255; transcendental phenomenology, 35
Pippin, Robert, 253
Pitkin, Hannah, 271
Plato, 4, 98–101, 112, 268
political freedom, 282,
political morality, 60, 148
political responsibility, 19, 61, 130–32, 137, 139, 149, 152, 237
political rights, 103, 132, 169, 172, 201, 239
political subjectivity, 10, 16
populism, 11
postmodernism, 14, 18, 238, 286
power, 8, 9, 12, 19, 25, 32, 33, 34, 37, 38, 39, 49, 50, 51, 58, 59, 60, 63–67, 72–75, 82, 84, 100, 102, 112, 130, 134, 136, 138, 139, 140, 144, 147, 153, 155, 157, 159, 162, 164, 165, 169, 170, 180, 192, 194, 203, 205, 207, 208, 209, 216, 223, 231, 232, 241, 244, 250, 252, 253, 256, 270, 299, 316, 317, 321
powerlessness, 144, 205
Proust, Marcel 115, 181–82; *Remembrance of Things Past,* 181
psychoanalysis, 23, 49, 52, 185–90
public freedom, 15, 20, 21, 100–103, 134, 163, 198, 225, 303, 308

rationalization, 11–13, 72, 82, 85, 263, 345
real abstractions, 213
reflective judgment, 11, 17, 20, 34, 49–52, 145, 171, 172, 217, 221, 225, 259, 271, 274–79, 287, 335
religious fundamentalism, 11

republicanism, 8; civic republicanism, 68, 81, 96, 103
revolution, 7, 16, 23, 32, 56–76, 103, 122, 158, 179, 248, 281, 284, 305
Rickert School, 37
Romanticism, 11
Rorty, Richard, 45, 117, 119, 230, 245, 256–57
Rousseau, Jean Jacques, 124; *Rêveries du promeneur solitaire*, 124

Said, Edward, 238, 278; "Reflections on Exile," 278
Sanford, R. Nevitt, 188
Sartre, Jean-Paul, 104, 174, 241
Schelling, Friedrich, 41, 91, 122
Schmitt, Carl, 8, 189, 285–86
Scholem, Gershom, 2, 3, 250
secularization, 12, 56, 181, 196, 206
Sedgwick, Eve Kosovsky, 182
Shoah, 26, 308
Simmel, Ernst 187; *Anti-Semitism: A Social Disease*, 187
Simmel, Georg, 35
Snow, Benjamin, 38
social contract, 75
social critique, 256
solidarity, 9, 14, 24, 75, 92, 129, 136, 141, 142, 146–49, 151–153, 158, 236, 238, 265, 272, 316, 319, 339
Stalinism, 23–24

Taylor, Charles, 125
Third Reich, 140
totalitarianism, 3, 22–26, 40, 72, 76, 80, 85, 95, 102, 104, 108, 147, 155, 160–62, 168–69, 174–77, 197–201, 206, 211–17, 222–24, 235, 241, 247, 249–50, 271, 273, 278
transcendental subject, 38, 257

United States, 1, 22, 32, 60, 156, 231, 232, 276
universalism, 10, 14, 16, 17, 20, 235, 241; anthropological universalism, 289; difference-sensitive universalism, 14; formal universalism, 152; liberal universalism, 17; metaphysical universalism, 143; moral universalism, 144
University of Frankfurt, 5, 26, 33, 34, 250
University of Freiburg, 5, 36, 45, 255

Vienna School, 36–37

Waldon, Jeremy, 102
Walzer, Michael, 230, 242
Weber, Max, 3, 8, 11, 13, 19, 81–84, 93–95, 100–102, 160, 180, 193, 199; *Ancient Judaism*, 193
Weimar Germany, 1, 19, 48, 101, 249
Wellmer, Albrecht, 53–54, 90
Wiggershaus, Rolf, 248
Wittgenstein, Ludwig, 47, 55, 255
Wolin, Richard, 254, 285
Wolin, Sheldon, 58–9

Young-Bruehl, Elisabeth, 105; *For the Love of the World*, 105

The authorized representative in the EU for product safety and compliance is:
Mare Nostrum Group
B.V Doelen 72
4831 GR Breda
The Netherlands

www.ingramcontent.com/pod-product-compliance
Lightning Source LLC
Chambersburg PA
CBHW030519230426
43665CB00010B/679